Power, culture and conflict in the coalfields

For my father
and
in memory of my mother

Power, culture and conflict in the coalfields

West Virginia and south Wales, 1900–1922

Roger Fagge

Manchester University Press

Manchester and New York

distributed exclusively in the USA and Canada by St. Martin's Press

Published by Manchester University Press
Oxford Road, Manchester M13 9NR, UK
and Room 400, 175 Fifth Avenue, New York, NY 10010, USA

Distributed exclusively in the USA and Canada
by St. Martin's Press, Inc., 175 Fifth Avenue, New York, NY 10010, USA

British Library Cataloguing-in-Publication Data
A catalogue record for this book is available from the British Library

Library of Congress Cataloging-in-Publication Data
Fagge, Roger.
    Power, culture and conflict : the coalfields of West Virginia and
South Wales, 1900–1922 / Roger Fagge.
        p.   cm.
    "Distributed exclusively in the USA and Canada by St. Martin's
Press."
    Includes bibliographical references.
    ISBN 0-7190-4745-5 (hc.)
    1. Coal miners–West Virginia–History–20th century.   2. Coal
miners–Wales. South–History–20th century.   3. Trade-unions–Coal
miners–West Virginia–Political activity–History–20th century.
4. Trade-unions–Coal miners–Wales, South–Political activity–
History–20th century.   I. Title.
HD8039.M62U62355   1996
322'.2'088622–dc20   95-37792   CIP

ISBN 0 7190 4745 5 *hardback*

First published 1996

00 99 98 97 96   10 9 8 7 6 5 4 3 2 1

Typeset in Great Britain
by Servis Filmsetting Ltd, Manchester
Printed in Great Britain
by Bookcraft (Bath) Limited

Contents

Acknowledgements

The research and writing of this book would not have been completed without the help of a number of people. First and foremost among these is Alastair Reid, who supervised the thesis upon which this book is based. His enthusiasm and intellectual incisiveness helped shape my ideas about this study, and my wider understanding of history. Various other individuals have also provided invaluable advice on parts, or earlier drafts, of this study. These include Barry Supple, Charlotte Erickson, Miles Taylor, Henry Pelling, Frank Wilkinson, Gwyn A. Williams, Kenneth O. Morgan, David Jarvis, Claire Fitzpatrick, and Andrew Bocking. My work has also greatly benefited from comments at various seminars, including those at Cambridge, Warwick, The Institute of Historical Research, and the University of South Australia at Adelaide. Two other individuals also merit special mention. Ron Lewis not only shared his immense knowledge with me, but also helped out on my arrival in Morgantown. Similarly Murray Couch took the time to show us the real mining community of Broken Hill, New South Wales.

The actual process of research was made easier by the staff at the libraries and archives I visited, particularly those at the West Virginia and Regional History Collection at WVU, the US National Archive, the Catholic University of America, the National Library of Wales, and Swansea University Library. Similarly grants from the Economic and Social Research Council, St. John's College, Cambridge and the University of Warwick all helped see this project through to a conclusion.

Although this study was begun whilst I was at Cambridge, it has been concluded at the University of Warwick. I have benefited enormously from the friendly atmosphere and intellectual stimulation of working with my colleagues within CAS and the Department of

History. I would particularly like to thank John King, Bernard Capp, Callum MacDonald, Bill Dusinberre, Roger Magraw (for his knowledge of social and labour history and, more importantly, Jazz!), as well as the other 'young' insurgents who have recently joined the Department, namely Penny Roberts, Patrick Major, Peter Marshall, Sarah Robinson, Rebecca Earle and Mark Levene.

My greatest debt though is to Tara, who has tirelessly supported my interest in militant miners. Without her help, this study, and so much else, would never have come to fruition. And finally, there is Miles, who arrived at the end of this project, and made everything worth while.

Abbreviations

AFL	American Federation of Labour
CLC	Central Labour College
CPGB	Communist Party of Great Britain
ILP	Independent Labour Party
IWW	Industrial Workers of the World
LRC	Labour Representation Committee
MAGB	Mining Association of Great Britain
MFGB	Miners' Federation of Great Britain
MMM	Miners' Minority Movement
MSWCA	Monmouthshire and South Wales Coal Owners' Association
RUDC	Rhondda Urban District Council
SDF	Social Democratic Federation
SPA	Socialist Party of America
SWMF	South Wales Miners' Federation
UMWA	United Mine Workers of America
UMWJ	*United Mine Workers' Journal*
URC	Unofficial Reform Committee

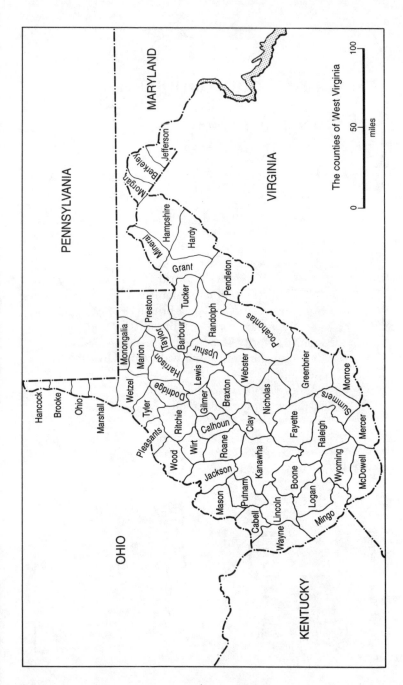

The counties of West Virginia

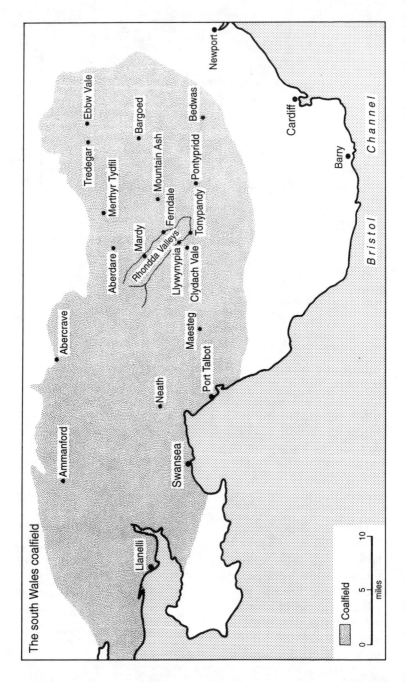

The south Wales coalfield

Coalfield

miles

x

Introduction

This book is an examination of the different patterns of protest in two major coal mining regions, and the way in which these were shaped by contrasting social relationships and cultural formations. It is intended primarily as a contribution to labour and working-class history, with particular reference to the way in which international comparisons can provide a fresh perspective on central themes within the discipline.

Context

Labour history in Britain and the US has undergone a significant transformation in recent years. During the 1960s and 1970s the subject was reinvigorated by the rise of the 'new' labour history which, rejecting the institutional accounts of the first labour historians, propounded 'history from below', and the primacy of class conflict. The result was a much broader understanding of working-class experience from the workplace to the community. The work of E. P. Thompson and Gutman, with their emphasis upon the way cultural factors shaped working-class responses to industrial society, was particularly influential within this context.[1]

However, encouraged by changes in the political climate of Western Europe and the US since the end of the 1970s, historians have recently taken a much more sceptical view of working-class formation and behaviour, and the theoretical underpinnings of the 'new' labour history. This has been particularly true in Britain where a number of historians have rejected Marxism in favour of a more consensual view of social relations, stressing sectional splits within the working-class (or classes) and strong, non-socialist continuities in the development of labour politics.[2] In the US, critics

1

have generally preferred to extend and revise the 'new' labour history, rather than totally abandon it. However, recent labour history has laid a heavy emphasis upon racial and gender fault lines within the US working-class.[3] Similarly, the abandonment of the teleological aspects of Marxism has led to a reappraisal of exceptionalist notions about US working-class politics.[4]

This greater emphasis upon complexity, and the revision of strict models within the broader discipline of labour history, is also apparent in the more specific historiography on coal miners. Seen as the most militant section of the industrial labour force, observers sought to explain such behaviour through models and ideal types which attempted to delineate as causal factors the work, social and cultural relations supposedly peculiar to mining. The most famous of these models was proposed by Kerr and Siegel, who suggested that miners constituted an 'Isolated Mass', removed from the rest of society, where protest becomes 'a kind of colonial revolt against far removed authority.'[5] Other, similar, arguments suggested that miners constituted an 'occupational community' and, traced back as far as Adam Smith, that the extreme form of exploitation prevalent in the coal industry made the coal miner the 'Archetypal Proletarian.'[6]

The relevance of such models to the reality of coal mining communities, however, was soon called into question; as was the original premise that coal miners are universally militant. Thus by the late 1950s Rimlinger, in a four nation international comparison, pointed out that there were variations in levels of conflict, with Anglo-American miners more strike-prone than their counterparts in France and Germany. As a result, he offered a revision of the 'Isolated Mass' theory which accepted the impact of 'the peculiar environment' of coal mining, yet also emphasised that this may be 'counteracted or reinforced by sociocultural factors.'[7]

A more fundamental and effective redefinition of the coal mining stereotypes began in earnest two decades later. The most influential of these new studies was a collection of essays edited by Harrison, which systematically deconstructed the myth of the 'Archetypal Proletarian' on a number of levels. What emerged was a picture of an occupation subject to different economic, geographic and cultural influences, one which could only be understood by examining the reality of historical experience, rather than 'ideal types'.[8]

Evidence of variety was reinforced in a number of subsequent studies, on various coalfields in various countries. Campbell for example provided a convincing picture of the differences between Coatbridge and Larkhall in the Lanarkshire Coalfield in the nineteenth century. He showed how the former developed at a faster pace, was subjected to more aggressive employers' strategies, and riven by ethnic divisions, all of which weakened the miners' industrial strength when compared to the more stable, homogeneous Larkhall.[9] In a similar vein, Shubert depicted the Asturian miners – whose leadership of the Asturian revolution in October 1934 conforms to some of the most heroic images of coal miners' struggle – as a community subjected to a number of divisions, which created a strong but 'volatile' industrial presence and prevented effective political organisation.[10] Hickey's study of the Ruhr miners also produced evidence of divisions at community level, particularly over ethnicity and religion, which created a relatively weak union movement and divided political organisation.[11]

Historians working on the US miners have also confirmed the a-historical nature of the mining stereotypes. These studies have shown an industry which experienced different rates of growth, different operator strategies, vast cultural (particularly ethnic) differences, and consequently different types and patterns of unionisation, strikes and political activity.[12]

It is in the context of this emphasis upon the complexity of the coal miner's experience, and the broader picture of fragmentation in labour history, that international comparisons can present a new perspective. For they offer the historian the opportunity to escape the constraints of national boundaries, and consider working-class formation and behaviour at a different level; one which can allow broader analysis of the variables in, and causes of, contrasts in the nature of communities and their patterns of protest. Indeed, with the abandonment by many historians of the teleological aspects of Marxism, and abstract theory in general, it could be argued that comparisons offer the opportunity to reconstruct labour history around an appreciation of the broader patterns linking specific historical structures and experiences. Despite this potential, however, comparative studies are still a relatively neglected option within mining and wider labour history, although Europe has been better served than Britain and America.[13]

3

West Virginia and south Wales

These two regions, and the time scale, were selected to allow consideration of miners' industrial and political protest. Both were major national and international producers of bituminous coal in this period (south Wales also had significant holdings of anthracite); with West Virginia, as the jewel of the Appalachian coalfield, representing one of the newer regions which fought its way into the world market, where it challenged established fields like south Wales. This economic importance was accompanied by a common tendency towards particularly high levels of conflict. However, of importance in the present comparison, the pattern of this conflict was very different, with West Virginia experiencing explosions of unrest amounting to what contemporaries described as 'civil war',[14] while south Wales experienced less violent but almost constant strike activity. Moreover, the two regions also presented an interesting contrast in terms of political organisation with south Wales embracing independent political activity by the end of this period, while West Virginia did not – a difference which allows an examination of political identities and the importance of organisational forms within these.

The miners in these two regions have not been compared before,[15] although there is an existing historiography on both coalfields. The literature solely, or partially, on West Virginia, has usually concentrated on the southern counties, and portrayed a particularly harsh picture of the coal operator's exploitation of the culturally diverse mining population. This can be seen from the contemporary account of Winthrop D. Lane, and the autobiography of Fred Mooney, who became Secretary-Treasurer of District 17 in this period, through to the more recent studies of Eller and Corbin.[16] The latter's work provided the first significant book solely on southern West Virginia, and besides emphasising the aggression of the coal operators, also argued that the inter-racial union struggles of the period were backed by a 'class conscious' Americanism, 'an ideology, containing values, beliefs, principles, and goals, as coherent, radical, and understanding of an exploitative and oppressive system as any ideology announced by Socialists, Communists and Wobblies.'[17] However, while Corbin's work expanded our knowledge of the West Virginia miners, his emphasis upon the translation of inter-racial unionism into a coherent, class based, political

4

language overplays the degree of political unity within the mining communities.

Historians have also shown a strong interest in the large black community in the West Virginia coalfield, with many noting the unusual system of race relations in this period.[18] Although there are differences of emphasis within these studies,[19] they all agree that black miners received better treatment at the workplace, and in the community than their counterparts in the rest of the south. Lewis has suggested, convincingly, that this greater equality, when combined with the social and economic exploitation of all miners, black and white alike, created the basis for the inter-racial struggles of the period.[20]

The south Wales miners have received far more attention than their counterparts in West Virginia. The literary traditions of the valleys has meant that there are a number of autobiographies and contemporary accounts on this period. Among the best of these are the autobiographies of Jack Jones, James Griffiths and Bert Coombes, who between them supply a picture of vibrant, self-conscious communities developing within the shadow of conflicting relationships in the coal industry.[21] A more politicised version of this was portrayed in the novels of miner and communist Lewis Jones, which depict a community struggling to discover its political, seen in this case as socialist, consciousness.[22]

Page Arnot's institutional accounts of the south Wales miners took a similar approach. While these volumes provided a narrative of the major events within the coalfield, and the severity of the conflict between miner and aggressive coal owner, they did so in a manner which often presented the mining communities as one-dimensional – much like the 'Archetypal Proletarian' image.[23] However, the greater attention paid to Welsh history in general in recent years has produced a more sophisticated understanding of the history of the coalfield. While an appreciation of the importance of conflict has remained central, more detail has emerged on economic development of the coalfields, the cultural context within which the mining communities grew, the resulting political identities, and variations present. Thus Morgan, whose work best encapsulates the above revisions, shows a restless mining population, particularly in the Rhondda, struggling within the confines of Welsh culture, and redefining it in the process.[24] Similarly G. A. Williams has illustrated the importance of Welsh radical traditions and their synthesis with newer ideas among the working-class of 'Imperial south Wales.'[25]

Although the most recent history of the SWMF tended to use the vocabulary of political development of Page Arnot,[26] the work of Morgan and G. A. Williams, along with Stead and C. Williams, has rejected the cruder versions of the 'class in itself/for itself' division. Instead, in concert with the broader trends in labour history, a less teleological view of political behaviour has emerged, with an emphasis upon continuity as well as change, and an awareness of the complexities within political identities.[27] Commenting on the wider issue of Welsh history, Dai Smith's words are particularly apposite in this context:

> The history of Wales is far more complex than we hitherto realised . . .
> The mists of Hegelian rhetoric, of a willed idealism about Wales, even
> the celebratory invocation of an internationalist working-class that
> was certainly more quick with life than its opponents ever were, must
> all give way to an emphasis upon the ambivalent, contradictory, lived
> history of the people of Wales whose experience, albeit patterned,
> cannot be summed up by words like 'community' or 'nation' nor by
> the flag waving of phrases like 'inferiority complex' or 'class con-
> sciousness'.[28]

The abandonment of the teleological aspects of Marxism, but a belief in the importance of conflict within industrial society, shaped by cultural and historical contexts, lies at the heart of this study. In this sense, whilst influenced by the recent, revisionist labour history discussed above, this book also owes more than a nod to the 'new' labour history pioneered by Thompson and Gutman.

The book is structured around these ideas. Chapter one outlines the basic economic facts of the industry in these two regions, includ- ing the differences in the form of development, and the shared insta- bilities present in the coal industry. Chapter two provides the central explanatory core of the study. It reveals fundamental differences in the nature of culture and community which dwarf any common experience related to the shared occupational base. The size, geogra- phy and structure of communities vary, as do the cultural mix of the two mining populations and their social conditions. Furthermore, these are overlaid by a dramatic contrast in power relationships, and consequently the ability to create independent structures within civil society.

Introduction

The effect of this upon the divergent forms of protest in West Virginia and south Wales is studied in subsequent chapters. Chapter three provides a detailed account of industrial conflict in both northern and southern West Virginia in these years. It reveals the degree of operator resistance to the UMWA, and the violent clashes which resulted. Chapter four, dealing with the same issues in south Wales, shows how the region's miners were able to organise and, as part of a stronger national union, mount frequent solidaristic, but less violent strikes.

Chapters five and six compare the different political identities that accompanied industrial conflict. The first reveals how the West Virginia miners were only sporadically involved in independent political activity, and united around a broad and at times ambiguous political identity. In contrast, chapter six shows how the south Wales miners organised politically, first through the Liberal party, and then Labour; reflecting a shift towards a more radical and solid political identity as coal miners within a broader labour movement.

Notes

1 Their classic contributions were H. G. Gutman, *Work, Culture and Society in Industrializing America: Essays in American Working-Class and Social History* (New York, Vintage Books, 1977); and E. P. Thompson, *The Making of the English Working-Class* (London, Gollancz, 1963).

2 See, for example, A. J. Reid, 'The Division of Labour and Politics in Britain, 1880–1920', in W. J. Mommsen and H. G. Husung (eds.), *The Development of Trade Unionism in Great Britain and Germany, 1880–1914* (London, Allen and Unwin, 1985); K. D. Brown, *The English Labour Movement, 1700–1951* (Dublin, Gill and MacMillan, 1982); P. Joyce, *Work, Society and Politics: The Culture of the Factory in Later Victorian England* (London, Methuen, 1982 edn.); E. F. Biagini and A. J. Reid (eds.), *Currents of Radicalism: Popular Radicalism, Organised Labour and Party Politics in Britain, 1850–1914* (Cambridge, Cambridge University Press, 1991); G. Stedman Jones, *Languages of Class: Studies in English Working-Class History, 1832–1982* (Cambridge, Cambridge University Press, 1983). For an overview, see A. J. Reid, *Social Classes and Social Relations in Britain, 1850–1914* (Basingstoke, Macmillan, 1992).

3 See D. Roediger, *The Wages of Whiteness: Race and the Making of the American Working-Class* (London, Verso, 1991); A. Saxton, *The Rise of the White Republic: Class Politics and Mass Culture in*

Nineteenth-Century America (London, Verso, 1990); A. Kessler-Harris, *Out to Work: A History of Wage-Earning Women in the United States* (New York, Oxford University Press, 1982); A. Baron (ed.), *Work Engendered: Towards a New Labor History* (Ithaca, Cornell University Press, 1991); R. Milkman (ed.), *Women, Work and Protest: A Century of US Women's Labour History* (London, Routledge and Kegan Paul, 1985). For a critique of US 'new' labour history, see H. Hill, 'Myth-Making as Labor History: Herbert Gutman and the United Mine Workers of America', *Politics, Culture and Society*, 2, 2 (1988), pp. 132–195.

4 For the debate on Exceptionalism, see E. Foner, 'Why is there no Socialism in the United States?', *History Workshop Journal*, 17 (1984), pp. 57–80; S. Wilentz, 'Against Exceptionalism: Class Consciousness and the American Labour Movement'; N. Salvatore, 'Response to Sean Wilentz'; M. Hanagan, 'Response to Sean Wilentz'; all in *International Labour and Working-Class History*, 26 (1984), pp. 1–24, 25–30, 31–6 respectively; and Wilentz 'A Reply to Criticism', *Ibid.*, 28, (1985), pp. 46–55.

5 C. Kerr and A. Siegel, 'The Inter-Industry Propensity to Strike: An International Comparison', in A. Kornhauser, R. Dubin and A. M. Ross (eds.), *Industrial Conflict* (New York, McGraw-Hill, 1954), p. 193.

6 For a discussion of these approaches, see M. I. A. Bulmer, 'Sociological Models of the Mining Community', *The Sociological Review*, 23, 1 (1975), pp. 61–92. See introduction to R. Harrison (ed.), *Independent Collier: the Coal Miner as Archetypal Proletarian Reconsidered* (Hassocks, Harvester, 1978) on the 'Archetypal Proletarian'. The most famous exposition of the latter view is N. Dennis, F. Henriques, and C. Slaughter, *Coal is Our Life: An Analysis of a Yorkshire Mining Community* (London, Eyre and Spottiswoode, 1956).

7 G. V. Rimlinger, 'International Differences in the Strike Propensity of Coal Miners: Experience in Four Countries', *Industrial and Labor Relations Review*, 12, 3 (1959), pp. 389–405.

8 Harrison, *Independent Collier*.

9 A. Campbell, *The Lanarkshire Miners: A Social History of their Trade Unions* (Edinburgh, John Donald, 1979).

10 A. Shubert, *The Road to Revolution: The Coal Miners of Asturias, 1860–1934* (Urbana, University of Illinois Press, 1987).

11 S. H. F. Hickey, *Workers in Imperial Germany: The Miners of the Ruhr* (Oxford, Oxford University Press, 1985).

12 See R. L. Lewis, *Black Coal Miners in America: Race, Class, and Community Conflict, 1780–1980* (Lexington, University Press of Kentucky, 1987); J. Gaventa, *Power and Powerlessness: Quiescence and Rebellion in an Appalachian Valley* (Urbana, University of Illinois

Press, 1980); M. Dubofsky and W. Van Tine, *John L. Lewis: A Biography* (New York, Quadrangle/New York Times Book Co., 1977); A. K. Powell, *The Next Time We Strike: Labor in Utah's Coal Fields, 1900–1933* (Logan, Ut., Utah State University Press, 1985); D. L. Miller and R. E. Sharpless, *The Kingdom of Coal: Work, Enterprise and Ethnic Communities in the Mine Fields* (Philadelphia, University of Pennsylvania Press, 1985); P. V. Fishback, *Soft Coal, Hard Choices: the Economic Welfare of Bituminous Coal Miners* (New York, Oxford University Press, 1992).

13 Studies on coal mining taking a comparative, or parallel approach (that is, chapters on individual countries, with a comparative theme), include Rimlinger, 'International Differences in the Strike Propensity of Coal Miners'; J. H. M. Laslett, *Nature's Noblemen: the Fortunes of the Independent Collier in Scotland and the American MidWest, 1855–1889* (Los Angeles, Institute of Industrial Relations, University of California, 1983); E. D. Weitz, 'Class Formation and Labor Protest in the Mining Communities of Southern Illinois and the Ruhr, 1890–1925', *Labor History*, 27, 1 (1985–86), pp. 85–105; K. Tenfelde (ed.), *Towards a Social History of Mining in the 19th and 20th Centuries* (Munich, Verlag C. H. Beck, 1992), particularly Section 1, pp. 53–310, and G. D. Feldman and K. Tenfelde (ed.), *Miners, Owners and Politics in Coal Mining: An International Comparison of Industrial Relations* (London, Berg, 1990). On labour history, see N. Kirk, *Labour and Society in Britain and the USA* (2 Vols.), (Aldershot, Scolar Press, 1994); J. Holt, 'Trade Unionism in the British and US Steel Industries, 1880–1914: A Comparative Study', *Labor History*, 18, 1 (1977), pp.5–25; James E. Cronin and C. Sirianni (eds.), *Work, Community, and Power: The Experience of Labor in Europe and America, 1900–1925* (Philadelphia, Temple University Press, 1983); I. Katznelson and A. R. Zolberg (eds.), *Working-Class Formation: Nineteenth-Century Patterns in Western Europe and the United States* (Princeton, Princeton University Press, 1986); D. Geary, *European Labour Protest, 1848–1939* (London, Croom Helm, 1981); J. Breuilly, *Labour and Liberalism in Nineteenth-Century Europe: Essays in Comparative History* (Manchester, Manchester University Press, 1992); Mommsen and Husung (eds.), *The Development of Trade Unionism in Great Britain and Germany*.

14 For example, W. D. Lane entitled his contemporary account of the mine wars, *Civil War In West Virginia: a Story of Industrial Conflict in the Coal Mines* (New York, B. W. Heubsch, 1921).

15 The exception is R. J. Fagge, 'A Comparison of the Miners of south Wales and West Virginia, 1900–1922: Patterns of Militancy', in Tenfelde (ed.), *Towards a Social History of Mining*, pp. 105–122. There

Introduction

have also been examinations of contemporary issues within the broader areas of Wales and Appalachia. See G. Day, 'The Reconstruction of Wales and Appalachia: Development and Regional Identity', *Contemporary Wales* (1987), pp. 73–89; and P. Clavel, *Opposition Planning in Wales and Appalachia* (Cardiff, University of Wales Press, 1983)

16 Lane, *Civil War in West Virginia* ; F. Mooney, *Struggle in the Coal Fields* [Ed. J. W. Hess] (Morgantown, West Virginia University Library Press, 1967). R. D. Eller, *Miners, Millhands and Mountaineers: Industrialization of the Appalachian South, 1880–1930* (Knoxville, University of Tennessee Press, 1982); D. A. Corbin, *Life, Work and Rebellion in the Coal Fields: The Southern West Virginia Miners, 1880–1922* (Urbana, University of Illinois Press, 1981). For accounts which are more sympathetic to the operators, see W. P. Tams Jr., *The Smokeless Coal Fields of West Virginia: A Brief History* (Morgantown, West Virginia University Library Press, 1963); W. Thurmond, *The Logan Coal Field of West Virginia: A Brief History* (Morgantown, West Virginia University Library Press, 1964); and Fishback, *Soft Coal, Hard Choices*.

17 Corbin, *Life, Work and Rebellion in the Coal Fields* , pp. 244–6.

18 The main works are J. T. Laing, 'The Negro Miner in West Virginia' (Unpublished Ph.D dissertation, Ohio State University, 1933); Lewis, *Black Coal Miners in America*, pp. 121–64; and J. W. Trotter Jr., *Coal, Class and Color: Blacks in Southern West Virginia, 1915–32* (Urbana, University of Illinois Press, 1991). The general works, particularly Corbin, *Life, Work and Rebellion in the Coal Fields*, pp. 61–86; and Fishback, *Soft Coal, Hard Choices*, pp. 171–97, also deal with the position of black miners.

19 Lewis, for example, convincingly disproves Corbin's claim that company towns were usually racially integrated: See *Black Coal Miners in America*, pp. 149–50. Similarly Trotter portrays a less positive picture of race relations than the other historians, arguing that, while 'black life . . . differed significantly from life in the Deep South', discrimination and racism were still prominent, and indeed got worse after the war. *Coal, Class and Color*, p. 3. See pp. 102–144 on the post-war position.

20 Lewis, *Black Coal Miners in America*, pp. 143–64.

21 J. Jones, *Unfinished Journey* (London, Hamish Hamilton, 1938); J. Griffiths, *Pages From Memory* (London, Dent, 1969); B. L. Coombes, *These Poor Hands* (London, Gollancz, 1939).

22 L. Jones, *Cwmardy* (London, Lawrence and Wishart, 1978 edn.); *We Live* (London, Lawrence and Wishart, 1978 edn.).

23 R. P. Arnot, *The South Wales Miners: A History of the South Wales Miners' Federation, 1898–1914* (London, Allen and Unwin, 1967); *The*

South Wales Miners: A History of the South Wales Miners' Federation, 1914–1926 (Cardiff, Cymric Federation Press, 1975).

24 K. O. Morgan, *Rebirth of a Nation: Wales, 1880–1980* (Oxford, Oxford University Press, 1981).

25 G. A. Williams, *The Welsh in Their History* (London, Croom Helm, 1982); *When Was Wales?: A History of Wales* (London, Penguin, 1985).

26 H. Francis and D. Smith, *The Fed: A History of the South Wales Miners in the Twentieth Century* (London, Lawrence and Wishart, 1980). For a critique of the language used in the latter, see P. Stead, 'And Every Valley Shall Be Exalted', *Morgannwg*, 34 (1980), p. 85; C.Williams, 'The South Wales Miners' Federation', *Llafur*, 5, 3, p. 50.

27 P. Stead, 'The Language of Edwardian Politics', in D. Smith (ed.), *A People and a Proletariat: Essays in the History of Wales* (London, Pluto Press, 1980), pp. 148–165; 'Establishing a Heartland – The Labour Party in Wales', in K.D. Brown (ed.), *The First Labour Party, 1906–1914* (London, Croom Helm, 1985), pp. 64–88; C. Williams, '"An Able Administrator of Capitalism?": The Labour Party in the Rhondda, 1917–1921', *Llafur*, 4, 4, pp. 20–30; and 'The South Wales Miners' Federation', *Llafur*, 5, 3, pp. 45–56.

28 D. Smith, 'Wales Through the Looking Glass', in *A People and a Proletariat*, p. 238.

1

The coal industry in West Virginia and south Wales, 1900–22

Although the exploitation of the Appalachian 'periphery' occurred later than most of the US, the pace of development was such that West Virginia soon became a major national and international producer. Production rose from 2.8 million tons in 1883 to 18.9 million tons in 1900, thereafter leaping to 59.6 million in 1912, and 80.8 million in 1921.[1] The growth of the labour force was similarly spectacular, rising from 28,017 in 1900 to 69,611 in 1912, and 116,726 in 1921.[2] In terms of the national industry, West Virginia was by 1909 the second largest coal producing State, when it accounted for 11.3% of total US production. This was, however, a long way behind Pennsylvania which accounted for 47.5% of the total.[3]

The south Wales coalfield grew at a much slower rate when compared to West Virginia, but significantly quicker than other British regions. By the 1850s it was already producing around 10 million tons annually, rising to over 16 million in the 1870s. Thereafter output jumped to over 41 million tons at the start of the new century, and then rose to a peak of 56.8 million in 1913. By 1922, amid annual fluctuations, it had reached 50.3 million tons.[4] The south Wales industry was far more labour intensive than West Virginia, with over 69,000 employed in 1880, increasing to nearly 148,000 in 1900, and over 233,000 in 1913. The peak in terms of manpower was 271,500 in 1920, after which there was a constant decline.[5] South Wales was even more significant within the national industry than West Virginia was in the US. It was the second largest field in terms of production from the 1830s, becoming the largest in 1913, when nearly 20% of Britain's coal came from the region.[6]

The importance of both these regions was increased by the quality of the coal they produced. The 1890 US Census, for example, commenting on the fledgling West Virginia industry, noted that 'no State in the Union is more favoured in the extent and diversity of its mineral deposits. Her coal embraces all grades of bituminous – steam, coking, and gas coals of the highest quality.'[7] These were spread throughout 17,280 square miles, mined in thirty-five counties,[8] ranging from the coking and steam coal of the northern Fairmont field to the southern coalfields, the eastern half of which – namely (running north to south) the New River, Winding Gulf, and Pocahontas fields – mined smokeless coals. The latter, although classified as bituminous coals, had a very low percentage of volatile matter, making them a good substitute for anthracite.[9]

Likewise south Wales produced a variety of good quality steam, house and industrial coals. The bituminous deposits covered most of the 1,000 square miles of the coalfield, with the large steam coal workings in the centre. The region also had rare supplies of good quality anthracite, which were located on the western edge of Glamorgan, and in Carmarthenshire.[10] Although by 1913 anthracite accounted for only 4.8 million tons of the nearly 57 million total of the coalfield, its importance was revealed by the fact that only 5.2 million tons of anthracite were mined the same year in the whole of Britain.[11]

The accessibility and condition of these deposits marked another variation between these two regions. In West Virginia the huge reserves were generally very close to the surface, allowing the majority of mining to take place via horizontal tunnels into hillsides, known as drifts. In 1909, 86.8% of the coalfield's production came from such mines, while 4.7% came from slope mines, and only 7.5% from shaft mines.[12] Although drift mines were usually smaller and contained less coal, they had several advantages over the deep shaft mines predominant in a region like south Wales. Not only was the opening of the mine cheaper (as was temporary closure during depressions), but problems of drainage, ventilation, and the transportation of coal and men, were not as great as with shaft mining.[13]

South Wales was also disadvantaged by being an older coalfield, which contributed to the problem of diminishing returns, whereby the coal seams became more distant requiring greater time and expenditure to mine. In 1913, for example, as much as 72% of the coal produced in the steam coal region was wound from pits that were at least twenty years old.[14] Nor were the seams of the same standard, with south Wales having more geological faults compared with other regions within Britain, let alone the thick, less faulted seams of West Virginia.[15] As will be seen later, the issue of payments for working in 'abnormal' places was to become a major source of contention between miner and owner.

The different geological conditions affected the levels of mechanisation in these two regions. By 1900, 13.42% of the West Virginia coal production was already machine rather than pick-mined. By 1922 this had risen to over 76%.[16] In contrast, by 1913 only 1.1% of south Wales coal was mined using machines, and even by 1927 the figure was only 7%.[17] This helps explain why the south Wales mines were much more labour intensive and, when combined with the fact that mines in the region were older, deeper, and more faulted, why productivity rates were so much lower than in West Virginia – particularly after the introduction of the 'Eight Hours Act' in 1908. In the Mountain State in 1912, where miners had less control of their working hours, an average of 885.9 tons was produced by each employee – part of an improving productivity rate.[18] In south Wales, in contrast, productivity per man per year was heading in the opposite direction, falling from 309 tons in 1883 to 222 by 1912.[19]

The disparity in the accessibility of coal deposits and ease of mining was, however, redressed somewhat by the geography of these two regions. For West Virginia may have had enviable mining conditions, but its landlocked position, mountainous terrain and sparse population, created a number of problems, particularly with regard to transporting coal. While the Baltimore and Ohio (B and O) railroad was able to provide a limited link from the northern Fairmont field to the Northern States from the middle of the nineteenth century, the major rail projects had to wait another three to four decades.[20] This was particularly true of the huge southern reserves which were not accessible until firstly the Chesapeake and Ohio (C and O) in 1873, and then the Norfolk and Western (N and W) in the 1880s, cut across the coal counties and connected them to the Virginia coast.[21]

Additions to the network aided the rapid development of the southern counties. In 1888, for example, McDowell county was integrated into the rail network by the N and W, via a tunnel under Flat Top Mountain. In 1892 the same railroad built an Ohio extension which gave the southern counties a crucial connection with the Great Lakes ports. With further links opening up the remaining coal deposits, the southern counties moved to the forefront of production. Thus McDowell became the largest county in terms of coal production in 1902, a position which it held until the 1930s. Fayette, Kanawha, and then slightly later Logan, Mingo, Raleigh and Mercer were also of great importance. With the addition of branch lines within the northern counties, Marion county became the third largest producer in the State by 1900, although it fell behind somewhat as production leapt in the southern counties. Harrison, Tucker and, by 1918, Monongalia counties were also among the ten most productive within the State.[22] It is important to note, however, that moving coal out of the State remained a problem throughout this period.[23]

In contrast to West Virginia, south Wales was in an ideal geographic position, close to the seaboard, thus eliminating the need for extensive rail journeys. By the 1860s there were rail links to three Cardiff docks, and a fourth dock was added at Barry in 1889 to meet increased production. By the early 1900s, the latter had become the world's major coal port, providing along with the other Cardiff docks, and lesser ports at Swansea, Port Talbot and Newport, an outlet for the rapidly expanding south Wales exports.[24]

The level of this export trade was remarkable. The Bristol channel ports handled over 40% of total British coal exports in the years between 1890 and 1913.[25] In terms of south Wales coal production, by 1913, 53% of the 56.8 million tons produced were exported (a figure which did not include the coal loaded for use by the steam ships on the outward voyage), compared to a national average of only 26%.[26] The only other region approaching the 29.88 million tons exported by south Wales was the North East with 23.02 million.[27] Indeed the South Wales export trade was so large that it accounted for nearly 33% of total world exports in the years between 1890 and 1910.[28]

The steam coal mined in the Rhondda lay at the heart of these figures, making up, by 1913, a quarter of the region's total exports.[29] This, in part, indicated the degree to which south Wales had benefited from the growth of steam shipping in the second half of the nineteenth century. Well situated in terms of imperial trade routes, the Bristol channel ports were able to supply south Wales coal for use by the admiralty, foreign navies, and the merchant fleet, as well as exports for developing economies around the world.[30] Thus by 1910 south Wales exports included 4.1 million tons to South America, 1.9 million to Egypt, 430,372 to Russia, 5.3 million to France, and 343,190 to Germany.[31]

Such far flung exports proved economic because of the relatively low freight rates, created by the expansion of steam shipping. Probably the most famous south Wales coal owner, D. A. Thomas, stressed the importance of this in a 1903 Paper to the Royal Historical Society. He noted that coal freights were 'now less than half what they were a generation ago', with in 1902, the 3,072 miles from Cardiff to Port Said costing only 5s 4d per ton, compared with a domestic rate of 6s 1d per ton for the rail journey from the Rhondda to London. This meant, 'Egyptian railways got their supplies of fuel as cheap, if not cheaper, say, than the Brighton or South Eastern.'[32] Significantly, in the same paper, Thomas also made a comparison with the New River and Pocahontas fields in West Virginia from 'which a great deal of coal is exported to Europe'. He noted that although these fields were 350–400 miles from the seaboard, rail freight rates on the C and O were only 0.1 d per ton per mile, compared with 0.575 d per ton per mile on the Taff Vale Railway for the twenty miles from the Rhondda to Cardiff.[33]

Therefore, despite the inhospitable geographical situation, other advantages allowed West Virginia to compete for markets with more established fields – including south Wales. This led the coal industry journal *Black Diamond* to note in 1900 that 'the Flat Top and Pocahontas coals seem to have a very strong place in foreign markets', and the following year that West Virginia coal was being used by the British navy.[34] Ten years later another trade journal, *Coal Age*, noted that the Consolidation Coal Company, the largest in the Fairmont field, had secured a new contract for 40,000 tons of steam coal for the Egyptian State Railways. It went on; 'this is the first time the latter company has asked for tenders for American coal.'[35]

West Virginia coal secured a further foothold within formerly British markets, during the first national British miners strike in 1912, when the British government bought over 1 million tons of the State's coal. It was reported that demand was such that the 'Consolidation Coal Co. is trying to buy coal to assist in taking care of English contracts'.[36] Similarly, two years later it was noted that West Virginia was sending large quantities of coal through Norfolk and Newport News. The reporter commented that there were at that time ten coal vessels flying foreign flags, including the British steamers 'Etaline' and 'Leslie'.[37] With US coal exports in general increasing from 3.5 million tons in 1899 to 21.3 million in 1917, it was clear that the south Wales' domination of the export trade was facing increased competition from the other side of the Atlantic.[38]

Although these two regions experienced different patterns of economic growth, they did share a similarly fragmented industrial structure – one which in many ways reflected a national similarity within US and British bituminous coal mining.[39] In West Virginia, the accessibility of the seams, and the consequent ease with which mines could be opened, encouraged a large number of small scale operations. In 1916 in Fayette County, for example, the State Department of Mines recorded no fewer than seventy-six companies producing coal, ranging from the DeWitt Fuel company producing 3,567 tons to the Boomer Coal and Coke Company producing 861,505.[40]

One of the largest and most longstanding exceptions to this pattern, was the Consolidation Coal Company in the Fairmont Field which, after its purchase of the Fairmont Coal Company in 1903, came into ownership of, or leased, thirty-two of the ninety-six mines in the field. In 1913, when there were seventy-two companies in the whole State producing over 200,000 tons each. Consolidation Coal was the largest, with 4.5 million tons (32% of the Fairmont field's output). Significantly, Consolidation Coal was owned by the B and O Railway.[41]

There were other large interests operating in the southern part of the State, some of which worked captive mines. The best example of this was found in the Pocahontas field, where the US Coal Commissioners noted 'a very great concentration in ownership of coal lands', most of it in the hands of the N and W railway.[42] The N and W had, along with the C and O, been taken over by the Pennsylvania Railroad in 1898, which in turn was linked to J. P. Morgan in New York. The latter was also connected with the US Steel Corporation which, in 1901, organised the US Coal and Coke Company, and began operations in Pocahontas. By 1913, US Coal and Coke had become the largest producer in West Virginia with nearly 5 million tons, and employing 3,900 men.[43]

Morgan had connections with other companies in Pocahontas, including the second largest producer, Pocahontas Consolidated Collieries Inc., as well as interests in New River and Kanawha. Other wealthy outsiders who carved out large holdings within the south included Samuel Dixon in New River, and William A. Coolidge and Albert F. Holden who created the US Coal and Oil

Company (which later became the Island Creek Coal Company). The latter led the way in industrialising Logan County, and by 1913 the company was the fourth largest producer in the State with nearly 2 million tons.[44]

On the whole, however, such large companies and combinations were counter-balanced by the large number of smaller producers. Thus, in 1916, even the huge US Coal and Coke produced less than a quarter of McDowell county's 19 million tons.[45]

There was a similar industrial structure in the south Wales coalfield. In the western, mainly anthracite region, where the mines were usually smaller, there were a particularly large number of companies. In 1910 the Home Office *List of Mines* recorded no fewer than sixty-six companies operating seventy-eight mines in Carmarthenshire. These ranged from a mine at Brynmawr employing two people, to one at Llanon with 547 men underground and 136 outside.[46] Although, as Church has pointed out, the Home Office lists conceal combinations and subsidiary companies which mined under different names,[47] the anthracite region was, considering its virtual monopoly of the product, surprisingly fragmented.This situation only changed in 1923 when there were consolidations leading to the Amalgamated Anthracite Collieries and United Anthracite Collieries companies. These two in turn merged three years later.[48]

There were more large companies and combinations in the rest of the coalfield, although even here they were not dominant. The main consolidations took place in the steam coal region, where D. A. Thomas built up the huge Cambrian Combine. Thomas had long advocated restricting competition in the coalfield, and in 1896 had attempted to secure an agreement involving output quotas. However, this was rebuffed by the other Rhondda owners, including Sir W. T. Lewis.[49] As a consequence, Thomas began acquiring various interests in the region which, by 1917, were producing 7.4 million tons.[50]

Other large operations included the Powell Duffryn Steam Coal Company which in the same year produced 4 million tons, the Ocean Coal Company 2.25 million, Benyon and Company 4.8 million and the combined United National and Burnyeat, Brown and Company 2.45 million.[51] Another large interest was the iron and steel firm Guest, Keen and Nettlefold of Dowlais, which had initially intended to operate captive mines, but had found the sale of coal so advantageous that by 1900 it was sending most of its coal to the open market, placing the company within the top twenty national producers.[52] Guest Keen and Nettlefold was also one of the companies which expanded its holdings in the immediate aftermath of the war.[53] As with West Virginia, however, these firms were not the norm. As Supple has pointed out such concentrations were 'insignificant compared with other heavy industries'. In 1913 the eleven largest firms in south Wales employed less than 40% of the labour force.[54]

One obvious consequence of the large number of coal companies in both these regions was their contribution towards the major fault of the bituminous industry; namely overproduction. As the period progressed, and coal from the newer fields like West Virginia poured onto the world market, supply began to exceed demand. Up to 1913 the rapid expansion in demand helped cover up some of these structural weaknesses, with world demand rising annually up to 1914 by around 4%. However, between 1913 and 1937 it rose by only 0.3%.[55]

The crunch came after the war, in the bitter decline of the 1920s and 1930s. South Wales was hit particularly hard, as its reliance on exports was undercut by the combination of fuel economies, the shift to oil for shipping, economic changes, and the maturing of other economies.[56] As an older coalfield, with falling productivity and more expensive coal, south Wales was ill prepared for the cold winds of competition. Nationally coal exports fell from 73.4 million tons in 1913, to 50 million by 1928 – barring the 79.4 million blip in 1923, courtesy of the US miners' strike. As a consequence, south Wales production fell from a peak of 56.8 million tons in 1913 to 35.2 million in 1934. In terms of manpower, the high of 271,000 in 1921 fell to under 140,00 in 1934.[57]

The social consequences of this collapse were traumatic. In the same year 37% of the labour force in Glamorgan were unemployed. Individual towns like Dowlais, Blaina and Merthyr experienced rates of over 70%.[58] It left Wales, to quote G. A. Williams, 'deracinated ... in terms of social disruption and identity crisis, the depression plays the same role in Welsh history as the famine in Irish.'[59]

The West Virginia industry, benefiting from its more easily mined coal, and lower labour costs, was not hit as hard. Production peaked in 1924 at 139.8 million tons, falling more gradually to 87.9 million by 1933. The labour force similarly declined from 121,280 in 1923 to 95,367 in 1934.[60] The social consequences, however, were similarly severe, with widespread hardship even for many of those employed. Some estimates, for example, suggest that the average per capita earnings for Appalachian coal miners fell from $851 in 1923 to $235 in 1933.[61] Furthermore the underdevelopment of the West Virginia economy, which was particularly pronounced even when compared to other mining regions, made the effects of decline even harder.[62]

The pattern of seemingly constant growth before the war, and the downturn in fortunes thereafter covered up the extent to which the bituminous industry had longstanding structural problems. Cyclical changes in demand and increasing competition had already made themselves felt throughout the industry prior to the post-war depression. Thus in West Virginia between 1897 and 1916, an average of only 220 days were worked each year, ranging from only 190 in 1915 to 249 in 1902.[63] With pressures already placed upon prices, the maintenance of profits depended on keeping costs, the largest of which was wages, down. In south Wales, even in the years preceding 1913, this resulted, as we shall see later, in a constant assault on customary rights and other payments. In West Virginia it encouraged the creation of a 'feudal' system of power relationships constructed with the intention of keeping a low wage, low cost industry.

This instability and cost cutting also helped encourage another less than attractive aspect of the industry; in the shape of high accident rates. In West Virginia from 1900–22 no fewer than 7,443 miners lost their lives at a rate of 5.45 per 1,000 employed.[64] In south Wales the rate was significantly lower, but higher within the national context. Between 1900–20, 1.65 per 1,000 lost their lives, compared with a national average of 1.23.[65] Nor were the majority of these miners killed in large scale disasters like the 1907 Monongah explosion in northern West Virginia which killed 359, or the 1913 Senghennydd disaster in south Wales in which 439 perished.[66] For, serious though such accidents were, the vast majority of miners were killed in isolated incidents.[67] In the West Virginia mines in 1922, for example, which was by no means a bad year for accidents, 183 miners were killed by falls of coal, slate and roof, 57 by coal cars, 3 by explosions, and 87 by 'other causes'. The individual accident records reveal that nearly all of these were separate incidents.[68] Nor does this complete the picture, as non-fatal accidents were even more common than fatal ones.[69] Thus in West Virginia in 1922, in addition to the 330 who lost their lives, another 542 were injured.[70]

The impact of this upon the mining communities in both these regions was tremendous. As one West Virginia miner recalled, 'not a week passed but what tragedy touched some home,'[71] while President William Brace told a SWMF conference in 1914 that 'it was appalling to think that neither the application of science nor anything else appeared to have been able to cope with the disasters in the Coalfield.'[72] The effects of accidents were particularly severe for women in the community who were often left alone in an environment which offered them little alternative means of support.[73]

In many ways the loss and injury within the mines represents a common thread in these two regions; one caused by cost cutting and carelessness in an unstable industry run with a good deal of incompetence and greed. Much of this instability was based on the precarious market position of the coal industry in these years, with a fragmented industrial structure encouraging over-production, at the same time as demand began to level off. Much of the greed was related to these problems, but it is difficult to ignore the evidence that the nature of coal mining itself encouraged an additional degree of harshness in the pursuit of profit, and a corresponding disregard for those actually digging coal.

The similarities between the two coalfields should not mask the different patterns of economic development that were also present. South Wales was an established coalfield long before West Virginia became a significant coal producing region. Its high quality coal which was mined from often faulted seams in older, deeper shaft mines found a ready market across the world. In contrast, West Virginia, although initially held back by its landlocked position, soon developed at a remarkable rate, utilising less faulted, more accessible coal, mined with a greater use of mechanisation. Playing these advantages to the full, the region soon began to challenge the dominance of the older coalfields. However, West Virginia' s challenge was not based solely on its natural advantages. As we shall see in subsequent chapters, it was also based on lower labour costs gained through a formidable assault on working conditions and wider civil rights.

Notes

1 These are calculated as long tons. West Virginia Department of Mines (WVDM), *Annual Report, 1927* (Charleston, 1927), p. 104. These figures do not include coke production which was (in short tons) 190,889 in 1883, 2.5 million in 1900, falling to 1.9 million in 1912, and 836,728 in 1921. *Ibid.*, p. 104.

2 West Virginia Mining, *Annual Report, 1985* (Charleston, 1985), p. 38.

3 US Bureau of the Census, *13th Census of the United States, Vol. 2: Mines and Quarries, General Reports and Analysis* (Washington D.C., 1913), p. 184.

4 R. Church, *The History of the British Coal Industry, Vol. 3, 1830–1913: Victorian Pre-eminence* (Oxford, Oxford University Press, 1986), p. 3; B. Supple, *The History of the British Coal Industry Vol. 4, 1913–1946: The Political Economy of Decline* (Oxford, Oxford University Press, 1987), p. 180; B. Mitchell and P. Deane, *Abstract of British Historical Statistics* (Cambridge, Cambridge University Press, 1971), pp. 115–17.

5 *Ibid.*, pp. 118–19.

6 Church, *The History of the British Coal Industry, Vol. 3*, p. 10; Supple, *The History of the British Coal Industry, Vol. 4*, p. 180.

7 US Bureau of the Census, *11th Census of the United States: Mineral Industries* (Washington D.C., 1892), p. 417.

8 West Virginia Coal Association, *His Majesty King Coal* (Charleston, 1938), p. 4; In 1922, 35 counties recorded some coal production, WVDM, *Annual Report, 1927*, p. 108.

9 The smokeless coals produced in these regions had a volatile matter of 16–24%, compared with 6–8% for anthracite. In comparison, the neighbouring Kanawha, Guyandotte (or Logan), and Williamson fields, which ran north to south in the western section of the southern region, produced coal with a 32–38% volatile matter. W. P. Tams Jr., *The Smokeless Coal Fields of West Virginia: A Brief History* (Morgantown, West Virginia University Library Press, 1963), pp. 15–16; W. Thurmond, *The Logan Coal Field of West Virginia: A Brief History* (Morgantown, West Virginia University Library Press, 1964), pp. 15–16.

10 H. S. Jevons, *The British Coal Trade* (Newton Abbot, David and Charles, 1969 edn.), pp. 94–9; Supple, *The History of the British Coal Industry, Vol. 4*, pp. 20–2.

11 F. A. Gibson, *Compilation of the Statistics of the Coal Mining Industry of the United Kingdom, the Various Coalfields Thereof, and the Principal Foreign Countries of the World* (Cardiff, 1922), p. 53.

12 US Bureau of the Census, *13th Census of the United States, Vol. 2*, p. 213.

13 *Ibid.*, p. 213; For good description of the access technology, see Church, *The History of the British Coal Industry, Vol. 3*, pp. 311–328.

14 R. Walters, 'Labour Productivity in the South Wales Steam Coal Industry, 1870–1914', *Economic History Review*, 28, 2 (1975), p. 295.

15 M. J. Daunton, 'Down the Pit: Work in the Great Northern and South Wales Coalfields, 1870–1914', *Economic History Review*, 34 (1981), pp. 582, 586; The Chief Mine Inspector commented on the relative ease of mining coal in West Virginia in, West Virginia Bureau of Mines, *Annual Report, 1899* (Charleston, 1899), p. 128; Buxton suggests that geological conditions in British mines were worse than in Germany, Poland and the US, but better than in Belgium, and similar to France and Czechoslovakia. N. K. Buxton, *The Economic Development of the British Coal Industry: From the Industrial Revolution to the Present Day* (London, Batsford, 1978), p. 180.

16 WVDM, *Annual Report, 1927*, p. 9.

17 Church, *The History of the British Coal Industry, Vol. 3*, p. 347; Supple, *The History of the British Coal Industry, Vol. 4*, p. 31.

18 Calculated using long tons from, West Virginia Mining *Annual Report, 1985*, pp. 38–9.

19 K. O. Morgan, *Rebirth of a Nation: Wales 1880–1980* (Oxford, Oxford University Press, 1981), p. 62. For a recent, detailed examination of the issue of productivity in south Wales, and Britain generally, see Church, *The History of the British Coal Industry, Vol. 3*, pp. 471–96.

20 P. Conley, *History of the West Virginia Coal Industry* (Charleston W. Va, Education Foundation, 1960), pp. 151–65; J. A. Williams, *West Virginia: a History* (New York, W. W. Norton and Co.,1984 edn.), pp. 51–2.

21 R.G. Lawrence, 'Appalachian Metamorphosis: Industrializing Society on the Central Appalachian Plateau' (Unpublished Ph.D dissertation, Duke University, 1983), pp. 34–45; R. D. Eller, *Miners, Millhands and Mountaineers: Industrialization of the Appalachian South, 1880–1930*, (Knoxville, University of Tennessee Press, 1982), pp. 65–85. Smaller amounts of coal were also transported by river. In 1905, for example, the WVDM reported that over 1 million tons of coal were 'floated out of the Great Kanahwa River', *Annual Report, 1905* (Charleston, 1905), p. 6.

22 Eller, *Miners, Millhands and Mountaineers*, pp. 73–5; pp. 132–40; WVDM, *Annual Report, 1930* (Charleston, 1930), pp. 88–9; Williams, *West Virginia*, pp. 110–14.

23 See, for example, Justus Collins to L. E. Tierney, 17 Jan 1902, Morgantown, West Virginia University (WVU), West Virginia and Regional History Collection, Justus Collins Papers (A+M 1824), Series 1, Box 1, File 1. Similarly a trade journal commented in 1903 that 'the railroads cannot keep pace with the output of the West Virginia mines.' *Black Diamond*, 31, 18 (31 Oct 1903), pp. 884–5.

24 M. Asteris, 'The Rise and Decline of South Wales Coal Exports, 1870–1930', *Welsh History Review*, 13, 1 (1986), p. 25; Jevons, *The British Coal Trade*, p. 111.

25 Asteris, 'The Rise and Decline of South Wales Coal Exports', p. 26; Church, *The History of the British Coal Industry, Vol. 3*, p. 35.

26 Asteris, 'The Rise and Decline of South Wales Coal Exports', pp. 26–7; Gibson, *Compilation of Statistics*, p. 78.

27 These were the only two British regions exporting more than 10 million tons: Supple, *The History of the British Coal Industry, Vol. 4*, pp. 12–13.

28 G. M. Holmes, 'The South Wales Coal Industry, 1850–1914', *Transactions Honourable Society of Cymmrodorion* (1976), p. 171.

29 E. D. Lewis, *The Rhondda Valleys: A Study in Industrial Development, 1800 to the Present Day* (London, Phoenix House, 1959), p. 134.

30 *Ibid.*, pp. 134–7; Asteris, 'The Rise and Decline of South Wales Coal Exports', pp. 27–33; A. J. Taylor, 'The Coal Industry', in D. H. Aldcroft (ed.), *The Development of British Industry and Foreign Competition* (London, Allen and Unwin, 1968), p. 41.

31 Gibson, *Compilation of Statistics*, pp. 100–8.

32 D. A. Thomas, 'The Growth and Direction of our Foreign Trade in Coal During the Last Half Century', *Journal of the Royal Historical Society*, 66 (1903), pp. 474–5.

33 *Ibid*, p. 474.

34 *Black Diamond*, 25, 11 (15 Sep 1900), p. 344; *Ibid.*, 26, 17 (27 Apr 1901), p. 549.

35 *Coal Age*, I, 4 (4 Nov 1911), p. 133.

36 *Ibid.*, I, 22 (9 Mar 1912), p. 725; *Ibid.*, I, 23 (16 Mar 1912), p. 759.

37 *Ibid.*, 6, 12 (19 Sep 1914), p. 485.

38 Recalculated as long tons from US Bureau of the Census, *The Statistical History of the United States from Colonial Times to the Present* (Connecticut, 1965), p. 356.

39 B. Supple, 'The Political Economy of Demoralization: The State and the Coalmining Industry in America and Britain between the Wars', *Economic History Review*, 41, 4 (1988), p. 569.

40 WVDM, *Annual Report, 1916* (Charleston, 1916), pp. 91–2.

41 R. M. Simon, 'The Development of Underdevelopment: The Coal Industry and its Effect on the West Virginia Economy, 1880–1930' (Unpublished Ph.D dissertation, University of Pittsburgh, 1978), pp. 430–2; WVDM, *Annual Report, 1913* (Charleston, 1913), pp. 25–6; G. F. Massay, 'Coal Consolidation: A Profile of the Fairmont Field of West Virginia, 1852–1903' (Unpublished Ph.D dissertation, West Virginia University, 1970), pp. 87–90.

42 E. E. Hunt, F. G. Tyron, and J. H. Willits (eds.), *What the Coal Commission Found* (Baltimore, Williams and Williams Co., 1925), pp. 91–2.

43 Eller, *Miners, Millhands and Mountaineers*, pp. 136–7, WVDM, *Annual Report, 1913*, p. 25.
44 Eller, *Miners, Millhands and Mountaineers*, pp. 134–5; WVDM, *Annual Report, 1913*, p. 25.
45 WVDM, *Annual Report, 1916*, p. 98; *Annual Report, 1927*, p. 107.
46 Home Office, *List of Mines in the United Kingdom of Great Britain and Ireland and the Isle of Man, 1910* (London, 1911), pp. 219–23.
47 Church, *The History of the British Coal Industry, Vol. 3*, pp. 402–3.
48 Supple, *The History of the British Coal Industry, Vol. 4*, p. 203.
49 Lewis, *The Rhondda Valleys*, p. 89.
50 *Commission of Inquiry into Industrial Unrest: No.7 District – Wales and Monmouthshire* (Parl. Papers, 1917–18, Cd.8868, XV), p. 6.
51 *Ibid.*, p. 6.
52 Church, *The History of the British Coal Industry, Vol. 3*, p. 406.
53 Supple, *The History of the British Coal Industry, Vol. 4*, pp. 202–3.
54 *Ibid.*, p. 34, see also pp. 361–77.
55 Supple, 'The Political Economy of Demoralization', p. 567.
56 Asteris, 'South Wales Coal Exports', pp. 41–3; Buxton, *The Economic Development of the British Coal Industry*, pp. 164–77.
57 Deane and Mitchell, *Abstract of British Historical Statistics*, pp. 116–21.
58 E. J. Hobsbawm, *Industry and Empire: From 1750 to the Present Day* (London, Penguin, 1969 edn.), p. 208.
59 G. A. Williams, *The Welsh in Their History* (London, Croom Helm, 1982), p. 178.
60 Recalculated as long tons from, West Virginia Mining, *Annual Report, 1985*, pp. 38–9.
61 Eller, *Miners, Millhands and Mountaineers*, p. 239. See pp. 237–42 for description of the depression.
62 See Simon, 'The Development of Underdevelopment', pp. 294–319 for details of dominance of coal, particularly in the southern fields.
63 WVDM, *Annual Report, 1916*, p. 12. This obviously led to irregular employment; Hunt et al, *What the Coal Commission Found*, p. 160.
64 WVDM, *Annual Report, 1922*, p. 317. Rate per 1,000 calculated from *ibid.*, and West Virginia Mining, *Annual Report, 1985*, pp. 38–9.
65 Calculated from Gibson, *Compilation of Statistics*, pp. 134–5.
66 *History of Monongah Relief Fund* (Fairmont, 1910), WVU, Monongah Mines Relief Fund Records (A+M 1733); Morgan, *Rebirth of a Nation*, p. 146.
67 Benson, 'Mining Safety and Miners' Compensation', Paper presented at 2nd International Mining History Congress, Bochum, 1989, pp. 3–4.
68 WVDM, *Annual Report, 1922*, pp. 318, 330–63.
69 Benson, 'Mining Safety and Miners' Compensation', pp. 4–5.

70 WVDM, *Annual Report, 1922*, p. 327.
71 J. Rogers, 'I Remember that Mining Town', *West Virginia Review*, 15 (7 Apr 1938), p. 205.
72 Special Conference, 2–3 Feb 1914, SWMF Minutes, p. 16, Swansea, South Wales Coalfield Archive, C.2.
73 D. Jones, 'Serfdom and Slavery: Women's Work in Wales, 1890–1930', in D. R. Hopkin and G. S. Kealey (eds.), *Class, Community and the Labour Movement: Wales and Canada, 1850–1930* (Wales, Llafur/Labour/Le Travail, 1989), p. 93.

2

Power, culture and community

Although sharing a common base within the coal industry, the coalfields of West Virginia and south Wales developed, as we saw in the last chapter, in different ways. This chapter will look at the subsequent formation of the mining communities in the two regions, and the contrasting social and cultural patterns which characterised them. The differences that emerge, in the cultural origins of the labour force, community structure, power relationships, social conditions, and community and cultural life, provide a basis for understanding the patterns of protest outlined in later chapters.

Cultural origins

The different timing and pace of economic growth in West Virginia and south Wales created a contrast in the pattern of immigration into the two regions. In south Wales, large scale immigration occurred in waves over a period of fifty years, ending in 1911, while in West Virginia immigration was restricted mainly to the early decades after 1900. This obviously had great cultural significance, as the new immigrants into south Wales in the period under discussion came into a society that was more established, and mining communities which had already constructed an identity. In contrast, many of the communities in West Virginia were quite literally 'new' and, therefore, had no pre-existing cultural identity. These differences were further widened by the contrasting make-up of the populations in the two coalfields.

The late economic development of West Virginia, and the relative shortage of native born labour, led to the creation of a distinctive, and culturally mixed labour force; made up of white Americans, black Americans, and European immigrants. The white Americans

27

were mainly native West Virginians, as well as a smaller number of immigrants from other States. They were spread throughout the mining counties, and numbered around half of the total labour force throughout this period.[1]

Black workers had been present in the State since before the civil war, when they had laboured, sometimes as slaves, in the early coal mines. Their numbers increased with an influx of immigrants from further south who were involved in the construction of the railroads and then, in many cases, stayed on to work in the coal industry.[2] During the period under discussion, black miners made up an average of around 20% of the labour force. Thus in 1900, there were 4,600 blacks in the West Virginia mines (22.7%), whilst twenty-two years later, there were 21,388 (19.9%).This amounted to the highest number in the US coal industry, as well as contributing, by 1920, to the State having 69% of the total black population of central Appalachia.[3]

The distribution of black miners within the State was far from even. They were most prominent in the southernmost counties, where they became the 'distinguishing characteristic' of the smokeless coalfields.[4] In McDowell and Mercer Counties by 1910, for example, they outnumbered the native whites.[5] In Kanawha, Fayette and Raleigh counties, black miners were more in proportion to the State average, whilst in the northern counties like Harrison and Marion, they were rarely employed until after the war, making up less than 4% in 1908.[6] In Marion in 1910, only ninety-six black miners were employed out of a total of 4,412, whereas by 1920 the figure had risen to 693 out of 6,033.[7]

European immigrants had also worked in the mines since the nineteenth century, becoming an increasingly important part of the labour force, although their origins had changed by this period. In the 1880s, around 20% of the labour force was registered as European, the vast majority of whom were from western Europe, particularly England and Ireland.[8] By the turn of the century, these miners were being replaced by the 'new' immigrants from southern or eastern Europe. In 1910 the State's Department of Mines reported thirty different nationalities employed across the coalfield, amounting to around 30% of the total. The largest national groups were Italian 12.5%, Hungarian 6.6%, Polish 3.1%, and Slavish 3.1%. Among the others were nine Welsh, and two Japanese.[9] The number of immigrants began to decline towards the end of this period, particularly with the dislocations of the war, and the subsequent immigration restrictions. By 1922, for example, the Italian presence had dropped to 6.8%, Hungarian to 4.7% and Polish to 2.8%.[10]

The south Wales mining communities were, in contrast, far more homogeneous, with immigrants coming largely from the bordering Welsh and English counties and, at times, from counties further removed. English immigration was particularly heavy into the central and eastern parts of the coalfield, with Baines suggesting that, 'there must have been as many people of English extraction in Glamorgan by 1901 as there were (Welsh-speaking) natives of rural Wales.'[11] In contrast, the western anthracite section of the coalfield remained, for geographical reasons, mainly Welsh. In Ammanford and Cwmamman Urban Districts, for example, over 80% of the populations still spoke Welsh in 1911.[12]

The Welsh and English core of the population was complemented by smaller numbers of other nationalities. In this period, Merthyr Tydfil, with 14,502 of the 41,115 male population in 1921 engaged in mining,[13] gained the reputation as 'the most cosmopolitan town in South Wales.'[14] The Irish were the largest minority, leading the Merthyr novelist Jack Jones to claim that they were 'almost as strong as us Welsh in my hometown.'[15] This probably reflected the concentration of the Irish in the working-class districts, as in 1911 only 3% of the population were of Irish descent.[16] Other nationalities were also present in the coalfield. The Welsh community at Abercrave, for example, were joined by 200 Spaniards in 1911. By the outbreak of the war Abercrave also had a small number of Portuguese, Belgian, French and German residents.[17] Italian immigrants also made their way into some of the valleys.[18] This cultural mix, however, was relatively insignificant when compared with the scale of ethnic diversity in the West Virginia coalfield.

The different composition of the labour force had a crucial influence on the type of culture which emerged in these two regions. As Gutman famously pointed out, workers 'bring more to a new or changing work situation than their physical presence.' [19] We need, therefore, to understand the cultural origins of the different groups, and their motivations for entering the coalfields.

Before the large scale penetration of the coal industry into West Virginia, the native mountaineers had led a largely rural existence, where 'two factors, land and family, were interwoven as the basic threads sustaining the fabric of life.'[20] In remote communities, the family provided the basis of the economic unit, the aim of which was self-sufficiency.[21] Society was intensely patriarchal, with a clearly defined role for women,[22] and although in many ways strongly individualistic, it was not motivated towards individual achievement or the acquisition of property. Consequently, wider kinship and community links were an integral part of the fabric of life, clustering around religion, 'common work', and gatherings on court and election days.[23] Religion was an important part of cultural life, with the Bible providing 'the source from which arguments are drawn for every important discussion of Church or State, or life in general'.[24]

When outside observers entered Appalachia in the late nineteenth century, they depicted the people as backward, violent, prone to running moonshine, feuding, and other lawless pastimes. To the eyes of the middle class, therefore, the economic integration of the region into the capitalist economy was tied to the idea of 'modernising the mountaineer', and bringing them culturally into the values of 'mainstream America'.[25] The issue of violence within pre-industrial society was particularly important, not least because it was sometimes used later on as an explanation for the violent nature of industrial conflict in the State. However, harsh though life was, it was actually the coming of the industrial order which introduced violence, rather than traditions within mountain culture. Even the famous Hatfield/McCoy feud was rooted in the social and economic changes generated by outside forces. [26]

The scale of economic change, and the way the coal and land companies amassed huge areas of land, often by dubious means, had a tremendous impact on the mountaineer's way of life.[27] This intensified the already significant pressure on land, and led many of the mountain people to sell up and leave the State, or else attempt to exist within the new framework. Of course, initially, the prospect of change was not frowned upon by everyone. Fred Mooney, later Secretary of District 17 of the UMWA, recalled his community welcoming the news of the coming of the lumber companies. However, the 'rejoicing at the coming of the mills soon turned into bitterness and chagrin at the devastation wrought by the cutting and marketing of the timber'.[28]

Some of the future coal miners worked in the lumber industry, which involved the men leaving to work in the logging camps. This gave them some experience of an industrial lifestyle, and eased the transition for the eventual move to the coal camps.[29] They were also, in the early stages of the industry, able to work on an 'obrero mixto' basis, working only part of the year to help support subsistence farming. In the Fairmont region, for example, the mines did not open in the summer until the 1890's.[30]

This option was not always taken up, however, as some of the mountain people refused to engage in mining, as they believed going underground would bring bad luck.[31] Those who did enter the mines were not always happy to accept the socially controlled world of the company – something which encouraged their reputation as unreliable and lacking in industrial discipline.[32] Ultimately, however, many of the mountaineers were forced into the coal camps where, as we shall see later, their pre-industrial existence in independent and self-sufficient communities, was replaced with dependency, isolation and instability.

The black migrants who flooded into the West Virginia coalfield also came from predominantly rural backgrounds. They were, however, faced with a different set of problems to the natives of the Mountain State. The migrants who fled to the North in this period, did so for two reasons. Firstly, to escape from the insecurity and poverty of rural living, and secondly to avoid the increasingly virulent racism in the South, manifested in the 'Jim Crow' laws and unpunished violence. In a study undertaken in the West Virginia coalfield in the 1930s, James Laing discovered that the '"pull" of high wages and increased opportunity' was a 'universal' reason for migration amongst the black miners, whilst the 'crop failures and bad conditions from which many of them came constituted a "push" which rendered the economic "pull" of the mining fields more effective.' Laing also noted the importance of 'better schools', and 'a greater opportunity for civic and personal liberty'.[33]

As has already been mentioned, some of the first blacks to migrate worked on the construction of the railroads. Whilst many of these workers stayed on to enter the mines, the demand for labour was such that the companies sent out recruiting agents to the South to attract other black migrants with false stories of the 'wonderful' conditions in the coalfield.[34] Howard B. Lee, a one-time Attorney General in the State, has written of how 'mass meetings were held in their churches where the spell binders described the opportunities offered in this new Eldorado'. The Eldorado was also opened up, in some cases, to prisoners who were released when the Southern

31

authorities emptied their jails.[35] Once the black population became established in the coalfield, many blacks migrated after receiving letters from friends who had already settled.[36]

The majority of the blacks who came to the State were single males, some of whom intended to bring their families to join them when they had saved enough to pay for the trip. Others had no intention of leaving their agricultural past behind, and had primarily short-term economic objectives. The State Bureau of Negro Welfare and Statistics noted in 1922 that many blacks 'worked, sacrificed and saved to buy a farm "down home", pay the indebtedness upon one already purchased or, after getting "a little money ahead", return to their old home.'[37] This process is underlined by the evidence for a heavy turnover of labour, which, as we shall discuss later, had a very important impact on the nature of the West Virginian mining communities.[38]

This mixture of motives was also characteristic of the wave of European immigrants who entered the coalfield. The majority of these immigrants also came from an agricultural background, although there was a substantial minority who had experienced the industrial mining environment. The US Immigration Commission calculated that in 1910, 75% of the foreign born workforce in southern West Virginia had been agricultural workers in their homelands, and many of them had never worked for cash wages. They also discovered that around 10% of the immigrant miners had previously worked in coal mining.[39] The majority of the experienced coal miners seem to have been of Hungarian and, to a lesser extent, Polish origin, with the majority of Italians having no experience of the coal mining environment.[40] As a consequence, the operators were very keen to recruit Hungarian miners,[41] although it is important to point out that immigrants in general were popular. For example Logan County operator, Walter Thurmond, believed that 'most of the immigrants made excellent miners.'[42]

The motivation for this immigration echoed the concerns of the black migrants, comprising both economic and wider interests. The chance to start a new life in the 'land of opportunity' obviously appealed to some. One miner recalled his father leaving Europe for the coalfield 'anxious to escape the tyranny of the power drunk despots of the fatherland; grateful for an opportunity to wrest out a livelihood in security and peace.'[43] Others had less idealistic reasons for making the journey. In his famous study of steel workers in the

US, Brody discovered that many European immigrants came with the strictly limited intention of earning the comparatively high wages on offer, and then returning to their homes. As he put it, 'a lowly job in the mills, however ill-paid and unpleasant, was endurable if it enabled the immigrant to leave in a few years with funds enough to resume his accustomed place in his native village.'[44]

As with some of the black migrants, this seems to have been repeated in the West Virginia coalfield. A 1912 State Mining Commission, for example, found that banks in the Fairmont region reported large sums of money sent back to Europe.[45] Further evidence is revealed in the relief records of the Monongah mine disaster of December 1907, in which 358 men lost their lives. The mine, which was in the Fairmont field, had a high proportion of European immigrants among the workforce. In the explosion 171 Italian, 52 Hungarian, 15 Austrian, 31 Russian and 5 Turkish miners lost their lives. The records reveal that a large number of the miners were supporting wives and families in their original homelands. For example, the files of Angelo, Celestino, Felice, Giacinto, and Vincenzo Berardo, all show that they left dependants in Duronia Del Sannio in Italy.[46]

Of course, this could mean that the victims were sending money back to pay the fares of their families to come and join them, or as in the case of Vincenzo, whose father was the recipient of the money,[47] possibly out of charity. However, although many of the migrants travelled without their families, and did sometimes later send for them,[48] there is every reason to believe that a good many intended to return home. Evidence for this can be found in the particularly high level of population turnover in the West Virginia coalfields, and the fact that so few foreign born miners chose to take out American citizenship – Only 10% of the foreign miners in the State were naturalised citizens in 1920, compared with a national average of 26%.[49]

The recruitment network was also similar to that of the black miners, encompassing both formal and informal contacts. Coal companies initially tried to recruit potential miners directly from their home countries, but after this was outlawed, they concentrated their attention on the new immigrants arriving at Ellis Island, and those within New York city. Company agents hired miners by offering 'free' travel to the coalfield, or by pretending the coalfield was close by.[50] Coming in 'on transportation' as it was termed, however, had a sting in the tail when the hapless migrant was often expected to work off the cost of his journey before he could leave the coalfield. This resulted in a number of allegations of 'debt peonage', leading to several investigations, including one after a complaint by the Italian Ambassador to the Secretary of State.[51] In 1907 a new State Immigration Bureau was established to try to recruit what the operators believed was a higher standard of immigrant.[52] The commissioner, John H. Nugent, a former President of District 17 of the UMWA, who had his salary paid by the coal companies, made several trips to Europe, including one in the summer of 1907, when he spent three months touring, paying special attention to England, Scotland, Wales, and Ireland.[53]

As with the black migrants, contact with friends and relatives already resident in the coalfield, was a common channel of communication to potential immigrants.[54] The relief fund files of the Monongah disaster are also enlightening in this context, as they reveal an interconnection between male relatives, as well as a large representations from particular towns and villages. For instance, of the 52 Hungarians who lost their lives, 15 came from Czeke. Similarly, many of the Italians who died came from Duronia del Sannio. Among these, there were several groups of victims with the same surname. As well as the five Berardos mentioned above, these included five Anciellos, three Basiles, and three Adducchios.[55] The five Turkish victims were also from the same town, Tenedos.[56] This would strongly suggest that the informal network of recruitment was the most prominent.

The migrants into the south Wales coalfield, whilst less of a cultural and ethnic mix, shared some of the characteristics of the groups who chose to enter the coalfields of West Virginia. The vast majority of them were young males, from primarily rural backgrounds, with a strong economic motivation for migrating, as well as a general interest in establishing a new life.[57]

Bert Coombes, who grew up in Herefordshire, recalled being 'fascinated by that light in the sky' from industrial south Wales, and the opportunity it offered to him as an eighteen year old who 'had decided I must get away somewhere'. To Coombes, the mining valleys represented a future where he could get 'good clothes, money to spend, to see fresh places and faces, and – well, many things'. It also meant he could escape what he saw as a bleak present: 'When I hear people extolling the joys of country living', he wrote, 'I think of the struggles of the small farmers as I knew them'.[58] Another miner, who migrated from Merionethshire around 1906, recalled having 'a desire to go for some years . . . I suppose I had been fired more or less by some of the advantages of going to south Wales. I wanted to get away from the farms, and I thought there would be an opportunity for more self-education in mining villages and that proved to be true.'[59]

The emphasis upon the hardship of rural life should not be missed, even when compared with the prospect of the rigours of the coal miner's existence. For example, in Cardiganshire in the early 1900s, considered the heartland of rural Welsh society, the 'way of life had changed little over the previous century'. Smallholdings were predominant on the poor upland soil, and the quality of food, housing, and consequently health, was poor. This led many to flee the county, with, by 1911 for example, a large number of Cardigan-born women resident in the Rhondda.[60] Even for areas with better agricultural conditions, the advantages of leaving for the coalfield were obvious. As Brinley Thomas has suggested, 'miners' earnings could easily reach a point at which they were distinctively superior to those of other trades: hence the incursion of such a large body of long distance immigrants.'[61]

The accessibility of the coalfield to potential miners meant that the informal networks of information were the main stimulus to migration. The migrant from Merionethshire commented on the fact that 'a big number from our valley' had gone to the coalfield,[62] and Coombes finally migrated to the distant fires of industrial south Wales with the help of a friend who had left a few months previously, and had arranged a job for him.[63] Likewise, Frank Hodges, who later became Secretary of the MFGB, heard at Woolaston in Gloucester, stories of 'fabulous wages' from 'Men who had left the village to go work in the mines' and returned for holidays. 'They spoke of the wages that could be earned, the joy that could be secured in life, and became accidentally the propagandists of the colliery companies, the recruiting sergeants of the colliery proprietors.' Hodges' father and eldest brother moved first to Abertillery and then sent back for the family, who left 'the fair and pleasant countryside' for the 'grimy, dusty and forbidding mining valley.'[64]

When Coombes recalled leaving rural Herefordshire for the south Wales Valleys, it is interesting to note that he wrote:

I carried the smell of the woodfire with me, and it has hung in my senses ever since. Little things like the thud of a falling apple, the crackle of corn being handled, the smell of manure drying on a warm day, the hoot of the owl from the orchard at night, and the smell of the new bread when my mother drew it from the stone oven on a long wooden ladle, are still very sweet to me. Every year the smell of drying grass makes me crave for the hayfields, but I have never since worked in them or been in my native place for anything more than a short visit. [65]

The fact that Coombes could recall this many years after leaving, is a subtle reminder of the 'cultural baggage' that the migrants brought with them to the mining communities. Harsh as it may have been, the very substance of rural existence was ingrained upon those who migrated, even those who intended settling permanently. This was something which linked the migrants to both the regions under discussion. Seeking a better life, they traded their agricultural roots for an industrial world, and discovered in the process that 'values stand to be lost as well as gained.'[66]

Community structure

The structure of the communities in these two regions, differed in many respects. The later and more rapid expansion of the West Virginia coal industry meant that the majority of coal mining communities were new in this period. Furthermore, whilst the greater number of pre-existing communities in the northern part of the State meant that the new coal mining settlements were sometimes erected at or near established towns, the vast majority, particularly in the south, were not.[67]

The reason for this was that the coal seams were usually remote from existing settlements in the sparsely populated State, which led to the construction of company coal towns (or coal camps as they were known early on), which were unincorporated. By the end of this period, the US Coal Commission calculated that just over 20% of the half-million bituminous coal miners in the US lived in incorporated towns with a population of more than 2,500. In West Virginia, however, only 6% of the miners lived in such towns, compared with 47% in Illinois.[68] Thus as many as 80% of the State's miners lived in company coal towns, compared with only 9% in Illinois.[69]

The individual surveys of the Coal Commission illustrate these points well. For example, one coal community in Logan County surveyed for the commission, lived around a mine that had been in operation for only seven years, and was expected to last only for another thirteen. Furthermore, the population of 317 were 16 miles from the nearest town (Madison), and 54 miles from the nearest town with a population of over 2,500 (St.Albins).[70] Another mine in Kanawha County was 21 years old, with a probable life of 100 years. Here the population of 192 were one mile from the town of Cedar Grove, and 17 miles from the nearest town with a population greater than 2,500, which was the State capital, Charleston.[71] Another, larger community, run by the Boomer Coal and Coke Company in Fayette County had 1,322 residents. This mine was 21 years old, with a probable life of 50 years. It was, however, closer to more established settlements, being two miles from Smithers, and 3 miles from the larger town of Montgomery.[72]

Similar evidence is provided by a survey conducted in the summer of 1920 by the US Children's Bureau. In its study of eleven representative Raleigh County mining communities, it discovered that all of the camps were between three and thirteen miles from the nearest large town, Beckley. The population of the communities ranged from 200 to 1,200.[73]

The isolation of many of these towns was not just a matter of distance. The above survey described the average town as 'practically a frontier settlement. It is remote and isolated, shut in by high, wooded hills, a straggling line of low houses in the wilderness . . . the distance in miles gives no idea of the inaccessibility', with lengthy, unreliable train services, and a walk of between a half and several miles to the nearest public road.[74] Similarly the Logan community described above was one mile from the nearest public road, although the bigger Fayette community did have nearly half of the company houses on a public road, which was part paved concrete, and the other two thirds 'dirt', 'narrow', and 'uneven'.[75]

One operator recalled conditions being so bad in the winter in the early part of this period, that the unpaved roads became unpassable. He also remembered that the journey between MacDonald and Bluefield could take as long as two days – a journey which in a car can be done in two hours. Under the circumstances, it is hardly surprising that the arrival of the first car in Raleigh County in 1910, led the miners in Tams to 'quit work and follow it up and down the town'! [76]

The south Wales mining communities shared the topography of the West Virginia, although they were different in terms of age, and geographic isolation. The mining towns were enclosed by steep-sided valleys into which, in the more populous parts of the coalfield, the mining settlements and population were, quite literally, crowded.[77] The size and density of this population was dramatically different to West Virginia. In 1911, Glamorgan had 1,383 persons per square mile, compared with an average for England and Wales of 618 persons per square mile. Even this figure, however, does not show the true extent of the population density for some parts of the coalfield, with 4,480 people per square mile in the Rhondda Urban District as a whole, and parts of the Rhondda as high as 6,400.[78]

The size of the mining labour force at particular mines, when compared to the figures presented above for West Virginia, under-lines this difference of scale. In 1913, the Home Office *List of Mines* noted that of the fifty-three collieries working in the Rhondda, forty-four employed over 500 men underground, while twenty-one employed over 1,000.[79]

As we saw in the last chapter, south Wales was already, by the late nineteenth century, an industrialised region. As G. A. Williams has pointed out for Wales as a whole, 'by the 1870s at the latest . . . the terrible dominion of the harvest and seasonal cycle had been broken and it was the rhythms of industry which had become the ultimate determinants of social life.'[80] This meant that, in contrast to West Virginia, many of the mining communities were not 'isolated' islands in an agricultural and rural sea, but were well established by the early 1900's with their own traditions, culture, and history.

Of course, the economic development of south Wales itself was not even, with a greater intensity in the eastern part, just as the West Virginian coalfield varied between north and south. However, unlike the southern part of West Virginia, many of the settlements in the western part of the coalfield were linked to previously rural com-munities. In the Carmarthenshire anthracite field, 'newer develop-ment more frequently took the shape of a linear expansion of existing nuclei along the major or minor thoroughfares.'[81] Thus James Griffiths recalled the merging of his village with a neighbour-ing one to form the mining community of Ammanford, when the new anthracite mines opened. As a consequence his father, who was the village blacksmith, had to adapt his business to the sharpening and tempering of collier's mandrels and hobnails.[82]

Nor did the communities around the anthracite mines have the same density of population, or employment as in the Rhondda. Thus in 1910, the Home Office *List of Mines*, recorded that of the seventy-eight mines registered in Carmarthen, four employed more than 500 men underground, one more than 400, three more than 300, and thirty-seven less than 100.[83]

On the question of isolation, it is also important to point out that while a good many of the miners did reside in the 'classic' south Wales mining valleys, like the Rhondda, others, as early as 1850, were resident in or dependent on larger, more diverse towns.[84] The large number of miners resident in the old iron town of Merthyr, mentioned earlier, illustrates this point. Furthermore, improved transport facilities allowed a more general flexibility, with miners able to live further from the pit and commute to work.[85] This offers a further contrast to the more isolated, newer West Virginian towns.

Power relationships

The different geographical and structural bases of the communities in these two regions were a significant influence on the formation of social relations, and the distribution of power within these. The importance of the newness of a community and the power this gave to the owners has been noted by historians. Waller, for example, has argued that in the Dukeries coalfield, 'the newness and isolation' of the pit villages explained the 'unusual authority and command of the employers.'[86] Mining communites that developed at a slower rate within a more established culture, however, were far from immune from the exercise of power by the owners. Hence, Williamson's description of Heddon, with its 'social order which was distinctly paternalistic', where two families dominated, providing the social amenities.[87] However, this form of control declined with the changing scale of the coal industry, in the move towards what Samuel calls the 'increasingly aggressive forms of capitalist intervention and management',[88] when the emphasis changed to controlling the workplace rather than dominating the social and cultural life of the communities. These differing patterns of social development were apparent in West Virginia and south Wales.

In the Mountain State the late, and rapid, penetration of corporate capitalism saw the coal operators seize control of large areas of

land, and with it legal and political power. One of the manifestations of this control was the company towns which the operators
built in the Appalachian wilderness. The system of social relations
that they fashioned in these settlements rarely allowed any development of independent initiatives. As they attempted to maximise their
profits, their policies – whether in the form of paternalism or blatant
exploitation, were directed towards controlling all aspects of social
life from above. The extent of this control has been described by
many writers, including Winthrop Lane, who wrote in 1921:

> The operators are not only the miner's employer, they are his landlord,
> his merchant, the provider of his amusements, the sanitary officer of
> the town, sometime the source of his police protection and patron of
> his physician, his minister and his school teacher . . . It is . . . in some
> ways a feudal civilization.[89]

The key to this control lay in the ownership of property. The miners
were not allowed to buy houses on company property, and it proved
very difficult to obtain land independently. Sometimes this was
because there was none available: as one miner told a Senate Inquiry
in 1913, 'there was no independent property that a man could either
lease or buy up' near his community.[90] In other cases there was a
limited amount of land or housing for rent or sale nearby at local
towns,[91] although it was another matter as to whether it could be
afforded.

The operators used the company houses as a method of controlling the labour force and, sometimes, as a source of profit.[92]
Residence in the company house did not grant the occupant normal
tenancy rights, and eviction was threatened if the miner stopped
work, for whatever reason.[93] The nature of these tenancy rights are
revealed in a letter from the manager of the Superior Pocahontas
Coal Company, George Wolfe, to operator Justus Collins. Wolfe
wrote, (ironically on the 25 December 1915), that 'our attorneys
claim that our houses are incidental to our business and that the
question of Landlord and Tenant at will does not exist, but the question is one of Master and Servant.'[94]

An examination of an actual lease for a company house reveals
the nature of this relationship. A White Oak Coal Company lease,
from the New River district, stipulated that 'it is expressly agreed
and understood that this agreement shall not operate or be con-
strued to create the relation of landlord and tenant between the

parties hereto under any circumstances whatsoever.' The insecurity
of the occupant is underlined by the clause which says the right of
occupancy will 'end and terminate whenever, from any cause whatsoever, the party of the second part shall cease to work for the party
of the first part . . .' The lease also had provision to deduct rent from
the miner's wages, and control the right of free association of the
resident – the occupant was not allowed 'to board or harbor on said
premises against the said wishes of the party of the first part . . .'[95]

The significance of the last point was underlined by Collins when
he told Wolfe in a letter, that he 'was the originator of the tenant
house contracts . . . and the original purpose in my mind . . . was to
exercise the right during strike times, and upon other extraordinary
occasions, to prevent undesirable people from roaming through our
property'.[96] The assertion of these property 'rights' proved, as we
shall see in the next chapter, one of the most powerful weapons in
the battle to prevent the miners from joining the UMWA. Strikes
were met with mass evictions, and the 'undesirable people' were
inevitably deemed to be union organisers. As one organiser in the
Fairmont field wrote in the *UMWJ* in 1900, 'we were notified to
leave at once. This we obeyed, as that is the custom down on
Watson's holy soil.'[97]

The operators' provision of the company store provided a further
avenue for control, and profit. Some forced their employees to buy
their goods at the store. One miner on Cabin Creek, claimed
employees were told 'that if they were going to trade at other places
they must work at other places; if they could buy goods at other
places cheaper, they could afford to work at other places cheaper.'[98]
While others, like Collins, rejected coercion,[99] the company store
allowed rich pickings. Throughout this period there were allegations that the prices in the company stores were artificially high.
This was accepted by the Coal Commission, which found that the
price of goods in the Kanawha region was 4.2% higher in company
stores, than in comparable independent stores. This was in spite of
natural advantages over independent stores, like the credit standing
of the mine company, or the fact that, as larger concerns, they are
more able to stand the problems associated with the irregularity of
the coal industry.[100]

In fact the Coal Commission may well have underestimated the
profits that could accrue to the company. The natural monopoly, in
some of the cases, allowed the company to charge very high prices.

As one mining family put it, 'we wouldn't trade at the company store at all, prices are so high there, if the other stores weren't so far away.'[101] The operators certainly seemed aware of the financial benefits available. The Fairmont merger in 1900, for example, allowed for profits of between 10% and 20% on sales in the company store.[102] Profits from company stores were also significant enough to be used to subsidise downturns in the demand for coal.[103]

The issue of profits from the store lay at the root of a dispute between Wolfe and independent merchants at Davy. Wolfe objected to the merchants delivering their goods in the company town, complaining that they were 'satisfied with very small profits', and that their competition had 'cut our powder profits from three thousand per year to eight hundred dollars'.[104] In a later letter, on the same issue, Wolfe spoke of store sales of $81,000 in 1914, and of a net profit on sales of 14%. He suggested that the company store could compete with the Davy merchants by copying the Raleigh Coal Company's Store, and making only 10% on sales, but selling more goods.[105]

Of course it would be wrong to suggest that all of the operators approached the use of the company store in the same way. Tams, for example, suggests the profits made from the company store 'varied widely', and that he 'operated on a margin considerably below that general among "private" stores in the area' – although he did admit that 'some companies took advantage of a near-monopoly, and charged all the traffic would bear.'[106] In practice, however, taking into account the unreliability of the coal industry, and the especially aggressive pursuit of profits that it encouraged, it would seem sensible to suggest, from the evidence above, that some thought the 'traffic' could bear a good deal.

The coal operators were also able to 'encourage' the use of the company store by issuing scrip – a paper ticket, or more commonly a metal coin, which provided credit for goods at the company store.[107] It was claimed that this was a 'convenience' for their employees, which allowed credit at the company store until payday.[108] While, for some at least, this may have been the intention, for others there were more manipulative reasons.

For scrip could often only be exchanged for goods at the company store or, when conversion to cash was available, only at a lower rate. Similarly if outside institutions exchanged scrip, it was usually at a reduced rate.[109] The result of the extensive use of scrip was that, sometimes intentionally on the part of the operators, families sunk heavily into debt. In her study of the Raleigh County mining communities, McGill noted that the unpredictability of earnings left 'most of the mine workers' families on credit.' She discovered that around 80% of the families were 'accustomed to using scrip', with some families 'constantly "scrip bound"', meaning that by pay day, they did not receive any cash.[110]

The operators' control of the company town opened the labour force up to other nefarious practices, which made further inroads into their social and economic well-being. These included numerous charges for the provision of 'services'. Lane, for example, found companies making deductions from wages of between $6 and $10 for a four-room house; $1 to $2 for the provision of a doctor, 50 c. to $1 for hospital service, 25 c. for sharpening tools, and 75 c. for a wash house, all per month.[111] The number and cost of these charges varied between different companies, with some making deductions for accident and burial funds, coal, and even cow feed ! [112] If we take these deductions into account, along with the issuance of scrip, it is easy to see how families could slide into debt. Using evidence for the wage returns of fifty miners presented in the evidence of the 1913 Senate Inquiry, Simon has calculated that in May 1912, the miners concerned received only 56% of their wages.[113]

The arbitrary and authoritarian nature of the way in which the companies operated these deductions is revealed in the details of a dispute at Pinnickinnick in 1900. After initially agreeing that the miners could choose their own doctor, the company reversed its decision, and introduced new charges for a candidate of the company's choice. A notice was issued telling the work-force that the new charges would be $1 per month for each married man, 50 c. for a single man, plus an extra $5 for obstetrical cases. It was followed by the warning that: 'There will be no exceptions to this clause, and you need therefore not ask, for if you cannot comply with the rules of our company you need not apply for work.'[114] The strike that resulted from these actions led the editor of the *UMWJ* to allege, somewhat colourfully, that the companies were employing 'beardless boys' from medical colleges, 'compelling the miners to pay these lively wages and supply them with subjects to experiment on.' [115]

Alongside these deductions, there were other methods of cutting the miner's wages. The company's control of the workplace in non-union mines gave them a free hand in deciding the amounts, if any, paid for dead work. Furthermore the gauge of the screens was sometimes adjusted to the company's advantage, and docking for impurities could be similarly arbitrary. The 1912 State Mining Commission, appointed by the Governor W. E. Glasscock admitted that there was evidence of 'some injustice to the miner' with regard to the latter.[116]

Perhaps the worst example of this form of exploitation, both symbolically and in terms of cost, was the shortweighing of coal. State law gave the miners the right to have a say in the selection of checkweighmen, but the laws were not properly enforced.[117] As a consequence, if there were scales, the weights were sometimes 'fixed' in the company's favour, or else completely ignored.[118] The most blatant example of this was payment by the car rather than the ton. In 1901, one miner from Ashland wrote to the *UMWJ* complaining of three different sizes of mine car in use, ranging from three tons and eight bushels, to three tons and fourteen bushels, all of which were priced at 46 c.. He told the editor, 'We don't have it quite as bad here as some of our brothers down the line below here', where the miners loaded cars, some of which had outside measurements of 10 ft 6 in long, 3ft 4 in wide at the bottom, 6 ft 4 in wide at the top, and 2 ft 8 in high. These cars were loaded for only 75 c.[119]

The introduction of larger cars was an obvious source of friction. The Assistant Superintendent of the Louisville Coal and Coke Company, A. M. Herndon, complained in 1905 of miners refusing to load new cars which were so large that the main entry to the mine had to have $1500 worth of work in order to allow them access. The protesting miners were given short shrift however, as they were sacked and placed on a blacklist 'so that they cannot get work in the Flat Top Field.'[120]

Nor was the loading of the cars always fair. In 1921, one miner described how, at times of a labour surplus, the miners had to 'heap' cars by 'what is known as the 0–2 hump', where 'the drivers are instructed to set their elbows at the edge of the miners' cars . . . and sight over their fingers, and if they could not see any coal over their fingers they would not let it stand until they could'.[121]

These abuses of power became central to the turbulent relations between the miner and operator in West Virginia. As the miner's song 'Miner's Lifeguard' put it;

You've been docked and docked, my boys,
You've been loading two for one;
What have you to show for working
Since this mining has begun?
Overalls, and cans for rockers,
In your shanties sleep on rails.
Keep your hands upon the dollar
And your eyes upon the scales

Chorus
Union miners stand together
Heed no operators' tale
Keep your hand upon the dollar
And your eyes upon the scale. [122]

The reference to the union is significant, as the battle to establish the UMWA was integral to the remedying of the arbitrary abuses of the operators. This is one of the most important reasons why, as we shall see in the next chapter, the union was so bitterly resisted. When, particularly in the war years, companies were forced to sign agreements with the UMWA, they were forced to adjust the abuses of their control of the workplace.[123]

Alongside the more obvious manifestations of operator power, like the abuses at the company store and the workplace, there were other more elaborate attempts at engineering the nature of life in the company town. The 'judicious mixture' of blacks, whites, and immigrants, described earlier in this chapter is a good example of this. Although the demand for labour necessitated tapping a variety of sources, there was also a definite attempt to build a culturally and ethnically divided workforce, that would split into its component parts, rather than unite against the operators. Black migrants, for example, were sometimes preferred by the operators, as they were considered 'less likely to complain'.[124] The segregation in the coal camps was a structural attempt to cement these differences.[125]

The provision of amenities in the company town also presented the operator with an opportunity to engineer social relationships. The provision of schools and churches are a good example of this, with some companies supplementing district funds to lengthen school terms and, within the mining camps, contributing by erecting a building, providing equipment, or helping pay the teacher's salary. The attitude to provision, however, varied between companies with 'some generous in their contributions', while 'others did little or nothing.'[126] The operator's role in providing facilities was matched by the control that they sought over them. As one miner on Cabin Creek put it, 'I don't like the schools; they seem to me to be controlled . . . by the company.'[127]

The size and isolation of the mining towns left many of the miners reliant on the company for the provision of churches. Some communities had no churches at all, while others were too small to have more than one church, which meant that different denominations would use the same building – sometimes the school house.[128] The Justus Collins papers provide salient evidence on the way some of the operators sought to exploit religion to their advantage. In 1902 the Catholic Church requested the right to build on company property. The request was greeted with enthusiasm as a similar arrangement had proved to the advantage of another coal operator when, during a strike, 'the Priest absolutely refused to allow his flock to have anything to do with the Union.'[129] Fifteen years later, at Winding Gulf, the company decided to help the black church goers build their own church, providing they could raise $200 in cash. The black preacher, M. L. Minter, was described as 'an able man', who 'has given very good satisfaction, and seems to have the interest of the company at heart.'[130]

The interference of the coal operators in the ostensibly public-funded education system is symptomatic of the substitution of the rule of the company for the rule of public, democratic institutions. In some ways, however, to speak of a substitution is an overstatement, as in many parts of the State there was very little to substitute for. The late and rapid development of the State's coal industry meant that, in many ways, the coal companies adapted and created the structures of legal and political life in the State, in much the same way as they constructed the company towns in the wilderness. A good example of this was the provision of law enforcement officers within the company town, and in the wider county.

In the early years of the coal industry, there was no official police force in the State, so the companies employed private police, or 'mine guards' as they became known, to enforce 'law and order'. According to Lee, many of those selected were of dubious backgrounds, whose remit was 'to keep the miners intimidated, to beat up, arrest, and even jail if necessary, any worker or visitor suspected of union activities around the camps'.[131] As the industry became more established, the operators concentrated on attempting to elect their men to the county post of sheriff. The latter had the right to appoint deputy sheriffs, who were paid by the company, and often came to 'police' the coal towns.[132] As we shall see later, the role of the deputies, particularly in Logan county, became one of the most contentious issues in this period.

The control of the legal structures of the company town and, often, the county, was buttressed by a web of influence that permeated all other aspects of the legal and political system. As the coal industry developed, the existing local elite threw in their lot with the 'modernisers', resulting in the main judicial and political posts being filled by those sympathetic to the coal operators. This control ranged from local to the State judiciary, from local politicians to State senators (who until 1913 were selected by the State legislatures, rather than a popular vote), and on to the State Governors, who despite sometimes mouthing phrases sympathetic to labour at election times, rarely erred from the path of supporting the coal interests.

The most obvious manifestation of the domination of the legal and political apparatus by economic interests, was the effort to prevent the incursion of the UMWA into the State, and the resulting violent outbreaks of industrial conflict. Indeed, attempting to talk of the role of law enforcement, from the deputy sheriff to the Governor, is almost impossible as, to a greater or lesser extent, their roles were intertwined with maintaining the feudal system of relations in the State. In West Virginia in these years, struggle was part of everyday life. Even when the huge explosions of industrial militancy subsided, or smaller strikes were broken or settled, the job of blacklisting, spying, intimidating, went on under the eyes of the 'authorities'.

The detail and evidence for this wider web of control will be discussed in the following chapter. It is important to establish now, however, that the formation of the mining communities, and the subsequent nature of life for the inhabitants, must be understood within the context of this control. The feudal relations within the State affected all facets of life, whether the inhabitants lived in incorporated, or unincorporated communities.

Of course, as it has been stressed throughout this chapter, it would be wrong to depict the operators as identical in their approach to the utilisation of their power. As we shall see in the discussion of conditions within the camps, there were variations between different operators, large and small companies, different regions, and over time. What it is important to stress, however, is that what can only be described as the absence of law and order within West Virginia, allowed, potentially, the operators a free hand in exploiting their employees. The desire for profits, in the notoriously unpredictable bituminous coal industry, when mixed with the peculiarly aggressive owners and managers that it attracted, meant that a system that allowed such abuses would, in varying degrees, be used.

In south Wales, the differing patterns of ownership, and wider input into social, political and judicial structures, created a different balance in the power relationship between owner and miner, when compared with West Virginia.

In the latter, the operator's control over the mining community was based on the domination of property, the most obvious manifestation of which was the company housing. In south Wales the pattern was entirely different, with the coal companies building few houses when compared with both West Virginia and other parts of the British coalfield. As early as 1873, a Royal Commission 'found that housing involved the coal owners to only a very minor degree.'[133] In 1919, the MSWCA submitted figures to the Royal Commission suggesting that 23.3% of houses in the coalfield were owned or leased by colliery companies, 19.3% owned by colliery workmen, and 57.4% by private landlords.[134]

The provision of company housing in south Wales was higher where the mines were established in more isolated, sparsely populated sections of the coalfield.[135] Thus the western anthracite district had the largest number of company houses. In contrast the eastern sections had a denser concentration of population, and the linear nature of colliery settlements, meant that new housing often formed an extension to existing coal communities, rather than a distinct new community. As Daunton points out, this meant that 'addition to the built up area was possible using the resources of the existing community, ploughing back the profits from the previous development and drawing upon an existing building industry.'[136] The fact that, as was discussed earlier, the majority of miners lived in the more populated eastern part of the coalfield underlines the impact of geographic isolation on the subsequent patterns of ownership.

There were some owners who attempted to construct communities that were in some ways comparable to those in West Virginia. In

the nineteenth century, for example, Sir William T. Lewis built terraces of company housing around his pits which K. O. Morgan has
suggested 'became virtually company towns on the model of the
United States.'[137] However, as we have seen, this was not the
common form of housing, nor, because they were the exception,
could they be operated with the same degree of impunity as in the
Mountain State.

For the majority of owners the attitude towards company housing
was quite different. In 1909, for example, the General Committee of
the Cambrian lodge, passed a motion concerning the sale of houses
by the Cambrian Combine. They 'resolved that a vote of thanks be
tendered to Mr D. A. Thomas and Mr Llewellyn for their generous
and considerate action in connection with the sale of company
houses to their workmen.'[138] Rather than seeing their role as provid-
ers of housing, Jones has suggested that coal owners only entered
into housing provision 'due to the rapid decline in the ability of
traditional agencies to provide sufficient accommodation in the
peak years of the coal industry.' This was the case after 1906, and
particularly 1914, when a relatively large number of company
houses were approved.[139]

As the motion from the Cambrian lodge shows, the miners were
keen to become owner-occupiers. The western anthracite district,
as well as having the highest number of company houses, also had
the greatest number of owner-occupiers, the majority of whom
owned their semi-detached houses.[140] In the rest of the coalfield, the
greater expense involved in building a house, meant that the most
common path to owning a home was via a building club. These
were made up of potential owner-occupiers, as well as 'men of substance', who would add prestige to the project, and sometimes
themselves partake in the scheme with the purpose of securing
houses for rent. The clubs were financed by the payment of monthly
shares which, when they reached a certain level, would be advanced
to a builder, who would construct the houses. The leases on these
were held by the trustees of the club, who negotiated a mortgage
with the banks. The occupant would then gradually pay this figure
off, eventually becoming the owner – something that could take
anything from five to twenty five years.[141] The importance of the
building clubs is revealed by the fact that by the late nineteenth
century, almost 25% of all the new houses erected in the coalfield,
were built using this process.[142] Building clubs remained important

in the early part of this period, although their use sharply declined after the War.[143]

The majority of housing was provided by private landlords. These ranged from wealthy individuals to joint stock companies, who 'almost invariably' constructed terraced settlements.[144] As we shall see later, the standard of these varied widely, and there is also evidence of private landlords attempting to assert their control over tenants. Edmund Stonelake, a local councillor in Aberdare, recalled how 'key money was demanded and some landlords let houses on condition that prospective tenants agreed to become customers at the landlord's shop' [145] Furthermore, while the coal owners did not own these houses, they were well aware that class interest gave them a degree of influence. A letter from the Ocean Coal Company in 1885 noted that 'a Colliery Company has much to gain by encouraging the public to build largely in its vicinity so as to secure their keep and support in any conflict they may be involved in with their workmen.' [146]

The different pattern of the ownership of housing in south Wales was representative of generally different social relationships. In the early nineteenth century, prior to the expansion of the industry, the small mining communities of the Rhondda, for example, possessed certain characteristics that were similar to West Virginia a century later. The miners lived in company houses and were paid monthly, sometimes in kind rather than cash, with deductions for 'services'. In 1832, the Anti-Truck Act prohibited payment in goods, or any form other than the 'current coin of the realm', although the Act was ignored by the coal owners of the Aberdare valley, because of the lack of inspectors.[147] However, the huge expansion of the industry in the 1870s, saw the proliferation of the sources of ownership and control, and the beginning of the intervention of public bodies. Furthermore, the greater freedom for the miners to organise, and the subsequent strength of the SWMF, meant that miners were able to collectively play a far greater role in shaping their own environment.

Certainly some aspects of control continued into the next century, and obviously the isolated communities were more open to such abuses. The issue of health deductions is one example that shows both the similarities and differences with the situation in West Virginia. In Mardy, for example, Arthur Horner recalled how the companies deducted money from the miners' wages to pay a doctor of the former's choice. Horner recalled how 'the doctors regarded themselves as virtually employees of the company'. The standard of care was also dubious, leading Horner to doubt whether one of the company's doctors 'had read a medical book since he first qualified.' Eventually, after a long battle the miners succeeded in getting their own doctor, and forming their own scheme.[148] A similar scheme had been in operation since the 1890s in Tredegar.[149]

What is significant here is the fact that the miners were able to oppose the attempt by the coal owners to impose their will from the top. A similar example lies in the field of education, where in 1914, The Annual Conference of the SWMF protested against the 'proposal of certain Education Authorities in the coalfield to hand over any phase of Mining Education to the coal owners or any other special interest.' They went on to 'strongly declare in favour of the democratic principle that all forms of Education shall be under the control of publicly-elected representatives of the people, and to this end we pledge ourselves to support our Labour Representatives in securing this.'[150]

The provision of social facilities by the coal owners likewise offers a variation with West Virginia. In the company towns the operators had little choice but to provide some facilities for their employees. In south Wales, the fact that the company did not create or, in a comparative sense, dominate the community, meant that such provision was optional. Of course some owners opted for philanthropic acts, either in the hope of encouraging quiescence, or from more genuine motives. Chapels and churches were the most common examples of such acts, as well as schools, libraries, hospitals and workmen's institutes.[151] However, on the whole, provision was not over-generous.[152]

This 'greater space' within civil society gave the developing mining communities a chance to create their own structures, and develop their own culture. As E. D. Lewis noted, Rhondda society 'owed but little to the leadership or patronage of the coal speculators', or those that followed them.[153] Even in the sphere of local government and administration, the coal owners' influence began to decline after the reforms of the 1880s, and the new century saw the political manifestations of the developing confidence of the new communities.

Similarly, the coal owners were not able to exert their influence through the legal and political system on the same scale as their West Virginian counterparts. Certainly, as we shall see in a later chapter, the authorities were far from impartial, and the communities were subjected to police harassment and surveillance, a far from independent judiciary, a biased press, and even the introduction of the army. However, the different legal and political framework did not allow the owners, even if they had wanted to, to employ law enforcement officers to beat and murder union organisers. Nor was the interference of the 'authorities' at local and national level as blatant as in West Virginia, where it was never accepted that the union had a right to organise. The operation of the legal system was influenced by a mixture of class interest, and the desire to preserve what the authorities defined as 'order', not to obscure a level of disorder that was remarkable even by the standards of the US.

Compared to West Virginia, therefore, power relationships were very different in south Wales. While the wider framework was not impartial, the coal owners did not and could not attempt to control the structures of civil society. Their attention was turned towards control of the workplace and the production process, something that was challenged by the strength of the union and, to a lesser extent, the imposition of government legislation on the mining industry.

Social conditions

In its study of 713 company controlled communities in the US coalfield, the Coal Commission painted a pretty dismal picture. Of the 71,000 company owned dwellings, 95% were made of wood, with over 66% 'finished on the outside with weather board, usually nailed directly to the frame', and roofs of composition paper. Less than 3% of these houses had bath tubs or showers, less than 14% had running water inside, although over 66% did have electric or gas light. Outside of the houses, 'company provision for recreation and amusement in the majority of communities is so meager as to be negligible', while the Public Health Service survey of sixty-four company controlled communities, undertaken as part of the Commission's work, suggested that 'there can be no question as to the general backwardness . . . as regards satisfactory methods of disposing of human excreta . . . Lack of proper sewage disposal methods may be ascribed to careless planning', and that 'control of disease carriers and communicable disease contacts appears to be an unknown art'[154]

52

This dreadful picture of the social conditions within the company coal communities was more than represented in West Virginia, where many of the company houses were situated. Thus McGill wrote of the eleven Raleigh County communities she studied: 'Uncertainty as to the probable lifetime of the mine makes for cheaply and hastily constructed houses, primitive sanitation, and other hardships – both sanitary and cultural – of pioneer life.' Her description of the overcrowded camps, with unclean water, no toilets, lack of pavements, and desperately poor housing, seems in character with much of the worst of the national study. She described the houses as being built to a general plan, made of wood, and the cheapest materials. They were damp, cold, and often had cracks and holes making them '"like paper" when the wind struck them'.[155] A similar point was made by a West Virginia miner in 1901, when he wrote to the *UMWJ*, 'I can't sleep for the wind whirling through the crack in my $ a month mansion.'[156]

Evidence for the meagre facilities in many of the towns is revealed in the Coal Commission surveys. One mine in Clay County, which received a rating of only 33.24 out of 100, had no street lights, no electric or gas lights in the houses, no recreation facilities of any kind, no wash house at the mine, no school, church, or library. Health provision was non-existent, with no doctor, or even first-aid equipment at the mine. The nearest hospital was twenty-four miles away, and the nearest independent doctor four miles away. The housing was also of a standard similar to that described by McGill. The report noted that 'houses are finished inside with rough boards and the walls are papered with rough brown paper or newspaper mostly. Big holes and crack in walls. Many houses not painted. Conditions bad.'[157] The monotonous, drab picture of the housing was pointed out in another settlement, where 'the houses are alike from one end of town to the other – and are all painted grey – Houses are generally in poor repair'.[158]

A more average community in Kanawha County, which received a rating of 49.46, did have gas lighting in four houses, although this had been provided by the occupants themselves. The town also had a company owned ball field, and a company owned school building, but no wash house at the mine. Medical facilities in the town consisted of first-aid equipment, with the independent doctor one mile away, and a hospital over four miles way along a 'very bad' road.[159]

Details of the poor sanitary conditions in the coal camps are revealed in the Public Health Service's survey of 123 communities. Of the fourteen West Virginia communities included in the survey (which included some incorporated towns), the highest total rating was 69.2 out of 100, and the lowest 16.4, with an average of 43.6.[160] Kayford, with a rating of 42.7, was the closest to average in the list. Here the water supply was fairly good, although 'with regard to the majority of privies it may be said that they are in such deplorable condition as to merit no consideration in the rating'. There were also no regular collections of rubbish, leading to 'considerable collections of waste', much of which was 'fed to hogs or chickens or thrown in the creek.' The provision of health care in the community was similarly poor, with a doctor who 'was much more interested in the abatement of a nuisance affecting his own residence than the preservation of the general public health.'[161]

The sanitary conditions in the coal camps obviously raised the spectre of disease. This was especially true in the many communities where water was piped from polluted creeks. The water supply to one Clay County community was described as 'very bad. Sewage flows into river water which is pumped to tank . . . River water piped from tank to some houses.' At another camp in Kanawha, the water supply was described as 'poor and insufficient', with residents avoiding the supplies from the creek, because they contained 'so much iron and mineral matter.' While some of the wells provided water that was fit to drink, another one, supplying twelve houses, and a school for blacks, led one black woman to comment that, 'I sure am glad you come to see it. God only knows t'aint fit to drink.'[162]

The connection between poor water supplies and infectious diseases was pointed out by the secretary of the State Board of Health. In 1912 he commented that 'a number of epidemics of typhoid fever have been directly traceable to the water supply, as the population of the State grows, so does the pollution of the streams.'[163] Six years later, typhoid was again high on the agenda. Three of the six epidemics in the previous year had been in coal mining camps. One of these broke out at Loma in Logan County, during August 1917. The investigation discovered that the miners had 'been rushed into partially completed houses where toilet facilities were inadequate and no protection existed at the open well.'[164]

Other diseases were also present in the coalfield. The above report provides evidence for outbreaks of smallpox, including one in the

Kanawha Valley, and another in Logan County, where Loma was again affected.[165] Two years later, an official in the Department commented that 'the State is never free from smallpox', as well as mentioning the presence of tuberculosis, the rate of which was 'cause for grave concern.'[166] Outbreaks of diseases like influenza also spread rapidly in the mining communities. During the 1918 epidemic, the southern counties of Mercer and McDowell were hit very hard. At Winding Gulf, they were forced to close public meeting places because of insufficient medical staff and facilities to cope with any outbreak there. The disease was described as particularly virulent, with new cases 'coming in at Bluefield at the rate of 100 per day', and 500 in two days at Huntingdon.[167] Other illnesses connected entirely with the mines were also a problem. In 1915, an official of the Rockerfeller International Health Commission, wrote to the Bureau of Mines describing a serious outbreak of hookworm in Kentucky and parts of West Virginia, due to poor sanitation within the mines.[168]

The attempts to combat disease were hampered by the lack of interest in, and critical underfunding of, health care. In 1918, for example, the State of West Virginia was giving barely two cents per capita, compared with a suggestion by the American Public Health Association that an appropriation of 25 cents would be desirable.[169] As a consequence, the coal mining communities received little attention, especially if they were far removed from the centres of population. This lack of interest in the health of the mining communities was reinforced by the fact that, as with every other agency in the State, certain officials in the Health Department had a direct interest in the coal industry.[170]

These poor social and health conditions were particularly hard on women. Coal mining communities are orientated around male labour and, usually, male needs. This was particularly true within the primitive company towns, where there were few opportunities for women to work outside of the home. Some took in boarders, or washing, some cleaned for company officials, and a few gained positions as nurses or teachers, but the vast majority were restricted solely to domestic labour. And, indeed, even those who were able to find outside work, still bore the weight of domestic responsibility on their shoulders. This was particularly arduous within the poorly provisioned company house and company town, where everything from food preparation to child rearing required both initiative and hard work.[171]

Of course, it would be wrong to suggest that circumstances in West Virginia offered the ideal setting for building a community with good social facilities. The remoteness of the mining camps, and their positioning in the hills and valleys, created certain problems associated with what the Coal Commission described as, 'natural location'. Furthermore, the pollution associated with the bituminous industry, inevitably affected the communities that surrounded the mines. This would be even worse where, as in the Fairmont field, large amounts of coke were produced.[172] However, the lack of foresight and care in the planning and positioning of towns made matters far worse, leaving coal dust, as Korson noted, everywhere – even on the fiddle.[173]

Indeed, contrary to the operators' claim that they were constrained by the nature of the environment, the Coal Commission's evidence suggests that good conditions were not always related to natural location. Hence, in forty-five company towns in West Virginia, there were ten which scored 75 points or over out of 100 points for natural location, yet only seven which scored in the same range for community conditions.[174] The scores for individual towns provides further evidence for the discrepancies. The Lundale and Latrobe mine, of the Logan County Coal Corporation, for example, scored 85.8 in the rating for community conditions, compared with a natural location rating of 50. In comparison, the Newlyn mine of the Newlyn Coal Company, scored 85 for natural location, but only 41.7 for community conditions.[175]

While many of the coal mining communities conformed to the generally poor conditions described above, there were other communities that were appreciably better. The 'model' town of Holden in Logan County is probably the best example of this. Established in 1903 by the US Coal and Oil Company, it was systematically planned and provided a range of facilities and services.[176] By the end of this period, 4,000 people lived there, 50% of whom were of foreign origin. The town provided boarding houses and recreation halls for different nationalities, a 'moving picture house', three schools, and the streets were paved with a concrete sidewalk in the central section. The 600 houses were made of wood, and in a 'good state of repair', although the yards were 'for the most part, rather small, and . . . there is little effort made towards improving them by gardens, trees, or grass.' There was also a company hospital with twelve beds, and travel was facilitated by the presence of a C. and O. railroad station.[177]

Another 'model' town was established at Widen, by the Elk River Coal and Lumber Company. Here, the houses had 'neat frame structures' and electric light, and the rubbish was collected regularly. There was a YMCA in the centre, with pool tables, a gymnasium, bowling alleys, a reading room, barber shop, and showers. Alongside a church and school, there was also milk from a company dairy, ten miles away, as well as an ice cream parlour, and an 'unusual feature', in the shape of a bank.[178]

Model towns such as Widen and Holden, however, only housed a small minority of the mining labour force in the State. Moreover, it would be wrong to claim that they were by any means perfect – as one commentator did when he described Holden as 'the model coal mining operation in the United States, if not the world.'[179] The town did receive a fairly good report from the investigator for the Public Health Service, but, in its overall sanitary rating, it still only received 54.9 out of a possible 100.[180] Similarly, at Widen, although the conditions were good, there was no running water in the houses, and none of the streets were paved.[181]

Perhaps the most important aspect of the 'model' towns was the example that they set. On one hand they were an example of what kind of community was possible, in spite of the inhospitable natural environment. On the other, they marked a different approach to the management of labour. This became particularly apparent amongst the larger companies in the latter part of this period. Concerns like US Coal and Coke, The Island Creek Coal Company, and Consolidation Coal, deliberately set out to improve social conditions in the mining camps, as part of a general change in labour policy, which also encompassed safety and a more sophisticated attempt to assert the idea of a community of interest between owner and operator – Consolidation Coal, for example, established an 'Employment Relations Department', in 1917.[182] The results of the Coal Commission illustrate the improved conditions that resulted, with several of the larger companies, coming nearer to the top of the scale.[183]

The motivation for this change in policy was not necessarily altruistic. In 1927, operator C. A. Cabell wrote that 'it is not altogether for humanitarian reasons that the modern mining towns are kept as sanitary as possible. There is a sound business reason for such activities . . . An epidemic of typhoid in a mining town would cost an untold amount of money.'[184] Later in his article, Cabell also mentions that such conditions would put the town on a 'blacklist'. This was related to the shortage of labour, which meant that miners were increasingly attracted to towns with better facilities. The significance of this is shown in relation to Holden, where an investigator noted that there was 'little labor turnover . . . some of the original Italian labor has lived in the village 27 years.'[185] The operators also hoped that, by providing better conditions, they would stem some of the criticism of those outside the industry, as well as the enthusiasm of the miners for the UMWA.[186]

Although the above process was important, it should, for this period at least, not be overstated. While the Coal Commission evidence, collected at the end of this period, shows improvements among the larger companies, on the whole, as the detailed evidence presented earlier suggests, conditions were not very good. There was, as we have seen, a variety, but the average was not high.

There is one significant factor which was divorced from the general social conditions of the company towns, but was, nevertheless, an integral part of the environment. Although many of the communities were small and isolated, their rural setting made many of them 'semi-agricultural villages.'[187] This meant that many of the families were able to grow crops, or keep livestock. McGill, for example, noted that in Raleigh County 'Chickens, hogs, and other domestic animals are kept almost as commonly as on the farms from which the miners come'.[188] Similarly, Arnold Miller, who grew up on Cabin Creek, and eventually became UMWA President, recalled how 'the hillsides were skinned up almost two-thirds of the way up the hill on both sides of the holler . . . and they were gardened.'[189]

A pamphlet from the operators' American Constitutional Association also stressed the prevalence of gardens, noting that the hillsides and bottom lands were frequently cultivated. They suggested that 53% of the forty-one towns in their 'survey' had gardens.[190] Evidence from the Coal Commission schedules suggest that this may have underestimated the proportion of communities where land was available for agricultural use. Many, regardless of their rating, seem to have had land available for gardens, poultry, and pasture for cows.[191]

The keeping of gardens, whether to improve the environment, or to grow food stuffs, was actively encouraged by the operators in the 'model' towns, where prizes and advice were sometimes given.[192] In

Logan County, for example, one company offered a $50 prize each summer for the best flowers and lawns.[193] Potential shortages of food also led some of the operators to encourage more agricultural pursuits. In 1917, scarcities caused by the war led Justus Collins to urge the planting of gardens at Winding Gulf and Davy. Seeds and fencing material were distributed, and cash prizes were to be offered.[194]

The cultivation of gardens and raising of livestock was often the responsibility of women. While this added to their already heavy workload, it did present a contrast to their main domestic chores, and also provided a supplement to both the diet and the family budget.[195] For some families, however, these activities were more than a supplement. As Miller put it, 'you gardened in those days or you didn't eat, it was just that simple'[196] – something which would have been true at times when the industry was slack. Keeping animals also had other uses, as we saw earlier in Kayford, where the rubbish-eating hogs partially solved the problem of disposing of 'garbage'.

The semi-agricultural nature of many of these communities was significant in another sense. Despite the drab conditions of many of the towns, these activities offered a link between the agricultural past of many of the miners and their industrial present, easing, as R. L. Lewis has suggested, the transition 'from peasant to proletarian'. This idea of a transitional culture was an important aspect of the cultural identity of the mining communities of West Virginia.[197]

In south Wales, the different size and structure of the communities in which most of the miners lived, meant gardens were not as common, and the migrant was plunged straight into a qualitatively different type of community. Whereas in some of the smaller anthracite communities, the residents were sometimes able to grow some of their own food, the majority, particularly in the steam coal region, were not.[198] One miner, who moved from the anthracite region to the Rhondda, recalled the different nature of life he found:

> in the west you see, there were farms there . . . gardens were there . . . we were not fully proletarianised . . . now when you came to the Rhondda they were fully proletarianised, you see it was only the odd person who dug his garden . . . It was what you may term a life connected with the pit entirely, I mean their social life, their religious life and everything else.[199]

This more urban basis of life indicates that the idea of a 'transitional culture', as applied to West Virginia, is not applicable to the mass of the south Wales miners, and therefore serves as a further point of contrast between the type of communities common to these two regions. When we add to this the fact that the miners were less mobile in south Wales, and that the communities were already established, less isolated, and more permanent, it becomes apparent that the region's mining communities were altogether more solid and less transitory. This created the basis for a far stronger sense of community than in West Virginia.

The more 'proletarian' nature of the south Wales mining towns created, in many ways, different social conditions to those found in West Virginia. One of the most obvious distinctions lay in the type of housing, with south Wales renowned for its ribbons of terraces, perched on the sides of valleys. However, although these were not 'camps' made up of wooden shacks, with hogs and chickens running loose, the south Wales mining towns were nonetheless, relative to the expectations and standards of the population, poor.

The 1917 Inquiry into Industrial Unrest in south Wales, investigated the social conditions of the region and pronounced a judgement that was almost as searing as that of the investigators of the US Coal Commission. They suggested that:

> The conviction that Capital and Labour are necessarily hostile, a conviction engendered by conflict in industrial matters, has been accentuated by the fact that the social conditions . . . are of an unsatisfactory character . . . the workers are deeply discontented with their housing accommodation and with their unwholesome and unattractive environment generally. The towns and villages are ugly and overcrowded; houses are scarce and rents are increasing, and the surroundings are insanitary and depressing. The scenery is disfigured by unsightly refuse tips, the atmosphere polluted by coal dust and smoke, and the rivers spoilt by liquid refuse from works and factories. Facilities for education and recreation are inadequate and opportunities for the wise use of leisure few.[200]

The effect of factors related to the mining industry like dust, dirt, subsidence, and scarring of the landscape, were serious. Coombes for instance recalled how 'black dust blew in through every open window', and how 'leaves were grey, and never green, and berries black before they were red.'[201] Added to this were specific social problems related to south Wales, rather than the industry in general.

One of the most serious was overcrowding – a distinct contrast to the partially full coal camps of West Virginia.

Overcrowding was caused by the inability of the agencies providing housing to keep up with the pace of growth of the labour force. Between 1901 and 1911, the population of Glamorgan increased by over 30%, but the number of houses by only around 25%.[202] This led to a shortage, by some estimates, of as many as 40–50,000 for the coalfield as a whole.[203] In the Rhondda the situation was particularly bad. The 1914 Health Report of the Rhondda Urban District Council revealed that in 1909, a peak year, 1,025 houses were built. Thereafter, however, the number declined with only 308 under construction in 1914. The situation was made worse by the fact that forty-three of the existing housing stock was condemned as unfit. Although twenty-two of these were later made habitable, this left only 287 new houses for a population increase of over 4,000 – a surplus, by the Council's calculations, of 2,300.[204]

The quality of housing was also fairly poor, although there is evidence of some improvement during this period. In his 1915 study, Jevons suggested that housing had improved over the last fifty years, partly due to Local Authority By-Laws, and was then of a higher standard than other parts of the British coalfield.[205] While housing in the coalfield may not have been the worst on the national scale, this was not saying very much. At the top end, some lived in three-up and three-down terraces,[206] while at the other, some inhabited what can only be described as hovels.

For example, Edmund Stonelake recalled that in Aberdare in the early 1900s, 'housing conditions were shocking, people were charged outrageous rents for rotten hovels.' Under his jurisdiction, the local Trades Council had carried out a survey of local housing in 1904. Some of the worst housing they discovered was in Abernant, where one row of houses were not higher than 5ft in to the eaves. Inside the one room was sometimes divided by a shawl, and an 'upstairs' created by a plank of wood placed on a partition, with a five step ladder. Stonelake described how the inhabitants had to 'crawl like a dog into a kennel', to gain entry.[207]

While the Abernant housing was probably among the worst, even the better five or six roomed houses were liable to be affected by the problems associated with bad positioning.[208] The 1917 Inquiry noted how in several of the valleys the houses were built on the less sunny side, often 'where it is impossible for any sunshine to penetrate the houses.'[209] Obviously, as in West Virginia, the valleys of south Wales did not offer the perfect conditions for building a community. However, the lack of attention paid to planning, and the consequent chaotic and piecemeal development produced a situation that, in its own way, was reminiscent of the Mountain State.

The sanitary conditions within the communities were also poor, although there was some improvement over time. The author Jack Jones recalled the 'two privies' shared by the twelve families in Tai-Harry-Blawd, in Merthyr, where he grew up at the end of the nineteenth century. These 'caves of concentrated stink', were often spurned in favour of using the left bank of the brook. The author recalled falling into the latter in his youth: 'Always I fouled myself and my clothes with human excrement with which the left bank, the bank on which we lived, was thickly overlaid.' On washing days, the water was often insufficient for the heavy use of the communal tap, and the women instead 'would go down to the brook when there was enough water to cover the many dead cats and dogs, and fill their buckets there.'[210]

In the Rhondda the situation was similar, with the river acting as the main sewer. There were some improvements in sanitary conditions from the 1890s, however, with the construction of a first sewer and, after the formation of the RUDC, a sustained effort that left nearly all the houses connected to sewers by the outbreak of war in 1914.[211] Even in 1910, however, the Labour and Trades Council reported on the flow of effluence into the river from local works and homes, creating strong odours, especially in summer.[212] In 1910, the council also began to incinerate rubbish at its eleven dumps, and water supplies were improved by the take-over and amalgamation of the two local water companies to form the Pontypridd and Joint Water Board.[213]

As in West Virginia, poor social conditions had special significance for women. Like their counterparts in the Mountain State, women in the south Wales mining communities had few job opportunities with, by 1911, only 14% of the female population over fourteen in work. The main source of employment was domestic service, however women were also present in professional positions as teachers and nurses.[214] Whether working or not, the majority of women, many of whom married young and had large families, faced a hard existence in the cramped and dirty mining towns. Cleaning and washing were a vital, but time-consuming, part of each week.

Similarly, managing the budget, preparing food, and looking after children all required constant effort.[215]

Women were not helped by the strict gender lines that ran through the community. Men were reluctant to help with domestic work; something which many women, at least publicly, concurred with. Indeed, those men who attempted to cross the line between work and home were sometimes ridiculed.[216] The lack of sympathy for the woman's lot from the majority of men, was shown over the issue of pit head baths. The use of home baths was problematic for women in a number of ways. The baths were heavy, and the boiling of water sometimes dangerous for children. Home bathing also meant that the men came into the house in their dirty and damp work clothes. This created mess, and an additional job for the woman, who had to dry the clothes for the next shift. Despite the burden this placed on women, many men were only reluctantly converted to the idea of pit head baths.[217]

The demands placed on women, within a generally unhealthy environment, took their toll. The mortality rate amongst women was high, particularly in the Rhondda where, in contrast to the rest of Wales and England, the death rate in the 20–44 age group was higher than for men.[218] Poor social conditions also had a deleterious effect on children's health. The figures for infant mortality were 'particularly shocking', with a figure of 380 per 1,000 for the five major boroughs of south Wales in 1911.[219] For the Rhondda, the infant mortality rate was an average of 160 per 1,000 for the ten years from 1904–1914, with illnesses like pneumonia, scarlet fever, whooping cough, and measles, among the causes.[220]

The health of the population was not helped by the scarcity of hospital facilities in the coalfield, which offered minimal coverage. In the Rhondda in 1897, there was only one hospital with ten beds, to serve a population of over 120,000. A further hospital was built on adjoining land in 1902, with a maximum of fifty-eight beds, and a smallpox hospital was completed in 1908 on top of Pen-rhys mountain. This, alongside a miners' cottage hospital at Porth, supported by subscriptions and donations, was the limit of the Rhondda's hospital provision up until 1914. [221]

The provision of educational facilities was somewhat better, due to the influence of the various national education acts – the Rhondda had 40 elementary schools by 1914.[222] However, the elementary schools in the coalfield were not always of a high standard,[223] and the 1917 Inquiry stated that 'evidence has been brought before us to show that the workers view with alarm the shortage of teachers and the consequent failure of the local authorities to provide proper education for the children.'[224] There were also insufficient open-air recreation grounds for either adults or children, and municipal buildings were rare, with no public libraries in the central Glamorgan section of the coalfield.[225]

The absence of such municipal facilities, however, were compensated for by other social centres like the workmen's institutes which, as we shall see later, became an integral part of the life of these communities. Furthermore, the large numbers of chapels in the mining towns provided a gathering place for the inhabitants – Mardy, for example, had six chapels, (three Welsh and three English), for its 9,000 residents at the end of the war.[226] There were also other public places, like the music hall, and the cinema, as well as a large variety of shops in most of the towns. In 1913, for example, there were 2,859 shops in the Rhondda Urban District alone [227] – a contrast with the single company store in many of the West Virginia mining towns.

The presence of such public areas and collective institutions helps explain, as we shall see, the different patterns of cultural and community life that emerged in south Wales and West Virginia.

Culture and community life

From the evidence that has been presented so far, it is clear that the cultural mix, structural base, power relationships, and social conditions of the mining communities were very different in these two regions. The West Virginia communities, if we recall, were mostly 'new' to this period, usually smaller, and geographically and culturally isolated. These factors were reinforced by the social relationships within the State, which saw most of the miners living in company towns which were, in many respects, feudal fiefdoms, isolated from constitutional, legal and political rights. This dramatically circumscribed the role for independent initiatives, and the right to free expression.

If isolation and exploitation are key terms in understanding the nature of these communities, then the idea of transition is of equal importance. On one hand this is related to the 'temporary', ephemeral nature of many of these communities; as an investigator in Mingo county put it, 'we have . . . a new community having little time for anything else beside work . . . The temporary character of the occupation lends an unstable element to the individual'.[228] Transition is equally applicable to the cultural configuration of the 'semi-agricultural villages', and the interaction between the agricultural and industrial lifestyle, that saw many drift back and forth between the two, returning home at harvest times, or more permanently, when savings had been accrued.

This idea of transition, however, is important in a more fundamental sense; namely mobility. Mobility of some sort is characteristic of many mining communities.[229] However, in West Virginia it was not only confined to those who returned home on a seasonal basis, but to a more general movement of population. These were communities that were in an almost perpetual state of motion. The level of this mobility was revealed in a letter from George Wolfe to Justus Collins in 1916. He wrote ' . . . we are practically losing men as fast as we can bring them in. We pay off every two weeks and after each pay-day there is a bunch that leaves'.[230] In a similar vein, a Coal Commission investigator described the community at the Monarch mine in Kanawha county, as being 'composed largely of a floating population'.[231]

The same term was used by McGill. She described how 'the population of these developing bituminous coal mining communities, unlike the typical anthracite district, is a floating one', with some families finding it 'impossible to remember the number of times they had moved.' McGill calculated the level of this movement, discovering that over 34% had been resident for less than a year, over 24% between one and three years, and only just over 2% for over fifteen years.[232] It remains open to question whether even this revealed the true level of mobility, as McGill was concerned with families, yet many of the miners were single, and would, as a consequence, find it easier to move.

The degree of mobility was encouraged by the boom and bust nature of the bituminous coal industry. It was also greatly influenced by the appalling social conditions within these towns, which left many fleeing to other towns or industries in the hope of finding better pay and conditions. As Wolfe tellingly put it in his letter to Collins, 'these men are all foreigners . . . they can go to Pittsburgh and work in the steel mills and make more money than they can make here, and have greater liberties in the way of living.'[233]

The degree of mobility in these communities, however, introduces something of a paradox. These may have been communities created entirely for the purpose of extracting coal, but the inhabitants clearly did not have a fixed definition of themselves as coal miners. As R. L. Lewis has suggested for black coal miners, many did not 'consider themselves permanent residents or even permanent miners.' Even for those who stayed, they only 'gradually' grew 'beyond their southern agricultural roots'.[234] The lack of identification with their occupational role was also underlined by the large number of children of miners who fled the coalfields for other industries, sometimes with the encouragement of their parents.[235] This was equally true for all of the ethnic groups in this period, whether they intended returning to the land, or leaving for another industry. This marked a very distinct contrast with south Wales where the identity as coal miners, within the working-class, was integral to the rationale of the communities.

The fluidity of community life and identities in the West Virginia coalfield was further reinforced by the diverse cultural mix of the company towns. As we have seen, the different groups of migrants had very different cultural origins, although they shared some of the same motivations for entering the coalfield. It would always be difficult, therefore, for the miners to form a common cultural base.

The most obvious manifestation of cultural diversity was the issue of black/white social relations, and the segregation of the mining camps. While this was not complete in the early settlements, and was never total, segregation became increasingly apparent during this period, particularly in the more established communities.[236] This covered both housing and social facilities. One operator described how there were six playgrounds in the mining camps of the Carbon Fuel Company, 'four for white and two for colored.'[237] Likewise, there were separate baseball teams, and in some towns, separate social celebrations on public holidays.[238] Segregation was also defined in State laws which covered, among other things, education and mixed marriages.[239]

Under such circumstances, it would seem inevitable that there would be conflict between these different groups, which would tend to polarise the communities. On the whole, however, the race relations within the coalfield were fairly stable during these years.

The most open friction between blacks and whites occurred when the industry first developed. In the turbulent conditions in the early camps, blacks who had been subjected to racism in the South mixed with mountaineers and whites from outside the State, in conditions which encouraged prejudice and mistrust.[240] In 1887 in the New River district, 3,000 black miners marched towards Fayetteville, to avenge the lynching of a black miner who had been accused of killing a mine foreman. There was further conflict in Mercer County in 1888 following a lynching, as well as 'many clashes' in McDowell County after the opening of black saloons.[241] John R. Williams, a Welsh miner from Aberdare, who was working in McDowell County in 1895, described how blacks had been 'shamefully abused and ill treated by white men, more to shame them.'[242]

However, by the early 1900s friction began to subside. The white mountaineers, in some cases, had never seen blacks before entering the coalfield,[243] and they 'never developed a deep prejudice'.[244] Race relations also improved more generally, not least because the labour shortages during this period prevented white miners from seeing their black counterparts as a threat to their jobs. The experience of life in the company town also had an effect. As R. L. Lewis has put it:

> As the heterogeneous racial and ethnic groups became accustomed to the new order imposed by the coal companies, a camaraderie among the workers sprouted out of the soil of common grievances against company rule and the common dangers which confront all who go down into the pits. As workers lived closer together in small isolated towns, discrimination generated by fear and ignorance soon dissipated, and racial-cultural animosity declined. When racial discrimination occurred in company-owned towns, the onus fell on the companies rather than other miners.[245]

The 'separate but equal' treatment of black and white miners in the company towns was of great significance. Black miners were allowed to vote, and given relatively good educational facilities. Moreover, although they were segregated, the different groups usually had similar standard housing, wages, and conditions.[246] This was revealed by the relative lack of discrimination at the workplace. Black and white worked side by side, and although blacks were usually prevented from becoming bosses, and were rarely employed as motormen, they were usually not discriminated against as machine men (a particularly sought after job), or in the mass of employment as loaders, pick miners, and labourers. The vast majority of blacks were engaged in these 'inside' jobs, despite the danger, not because of racism, but because the jobs allowed greater freedom, and were better paid.[247]

Of course friction between black and white had not completely disappeared. Thus In Mercer County in 1912, a black man accused of attacking a white girl was lynched after being seized from the sheriff.[248] In similar circumstances, a black man was murdered by a mob in Logan County in 1919, after being taken from deputies. This incident brought a stinging rebuke from the State Governor, John Cornwell, who complained to Sheriff Don Chafin that 'it is passing strange that, with the reputed number of deputy sheriffs in your County, prisoners in the hands of officers of the law cannot be protected from violence.'[249]

The presence of foreign-born miners in the coalfields added a further dimension to race relations. The immigrant miners were initially greeted with a mixed reaction by both black and white, because it was feared that they would work for lower wages. However, as they became more established, their prominent role in strike activity, and support for the UMWA, led to greater acceptance.[250] This did not prevent a certain amount of friction continuing between the immigrants and black miners. According to Laing this was usually caused by the immigrants trying to become 'American', and adopting racist characteristics.[251]

Nor were the immigrant miners a culturally homogeneous block. Fred Mooney, for example, recalled organising one local in Monongah, 'in which about twenty-seven different languages were spoken.'[252] Different nationalities could also exhibit rivalries within the coal camp, as could regional sub-groups within the national group.[253] Thus in the Fairmont Field in 1915, a miner killed a fellow Italian from his home town because of a feud relating to their membership of different Mafia organisations at home.[254] There could also be generational differences, when the children of immigrants spoke English and grew up understanding, but not able to speak, their mother tongue.[255]

Internal fissures were also present within the black community. Natives of Virginia and West Virginia sometimes thought themselves superior to migrants from the South, whom they considered to have lax morality, while divisions between church and non-church members sometimes led to discord.[256] Gender was also controversial, with black women who stepped outside the conventional domestic sphere exacting stinging criticism form their male counterparts.[257]

The violent conflict that occurred between and within ethnic groups was part of a larger pattern of violence and disorder throughout the coalfield. Indeed, when we take into account the level of this violence, it further puts into perspective the relative lack of conflict along solely racial lines. Again, conflict was worse in the early coal camps, but it remained a significant factor in community life throughout this period.

The level of violence shocked John R. Williams, who found it a distinct contrast to Aberdare. He wrote, 'it is nothing unusual here to find four or five fellows shot dead, and it is quite unusual if this is not the case on pay day nights which, thank God, only come once a month.' He added, gloomily, 'such is life in West Virginia'.[258] Twenty-eight years later, the investigator in Mingo County who described the temporary nature of the communities, also described them as 'lawless', where 'trouble in the shape of murder and sudden death is common.'[259] The linking of mobility and lawlessness as important characteristics of these communities, was also made by the Coal Commission investigator who described the 'floating' population at the Monarch mine. She continued, 'in one section, particularly, there was an air of general lawlessness. The State Police had raided the place on the previous day, following the murder there of a Prohibition officer the week before . . . The strife between families was such that the women fought openly in church.'[260]

Trouble could flare over many issues. Elections often brought violence to the fore, as in 1904, when eight men, including the local sheriff, were killed in Fayette County during election week.[261] The enforcement of prohibition, as at the Monarch mine, was another cause of conflict. The Vice President of the Raleigh-Wyoming Coal Company wrote to Governor Morgan in 1921, claiming that since the company opened a mine at Edwight in Raleigh County, they had had trouble with moonshiners and bootleggers. He complained of 'a number of murders . . . the moonshiners resented our attitude in prohibiting the sale of liquor in our camp.'[262]

In this environment there were inevitably those who made a living from their criminal activities. In Mercer County one of a number of 'blackhands' who extorted money from miners, was shot dead by an Italian miner on the advice of the County's Prosecuting Attorney.[263] Similarly, a 'desperado of the coalfields', Matt Jarrell, shot dead the socialist Marshall Of Eskdale, S. F. Nantz, when the latter tried to arrest him.[264]

Violence and lawlessness was also present on a more general level. Tams, for example, recalled that the railway bridge across New River at Thurmond, was 'somewhat hazardous' to cross at night – on one occasion, after pay day, a murder victim was discovered on the bridge.[265] Social gatherings were another source of potential violence. Rogers remembered how dances in the communities often ended in fights. He wrote, 'it is not easy for a youngster to erase from his mind the horror of a crimson gash laid open from forehead to chin by the swift slash of keen steel.'[266] Unpopular mine officials were also the target of threats. One example of this was contained in the report of a spy employed by the Baldwin-Felts agency. His report claimed that a Kyle Boyd 'would do Mr Riley injury if he could get a chance. He stated that Mr Riley ought to be killed. Mr Riley is likely to be done some harm if he goes out in the night time.' – Riley was the manager of the Superior Pocahontas Coal Company at Hallsville.[267]

In many ways it is appropriate that officials like Riley should have been on the receiving end of threats like the above. After all, the coal operators had arrogantly asserted their aim of civilising the wilderness of West Virginia, but in fact had, through their greed and disrespect for their workforce, created the circumstances where such violence could flourish. The abuses of power through the use of the violent mine guards, and the absence of legitimate law enforcement in the 'feudal' company towns hardly make the level of this violence surprising. As a reminder of this, it is interesting to note that the spy who reported the threat against Riley, also wrote 'the people claim that the Coal Company purchased a box of Winchesters a few days ago and it has a good effect on them. They are afraid if they raise a disturbance, they will be killed or sent to jail.'[268]

Not that companies were so vigorous in their response to violence against ordinary citizens. In the case of the murder at Thurmond, there was no attempt at finding the culprit, and an inquest assessed a fine of $20, with $28 costs, after passing a verdict of suicide. The fine was levied to pay the burial costs. As Tams put it, brawls and murder 'were treated quite casually by the authorities.'[269]

So far in this section, we have seen that the mining population in West Virginia was mobile, 'transitional', divided, and subject to high levels of violent and lawless behaviour. While the heterogeneous workforce was not dramatically split along ethnic lines and, indeed, had even formed a degree of unity, this was very much based upon a reaction to exploitation, rather than a distinctive cultural identity and common definition of community. Indeed, it is sometimes difficult to consider the flux of life in the mining camps of West Virginia constituting a 'community' in the cultural sense.

The lack of religious unity is another example of the cultural divisions in the labour force. Unlike south Wales, religion was not a cultural binding force. In the first place, facilities were segregated, whether in terms of separate buildings, or separate meetings in the same building, thus preventing the population meeting as one. Furthermore, there were obvious doctrinal differences among the workforce, not only between Catholic and Protestant, but among various Protestant sects.

Many of the immigrants who entered the coalfield were catholics. They stuck to their religious roots, publicly celebrating the various Saints Days, or 'Big Sundays' as they were called,[270] as well as pushing for their own places of worship. Rogers, for example, recalled how at Minden, 'two churches were eventually erected to satisfy the cross currents of religious hunger . . . For those of Roman Catholic faith, an inconspicuous tabernacle . . . was raised on the brow of No.5 hill. The Protestants built their edifice on lower ground.'[271] As a minority, however, the immigrants were not exempt from being patronised or discriminated against. Thus, coal operator A. B. Fleming wrote in 1901 about how 'in general, the Slavonic peoples, and Italians are the most numerous and destitute of the Scriptures.'[272]

Not that all of the immigrants were Catholic. Others, like Arnold Miller's family, who came from Hummel in Germany, were Protestants, 'raised religiously in the Dunkard belief that adhered strictly to the Bible as it was written.'[273] This fundamentalism was shared by many of the native white miners who, as we saw earlier, had a very literal approach to the Bible. In the coal camps the white miners were split, however, among numerous sects, including 'hard shell', 'soft shell', and 'free will' Baptists, and smaller groups like the Church of God, and the Holiness Church (or Holy Rollers).[274] The latter were renowned for their enthusiastic worship, which included shouting, and participants' bodies being hurled across the room during services.[275]

The shared fundamentalism of these sects did not provide the various adherents with a joint approach to religion, however literally they claimed they were interpreting the bible. Fred Mooney, whose family were members of these sects, described them as 'intolerant in their attitude toward one another's religion, political views, and affiliation', although they were 'charitable in the broad sense of the word.'[276]

The vast majority of the black miners in the State were Baptists, with the rest following forms of Methodism and Presbyterianism. Part of the former's success can be explained by the lack of restrictions they placed on establishing new churches. Key to this was the Baptists' willingness to allow miner-preachers, whereas the Methodists favoured trained preachers.[277] As with the native whites, black miners were often divided by their religious preferences. Thus, although both Methodist and Baptist would sometimes use the same building, there was little mixing between the two and, indeed, there was a good deal of sectarianism.[278] Moreover, there were also differences in the 'style of religious expression' within the black Baptists, with those from the Virginias tending to favour 'mainstream practices', while those with Southern origins, 'adhered to practices more in keeping with their rural folk origins.'[279]

The nature of the social relationships within the company town, as we saw earlier, allowed the operators to use religion as a further way of encouraging quiescence in the workforce. Some, of course, provided no facilities or support within their communities, while others provided both the building and paid the salary of the minister.[280] Some of the larger companies also helped finance tours by national religious figures, as in October 1916, when the *McDowell Times* reported that R. L. Peters' 'one of the greatest evangelists in this country' was making a number of speeches in McDowell County. His trip was made possible by free travel on the Norfolk and Western railway.[281]

The partiality of the paid ministers, however, tended to alienate many in the mining community.[282] This explains why the miner-preachers were so popular, particularly among the Baptists, as they were not reliant on, or subject to, the operators. Itinerant preachers who travelled around the coalfield, were also popular with the miners, and consequently unpopular with the operators. In 1907, a Mr Bettes, the 'Cow Boy Preacher', attempted to sue the Superior Pocahontas Coal Company, after he was assaulted by five men at Hallsville. His popularity among the residents of Hallsville is revealed by the comments of T. L. Felts' spy in the town, who wrote that 'nearly all the people here seem to take the Preacher's part', and that 'I believe that most of the men who have left Mr Riley's works will return as soon as the Cow Boy Preacher leaves'- an obvious reference to his involvement in a strike.[283] The company church and minister was also disliked on religious grounds, as the fundamental-ists considered that members 'do not have religion', because they played cards, wore make-up, and drank.[284]

Although religion cannot be seen as a form of cultural binding for these communities, it did at least, taking into account the sparse facilities in many of these towns, provide some form of social life for the different groups. The black churches in particular played an important role in the social sphere of the black community, pro-viding a continuation and link with the cultural traditions that the migrants had left behind. Funerals proved an especially popular form of social interaction as, to a lesser extent, did marriages and baptisms. In addition, the churches sometimes provided socials, fes-tivals, plays, and societies for young people.[285]

Other leisure activities, not connected with churches, also reflected the cultural past of the different groups that constituted the population of the mining towns. The semi-agricultural nature of many of these communities meant that hunting and fishing remained a popular pastime in the coal camps.[286] Indeed, so much so that the opening of certain hunting seasons interfered with the production of the mines. In September 1916, for example, Mines One and Three at Winding Gulf saw the number of cars loaded in a day drop from nineteen to ten, with the start of the squirrel season.[287] Laing also noted the importance of hunting dogs to fami-lies. He wrote of 'one mine . . . where the miners had hardly enough food to keep them from being hungry'. Yet a black woman showed Laing 'with a great deal of pride', thirteen hunting dogs belonging to her husband.'[288]

In terms of communal leisure, baseball, where the facilities were available, was one of the most popular activities. Teams represented different communities, as well as black and white sections of the same camps. Competition was fierce, leading to spectators running on the pitch, fighting, and even in the case of a match on Loop Creek, a gun fight between two mine guards on different teams.[289] Other pastimes were even more dependent upon provision of facil-ities. Where they existed, facilities to show films, YMCA's, bowling alleys, and pool rooms were well utilised. McGill found that the inhabitants of six of the eleven Raleigh County communities she surveyed had, or were near to, 'motion-picture houses showing pictures usually two or three times a week.' The only other 'commercial amusement' was a pool room in three of the camps. [290]

The absence of facilities inevitably led to the following of less formal pursuits. The tiring nature of work and lack of cash encouraged many to just meet and talk after work. A miner on Cabin Creek stated that in the evenings miners mostly 'eat their suppers and crash and dress and sit around and smoke and go to bed to rest for the next day', which, he suggested, 'was the usual miner's occupation up by me.'[291] Gathering in groups, or 'loafing', was particularly popular among black miners, as it continued a tradition from their agricultural past. The subjects of discussion were varied, but Laing suggested that these groups performed an important social role, providing both amusement and 'informal agencies of communication and control.'[292]

The importance of such oral communication was reinforced by the fact that education and reading were not a major element in the leisure patterns of these communities. The absence of library and educational facilities, the lack of a tradition of self-education, and the high level of illiteracy were the main causes of this.[293] There were some, like Fred Mooney, who were interested in self-education. He recalled reading various authors when he was younger, including Upton Sinclair, Jack London, Victor Hugo, Plato, and Marx, among others – although of the latter Mooney wrote, 'Marx himself I could not absorb. His work was too difficult for I had only reached the sixth reader in public school.'[294]

This did not seem to have diminished Mooney's knowledge, however, as John L. Spivak discovered when he visited the coalfield for the American Civil Liberties Union. He noted that 'Fred was knowledgeable on labor history. I had some elementary courses . . . but from Fred I got a post-graduate course'. He also described how District 17 President, Frank Keeney, was proud of his own self-education, and the fact that he had married a school teacher.[295]

Mooney and Keeney, however, were probably exceptions to the rule in what was, generally, an oral rather than literate culture. Certainly, as we shall see when we look at south Wales, there were not the same traditions or institutions of self-education. This is perhaps underlined by the lack of written material left by the West Virginia miners in this period. The only autobiography was Mooney's, and there were no novels written by miners – another indication of the transience and impermanence of these communities.

If reading did not absorb the remaining leisure time of the population of the camps, there were many other activities that did. Gambling, usually over playing cards, was popular both between miners, and with professional players who sometimes entered the communities to swindle the inhabitants on pay days.[296] Similarly, drinking, dancing, and sex, all played a part in easing the hardships of the miner's life.

Alcohol would be either bought from pedlars, or brewed by the miners themselves. This was in spite of the concerns of operators, the union, and teetotal members of the community. One miner lamented in the *UMWJ*, that 'drink is our worst enemy today in West Virginia. Oh, my brothers, will you stop and think of the houses left desolate by intemperance.'[297] The extent of what *Coal Age* called 'The Liquor Problem in Mining Communities',[298] is revealed in a comment by Tams, who noted that 'Raleigh County was officially dry, but in actual practice quite wet indeed.'[299]

Music and dance were an important part of the cultural traditions of all sections of these communities, and provided a local source of entertainment. One immigrant recalled:

> Next to the Sunday afternoon baseball games, nothing appealed more to me than the dances sponsored pay-day night by a local chapter of the Lithuanian lodge ... Far into the night fiddles squeaked and accordions wheezed; shuffling, scraping feet made the flimsy walls groan and quiver; uproarious laughter mingled with half-barbarous gypsy tunes brought over by the musicians from their mother countries. Every man, woman and child, sometime during the shindig, could be counted on to join in the polka.[300]

Bands were also popular for both white and black miners, playing on public holidays and at communal gatherings.[301] Music, in the shape of ballads, also provided an avenue for expressing grievances about life within the coal camps. As a form of oral communication, these were well-suited to the mobile labour force, telling stories of accidents, strikes, and exploitation.[302]

Prostitution was also common in the coalfield. The most famous example of this was the red light district of 'Cinder Bottom' at Keystone in McDowell County. In 1911, among the population of 2,500, 75% of whom were black or foreign-born, there were twenty five houses which served as brothels. All nationalities were represented, 'along with saloon keepers, gamblers, bouncers, thieves, pimps, and panhandlers.'[303] Sex had a wider significance within the context of the dreary coal camps, taking on, according to Ross, 'terrific proportions'. Whether he was talking about quality or quantity, or both, sexual activity, particularly outside marriage, placed a strain on the traditional moral values of some of the more conservative elements in the company town.[304]

Other leisure activities also created divisions within these communities. The example of the miner who complained of intemperance suggests that there were deep divisions over 'morality' within the community, especially between those of fundamentalist bent, and those who were not. The tensions between the 'godly' and the 'ungodly' were not restricted to the dislike of alcohol and sex. Thus in Glen Jean, the practice of fighting wild cats and bull terriers on a Sunday was halted after women church members 'put up such a fight against this amusement that the County Authorities had to stop it.'[305] Within the black community, what were seen as 'lax standards' of morality, drove a further wedge between church and non-church members, and natives of the Virginias, and those from further South.[306]

The fragmentation of leisure pursuits fits well into the general picture of the culturally 'splintered world'[307] of the West Virginia miners. The absence of the opportunity to organise and create their own stuctures within the social framework of the mining camp, meant that even in the sphere of leisure, the areas for voluntary association were absent. Certainly, as we saw earlier, there were no opportunities to build and run workmen's institutes, let alone places to organise and debate through the UMWA. The latter did attempt to organise picnics and parades, such as on Labor Day and the Fourth of July; [308] however its inability to enter the coal camps, and hence permeate the culture of the communities, denied it a pivotal role in that culture.

If the nature of culture and community in West Virginia was fragmented and transitory, the evidence presented thus far would suggest a very different cultural configuration in the valleys of south Wales. As we have already seen, south Wales experienced dramatic changes in this period, but it did so more slowly, over a longer period. Moreover, it was made up of generally larger, less isolated communities, which were more 'proletarian' than their equivalents in the Mountain State, and were formed by a culturally more homogeneous population. Furthermore, the different social and power relationships within these communities allowed a far greater freedom of voluntary association, and the ability to create independent structures within civil society.

One of the principal resulting differences in the type of communities in these two regions lay in the levels of mobility within the population. Although the mining population in south Wales was far from static,[309] there was less mobility than in West Virginia, and that which there was was usually internal, with migrants tending to stay within the industry.[310] Moreover, whereas the sons of the West Virginia miners actively sought a different occupation from their fathers, in south Wales (and Britain generally), the vast majority of sons followed their fathers into the industry.[311] This meant that the old adage of 'once a miner always a miner', which Church describes as 'close to the truth' for Britain,[312] gave the south Wales miners a far stronger identification as coal miners than their West Virginia counterparts, which was reinforced by the other more permanent aspects of their communities.

The greater homogeneity of the labour supply in south Wales, and the slower pace of development of the coalfield further reinforced the basis for the formation of a common culture. As we saw earlier, immigrants did come from various sources, and within a purely British context, it would not be unreasonable to describe the south Wales coalfield as cosmopolitan in these years.[313] However, relative to the US, and in particular West Virginia, the pattern of life and culture in the mining towns was considerably less diverse – certainly there were no towns with inhabitants possessing the twenty-seven languages encountered by Fred Mooney. Furthermore, the communities were not subject to the structural divisions of segregation, and the manipulations of the 'judicious mixture'.

There were, of course, some linguistic differences within the communities, principally between Welsh and English speakers. However, by this period, the anglicisation of language in the most populous parts of the coalfield was undermining this as a source of division. The exact speed at which this anglicisation occurred has long been the subject of controversy in Welsh history. However, if we accept Dudley Baines' recent revisions, it seems clear that the higher number of migrants from England would have accelerated the decline of the Welsh language in the coalfield at a faster rate than has sometimes been thought.[314] Certainly by this period, English was becoming the main language of the central steam coal region, although the western anthracite region remained almost exclusively Welsh speaking.[315] In the Rhondda, for example, the 1911 census revealed that of the 139,335 population, 60,056 spoke English only, 6,100 Welsh only, and 70, 696 English and Welsh.[316]

This decline in the use of Welsh cannot be explained solely by the influx of migrants from England. As with the European immigrants who worked in the West Virginia coalfield, linguistic divisions opened up between different generations. Thus Jack Jones, originally knew Welsh from his home, but after mixing with English, Scottish and Irish children 'became more fluent in English than in my native language.' This led on at least one occasion to an argument with his father who resented his son replying to questions in English.[317] This type of division seems to have been increasingly common, with E. D. Lewis suggesting that 'for one family in every four in which the parents spoke Welsh, the children were being brought up in ignorance of it. The sequence was already becoming painfully clear: parents usually Welsh, children mainly English, next generation entirely English.'[318]

While anglicisation may have had disastrous implications for the Welsh language, it did help prevent polarisation, and became part of the evolving culture of these communities. The shift to the use of English in union meetings and publications was a good example of this, with the Welsh language losing out to the fact that, taking into account those who were bilingual, English was the most common language, and indeed the only one that the mass of migrants from England understood. Indeed, the use of English was not necessarily a hindrance to aspiring union officers, even in areas where Welsh was more common. Frank Hodges, for example, was elected to the post of Garw miners' agent, despite thinking that as an English speaker he stood no chance.[319]

Although language may not have split the workforce, divisions were not entirely absent. One miner recalled how 'the people that were disliked in the Clydach Vale and in the Rhondda, were the North Walians. They didn't like them at all.'[320] More prominent (and predictable), was the attitude to the more easily identifiable minorities in the valleys. The Spanish who moved into the wholly Welsh community at Abercrave initially experienced resentment, with accusations that they were favoured at the coal face, and lived in disgusting conditions. The situation led one of the Spanish leaders to appeal; 'Fellow workers of Abercrave do not besmirch the fair reputation of the Welsh collier'.[321] Despite suspicion of the different religious and cultural practices of the Spanish, the fact that they were active politically and in the SWMF, eased their acceptance. Significantly, the newer migrants into the town also tended to support this group, with some later citing the influence of the Spanish in their political radicalisation.[322]

Resentment against racial minorities sometimes took a more aggressive form. The most prominent example of this in this period were the anti-Jewish disturbances in Tredegar in 1911. In August, 160 Jews in Tredegar found themselves 'under attack' by rioters, who looted shops. Rioting then spread to Ebbw Vale, Rhymney, Bargoed, Gilfach and Sehnghenydd. The cause of these riots was, ostensibly, what was seen as the association between high rents and the Jewish community. However, as Holmes has pointed out, the riots also occurred at a time of profound social unrest due to the Cambrian dispute and the great railway strike of 1911, and were connected with a general resentment against the trading community.[323]

Such incidents should, however, be placed in perspective. As Francis has correctly noted, 'racism and jingoism were as prevalent in south Wales as anywhere else in imperial Britain in the early part of the twentieth century.'[324] Moreover, with a society that was undergoing such fundamental changes, and the ferocity of the industrial conflict that accompanied it, it is perhaps not surprising that this racism should have occasionally taken so violent a form. On the whole, however, if only because the minorities were so small in the coalfield, racism was not a significant barrier to building a community identity.

The assimilation of migrants into these communities, and the synthesis of values that resulted, was a much smoother process than in West Virginia, and not based solely upon a recognition of an equal share in exploitation. Certainly the fact that migrants entered communities which were part of an established, albeit changing, culture, was very different from the cultural vacuum of the isolated West Virginia coal camps. In the nineteenth century, the existing culture was particularly resilient, with the native Welsh showing 'a marked capacity for stamping their own impress on all newcomers.'[325] However, by the beginning of this period the sheer size of the non-Welsh migration meant that, as with language, culture was being remade and reconstructed.

The spread of Nonconformity throughout Wales in the nineteenth century was dramatic, and it became enmeshed within the fabric of life in the mining valleys of the south. As K. O. Morgan has suggested, Nonconformity 'was surging on into the industrial valleys simultaneously with the industrial process itself. Places like Merthyr Tydfil, Aberdare, Neath, and Llanelli were, by the eighties, citadels of dissent, their ministers and deacons a new elite of popular leadership.'[326] Furthermore, while the different denominations within Nonconformity, which included the Congregationalists or 'Independents', Baptists, and Methodists, had certain doctrinal differences, there was a far greater sense of unity than amongst the different religious groups in the West Virginia coalfield.[327]

Although the strict rules of chapel membership kept the official membership small, their social importance was manifestly larger. In the Rhondda, 'by 1860, the Dissenting Chapels . . . had become real fields of mental as well as spiritual activity. They gave to the ordinary working man scope for exercising his initiative and administrative capacities'.[328] Alongside a leadership role, the chapels provided a meeting place, sponsored debates and cultural activities and through their campaigns for disestablishment, temperance, and land reform they made a significant contribution to the political hegemony of the Liberal Party. All of these were buttressed by a clear moral approach to life and faith, presented in the most forceful manner. As Frank Hodges recalled, 'we used to say we could hear the sinners sizzling twice every Sabbath when he (their preacher) was in the pulpit.'[329]

The religious bent of the coalfield, and its role in binding the mining community together, was not missed by the US *UMWJ*. In 1900 they glowingly described a miner's chapel built 750 ft underground at Myndd Newydd, near Swansea, where ecumenical services were held in Welsh. They described how 'the sense of the common danger of their perilous occupation tends to intensify the veneration and devotion . . . scoffers are unknown there, and it is admitted that the Myndd Newydd pit has an unusual proportion of sober, upright workmen.'[330]

Like the anglicisation of language, the hegemony of Nonconformity was increasingly undermined in this period, as it was unable to attract many of the new English immigrants. However, the true dimension of this drift away from Nonconfomity was temporarily covered up in the early part of this period by the explosion of religious fervour that swept through the valleys in 1904–5.

South Wales had a long tradition of religious revivals, with industrial districts having 'consistently generated a revivalistic atmosphere.'[331] Led by the former miner, Evan Roberts, however, the revival of 1904–5 was on an entirely different scale. Unorthodox in his outlook, Roberts claimed to have religious visions, including seeing the devil 'grinning' at him in his garden.[332] This eccentric approach exemplified the popular and spontaneous nature of the revival. As Hall has suggested:

> Whatever else it was, the Welsh revival was a remarkable example of popular religion: it came from the people, from the ordinary folk of the mining valleys and villages of the countryside; their emotions and their religious aspirations shaped it, and they consistently repudiated professional ministerial guidance or other attempts to guide and control it along lines traditional to revivals of the past.[333]

The populist fundamentalism was conveyed in the revival's four articles of faith. They were: firstly, a confession to God of all sins hitherto unconfessed; secondly, the giving up of everything doubtful; thirdly, open confession of Christ; and fourthly, ready and immediate obedience to every impulse of the spirit.[334]

The 'riot of religious sentiment' [335] that was unleashed had a profound, if temporary, effect. Thus, James Griffiths recalled how after a visit by Roberts, services were held down the mine, and the family home was turned into a chapel.[336] Another miner who 'converted' during the revival, remembered how, 'it was nothing to go into the work and see all the timber chalked out and on the trams . . . people would be chalking to give attention to church quotations and scripture, it was a common thing.'[337]

The act of conversion was one of the high points of the meetings, which were charged with an almost hysterical atmosphere which would not have been alien to the holy rollers of West Virginia. A sympathetic observer in the south Wales valleys at the time of the revival, described how Roberts would approach someone in the audience who was 'surely an impossible case', eventually getting the person to kneel and pray, the effect of which reduced the congregation into 'tears and songs that alternate between sobs and exaltations', further heightened at the 'sound of the broken confessions', when 'Ebenezer chapel is taken to the awe of eternal things.'[338]

The 'eternal' enthusiasm, however, was not without its material consequences, as in the case of the Reverend Daniel Jones of Loughor Calvinist Methodist chapel, who resigned in protest after £60 damage was done to his chapel during a revival meeting.[339]

The remarkable nature of the revival, and its claimed conversion of 100,000, was matched by the speed with which its influence waned. Both Frank Hodges and James Griffiths remembered how they temporarily succumbed to the enthusiastic outburst before, as the former put it, 'reason again began to play its part, and a greater sense of reality was restored.'[340] Certainly the revival, rather than heralding a new growth of spirituality as many adherents had believed, was, in many ways, a sign of quite the opposite. As the dominance of the chapel was being undermined, the space was created for an outburst of energy created by the powerful, and sometimes contradictory, emotions and forces that were unleashed.

Before the dust had settled from the revival, all the main denominations were losing members. Burdened by debt, and increasingly out of touch with the ideals and pursuits of the masses in the mining towns, by the outbreak of war the signs of a new social hegemony were apparent, with politics and secular ideas increasingly replacing religion.[341] Some were able to move, and even influence, the changing tide, such as the Reverend R. J. Campbell, friend of Keir Hardie, whose *New Theology* provided a religion more relevant to the turbulent times. Similarly, a number of Nonconformist ministers openly supported the ILP, and the idea of an independent, rather than compromised labour politics. The most prominent, if colourful, example of this trend was T. E. Nicholas of Seion Congregational Church, Glais, who was editor of the Welsh section of the *Merthyr Pioneer*, was imprisoned in the war, and became a founder member of the CPGB in 1920.[342]

Although the influence of Nonconformity declined, its importance was felt throughout this period, even on those who eventually rejected its spiritual control. Several of the leading socialists of the period, like Horner, Cook, and Griffiths had a religious training which they later translated into a political currency. Horner, for example, wrote that 'for a long time I was trying in my own mind to wed Christianity to Socialism and only slowly did I reach the point of accepting the materialist conception of history and the struggle of the working-classes as the only way to emancipation.'[343] The fiery language, and moral certitude, as well as the democratic, communal dimension of the chapel, were all bequeathed to the likes of Horner, who became the new spokespeople for a different type of crusade.

The bedrock of the changing culture of the mining towns lay in the rise of organisations and institutions which initially co-existed, and then replaced the chapel as the social and cultural centres of life. In the greater 'space' within civil society in south Wales, relative to West Virginia, and in the climate of conflict and social division in these years, it is not surprising that the miners constructed these new institutions themselves. In the process they synthesised old and new values and definitions of community into a distinctive culture based on their occupational position.

Considering the prominent role that conflict played in defining cultural identities, it is somewhat inevitable that the SWMF filled a good deal of this 'space', performing a concrete social and political role, in distinct contrast to the position of the UMWA in West Virginia. The industrial and political influence of the 'Fed' and other political organisations will be examined in the subsequent chapters. It is important to establish here, however, that the solidarity of these communities, rooted in their common occupation, experience and struggle, was cemented by the free association at industrial and political meetings which were largely unavailable in West Virginia. This political dimension to the formation of a communal culture should not be underestimated.

The workmen's institutes and libraries of the mining towns are one of the best examples of the self-organisation and voluntary association in the south Wales coalfield. Unlike the diversified, frag-mentary pattern of social life in West Virginia, the institutes, under one roof, provided everything from a meeting place, to leisure activ-ities, to a welfare role within the community.

The institutes offered a range of leisure pursuits. Traditional Welsh culture was supported in the shape of the eistedfodd, with special committees established for the purpose and, in the case of Bargoed in 1908, £35 prize money for, among other things, the best male voice choir.[344] A case was later provided in the hall to house the Bargoed male voice shield.[345]

Less traditional than the eistedfodd, were the sporting activities which occurred within the institutes. Billiards was one of the most popular examples of this, with a Billiard Sub-Committee at Bargoed. On one occasion this called for a 'better class table' than the 3/4 length suggested by the main committee. Those who played at Aberbargoed were obviously under-represented on the Sub-Committee, as their request for a new table was rejected in favour of them receiving the old one from Bargoed.[346]A competitive element was also introduced with a 'billiard's handicap'. In return for an entrance fee of 6*d*, competitors had the opportunity to win a cue and case, a turkey, a goose, or a duck.[347]

More vigorous sporting activity was available at the gymnasium club, which used both a room inside the hall, as well as practising outside. The stipulation that 'no wrestling or boxing will take place', by the Bargoed Committee in May 1909, seems to have been later rescinded, as the records for 1912 reveal the provision of a punch bag and gloves at Aberbargoed.[348]

For those in search of more leisurely entertainment, the institutes provided theatre and variety shows. In February 1920, the Mardy Committee agreed to 'kindly accept' the offer of the Mardy Dramatic Society to perform 'Change', the proceeds of which were to go to charity.[349] Professional performers from outside the mining communities were also keenly sought. In 1915, for example, the Ogmore Vale Committee placed an advert in *The Stage*, and *Performer*, stating that the hall was 'open for bookings to Dramatic and Opera Companies during the winter months.'[350]

Seemingly more popular than all of the above, were the provision of film shows. As early as April 1908, the minutes of the Bargoed Institute mention the presence of a 'Cinematograph',[351] and by June 1912, the Ogmore Vale Institute had established a Bioscope Committee, and arranged an ordering service for films.[352] By 1915, a fairly sophisticated organisation had been established, with for example, the adoption of 'Gaumont's list for the week beginning 20 September. For the first three days, a full programme of 6,235 foot of film was to be offered, along with a special programme for children on a saturday afternoon. During the latter half of the week, various films were shown, including 'Saved from the Sea', 'A Race for a Crossing', and 'Sophie's Fighting Spirit.'[353]

Other institutes, like the one at Mardy, were slower to pick up on the demand for cinema. Here, it was not until January 1919 that the committee decided to appoint two 'conversant with electricity to go around the cinema halls and workmen's halls to see how things are workable, and the cost of running the same.'[354] By July 1919, an operator had been appointed, a Picture Committee established, and salaries were being assessed. A year later, demand was such that 'the auditors suggested that another secretary and treasurer should be appointed for the picture show cinema, as there was so much work.'[355]

The enthusiasm for the cinema shows sometimes led to unforeseen difficulties. In August 1920, a Mardy Committee member, John Morgan, appealed to the audience to 'keep order on Friday evening', and a police constable was requested to attend for a few weeks.[356] In July 1921, committee member Fred Evans was forced to resign over a different type of misdemeanour – he was caught letting people into a cinema show without a ticket.[357]

Although other institutes, like the one at Tredegar, did not establish their own cinemas until the 1930s, 'quite a number', to quote Hogenkamp, 'had their main hall equipped with screen and projection booth.'[358] For those that possessed them, like Bargoed, Ogmore Vale, and Mardy, cinema was important in terms of entertainment as well as wider culture, with the enthusiasm further encouraging the shift towards greater anglicisation and, indeed, Americanisation.

The institutes played an even more important cultural role, through the provision of libraries and rooms for working-class education, which was so popular among the miners. This interest in education, particularly under the auspices of the CLC, was an integral part of the 'literate' culture of the south Wales valleys, as opposed to the 'oral' culture of West Virginia. The interest in education and literature had long been a central part of Welsh culture, however, the classes and libraries of the institutes synthesised this tradition into a new, more distinctly political and working-class form.

The institute libraries were a particular source of interest and pride within these communities. They were frequently supplemented, and improved with grants from the committees, and gifts from benefactors.[359] A large variety of books and magazines were held and, where there were separate branches of an institute, they were moved around to give variety. In 1908, for example, the Library Committee at Bargoed decided to change the books every three months between the reading rooms at Bargoed, Aberbargoed, and Gilfach.[360] The popularity of the libraries was revealed by the printing of 2,000 lending forms in September 1909.[361]

The continual growth of the libraries saw them amass huge numbers of books, and expand their importance within the community. Thus, by 1930, the library at Tredegar, where Aneurin Bevan chaired the Book Committee, held over 70,000 volumes. These were used heavily, with 60,000 volumes borrowed a year, at a rate amounting to nearly three for every member of the population.[362]

This appetite for learning was reinforced by the education classes of the County Education Authorities, the WEA, and the CLC.[363] The latter was formed after the SWMF inspired secession from Ruskin College in 1908. This was caused by the sacking of the Ruskin principal, Dennis Hird, who had been ordered to sever his connections with the militant Rhondda based 'Plebs League'. A strike by the students followed, and eventually the CLC was established in London, financed by the SWMF and the rail unions.[364]

Miners from the coalfield had been sent on scholarships to Ruskin, financed by the SWMF. These had included Frank Hodges and Noah Ablett, the latter of whom was prominent in the Ruskin strike, and was to become the principal theorist and spokesperson for the militant syndicalism of the period. The scholarship system continued with the CLC, only this time the courses they studied were more openly political. As G. A. Williams has suggested, 'the syllabus was demanding, rigorous with Marx and Marxist classics, Joseph Dietzgen, science, biology and Marxist history.'[365] The students, who included Aneurin Bevan, Ness Edwards and James Griffiths, spent two years at the college before returning, often to teach within their own communities.[366]

By 1917, it was calculated that of the CLC's forty-one classes, nineteen were held in the south Wales coalfield, and eight of these in the Rhondda, where over 500 students were registered.[367] The importance of these classes to the young miners who attended them is revealed in Arthur Horner's autobiography. He recalled:

> The lecturer was Theodore Griffiths and we paid twopence a lecture. I used to start for the pit at 5 a.m., rush home to take a bath and then get to the lecture. I often fell asleep before the end, but to this day I marvel at how much education in economics, sociology and other subjects I was able to absorb.[368]

The political nature of these classes was not appreciated by all observers. The 1917 Inquiry, for example, described the CLC classes as 'centres of social and political activity', where the study of economics was 'degraded into a gross materialistic conception of cause and effect.'[369] The working-class dimension on education, however, became entwined with the wider political changes within the valleys.

Alongside the prominent role in the provision of facilities for leisure and education, the institutes were also a focal point for welfare provision, sometimes linking together different parts of the community. The most obvious example of this occurred during strikes and lockouts, with joint efforts by the institutes and local SWMF lodges (The fact that the committees of both organisations often had similar membership, make such co-operation unsurprising). In 1921, for example, the Mardy Institute took out a loan to pay half of the weekly cost of the strike soup kitchen, the loan for which was drawn 'in conjunction with the federation officials.'[370] The institutes also worked with other sections of the community, such as religious groups. Thus in 1912, the Aberbargoed hall was opened up to a religious group who had allowed 'their place of worship for the soup kitchen' during a strike.[371]

The welfare role was not, however, confined to strikes. In 1920, the Mardy Institute held a meeting to put pressure on the RUDC over the housing crisis,[372] and during a period of bad trade in 1921, the same committee asked the Chairman and Treasurer to 'interview Mr Williams, schoolmaster and Mrs Humphreys, schoolmistress respectively as to the possibility of children . . . being in need of food.'[373] Furthermore, the miners' own medical schemes, which were briefly mentioned earlier as a good example of self organisation, were also often run from the institutes. Again at Mardy in 1920, the 'Medical New Scheme Committee' was granted £200 towards turning the 'Iron building' into a surgery, with the installation of a railing, and painting and decorating.[374]

So far, by looking at the chapel and the workmen's institutes, we have focused on two of the most important examples of community life, revealing not only the variety of this life, but the degree to which voluntary association and self organisation permeated its very substance. The variety of life, however, was even richer than the study of these two institutions has suggested, and its vigour reveals a good deal of the tension and dislocation underlying the culture of this period; particularly the discrepancy between Nonconformist notions of society, and the actual reality. As Francis and Smith have written, this was 'a society . . . intent on bolstering its much professed spirituality with a strong dose of the materialism that was its raison d'être'.[375]

The large number of shops and markets within the coalfield suc-
coured material needs, as well as providing places for social interaction. In Lewis Jones' *Cwmardy*, for example, the barber's shop
served as a 'local parliament.'[376] Leisure pursuits were even wider
than those organised by the institutes. Pastimes like whippet racing,
handball, cycling, boxing, wrestling, football and rugby, all had
their followers, and the travelling fairs and circuses met with great
enthusiasm.[377]

The proximity of unspoilt countryside provided a less elaborate
and cheaper form of escape from the mining town. As Coombes
described it, 'away from the dirt of the village one had only to walk a
few hundred yards and there was a wonderful valley that made me
gasp with amazement.'[378] As well as seeking peace and solitude,
some, like Frank Hodges and Aneurin Bevan, would walk with
others, further discussing and hammering out opinions and ideas.[379]

To those with a moralistic outlook, there were also distinctly less
seemly leisure pursuits. As in West Virginia, gambling was popular,
with one resident at Maesteg recalling that 'everybody gambled,
church people and all'[380] Similarly, in 1908, the Bargoed Institute
was forced to reprimand gamblers, and issue a notice threatening
expulsion for those who were caught.[381] The latter incident seems to
have been caused by the discovery of betting on a game of billiards –
one of a number of pastimes that was open to such practices. Indeed,
betting was so widespread in the coalfield, that it was brought to the
attention of the Select Committee on Betting in 1923.[382]

The pub and consumption of alcohol was, as in West Virginia, an
even more controversial issue. The spread of the temperance movement from the 1870s saw many 'taking the pledge', and a good deal
of hectoring of those who did not. Mabon, the epitome of respectable, Nonconformist trade unionism, complained to a SWMF No.1
Rhondda District meeting in March 1901, that:

> he would invite the Clydach Vale men . . . to pay the strike money in
> places other than the public houses. The wailings which came to him
> last week were something terrible, of women who explained that the
> money was spent by their husbands before they got home after being
> paid. Let them do something in honour of their reputation as social,
> moral and religious men by removing this blot.[383]

Although the revival heightened the interest in temperance, there
were many who preferred frequenting pubs and drinking,

sometimes to excess. As one miner recalled, reminiscent in this sense of West Virginia, there was 'a lot of drunkenness. And nearly every Saturday night a lot of fighting'.[384] Suffice to say, however, that the fighting did not produce the harvest of bodies that so frightened the hapless John Williams in the mining camps of McDowell County.

The patronage of the pub and gambling were as inevitable a by-product of the nature of life in these mining towns, as the passion for rugby, or the escapism of the cinema. They were part of the bustling, vibrant, and at times contradictory life in these towns. Of course, it was in the field of leisure, that part of the clash of values, leading to the declining influence of Nonconformity, occurred. This concerned both the use of leisure time, and the inflexibility of the chapel's designation of certain forms of leisure as 'ungodly'.

However, it would be wrong to see this clash of values as being solely related to spiritual matters, or restricted entirely to the post-1900 period. It was also part of an attempt by the middle class to smother these communities under a blanket of respect-ability,[385] in a vague echo of the 'civilising' ethos so farcically applied to Appalachia. Thus in 1856 Walter Coffin, J. P., MP and coal owner said of the miners of the Lower Rhondda that, 'a more respectable body of men . . . does not exist.'[386] However, as E. D. Lewis has noted, 'side by side' with the cultural growth associated with Nonconformity, 'there was a less exalted and more earthy side of Rhondda life'. He went on, 'it has been facetiously said that the Rhondda Valley in the second half of the nineteenth century contained more temples for the worship of God and more edifices for the worship of the devil than any other mining area in Britain.'[387]

These contradictions, which made the respectable collier of Mabon as much a myth as the archetypal proletarian that suppos-edly hatched fully fledged from the shell of the Nonconformist egg, were part of the substance of these communities, both collectively as well as within individuals – the drinking and fighting preacher, Dai Cannon, in the novel *Cwmardy* may be seen metaphorically as a symbol of this.[388] However, although at times contradictory, culture was always collective, and popular. As culture shifted towards its more anglicised and secular juncture, the contradictions remained, but they were not ones that divided the communities, rather they further drew them together.

The cultural patterns which emerged in south Wales therefore were very different from those found in the West Virginia coalfield. In the latter, the communities were newer, smaller, more isolated, and populated by a culturally heterogeneous population. Moreover, they developed within a framework which gave the coal operators immense power over virtually every aspect of life – power which they exercised with vigour. While the level of exploitation at times engendered a degree of unity among the inhabitants of the company town, this did not extend to the formation of a common culture. What emerged was a fragmented culture that, beyond its reactive element, was only partially related to the economic world of coal mining.

In contrast, the older, larger, more integrated communities in south Wales, emerged within an existing social framework which not only provided a cultural context, but granted greater space for their self-development. Under such different circumstances, in place of the fragmentation, heterogeneity and transition of West Virginia, south Wales developed a more homogeneous, and collective culture, directly related to the industrial world of the coal miner. A difference which, as we shall see in the following chapters, helps explain the contrasting pattern and form of industrial and political protest in these two regions in this period.

Notes

1 For example, in 1910, the West Virginia Department of Mines reported that just over 46% of the miners in the state were of white native stock. West Virginia Department of Mines (WVDM), *Annual Report, 1910* (Charleston, 1910), p. 104.

2 J. T. Laing, 'The Negro Miner in West Virginia', (Unpublished Ph.D dissertation, Ohio State University, 1933), pp. 60–72.

3 K. R. Bailey, 'A Judicious Mixture: Negroes and Immigrants in the West Virginia Mines, 1880–1917', *West Virginia History*, 34 (1973), p. 144; WVDM, *Annual Report, 1922* (Charleston, 1922), p. 13; Laing, 'Negro Miner In West Virginia', pp. 75–6; R. L. Lewis, 'From Peasant to Proletarian: The Migration of Southern Blacks to the Central Appalachian Coalfields', *Journal of Southern History*, 55, 1 (1989), p. 82.

4 J. B. Thomas, 'Coal Country: The Rise of the Southern Smokeless Coal Industry and its Effect on Area Development' (Unpublished Ph.D dissertation, University of North Carolina, 1971), p. 178.

5 In 1910 there were 5,275 blacks and 4,471 white Americans employed at the mines and coke ovens of McDowell County. WVDM, *Annual Report, 1910*, p. 105.

6 R. M. Simon, 'The Development of Underdevelopment: The Coal Industry and its Effect on the West Virginia Economy, 1880–1930', (Unpublished Ph.D dissertation, University of Pittsburgh, 1978), p. 233, and table, p. 235.

7 WVDM, *Annual Report, 1910*, p. 105; *Ibid.*, *Annual Report, 1920* (Charleston, 1920), p. 260.

8 Bailey 'Judicious Mixture', p. 144.

9 WVDM, *Annual Report, 1910*, p. 104.

10 WVDM, *Annual Report, 1922*, p. 13

11 D. Baines, *Migration in a Mature Economy: Emigration and Internal Migration in England and Wales, 1861–1900* (Cambridge, Cambridge University Press, 1985), pp. 276–8. Baines suggests a slightly earlier date for the arrival of large numbers of English immigrants than the established view. See B. Thomas 'The Migration of Labour into the Glamorganshire Coalfield, 1861–1911', *Economica*, 10 (1930), pp. 275–94.

12 I. Matthews, 'The World of the Anthracite Miner', *Llafur*, 6, 1 (1992), p. 99.

13 *Census of England and Wales, 1921: County of Glamorgan* (London, 1923), pp. 32–3.

14 K. O. Morgan, 'The Merthyr of Keir Hardie', in G. Williams (ed.), *Merthyr Politics: The Making of a Working-Class Tradition* (Cardiff, University of Wales Press,1966), p. 60.

15 J. Jones, *Unfinished Journey* (London, Hamish Hamilton, 1938), p. 113.

16 Calculated from *Census of England and Wales, 1911* (Parl. Papers, 1912–13, Cd.7017, IX), p. 247.

17 D. Smith and H. Francis, *The Fed: A History of the South Wales Miners in the Twentieth Century* (London, Lawrence and Wishart, 1980), p. 11.

18 N. Evans, 'Immigrants and Minorities in Wales, 1840–1990: A Comparative Perspective', *Llafur*, 5, 4 (1991), p. 9.

19 H. G. Gutman, *Work, Culture, and Society in Industrializing America: Essays in American Working-Class and Social History* (New York, Vintage Books, 1977 edn.)

20 R. D. Eller, *Miners, Millhands, and Mountaineers: Industrialization of the Appalachian South, 1880–1930* (Knoxville, University of Tennessee Press, 1981), p. 38.

21 D. Billings, K. Blee, and L. Swanson, 'Culture, Family and Community in Preindustrial Appalachia', *Appalachian Journal*, 13, 2 (1986), pp. 155–6.

22 Eller, *Miners, Millhands, and Mountaineers,* p. 31; R. G. Lawrence, 'Appalachian Metamorphosis: Industrializing Society on the Central Appalachian Plateau, 1860–1913' (Unpublished Ph.D dissertation, Duke University, 1983) pp. 81–3; H. M. Caudill, *Night Comes to the Cumberlands: A Biography of a Depressed Area* (Boston, Little Brown and Co., 1963 edn.), p. 80.

23 Eller, *Miners, Millhands, and Mountaineers* , pp. 33–7; Billings et al., 'Culture, Family and Community in Preindustrial Appalachia', pp. 155–6.

24 J. C. Campbell, *The Southern Highlander and his Homeland* (Lexington, University Press of Kentucky, 1969 edn.), p. 178.

25 Eller, *Miners, Millhands, and Mountaineers,* pp. 39–44.

26 See A. L. Waller, *Feud: Hatfields, McCoys, and Social Change in Appalachia, 1860–1900* (Chapel Hill, University of North Carolina Press, 1988); and G. B. McKinney, 'Industrialization and Violence in Appalachia in the 1890s', in J. W. Williamson ed., *Appalachian Symposium* (Boone, N.C., Appalachian Consortium Press, 1977), pp. 131–142.

27 Some of the mountaineers presented easy prey to prospective buyers. Offers of what were, in reality, pitiful amounts of money, were sometimes backed up with leases which supposedly sold only minerals underneath the ground. Sellers later discovered, however, that the buyer had the right to gain access how and where they wanted. In addition, the coal and land companies took advantage of the confused records of ownership and, using the courts (which inevitably worked in their favour), cheated the mountaineers out of large amounts of land. Eller, *Miners, Millhands, and Mountaineers,* pp. 54–8; Caudill, *Night Comes to the Cumberlands,* pp. 71–6; H. Lewis, 'Fatalism and the Coal Industry? Contrasting Views of the Appalachian Problem', *Mountain Life and Work,* 45 (1970), p. 8.

28 F. Mooney, *Struggle in the Coal Fields* [ed. J. W. Hess] (Morgantown, West Virginia University Library Press, 1967), p. 5.

29 Eller, *Miners, Millhands, and Mountaineers,* pp. 126–7.

30 G. F. Massay, 'Coal Consolidation: Profile of the Fairmont Field of West Virginia, 1852–1903' (Unpublished Ph.D dissertation, West Virginia University, 1970), p. 194.

31 H. B. Lee, *Bloodletting in Appalachia: The Story of West Virginia's Four Major Mine Wars and Other Thrilling Incidents of its Coal Fields* (Morgantown, West Virginia University Library Press, 1969), p. 4.

32 Billings et al., 'Culture, Family and Community in Preindustrial Appalachia', p. 163; Eller, *Miners, Millhands, and Mountaineers,* pp. 63–4; E. A. Cubby, 'The Transformation of the Tug and Guyandot

Valleys: Economic Development and Social Change in West Virginia, 1888–1921' (Unpublished Ph.D dissertation, Syracuse University, 1962), p. 256; Caudill, *Night Comes to the Cumberlands*, p. 97; E. E. Knipe and H. M.Lewis, 'The Impact of Coal Mining on the Traditional Mountain Subculture', in J. K. Moreland (ed.), *The Not So Solid South: Anthropological Studies in a Regional Subculture* (Athens, Ga., University of Georgia Press, 1971), p. 29.

33 J. T. Laing, 'The Negro Miner in West Virginia', *Social Forces*, 14 (1936), p. 418.

34 M. Kline, 'Growing up on Cabin Creek: An Interview with Arnold Miller', *Goldenseal*, 7, 1 (1981), p. 41.

35 Lee, *Bloodletting in Appalachia*, pp. 6–7.

36 W. P. Tams Jr., *The Smokeless Coal Fields of West Virginia: A Brief History* (Morgantown, West Virginia University Library Press, 1963), p. 61.

37 WVBNWS, *First Annual Report*, p. 39.

38 Laing, 'The Negro Miner in West Virginia', pp. 135–7; Lewis, 'From Peasant to Proletarian'.

39 Thomas, 'Coal Country', p. 197.

40 Cubby, 'Transformation of the Tug and Guyandot Valleys', pp. 256–7; Lawrence, 'Appalachian Metamorphosis', pp. 187–9.

41 See Herndon to Collins, 20 Jul 1905, Morgantown, West Virginia University (WVU), West Virginia and Regional History Collection, Justus Collins Papers (A+M 1824), Series 1, Box 1, File 6; Wolfe to Collins, 5 October 1913, *Ibid.*, Box 12, File 80.

42 W. Thurmond, *The Logan Coal Field of West Virginia: A Brief History* (Morgantown, West Virginia University Library Press, 1964), p. 63.

43 J. Rogers, 'I Remember the Mining Town', *West Virginia Review*, 15 (7 Apr 1938), p. 203.

44 D. Brody, *Steelworkers in America: The Nonunion Era* (Cambridge, Mass., Harvard University Press, 1960), pp. 96–111.

45 *Report of West Virginia Mining Investigation Commission, Appointed by Governor Glasscock on the 28th Day of August, 1912* (Charleston, 1912), p. 16.

46 Monongah Mine Relief Fund Records (A+M 1733), WVU, Box 1, Files 26–30; *History of the Monongah Mines Relief Fund* (Fairmont, 1910), in collection.

47 Vincenzo Berardo's father declared under oath before the Mayor of Duronia del Sannio that his son sent money home, and produced three receipts to prove it. He duly received $200 from the fund. *Ibid.*, File 30

48 Lawrence suggests that the Hungarians were more likely to do this, 'Appalachian Metmorphosis', p. 189.

49 E. E. Hunt, F. G. Tyron, and J. H. Willits (eds.), *What the Coal Commission Found* (Baltimore, William and Williams Co.,1925), p. 137.

50 Eller, *Miners, Millhands, and Mountaineers*, p. 173; Bailey, 'Judicious Mixture' p. 143; Cubby, 'Transformation of the Tug and Guyandot Valleys', p. 256.

51 Bailey, 'Judicious Mixture', pp. 143–8; Eller, *Miners, Millhands, and Mountaineers*, pp. 173–4.

52 Simon, 'Development of Underdevelopment', pp. 231–6.

53 Charleston *Labor Argus*, 3 Oct 1907, p. 1.

54 Thurmond, *The Logan Coal Field*, p. 61.

55 There were several groupings of surnames from the same towns in Italy. See *History of Monongah Mines Relief Fund*, pp. 29–39, in Monongah Mine Relief Fund Records, for details.

56 Monongah Mines Relief Fund, File 302.

57 A 1917 Parliamentary Inquiry noted the large number of single male immigrants. They pointed out that Monmouthshire had the highest proportion of males in England and Wales, with 912 women to 1,000 men. Glamorgan was not far behind with 924 to 1,000; *Commission of Inquiry into Industrial Unrest: No.7 District – Wales and Monmouthshire* (Parl. Papers, 1917–18, Cd. 8668, XV), p. 16.

58 B. L. Coombes, *These Poor Hands* (London, Gollancz, 1939), pp. 7, 8, 11.

59 Interview with Jim Vale, pp. 1–2, Swansea, South Wales Miners' Library (SWML), Oral History Collection.

60 D. Jones, 'Serfdom and Slavery: Women's Work in Wales, 1890–1930', in D. R. Hopkin and G. S. Kealey (eds.), *Class, Community and the Labour Movement: Wales and Canada, 1850–1930* (Wales, Llafur'Labour/Le Travail, 1989), pp. 86–100.

61 Thomas, 'Migration of Labour into the Glamorganshire Coalfield', p. 290.

62 Interview with Jim Vale, p. 1, SWML, Oral History Collection.

63 Coombes, *These Poor Hands*, p. 10.

64 Frank Hodges, *My Adventures as a Labour Leader* (London, George Newnes, 1925), p. 3.

65 Coombes, *These Poor Hands*, p. 16.

66 E. P. Thompson, 'Time, Work-Discipline and Industrial Capitalism', in A. Giddens and D. Held (eds.), *Classes, Power and Conflict: Classical and Contemporary Debates* (Macmillan, Basingstoke, 1982), p. 308.

67 J. A. Williams, *West Virginia: A History* (New York, W. W. Norton and Co., 1984 edn.), p. 139; P. Conley, *History of the West Virginia Coal Industry* (Charleston, W. Va., Education Foundation, 1960), p. 171.

68 Hunt et al., *What the Coal Commission Found*, pp. 136, 139–40.

69 Williams, *West Virginia*, p. 139.
70 Schedule for Boone 2 and 3, Logan County. Suitland, Washington National Records Center (WNRC), Records of US Coal Commission (RG 68), Records of Division of Investigation of Labor Facts, Living Conditions, Schedule 62, 'Completed Mining Community 'A' Schedules, with Camp Ratings', Box 31.
71 Schedule for Monarch Mine, Kanawha County, US Coal Commission, 62, Box 28.
72 Schedule for Boomer Coal and Coke Company Mine no.2 North, No.2 South, 3 and 4, Fayette County, *ibid*.
73 Department of Labor, Children's Bureau, *Welfare of Children in the Bituminous Coal Mining Communities in West Virginia* (by N. P. McGill, Bureau Publ. No.117, Washington D.C., 1923), p. 2.
74 *Ibid.*, p. 6.
75 Schedule for Boone 2 and 3, Logan County; Schedule for Boomer Coal and Coke Company Mine no.2 North, No.2 South, 3 and 4, Fayette County, US Coal Commission, 62, Box 28 and 31 respectively.
76 Tams, *Smokeless Coal Fields of West Virginia*, pp. 53–5.
77 *Commission of Inquiry into Industrial Unrest*, p. 12; Francis and Smith, *The Fed*, pp. 8–9.
78 *Commission of Inquiry into Industrial Unrest*, p. 14.
79 Lewis, *The Rhondda Valleys*, p. 100; See also G. M. Holmes, 'The South Wales Coal Industry, 1850–1914', *Transactions of the Honourable Society of Cymmrodorion* (1976), pp. 203–4.
80 G. A. Williams, *When was Wales? A History of the Welsh* (London, Penguin, 1985), p. 176.
81 R. Church, *The History of the British Coal Industry Vol. 3, 1830–1913: Victorian Pre-eminence* (Oxford, Oxford University Press, 1986), p. 615.
82 J. Griffiths, *Pages From Memory* (London, Dent, 1969), p. 5.
83 Home Office, *List of Mines in the United Kingdom of Great Britain and Ireland and the Isle of Man, 1910* (London, 1911), pp. 219–222.
84 Church, *The History of the British Coal Industry, Vol. 3*, p. 614.
85 *Ibid.*, p. 615.
86 R. J. Waller, *The Dukeries Transformed: The Social and Political Development of a Twentieth-Century Coalfield* (Oxford, Oxford University Press, 1983), p. 292.
87 B. Williamson, *Class, Culture, and Community: A Biographical Study of Social Change in Mining*, (London, Routledge and Kegan Paul, 1982), pp. 17, 21–3.
88 R. Samuel, *Miners, Quarrymen and Saltworkers* (London, Routledge and Kegan Paul, 1977), pp. 73–4.
89 Lane, *Civil War In West Virginia*, p. 17.

90 US Senate, Committee on Education and Labor, *Conditions in the Paint Creek District, West Virginia*, 63 Congress, 1 Session (Washington D.C., 1913), Pt. 1, p. 789. See also Schedules for Thacker Mine no.11, Mingo County, and Paint Creek Coal Company Mine (serial 69) in Kanawha County, US Coal Commission, 62, Box 29.

91 For example, Monarch Mine residents could buy lots in Cedar Grove, one mile distant. Schedule for Monarch Mine, Kanawha County, *ibid.*, Box 28

92 Massay, 'Coal Consolidation', p. 198.

93 Hunt et al., *What the Coal Commission Found*, pp. 148–9.

94 Wolfe to Collins, 25 Dec 1915, Collins Papers, 1, Box 13, File 93. Collins was one of the major Southern operators and, characteristically, vigorously anti-union. Alabaman born, he opened his first mines in West Virginia in 1888, expanding his interests in the following years. These included mines in the Pocahontas and New River fields and, in 1909, the large scale 'Winding Gulf Colliery Company', in the new Winding Gulf field. See typed obituary in Collins Papers, Series VII, Box 56, File 6.

95 See copy of complete lease in 'Lawrence Dwyer File', WNRC, Records of the Federal Mediation and Conciliation Service, (RG 280), File 170/1185.

96 Collins to Wolfe, 27 Dec 1915, *ibid.*, Box 13, File 93.

97 *UMWJ*, 24 May 1900, p. 2.

98 *Conditions in the Paint Creek District*, 1, p. 776.

99 Collins to Wolfe, 27 Dec 1915, Box 13, File 93.

100 Hunt et al., *What the Coal Commission Found*, pp. 152–4.

101 *Welfare of Children in the Bituminous Coal Mining Communities in West Virginia*, p. 72.

102 Simon, 'Development of Underdevelopment', p. 210.

103 Tams, *Smokeless Coal Fields of West Virginia*, p. 25.

104 Wolfe to Collins, 25 Dec 1915, Collins Papers, 1, Box 13, File 93.

105 Wolfe to Collins, 26 Dec 1915, *ibid.*

106 Tams, *Smokeless Coal Fields of West Virginia*, p. 52.

107 R. W. Craigo, 'West Virginia Coal Company Scrip', *Goldenseal*, 5, 4, (1979), pp. 68–71.

108 Tams, *Smokeless Coal Fields of West Virginia*, p. 52; This point is supported by C. A. Shifflett. See *Coal Towns: Life, Work and Culture in Company Towns of Southern Appalachia* (Knoxville, University of Tennessee Press, 1991), pp. 182–3.

109 One miner told the Senate Inquiry that the companies only gave 90 c. cash for each $1 scrip: *Conditions in the Paint Creek District*, 1, pp. 219–223; Lawrence, 'Appalachian Metamorphosis', pp. 161–2.

110 *Welfare of Children in the Bituminous Coal Mining Communities in West Virginia*, pp. 71–2. For a more sympathetic interpretation of the operator's motivations in using scrip, and the wider role of the company store, see Shifflett, *Coal Towns*, pp. 176–89; and P. V. Fishback, *Soft Coal, Hard Choices; The Economic Welfare of Bituminous Coal Miners* (New York, Oxford University Press, 1992), pp. 133–51.

111 Lane, *Civil War in West Virginia*, pp. 23–5.

112 See schedules for Monarch Mine, Kanawha County, US Coal Commission, 62, Box 28; For example of cow feed, Thacker Mine No.11, Mingo County, Box 29.

113 Simon, 'Development of Underdevelopment', p. 215.

114 *UMWJ*, 9 Aug, 1900, p. 1.

115 *UMWJ*, 23 Aug, 1900, p. 4.

116 *Report of the West Virginia Mining Investigation Commission*, p. 7. See Simon 'Development of Underdevelopment', pp. 199–207, for evidence of the company 'larceny' at the workplace.

117 *Ibid.*, p. 204.

118 Simon 'Development of Underdevelopment', pp. 204–5.

119 *UMWJ*, 7 Feb 1901, p. 7.

120 Herndon to Collins, 20 Jul, 1905; 22 Jul 1905; 29 Jul 1905; Collins to Herndon, 22 Jul 1905, Collins Papers, 1, Box 1, File 6.

121 US Senate, Committee on Education and Labor, *West Virginia Coalfeld Hearings*, 67 Congress, 1 Session (Washington D.C., 1921–2), Volume 1, p. 32.

122 G. Korson, *Coal Dust on the Fiddle: Songs and Stories of the Bituminous Industry* (Hartborough, Penn., Folklore Associates, 1965 edn.), p. 414. The song is probably better known as 'A Miner's Life': See B. Reiser and P. Seeger, *Carry it On !: a History in Song and Picture of the Working Men and Women of America* (Poole, Blandford, 1986), pp. 90–1. It was also popular within British mining communities: See Dick Gaughan's recorded collection of Scottish miners' songs, *True and Bold: Songs of the Scottish Miners* (Released by the Scottish TUC, 1985).

123 See Wolfe to Collins, 27 Aug 1917, Collins Papers, 1, Box 15, File 105.

124 Bailey, 'Judicious Mixture', p. 156.

125 Lewis, *Black Coal Miners in America*, pp. 149–51.

126 *Welfare of Children in the Bituminous Coal Mining Communities in West Virginia*, p. 20.

127 *Conditions in the Paint Creek District*, 1, p. 773.

128 W. J. B. Livingston, 'Coal Miners and Religion: A Study of Logan County' (Unpublished Doctor of Theology dissertation, Union Theological Seminary, Richmond, Va., 1951), pp. 179–80; Schedule for Boone 2 and 3, Logan County, U.S. Coal Commission, 62, Box 31.

129 Jairus Collins to Justus Collins, 21 Oct 1902, Collins Papers, 1, Box 1, File 2.
130 Wolfe to Collins, 31 Mar 1917; Collins to Wolfe, 3 April 1917, Ibid., File 101, Box 14.
131 Lee, *Bloodletting in Appalachia*, p. 11.
132 Eller, *Miners, Millhands, and Mountaineers*, pp. 214–5.
133 P. N. Jones, *Colliery Settlement in the South Wales Coalfield, 1850–1926* (University of Hull, Occasional papers in Geography, No.14, 1969)
134 M. J. Daunton, 'Miners' Houses: South Wales and the Great Northern Coalfield, 1880–1914', *International Review of Social History*, 25 (1980), pp. 145–6.
135 Jones, *Colliery Settlement in the South Wales Coalfield*, p. 46.
136 Daunton, 'Miners' Houses', p. 166.
137 Morgan, *Rebirth of a Nation*, p. 69.
138 General Committee, 18 Dec, 1909, Cambrian Lodge Minutes, 31 May 1906 - 12 Oct 1910, Swansea, South Wales Coalfield Archive (SWCA), A.2.
139 Jones, *Colliery Settlement in the South Wales Coalfield*, p. 45.
140 *Ibid.*, p. 42.
141 Daunton, 'Miners' Houses', pp. 147–8; Church, *The History of the British Coal Industry*, Vol. 3, pp. 602–3; Jones, *Colliery Settlement in the South Wales Coalfield*, pp. 43–4.
142 Church, *The History of the British Coal Industry*, Vol. 3, p. 603.
143 Daunton, 'Miners' Houses', p. 169.
144 Jones, *Colliery Settlement in the South Wales Coalfield*, pp. 42–3.
145 E. Stonelake, *Autobiography of Edmund Stonelake* [ed. A. Mor-O'Brien] (Bridgend, Mid Glamorgan Education Committee, 1981), p. 103.
146 Quoted in Jones, *Colliery Settlement in the South Wales Coalfield*, p. 47.
147 Lewis, *The Rhondda Valleys*, p. 181. See pp. 180–196 for more detail.
148 A. Horner, *Incorrigible Rebel* (London, MacGibbon and Kee, 1960), pp. 61–2.
149 M. Foot, *Aneurin Bevan, 1897–1945* (London, Paladin, 1975 edn.), pp. 66–7 for details.
150 SWMF Annual Conference 1914, SWMF Minutes, 1914, SWCA, C.2.
151 L. J. Williams, 'The Coalowners', in D. Smith (ed.), *A People and a Proletariat: Essays in the History of Wales, 1780–1980* (London, Pluto Press, 1980), p. 106.
152 Lewis, *The Rhondda Valleys*, p. 218.
153 *Ibid.*, p. 217.
154 Hunt et al., *What the Coal Commission Found*, pp. 142–148.

155 *Welfare of Children in the Bituminous Coal Mining Communities in West Virginia*, p. 6, sanitation, pp. 14–18, housing, p. 10, mining town, pp. 6–10.

156 *UMWJ*, 5 Dec 1901, p. 8.

157 Schedule for Queen Shoals Mine, Clay County, Coal Commission, 62, Box 29. The comments are written longhand underneath the final section.

158 Paint Creek Coal Mining Company mine, serial number 69, in Kanawha County, *ibid.*, Box 29. Comments on separate sheet attached to rear.

159 Monarch mine, Kanawha County, *ibid.*, Box 28.

160 The scale was worked out as follows: environment and habits of population, up to 3.0; water supply, up to 40.0; disposal of human excrement, up to 32.0; general sanitary control, up to 12.5; disease prevention activities, up to 12.5. 'Summarised Report on the Sanitation of 123 Communities in the Bituminous Districts of 9 States', by the US Public Health Service, p. 4, WNRC, Records of US Coal Commission, Office of George Otis Smith, Public Health Service Sanitary Surveys of Coal Communities, 13, Box 7. West Virginia figures in Table 21.

161 'Sanitary Survey of Kayford, Kanawha County, West Virginia', by US Public Health Service, *ibid.*

162 The first mine was the York Roland in Clay County, the second was the Paint Creek Coal Mining Company Mine (Serial 69), in Kanawaha County. US Coal Commission, 62, Box 29.

163 *Biennial Report of the West Virginia Department of Health, 1910–11* (Charleston, 1912), p. 6.

164 *Annual Report of the West Virginia State Health Department, 1918* (Charleston, 1918), pp. 41, 36.

165 *Ibid.*, pp. 41, 36.

166 *Annual Report of West Virginia State Health Department, 1920* (Charleston, 1920), p. 103.

167 Wolfe to Justus Collins, 7 Dec 1918; Wolfe to Berkeley, 7 Dec 1918 (two letters and a telegram), Collins Papers, 1, Box 16, File 110.

168 W. Rose to V .H. Manning, 10 Aug 1915, WNRC, Bureau of Mines (RG70), Box 169, File 53.

169 *Annual Report of the West Virginia State Health Department, 1918*, p. 15.

170 For example, Dr. J. E. Robins was a member of the State Board of Health in 1911, at the same time as being President of the Harrah Coal Land Company. Collins to Robins, 14 Nov 1911, Collins Papers, 1, Box 10, File 64.

171 Trotter, *Coal, Class and Color*, pp. 90–1; Shifflett, *Coal Towns*, pp. 82–3.; C. G. Bindocci, 'A Comparison of the Roles of Women in Anthracite and Bituminous Mining in Pennsylvania, 1900–1920', in K. Tenfelde (ed.), *Towards a Social History of Mining in the 19th and 20th Centuries* (Munich, Verlag C. H. Beck, 1992), pp. 682–7.

172 Massay, 'Coal Consolidation', pp. 203–4.

173 Korson, *Coal Dust on the Fiddle*, p. 31.

174 See table XLVI, 'Bituminous Coal Fields of the United States: Relative Standing of 264 Company-Controlled Communities Rated by Agents in the Field on Natural Location and on Community Conditions with a basis of 100 points for each', US Coal Commission, 62, Box 33.

175 See hand written table on General Community and Natural Location Ratings for 364 Company Controlled Communities, *ibid.*, 62, Box 33.

176 Cubby, 'Transformation of the Tug and Guyandot Valleys', pp. 251–4.

177 'Sanitary Survey of the Island Creek Coal Company's Settlement at Holden, Logan County, West Virginia', by US Public Health Service, US Coal Commission, 13, Box 7.

178 Lane, *Civil War In West Virginia*, pp. 32–3.

179 Quoted in Eller, *Miners, Millhands and Mountaineers*, p. 190.

180 'Sanitary Survey of the Island Creek Coal Company's Settlement at Holden', US Coal Commission, 13, Box 7.

181 Lane, *Civil War In West Virginia*, p. 32.

182 Eller, *Miners, Millhands and Mountaineers*, pp. 219–21.

183 See hand written table on General Community and Natural Location Ratings, US Coal Commission, 62, Box 33.

184 C. A. Cabell, 'Building a Model Mining Community', *West Virginia Review* (Apr. 1927), p. 208.

185 'Sanitary Survey of the Island Creek Coal Company's Settlement at Holden', US Coal Commission, 13, Box 7.

186 Simon, 'Development of Underdevelopment', pp. 396–400; Eller, *Miners, Millhands and Mountaineers*, p. 221.

187 Lewis, 'From Peasant to Proletarian', p. 88.

188 *Welfare of Children in the Bituminous Coal Mining Communities in West Virginia*, p. 17.

189 Kline, 'Growing up on Cabin Creek', p. 38.

190 American Constitutional Association, *Life in a West Virginia Coal Field* (Charleston, 1923), pp. 54–5.

191 Question 9 in section X of the schedules for individual communities asked about the availability of such land. In the schedules for nine, randomly selected, mixed quality communities, there was land available for such use in every case. The nine were: mine No. 2 North, No.2 South, 3 and 4, Fayette County; Monarch Mine, Kanawha County; Box 28; Boone Mine No.10, Logan County; Queen Shoals Mine, Clay

County; York Roland Mine, Clay County; Thacker Mine No.11, Mingo County; Box 29; Brooklyn Mine, Fayette County; Ragland Coal Company Mine, Raleigh County; Boone No. 2 and 3, Logan County, Box 31; Records of US Coal Commission, 62.

192 Lewis, 'From Peasant to Proletarian', p. 89.

193 Schedule for Island Creek No.11 and 12, Logan County, US Coal Commission, 62, Box 31.

194 Collins to Wolfe, 11 Apr 1917, Collins Papers, 1, Box 15, File 102.

195 Trotter, *Coal, Class and Color*, pp. 90–1; Shifflett, *Coal Towns*, pp. 82–3.

196 Kline, 'Growing up on Cabin Creek', p. 38.

197 Lewis 'From Peasant to Proletarian', pp. 77–102; Corbin, *Life, Work and Rebellion in the Coal Fields*, pp. 33–4.

198 Griffiths described how miners would plant a row in the farmers field, in return for which they would help out at harvest time, *Pages From Memory*, p. 10. Matthews, 'The World of the Anthracite Miner', p. 98.

199 Interview with D. D. Evans, pp. 23–4, SWML, Oral History Collection. He also noted that after 1926, the anthracite region itself was becoming increasingly proletarianised.

200 *Commission of Inquiry into Industrial Unrest*, p. 23.

201 Coombes, *These Poor Hands*, p. 27.

202 H. S. Jevons, *The British Coal Trade* (Newton Abbot, David and Charles, 1969 edn.), pp. 126–30.

203 *Commission of Inquiry into Industrial Unrest*, pp. 33–4.

204 RUDC, *Report of the Medical Officer of Health and School Medical Officer for the Year, 1914*, p. 79.

205 Jevons, *The British Coal Trade*, pp. 126–30; A. R. Griffin, *The British Coal Mining Industry: Retrospect and Prospect* (Buxton, Moorland Publishing Co., 1977), p. 159.

206 Smith, 'Tonypandy 1910', p. 171.

207 E. Stonelake, *The Autobiography of Edmund Stonelake*, pp. 105, 21.

208 B. Supple, *The History of the British Coal Industry, Vol. 4, 1913–1946: The Political Economy of Decline* (Oxford, Oxford University Press, 1987), p. 459.

209 *Commission of Inquiry into Industrial Unrest*, p. 12.

210 Jones, *Unfinished Journey*, pp. 16–18.

211 Lewis, *The Rhondda Valleys*, pp. 210–12.

212 Smith, 'Tonypandy 1910', p. 172.

213 Lewis, *The Rhondda Valleys*, pp. 210–12.

214 D. Jones and L. J. Williams, 'Women at Work in Nineteenth Century Wales', *Llafur*, 3, 3 , pp. 20–32.

215 D. Jones, 'Counting the Cost of Coal; Women's Lives in the Rhondda, 1881–1911', in A. V. John (ed.), *Our Mother's Land: Chapters in Welsh Women's History, 1880–1939* (Cardiff, University of Wales Press, 1991), pp. 112–24; R. Crook, '"Tidy Women": Women in the Rhondda Between the Wars', *Oral History Journal*, 10, 2 (1982), pp. 40–5.

216 *Ibid.*, p. 42.

217 N. Evans and D. Jones, '"A Blessing for the Miner's Wife": The Campaign for Pithead Baths in the South Wales Coalfield, 1908–50', *Llafur*, 6, 3 (1994), pp. 5–28; Jones, 'Counting the Cost of Coal', p. 128.

218 *Ibid.*, pp. 124–7.

219 Morgan, *Rebirth of a Nation*, p. 71.

220 RUDC, *Report of the Medical Officer of Health and School Medical Officer for the Year, 1914*, p. IX; Dot Jones, 'Serfdom and Slavery', p. 95.

221 Lewis, *The Rhondda Valleys*, p. 213.

222 Morgan, *Rebirth of a Nation*, pp. 70, 105; Lewis, *The Rhondda Valleys*, pp. 214–17.

223 Hodges, *My Adventures as a Labour Leader*, pp. 5–6.

224 *Commission of Inquiry into Industrial Unrest*, p. 34.

225 *Ibid*, pp. 12–13.

226 S. Macintyre, *Little Moscows: Communism and Working-Class Militancy in Inter-War Britain* (London, Croom Helm, 1980), p. 25.

227 Jones, 'Serfdom and Slavery', p. 92.

228 Walker Report, Daily Reports of Field Investigators, Mar-Aug 1923, US Coal Commission, Division of Investigation of Labor Facts, Labor Relations Section, 161, Box 70.

229 Supple, *The History of the British Coal Industry, Vol. 4*, pp. 488–9.

230 Wolfe to Collins, 30 Jul 1916, Collins Papers, 1, Box 14, File 96.

231 Monarch Mine Schedule, Kanawha County, US Coal Commission, Box 28.

232 *Welfare of Children in the Bituminous Coal Mining Communities in West Virginia*, pp. 4, 7.

233 Wolfe to Collins, 30 Jul 1916, Collins Papers, 1, Box 14, File 96.

234 Lewis, 'From Peasant to Proletarian', p. 86.

235 Laing, 'Negro Miner in West Virginia', pp. 390–1; Kline, 'Growing up on Cabin Creek', p. 41.

236 Lawrence, 'Appalachian Metamorphosis', p. 179; Laing, 'Negro Miner in West Virginia', p. 480; Lewis, *Black Coal Miners in America*, pp. 149–52; Trotter, *Coal, Class and Color*, pp. 27–8.

237 Cabell, 'Building a Model Mining Community', p. 210.

238 Rogers, 'I Remember that Mining Town', p. 205; Lewis, *Black Coal Miners in America*, pp. 149–50.

239 Trotter, *Coal, Class and Color*, pp. 27–30, 128–30.
240 WVBNWS, *First Annual Report*, pp. 11–14.
241 Laing 'Negro Miner in West Virginia', pp. 493–6.
242 A. Conway (ed.), *The Welsh in America: Letters from the Immigrants* (Minneapolis, University of Minnesota Press, 1961), p. 208.
243 WVBNWS, *First Annual Report*, pp. 11–14.
244 Eller, *Miners, Millhands and Mountaineers*, p. 172.
245 Lewis, *Black Coal Miners in America*, p. 156.
246 Eller, *Miners, Millhands and Mountaineers*, pp. 171–2; Lewis, *Black Coal Miners in America*, pp. 152–6.
247 *Ibid.*, p. 143–6; Laing, 'Negro Miner in West Virginia', (*Social Forces*), pp. 418–19; Fishback, *Soft Coal, Hard Choices*, pp. 176–92. Trotter, however, takes a more sceptical view, suggesting that there was discrimination at the workplace, and that it increased after the war. See *Coal, Class and Color*, pp. 102–10.
248 *Moundsville Echo*, 6 Sep 1912.
249 Cornwell to Chafin, 16 Dec 1919, Morgantown, WVU, John J. Cornwell Papers (A+M 952), Series 35, Box 139. The wording of the Governor's reply perhaps underlines the fact that such an event was unusual in West Virginia, particularly when compared with the South.
250 Bailey, 'Judicious Mixture', pp. 150–1; See Charleston *Labor Argus*, 17 Jun 1909, p. 1.
251 Eller, *Miners, Millhands, and Mountaineers*, p. 172; Laing, 'Negro Miner in West Virginia', p. 474.
252 Mooney, *Struggle in the Coal Fields*, p. 60.
253 Mildred Beik has made this point very strongly in her study of Windber, Pennsylvania, where she discovered internal stratification and divisions within ethnic groups. M. E. Beik, 'The Competition for Ethnic Community Leadership in a Pennsylvania Bituminous Coal Town, 1890s-1930s', in Tenfelde, *Towards a Social History of Mining*, pp. 223–41.
254 Bailey, 'Judicious Mixture', p. 155.
255 Tams, *Smokeless Coal Fields of West Virginia*, pp. 62–3.
256 Laing, 'Negro Miner in West Virginia', pp. 456–9.
257 Trotter, *Coal, Class and Color*, pp. 52, 167.
258 Conway, *The Welsh in America*, p. 209.
259 Walker Report, US Coal Commission, 161, Box 70.
260 Monarch Mine Schedule, Kanawha County, US Coal Commission, Box 28.
261 Tams, *Smokeless Coal Fields of West Virginia*, p. 58.
262 C. Scholz to E. F. Morgan, 8 Apr 1921, Morgantown, WVU, Ephraim F. Morgan Papers (A+M 203), Box 4, File 5. Scholz wrote again to Morgan three months later about a gun battle at the headwaters of

Hazy Creek between a posse led by a deputy sheriff and moonshiners, which left one person dead. Scholz to Morgan, 8 Jul 1921, Box 8, File 1

263 Bailey, 'A Judicious Mixture', p. 155.

264 Nantz was one of those imprisoned during the Paint Creek strike. Huntington *Socialist and Labor Star*, 25 Dec 1914, p. 4.

265 Tams, *Smokeless Coal Fields of West Virginia*, pp. 58–9.

266 Rogers, 'I Remember that Mining Town', p. 205.

267 The report was sent to Riley. T. L. Felts to P. J. Riley, 19 Mar 1907, Collins Papers, 1, Box 2, File 11.

268 *Ibid.*

269 Tams, *Smokeless Coal Fields of West Virginia*, pp. 58–9.

270 Bailey, 'A Judicious Mixture', p. 153.

271 Rogers, 'I Remember that Mining Town', p. 204.

272 Quoted in Massay, 'Coal Consolidation', p. 216.

273 Kline, 'Growing up on Cabin Creek', p. 36.

274 Livingston, 'Coal Miners and Religion', pp. 224–5; Mooney, *Struggle in the Coal Fields*, pp. 1–2.

275 5 M. Ross, *Machine Age in the Hills* (New York, Macmillan, 1933), p. 72.

276 Mooney, *Struggle in the Coal Fields*, p. 4.

277 Laing, 'Negro Miner in West Virginia', pp. 425–6.

278 *Ibid.*, p. 425.

279 Lewis, 'From Peasant to Proletarian', pp. 94–5.

280 Massay, 'Coal Consolidation', p. 215.

281 *McDowell Times*, 27 Oct 1916, p. 1.

282 Corbin, *Life, Work and Rebellion in the Coal Fields*, pp. 149–50; Laing, 'Negro Miner in West Virginia', p. 426.

283 T. L. Felts to P. J. Riley, 19 Mar, 1907; 21 Mar 1907, Collins Papers, 1, Box 2, File 11.

284 Livingston, 'Coal Miners and Religion', p. 186.

285 Laing, 'Negro Miner in West Virginia', pp. 412–14; Lewis, 'From Peasant to Proletarian', pp. 95–6; Trotter, *Coal, Class and Color*, pp. 102–3.

286 Kline, 'Growing up on Cabin Creek', p. 39.

287 Table for Winding Gulf, Mines One and Three, September 1916, Collins Papers, 1, Box 14, File 98.

288 Laing, 'Negro Miner in West Virginia', p. 407.

289 Tams, *Smokeless Coal Fields of West Virginia*, pp. 58–60; Rogers, 'I Remember that Mining Town', p. 205; Kline, 'Growing up on Cabin Creek', p. 41.

290 *Welfare of Children in the Bituminous Coal Fields in West Virginia*, p. 58.

291 *Conditions in the Paint Creek District*, p. 772.
292 Laing, 'Negro Miner in West Virginia', pp. 394–5.
293 *Ibid.*, p. 393; WVBNWS, *First Annual Report*, see table, p. 26.
294 Mooney, *Struggle in the Coal Fields*, pp. 7–8, 48.
295 J. L. Spivak, *A Man and His Time* (New York, Horizon Press, 1967), pp. 63–4.
296 Tams, *The Smokeless Coal Fields of West Virginia*, pp. 55–6.
297 *UMWJ*, 7 Jun 1900, p. 2.
298 *Coal Age*, 1, 1 (14 Oct 1911), p. 25; 1, 2 (21 Oct 1911), p. 56; 1,3 (28 Oct 1911), p. 30.
299 Tams, *The Smokeless Coal Fields of West Virginia*, p. 55
300 Rogers, 'I Remember that Mining Town', p. 205.
301 1 Laing, 'Negro Miner in West Virginia', pp. 418–19.
302 Korson, *Coal Dust on the Fiddle*, pp. 17–22.
303 Lewis, *Black Coal Miners in America*, pp. 151–2; Bailey, 'Judicious Mixture', p. 158.
304 Ross, *Machine age in the Hills*, p. 118.
305 Tams, *The Smokeless Coal Fields of West Virginia*, p. 56.
306 Laing, 'The Negro Miner in West Virginia', p. 400.
307 This term is used by M. Davis, see *Prisoners of the American Dream: Politics and Economy in the History of the US Working-Class* (London, Verso, 1986), pp. 3–51.
308 See *Labor Argus*, 7 Jun 1906, p. 4; 19 Jul 1906, p. 4; 6 Sep 1906, p. 1.
309 Francis and Smith, *The Fed*, p. 7.
310 Supple, *History of the British Coal Industry, Volume 4*, p. 489.
311 Church, *History of the British Coal Industry, Volume 3*, pp. 224–235.
312 *Ibid.*, p. 226.
313 Francis and Smith, *The Fed*, p. 10.
314 Baines, *Migration in a Mature Economy*, pp. 276–7; B. Thomas, 'Wales and the Atlantic Economy', in *ibid* (ed.), *The Welsh Economy: Studies in Expansion* (Cardiff, University of Wales Press, 1962), pp. 26–9.
315 Lewis, *The Rhondda Valleys*, pp. 241–2; Williams, *When was Wales?*, pp. 245–6.
316 Lewis, *The Rhondda Valleys*, p. 242.
317 Jones, *Unfinished Journey*, p. 22.
318 Lewis, *The Rhondda Valleys*, pp. 242–43.
319 Hodges, *My Adventures as a Labour Leader*, pp. 59–62.
320 Interview with Bryn Lewis, p. 18, SWML, Oral History Collection.
321 Francis and Smith, *The Fed*, pp. 11–12.
322 *Ibid.*, pp. 11–12.
323 C. Holmes, 'The Tredegar Riots of 1911: Anti-Jewish Disturbances in South Wales', *Welsh History Review*, 2, 2 (1982), pp. 214–225.

324 H. Francis, *Miners against Fascism: Wales and the Spanish Civil War* (London, Lawrence and Wishart, 1984), p. 34.
325 *Commission of Inquiry into Industrial Unrest*, p. 15.
326 Morgan, *Rebirth of a Nation*, p. 14.
327 *Ibid.*, p. 17.
328 Lewis, *The Rhondda Valleys*, p. 195.
329 Hodges, *My Adventures as a Labour Leader*, p. 20.
330 *UMWJ*, 12 Apr 1900, p. 3.
331 E. T. Davies, *Religion and the Industrial Revolution in South Wales* (Cardiff, University of Wales Press,1965), p. 55.
332 B. Hall, 'The Welsh Revival of 1904–5: A Critique', in G. C. Cuming and D. Baker (eds.), *Popular Belief and Practice: Papers Read at the Ninth Summer Meeting and Tenth Winter Meeting of the Ecclesiastical History Society* (Cambridge, Cambridge University Press, 1972), p. 291.
333 *Ibid.*, p. 293.
334 H. E. Lewis, *With Christ Among the Miners* (London, Allen and Unwin, 1906), p. 70.
335 Hodges, *My Adventures as a Labour Leader*, p. 18.
336 Griffiths, *Pages From Memory*, p. 11.
337 Interview with T. Jenkins, p. 2, SWML, Oral History Collection.
338 Lewis, *With Christ among the Miners*, p. 81.
339 Hall, 'The Welsh Revival', p. 299.
340 Hodges, *My Adventures as a Labour Leader*, p. 18; Griffiths, *Pages from Memory*, p. 11.
341 Jevons, *The British Coal Trade*, p. 125; Morgan, *Rebirth of a Nation*, pp. 135, 197.
342 C. Turner, 'Conflicts of Faith? Religion and Labour in Wales, 1890–1914', in Hopkin and Kealey, *Class, Community and the Labour Movement*, pp. 73–8.
343 Horner, *Incorrigible Rebel*, p. 14.
344 General Committee, 25 Feb 1908; 10 Nov 1908, Bargoed Workmen's Hall and Institute: Annual, General and Committee Minutes, 10 Feb 1908 – 3 Sep 1912, pp. 11, 46, SWCA, A.1.
345 General Committee, 5 Jan 1909, *ibid.*, pp. 54–6.
346 General Committee, 29 Feb 1908; 27 Apr 1908; 23 Jun 1908, *ibid.*, pp. 13, 23, 30.
347 7 Billiard Committee, 17 Nov 1908, *ibid.*, p. 49.
348 General Committee, 4 May 1909; 25 May 1909; 14 May 1912, *ibid.*, pp. 75, 79, 297.
349 Special Committee, 16 Feb 1920, Mardy Workmen's Hall and Institute: Annual, General and Committee Minutes, 27 Nov 1918 – 20 Aug 1925, p. 49, SWCA, A.1.

350 Cinema Sub-Committee, 14 Sep 1915, Ogmore Vale Workmen's Hall and Institute: Annual, General and Committee Minutes, 19 Mar 1914 – 12 Mar 1927, SWCA, A.1.
351 General Committee, 27 Apr 1908, Bargoed Workmen's Hall and Institute Minutes, p. 21.
352 Bioscope Committee, 3 June 1912, Ogmore Vale Workmen's Hall and Institute Minutes.
353 Cinema Sub-Committee, 14 Sep 1913, *ibid.*
354 General Committee, 1 Jan 1919, Mardy Workmen's Hall and Institute Minutes, p. 4.
355 Although this was later turned down. General Committee, 23 Apr 1919; 29 May 1919; 18 Jun 1919; Annual Meeting, 21 July 1920, *Ibid.*, pp. 13, 16, 20, 66.
356 General Committee, 19 Aug 1920, *ibid.*, p. 72.
357 General Committee, 15 Jul 1921, *ibid.*, p. 109.
358 B. Hogenkamp, 'Miners' Cinema in South Wales in the 1920s and 1930s', *Llafur*, 4, 2 (1985), pp. 68, 64.
359 For example, Committees at Bargoed granted £20 for purchasing books on 23 Jun 1908, another £30 on 17 Aug 1908, £10 each quarter on 10 Nov 1908, Bargoed Workmen's Hall and Institute Minutes, pp. 31, 37, 45.
360 General Committee, 27 Apr 1908, *ibid.*, p. 23.
361 General Committee, 14 Sep 1909, *ibid.*, p. 96.
362 J. Campbell, *Nye Bevan and the Mirage of British Socialism* (London, Weidenfeld and Nicholson, 1987), p. 21.
363 Jevons, *The British Coal Trade*, p. 125; Hodges, *My Adventures as a Labour Leader*, pp. 13–16.
364 Horner, *Incorrigible Rebel*, pp. 47–9.
365 Williams, *When was Wales?*, p. 244.
366 Griffiths, *Pages From Memory*, pp. 24–6.
367 *Commission of Inquiry into Industrial Unrest*, p. 18.
368 Horner, *Incorrigible Rebel*, p. 49.
369 *Commission of Inquiry into Industrial Unrest*, p. 18.
370 General Committee, 28 May 1921, Mardy Workmen's Hall and Institute Minutes, pp. 102–3.
371 General Committee, 11 Mar 1912, Bargoed Workmen's Hall and Institute Minutes, pp. 290–1.
372 Special Committee, 13 May 1990, Mardy Workmen's Hall and Institute Minutes, p. 55.
373 General Committee, 16 Feb 1921, *ibid.*, p. 87.
374 Special Committee, 15 Dec 1919; 14 Jan 1920; 12 Feb 1920; 16 Feb 1920; 18 Mar 1920, *ibid.*, pp. 39, 44, 47, 48, 53.
375 Francis and Smith, *The Fed*, p. 3.

376 L. Jones, *Cwmardy* (London, Lawrence and Wishart, 1978 edn.), p. 9.
377 Morgan, *Rebirth of a Nation*, pp. 72–3; Smith, 'Tonypandy', p. 171; L. J. Williams, 'The Road to Tonypandy', *Llafur*, 1, 2, p. 7; Interview with T. Jenkins, pp. 7–8, SWML, Oral History Collection; Lewis, *The Rhondda Valleys*, pp. 223–4.
378 Coombes, *These Poor Hands*, p. 27.
379 Hodges, *My Adventures as a Labour Leader*, p. 16; Foot, *Aneurin Bevan, 1897–1945*, p. 60.
380 Interview with J. Davies, pp. 6–7, SWML, Oral History Collection.
381 Billiard Committee, 17 Nov 1908, Bargoed Workmen's Hall and Institute Minutes, pp. 49–50.
382 See Morgan, *Rebirth of a Nation*, p. 198.
383 District meeting, 4 Mar 1901, Rhondda No.1 District Minutes, p. 15, SWCA, K 10 A.
384 Interview with B. Lewis, p. 14, SWML, Oral History Collection.
385 See Williams, *When was Wales?*, p. 234.
386 Lewis, *The Rhondda Valleys*, p. 196
387 *Ibid.*, p. 223.
388 Jones, *Cwmardy*, pp. 72–3.

3

Civil war in the
West Virginia coalfield, 1900–22

Industrial conflict in West Virginia in this period was fought over one central issue: the right to organise. For the operators, their huge competitive advantages rested upon maintaining the feudal relationships and appalling social conditions in the State and, therefore, keeping the UMWA out. For the miners on the other hand, the main hope for remedying the deprivations and exploitation of the company town came through membership of the UMWA. This situation was summed up at the end of this period by Senator W. S. Kenyon, who commented:

> Here we have the situation of two determined bodies trying to enforce what they believe are rights, which rights are diametrically opposed to one another, and we have the situation of an irresistible force meeting an immovable body. In such cases there can be nothing but trouble.[1]

Of course the basis for battle between these two sides was far from equal. The miners were hampered by the fragmented culture and isolation of the mainly small mining communities, which presented a practical barrier against organising protest. Even more of an impediment however was the overarching power of the operators, who were able to utilise a huge arsenal of 'legal' and illegal tactics against any internal opposition. This explains why conflict took the form of periods of constant, but relatively low level unrest, followed by huge explosions of militancy. The number of days lost was, therefore, secondary to the intensity of conflict – these were not so much strikes as civil wars.

Despite the remarkable displays of militancy by the West Virginia miners, the operators generally succeeded in their aim. In 1900 the UMWA recorded only 421 members amongst the 28,017 miners in the State.[2] By the mid 1920s, with the decline in the industry's fortunes and the growth of the open shop movement, the UMWA was faring little better, having been defeated in the areas where it had established a presence.[3]

The gains that had been made prior to this were substantial, although never stable. For example, the UMWA had organised over 18% of the State's miners by 1903, only to witness a drop to 2.1% by 1912, before rising again by the end of the decade.[4] Individual years also witnessed fluctuations. Thus District 29, newly organised in the New River District, saw membership drop from 1,367 in December 1914, to only 296 in November 1915.[5] Peak membership for the whole State was in 1918–20 when, with the help of the Federal Government's intervention during the war, as many as 50% of the West Virginia miners were organised.[6] Ultimately, however, it would not be until the Federal Government intervened again under the New Deal that West Virginia would become solidly union. When in 1933 the National Industrial Recovery Act became law, it took just over a week to organise the whole State, and only two days for the infamous Logan County, the most impregnable of the non-union counties [7] – which proved testimony to the fact that it was only intimidation that kept the miners from joining the union.

The West Virginia miners had been active in strikes and unions as long as the coalfield had been in existence. In the 1880s there were a number of instances of union activity, with the Knights of Labor, National Federation of Miners and Mine Laborers, and the National Progressive Union of Miners and Mine Laborers all present. While these were never consistently successful, the 1880s revealed a trend in labour organisation which differentiated the State from the rest of the South, with black and white miners sometimes overcoming racial divisions and forming 'strong and viable interracial Local Unions'.[8] This trend was continued when, in 1890, the first convention of District 17 of the newly formed UMWA, elected black union activist Horace Smith to the Vice Presidency. He was succeeded in the post by other black officers, including J. J. Wren, who assumed the Presidency of District 17 on the death of the incumbent Michael Moran. While black-white frictions were apparent even during the 1890s, and interracial unionism proved more fragile in the immediate future, this legacy provided the basis for larger interracial struggles in the coalfield, particularly in 1913–14 and 1919–22.[9]

Other characteristics of later labour protest also came to the fore in the 1890s. In 1892, a strike in the Fairmont field, where the UMWA 'had but recently obtained a firm foothold', ended in defeat and loss of union recognition when the national organisation refused to support the strike, which had been called without their permission.[10] The division between the national union and local miners was symptomatic of things to come, as was the sacking of the strike leaders, which revealed the increasingly aggressive attitude of the operators.

The general strikes of 1894 and 1897 further underlined the pattern for future years. Support in West Virginia was sporadic in 1894, and only 30% of miners answered the call in 1897 – 80% of whom were in Kanawha and Fayette Counties. The UMWA placed a high priority on trying to organise the State, and a large number of organisers were despatched. Other interested parties, including Eugene V. Debs, also made appearances to try and generate support, but despite warm receptions, had little success. The operators managed to win the strike by using both carrot and stick. Bonuses were granted to buy off potential strikers, injunctions were issued against those who did answer the call, and 200 were arrested for contempt, twenty-seven of whom were jailed.[11]

The subsequent 1898 agreement between the UMWA and key northern operators covering the Central Competitive Field – Illinois, Western Pennsylvania, Ohio and Indiana – set the seal on the position of West Virginia. The West Virginia operators refused to attend, the majority preferring to maintain lower wages and other forms of exploitation that non-union status granted them, rather than grant an eight hour day and other concessions. This, combined with the natural advantages of the high quality product which was rapidly increasing its market share, made the State a threat to all the signatories of the 1898 Agreement.[12] As Perlman and Taft put it, 'a non-union or rather anti-union West Virginia was a gun pointed at the heart of industrial government in the bituminous coal industry.' [13]

The operators and miners in the Central Competitive Field, therefore, had a joint interest in ensuring that West Virginia was brought into the fold. This common interest, however, was repeatedly described as a 'conspiracy' by the West Virginia operators, and in future years it became one of their central justifications for resisting the UMWA. The Congressional Hearing into the Paint Creek strike, for example, was told by operator Charles Cabell, that the strike was caused by 'the desire on the part of the United Mine Workers . . . to keep their promises to the operators of the four competitive States.'[14] A West Virginia Mining Association pamphlet was even more forthright, claiming that 'Pennsylvania and Ohio operators are stirring the union to action . . . It is an operators' battle and the miners are being used as tools of operators in the competitive States.'[15]

The argument remained the same at the end of this period.[16] During the 1921 Senate Inquiry, the representative of the Williamson Operators' Association, Z. T. Vinson, claimed that:

> Every single, solitary disturbance, every murder, every assassination that has been committed in the coal industry in West Virginia is traceable to this unannounced policy of organisation to own the property themselves. That was the policy that they announced back in 1898, when they entered into arrangement with the operators in the northwest to unionize West Virginia.[17]

The confusion in the above argument reveals how much the 'conspiracy' claim was a convenient peg upon which the West Virginia operators could hang their rather weak case. After all, Vinson on one hand accused the UMWA of wanting complete appropriation of property after its 1912 adoption of the 'full social value' clause in its constitution,[18] yet on the other hand he claimed an alliance with the northern operators – a rather strange and improbable alliance of communism and capitalism !

In reality, the two sides had an obvious shared interest in bringing West Virginia into the inter-state conference, and one which was neither secret or surprising. Indeed, the only conspiracy lay firmly in the court of the West Virginia operators who realised that granting union rights to their employees, and entering into agreements with other operators, would damage their competitive advantages and, consequently, profits.

The State of West Virginia, therefore, entered the new century as unpopular with northern operators, as it was with union coal miners. One Illinois miner wrote to the *UMWJ* claiming that the West Virginia miners 'seem to be in a hypnotic sleep',[19] while an editorial exclaimed 'the miners of West Virginia must have a peculiar cast of mind. They know they are not only harming themselves by the peculiar attitude they assume, but they are also harming their fellow miners everywhere'.[20]

Such criticisms angered those working for the union in West Virginia. District 17 official, George Scott, told an Iowan critic, 'this is not Iowa brother . . . Shall we drag you western people down to our level, or will you have patience with us and be proud that at least we are trying in spite of our environments to come your way?'.[21] He later explained that organising the State was a 'herculean task', with 'physical conditions, the geography of the State, the isolated condition of one mount from another, the absence of meeting places . . . leading to our deplorable, disorganised shape you find us in.'[22]

Just how difficult organising would be was discovered in 1900–02, when the union launched a vigorous organising drive, and ran head on into natural and man-made barriers. The organisers, who included veteran activist Mother Jones, soon became acquainted with the increasingly brutal activities of the operators. Intimidation and acts of violence were commonplace across the State. In September 1901, one organiser wrote from the Elkhorn Field telling UMWA President John Mitchell that he had been assaulted and threatened. 'I am willing to go anywhere else', he complained, 'but I cannot endure this but little longer.'[23] In the same area, organiser William Warner received similar treatment when he was told by local law officers to leave the County if he valued his life. He told Mitchell, 'such is the abuse that we receive at the hand of men commissioned as officers of the law. The facts are that there is no law in this State for a working man especially if he is a union man.' He appealed to Mitchell to be relieved, as he did not 'wish to work in a region where the officers of the law are assassins.'[24]

Organising drives were further hampered by the immediate sacking of union members, and even the temporary shutting down of mines to break Locals. The latter happened in the Fairmont region in July 1901, where organiser William Warner 'found none who are not in favour of the organisation'. The dominance of the newly established Fairmont Coal Company which 'owns every mine between Clarksburg and Fairmont', however, meant that union membership led to an immediate discharge.[25] Similarly, in Kanawha a local miner complained of the company deliberately sacking union men who had large families.[26]

The courts proved their anti-UMWA credentials, refusing to oppose the eviction and intimidation of union members. John H. Walker, for example, wrote from Mount Carbon telling Mitchell that legal action in defence of a sacked miner would probably be unsuccessful, as 'the court is practically controlled by the operators.'[27] The operators' much favoured injunctions were also passed with ease, particularly where a strike was in progress. A strike in the Thacker field was beaten by injunctions, alongside the use of deputies, strike breakers and intimidation.[28] In one case, five union miners were prevented from appearing before a Grand Jury by being falsely arrested on contempt charges.[29]

Other, more unpredictable, problems were also thrown in the path of the organisers. Union members at Keystone distributed leaflets warning men that a local company was looking for strike breakers to work in Kansas and the Indian territory. However, Crawford wrote to Mitchell, 'strange to say those bills had just the opposite effect to what they intended . . . the result was that the agents hunting scabs never have been so successful in so short a time.' The somewhat bemused Crawford told Mitchell, 'I write this merely to give you an inside peep into the character and disposition of the people of this coalfield.'[30]

The hapless Crawford also experienced first hand the use of guns within labour disputes, when he told a UMWA NEB meeting that Kentucky miners on the border with West Virginia had already been 'induced to desist' from using their winchesters to stop 'scabs'.[31] Violence, however, did occur after a US martial shot a union miner. Crawford told Mitchell that twenty Kentuckyans who came across the river looking for revenge, told him that 'if the striking miners could not work in the Thacker mines that no-one else ever should.' He wrote, 'I am a man of peace and do not wish to make myself a party to lawlessness although the aggressiveness of the companies and the deputy United States marshals certainly justifies it.'[32]

Other unforeseen problems arose, including the bribing of union organisers. Both William Warner and Polish organiser Albert Manka were dismissed in August 1901 after being accused of accepting bribes, although the former was subsequently reinstated.[33] Cleavages between the local and national union were also re-opened, as the local miners complained of insufficient funding and support. 'Some think that the union is other States, and also the national organisation don't care anything about West Virginia', a Tyrconnell miner claimed [34], while the President of a Local Union at Matewan complained that 'we are not being treated right here . . . if there is not more attention paid to the actual needs of our men in justice to myself and men I will resign and in this declaration I voice the sentiments of all the officers of our L.U.' Help was subsequently given to Matewan, and the Local Union later conveyed their thanks.[35]

The West Virginia campaign also revealed a split within the national leadership between Mitchell and Vice President T. L. Lewis. The latter was given charge of organising the campaign, but he refused to co-operate. In one instance Lewis' claim that 'he was not directing affairs' received a firm rebuff from Mitchell, who told him 'your instructions were to supervise work of organising and carry out policy outlined by me and endorsed by unanimous vote of National Executive Board. Let me know if you intend to carry out these instructions.'[36] This did not have the required effect as, much to Mitchell's disapproval, two weeks later Lewis left the coalfield due to 'urgent matters' at home.[37] The return home, and the general disinterest in the West Virginia situation, however, were not connected with 'urgent matters', but Lewis' intriguing against Mitchell in support of a possible leadership challenge.

Taking into account the other problems the union encountered, the absence of Lewis probably did little to damage the organising drive. Mitchell told the National Conference in January 1902 that the UMWA had increased its membership in West Virginia to 5,000 in eighty Locals, but that the 'antagonism to our organization on the part of the operators of West Virginia', which was 'more pronounced than ever before', was scuppering further advances, and any hope of a joint conference between operators and miners similar to the union fields.[38] Indeed the District 17 Convention at Huntington in October 1901, which had called for a joint conference, was rejected in the most emphatic style – the operators sacked many of the conference delegates.[39]

On 18 March 1902, the State's miners held another convention, this time formulating a wage scale which they sent to the operators with the offer of a conference. This was again refused and a strike was called for 7 June 1902, with particular emphasis placed upon the Fairmont district.[40]

The West Virginia strike may have been overshadowed by the more successful Pennsylvania anthracite strike which ran concurrently, but it was nevertheless a landmark in the State's history, with 80% of the miners answering the strike call.[41] It was also equally significant as it revealed the true dimensions of the operators' power within the State, which could subdue even such large numbers of strikers.

In the Fairmont district, under the leadership of Thomas Haggerty and his deputy, Mother Jones, over 150 men marched from a unionised mine at Flemington, led by a band and 'colour guard with American and Italian flags'.[42] They travelled between mining towns hoping to encourage support for the strike. On 9 June, however, the Fairmont Coal Company obtained an injunction against the marchers from the Marion County Circuit Court, which led to the arrest of Haggerty. This was followed a few days later, by further injunctions, granted by Federal Judge, John Jay Jackson. These effectively prevented strike agitation, including marches, even on premises that were leased to the strikers. This resulted in the arrest of Mother Jones and the other main strike leaders.[43]

Following legal delays and strict bail conditions which kept the leaders away from the strike zone, the cases finally came to court at the end of July. Several of the accused were sentenced to sixty days imprisonment, although Mother Jones was given a lecture and a suspended sentence.[44] Jackson, a prominent friend of local coal operators, made clear why he had issued the dubious injunction and subsequent rulings. He told the court, in what Williams has described as 'a ringing declaration of capitalist class-consciousness', that the time had come to face 'what must soon transpire in this country – the conflict between two elements of society.'[45] Samuel Gompers, leader of the AFL, retorted that 'I would not only disregard the injunction of Judge Jackson, but I would violate it and trample it under foot.'[46] The injunctions, however, served their purpose, and the strike collapsed in the Fairmont field before the end of July.

The strike continued in the southern part of the State, complete with mine guards, injunctions, and in the New River field, the introduction of the State militia.[47] The strike in the Kanawha region was also hampered when supplies destined for the strikers were sidelined by the C and O railroad, until a Kentucky court forced their release.[48] Eventually the miners in the Kanawha valley, who had struck in the largest numbers, achieved a settlement in early October, which granted around 7,000 miners various concessions, including union recognition, a nine hour day, checkweighmen and the right to trade at any store.[49]

The failure of the 1902 strike across most of the State, graphically illustrated the difficulties in organising and sustaining strike activity in West Virginia; something which was further underlined when in 1904, the Cabin Creek operators reneged on a new Kanawha agreement and drove the union off the creek.[50]

The loss of Cabin Creek was symptomatic of the ever tightening noose of operator power. The Baldwin-Felts mine guards were acting with increasing impunity in the central and southern parts of the State, where operators like Justus Collins believed they were imperative to normal operations. In a letter to fellow operators concerning the setting up of the Tug River Operator's association in 1906, Collins proposed that they 'employ Mr T. L. Felts with his force to keep out strike agitators and undesirable characters', as he claimed, 'we will sooner or later be confronted with an organization of the miners.'[51] Not all operators were quite as enthralled with the idea as Collins, however, and four years later he was told that there was some reluctance to employ the Baldwin-Felts agents in the Winding Gulf field as they 'beat up people around the job'. However, the correspondent did believe that the dissident operators would acquiesce in the end.[52]

The Baldwin-Felts agents became one of the most important issues in what the UMWA President, John P. White, called 'one of the greatest industrial conflicts our organisation has ever engaged',[53] when the Kanawaha region experienced a major strike in 1912–13. The strike proved a watershed in a number of ways. The large scale violence and intensity of the dispute indicated the depths of distrust and hatred between operator and miner, and the willingness of the miners to defend themselves. This was tied to a resurgence of inter-racial strike activity as white, black, and immigrant miners, joined together to challenge the operators' transgressions.

Furthermore, the distinction between the operators and the legal and governmental apparatus of the State became invisible, with widespread abuses of civil rights by State authorities. In this sense the strike, or 'labor war', marked a new dimension to protest which lasted in the southern coalfields until the Mine Wars in 1919–21. As Fred Mooney told the 1921 Senate Inquiry, the Mingo disorders were 'exactly of the same nature' as those of 1912–13.[54]

The strike began on 20 April 1912, after the Kanawha operators refused to sign a new agreement and insisted on returning to wages and conditions comparable with the non-union field.[55] It was partially settled two weeks later when three quarters of the operators agreed a compromise and signed a new contract. The Paint Creek operators refused however, and the strike continued there, and was joined in August by non-union miners on Cabin Creek.[56]

As soon as the strike began the operators brought in large numbers of Baldwin-Felts agents to act as mine guards, who began evicting miners from company houses. 'Personal belongings were dumped beside the railroad tracks or in the creek bed, the only property not owned by the coal companies', leaving the strikers to move to a UMWA tent colony at Holly Grove.[57] The guards were commissioned as deputies by the operator controlled sheriff,[58] and they proceeded to intimidate the strikers. An investigator for the Commission on Industrial Relations was told how 'instead of trying to be decent to the strikers', the guards 'began to abuse them and pick fights.'[59] Similarly a reporter on the *Charleston Gazette*, who visited Paint Creek in June 1912, noted that 'the miners are quiet and sullen. The guards go around with short Winchester rifles . . . They patrol the entire property, and their guns are never out their hands. This the miners resent bitterly – they hate the sight of the guards.'[60]

Nor were the guns for show, and before long a cycle of violence was set in motion. Fred Mooney recalled how after mine guards began firing into the tent colonies, the strikers decided that they should be 'given a dose of their own medicine', and began to arm themselves. In one instance several boxes of Springfield rifles, and 10,000 rounds of ammunition were delivered to Holly Grove.[61] A series of skirmishes followed, and the first death seems to have been that of an Italian miner on 5 June.[62] By the end of July the scale of the fighting had intensified, and miners and guards engaged in a fierce battle at Mucklow, with further loss of life. One report claimed over 3,000 shots were exchanged in the battle.[63] This led to the introduction of the State militia and, when the violence continued, the first declaration of martial law on 2 September.

On the declaration of martial law the State militia began collecting arms from the protagonists. During the first few days 1,875 high power rifles, 556 pistols, 6 machine guns and 225,000 rounds of ammunition were seized (including 2 machine guns and 15,000 rounds of ammunition belonging to just one operator).[64] It was clear, however, that this did not reflect the true figure, as some chose to hide their guns rather than give them up. For example, one miner was sentenced by the military courts for saying, 'the other miners are fools for giving the soldiers their rifles. I kept mine, a rusty old Springfield.'[65] The imposition of martial law did encourage a period of relative peace, and the militia were withdrawn in the middle of October.[66] However, violence in the strike zone restarted, and was to continue throughout the strike, leading to two more declarations of martial law in November 1912, and February 1913.

The catalogue of intimidation and violence continued on both a small and large scale. An Italian miner told the Senate Inquiry how a mine guard shot a striker in the face on a train:

> This fellow was between the car, across the door, talking to another fellow, and the guard came in and he said, 'Man, go on and get your seat.' This fellow says, 'I can't get no seat.' He says, 'I will make you get your seat.' He says, 'All right', and he walked back through the door in the closet and shot through the door.[67]

The worst of the large scale violence happened in February 1913, and led to the third period of martial law. It began with the operators' use of the so-called 'Bull Moose Special'. The latter was a specially constructed armoured train, built by the C and O Railroad Company, and manned by mine guards with rifles and two machine guns.[68] On 7 February the train moved through the tent colony and fired shots into the striking miners' tents, killing one miner fleeing with his children, and wounding a woman. Who began the firing was, as with everything else in the strike, a matter of dispute. The miners universally claimed the first firing came from the train, while the operators and their newspapers claimed otherwise.[69]

Whoever initiated the trouble, the use of the Bull Moose Special and the firing of machine guns at tents clearly illustrated the lack of regard that the operators had for the strikers' lives. It also led, inevitably, to more violence. A number of armed miners began a march on Mucklow on 10 February, and were intercepted by mine guards. When the battle ended, sixteen lay dead – twelve miners and four mine guards. The militia were also installed for the third time.[70]

The operation of martial law and the activities of the militia were, in themselves, highly controversial. As Gompers suggested in his swingeing attack on 'Russianized West Virginia', during periods of martial law 'military government had eliminated civil government', which was part of 'the powerful and subtle conspiracy between organized capital and the governmental agents of the State', which 'steals from the workers the liberty they think and are told they have.'[71]

The principal abuse concerned the operation of the military

courts during periods of martial law. Governor Glasscock, contra-
dicting the State's constitution, had suspended the right of *habeas
corpus,* and allowed strikers to be tried before a Military Commission.[72] Such was the partiality of the State courts that the miners'
appeal against the suspension of *habeas corpus,* which was initially
supported by a County Court, was then rejected by the State's
Supreme Court.[73] A dissenting judge, Ira E. Robinson attacked the
decision, asserting that Glasscock:

> cannot use the militia in such a way to oust the laws of the land . . . By
> the power of the militia he may, if the necessity exists, arrest and detain
> any citizen offending against the laws; but he cannot imprison him at
> his will, because the constitution guarantees to that offender trial by
> jury, the judgement of his peers.[74]

UMWA lawyer, A. M. Belcher, was equally aghast at the decision.
He told President John P. White, 'this Court has gone much further
than any Court in the Union . . . In fact it is the only Court in the
United States that has held that Military Commissions can try civil-
ians.'[75]

The prisoners were not only denied trial by jury, but were prevented from having their own counsel. They were also tried in large
numbers, sometimes as many as thirty at a time.[76] The sentences
were equally arbitrary. The miner mentioned earlier, who claimed
the strikers should have kept their rifles, was sentenced to sixty days,
while another defendant, on the same day, received six months for
possession of a gun.[77] The Governor evidently approved of the sentences as a form of deterrent. He wrote to an acquaintance in
November 1912 that 'our military court has been doing some good
work and some of the offenders are receiving pretty severe punish-
ment.'[78] Later he claimed that the sentences were not meant to be
served, but to keep those arrested away from the strike zone.[79]
Certainly the prisoners were later released, although mostly under
the Governorship of Henry D. Hatfield.

Even the arrest and detention of the accused was unsatisfactory.
The arrests were usually made by mine guards, who were commissioned as deputies or special agents.[80] Moreover, the investigator
from the Commission on Industrial Relations reported that 'the
militia began arresting the strikers in droves and confining them in
what was known as a "Bull Pen"'. He went on to complain that men
were sometimes held and then released without charge, and that

they were not told their sentences until it had been approved by the Governor.[81] The partiality of the system, with the overwhelming emphasis upon arresting strikers, underlines the fact that the military courts assisted the campaign to break the strike rather than just maintaining law and order. This was perhaps best symbolised by the fact that the militia aided the operators in the task of evicting striking miners[82] and that, after the end of periods of martial law, some stayed on as guards in the employ of the operators.[83]

The abuse of civil rights came to a head with the third declaration of martial law. The military issued a number of warrants and arrested over 150 strike activists, including Mother Jones, UMWA organiser Paul Paulsen, and the editor of the Charleston *Labor Argus*, Charles Boswell.[84] It was the arrest and treatment of the 83 year old Mother Jones which was to precipitate the greatest uproar.

The final stages of the Paint Creek strike, and the bulk of the outcry, occurred under the Governorship of Hatfield, who came into office on 4 March. He declared himself to be intent on finding a settlement to the dispute and, as if to prove the point, went immediately to the strike zone and, so he later claimed, began treating the sick. One of the first he saw was Mother Jones who was suffering from pneumonia. She was subsequently shifted to a hospital in Charleston, but was returned into custody on her recovery.[85]

The outcry over her initial arrest and subsequent detention focused national attention on the West Virginia strike situation. The greatest anger was expressed by UMWA Locals incensed at the treatment of the 'miners' angel'. There were numerous appeals sent to the national union by Locals calling for a national strike to press for her release.[86] Although the union opposed this, the leadership sent an urgent telegram on behalf of the UMWA, to the Secretary of Labor (and former UMWA official), William B. Wilson, claiming that Mother Jones and others were 'unlawfully imprisoned', and denied constitutional rights in a manner, they claimed, 'without parallel in American history.'[87]

Numerous other letters flooded into Wilson from across the country, from both organisations and individuals. A member of the Arizona State legislature asked 'whether it is possible for the Government of the United States to render her (Mother Jones) any assistance',[88] while another correspondent complained of harassment of 'an old woman whose only crime is her loyalty to the proletariat.'[89]

Nor was Mother Jones silent on her incarceration and the situation in West Virginia. She wrote from the military prison at Pratt to Senator W. E. Borah, telling him that 'the wretches have pleaded with the State to do something for them but in return they got the jails and bullets from the public officials.' She went on to tell him that she was a military prisoner, which was 'just what the old monarchy did (to) my grandparents ninety years ago in Ireland.'[90]

The letter from Mother Jones was written in thanks for Borah's Senate resolution calling for a national investigation into conditions in West Virginia. This was not taken up by the 62nd Congress. However, following intensive lobbying by Gompers, the UMWA, and Secretary of Labor Wilson, a resolution proposed by majority leader Kern was passed by the 63rd Congress.[91] The hearings, which were conducted by a subcommittee of the Senate Committee on Education and Labor, began in Charleston on 10 June. They were eagerly greeted by the miners and their supporters. The Huntington *Socialist and Labor Star* proclaimed on its front page 'United States of America Invades West Virginia', followed by the claim that the aim of the inquiry was 'to guarantee to its citizens a republican form of government and relief from military tyranny.'[92] In contrast, the investigation was opposed by the operators and Governor Hatfield, who were less than enthusiastic about the national spotlight shining on West Virginia.[93]

In the meantime, the strike was coming to a somewhat messy end. Hatfield had been involved in negotiations with UMWA representatives Thomas Haggerty, District 17 President Thomas Cairns, National Vice President Frank J. Hayes, and John P. White, and the strike seemed destined for an early finish when the Paint Creek Colliery Company, representing around 2,500 (50%) of the strikers, settled on 21 March.[94] The other operators, however, rejected these terms and, on 14 April, Hatfield announced a proposed settlement. It contained a vague right to organise (but no recognition of the UMWA), a nine hour day, semi-monthly pay day, the right to checkweighmen, and a guarantee of no discrimination against miners using independent stores.[95]

These terms were welcomed by the operators, but were less popular with the miners. After all, the settlement did nothing to prevent the deployment of mine guards, nor did it provide a clear right to belong to the UMWA – the two central issues of the strike. Furthermore, no wage increase was provided for, the nine hour day was already common in the State, and checkweighmen were already, supposedly, provided for in State law. As Williams has suggested, 'it was a measure of the cynical traditions of West Virginia justice and politics that Hatfield considered it a breakthrough to promise enforcement of laws already on the books'.[96]

For the strikers, however, there was worse to come. When it became clear that they would probably reject the settlement, the Governor issued the so-called 'Hatfield Ultimatum', which warned the miners to accept the proposals or face the sternest consequences – probably being driven from the State.[97] Under such pressure, Haggerty and Cairns urged acceptance of the deal and, on 27 April, amid allegations of vote rigging and packing, a delegate conference reluctantly concurred.[98] This, however, was not the end of the matter. Revealing a large fissure in the union ranks between the 'outsider' leaders like Haggerty, Cairns and national organiser Vasey, and the newer, more militant local activists, some miners refused to accept the Hatfield agreement, and stayed out on strike. The situation was further complicated by the refusal of some of the companies to take back strikers.[99]

Hatfield's response was to ignore the operators' actions, while lashing out at those supporting the strike. On 9 May, having already suppressed the Charleston *Labor Argus*, he sent militia men to the Huntington *Socialist and Labor Star*, which had agitated against the settlement, but was outside the martial law zone. Type and printing materials were destroyed, documents confiscated, and the editor, W. H. Thompson, and four others were arrested. The prisoners were then taken to Kanawha County jail and Thompson's house was raided, in spite of protests from the local sheriff, who insisted that warrants were needed.[100] Hatfield later claimed that they could have been released immediately if they had guaranteed that 'they would cease their activities in attempting to bring about insurrection and riot, as well as the encouragement of the strike'.[101]

Thompson's stay in jail was relatively short. The increasing attention being focused on West Virginia, and the relative quiet in the strike area, led to the release of the prisoners held under martial law. Mother Jones was set free on 8 May, and Thompson and a number of others two weeks later, probably due to the intervention of a committee from the SPA, led by Eugene V. Debs, which was investigating conditions in the State.[102] Martial law was eventually ended in June, when the last five militia men left Paint Creek.[103]

The strike itself continued to ebb and flow through June and July, with unrest caused by the terms of the settlement and the operation of a blacklist. The Cabin Creek miners eventually returned at the beginning of August.[104] The situation was further complicated by unrest in the New River field which had recently been divided from District 17 to form District 29 of the UMWA. The success of organising drives created substantial pressure for a strike, which came to a head by the end of June. By the beginning of July, however, a two year agreement had been hammered out.[105]

The strike may have ended by late summer 1913, but the split within union ranks remained. Allegations about the activities of Haggerty and Cairns had arisen prior to the strike, and their conduct of the dispute generated further criticism. In January 1912, the UMWA conference was presented with evidence that the executive elections for District 17 were fixed, with vote rigging, opened ballot boxes, and a suspiciously high turnout.[106] Under UMWA rules the complaint should have been dealt with locally, but evidence was produced to suggest those making the charges were not given a fair hearing. As a consequence, the conference decided to put the matter before the UMWA International Executive Board.[107]

Nothing happened as a result of the allegations, but the resentments resurfaced with great force towards the end of the Paint Creek strike. Many of the local miners became incensed by what they saw as too close a relationship between the leadership and Hatfield. Of particular concern was the support for the Hatfield agreement, and the approval of the maintenance of martial law. One local paper, for example, reported on 20 May that 'the representatives of labor have been in favour of continuance of martial law until it was assured that the agreement reached which ended the strike would be carried out in good faith.'[108]

The implications for those opposing the settlement were clear, as was the fulsome praise Haggerty lavished upon Hatfield. With some of the strikers still in jail, Haggerty enthused, 'I want to say that I heartily approve of Governor Hatfield's efforts to restore peace and harmony ... His efforts command the support of the working man, instead of their censure and ridicule.'[109] Similarly, a few days later, Haggerty spoke of the 'wonderful part the present Governor has played'.[110] Hatfield seemed equally impressed with the miners' leader, commenting that 'I am glad to have Mr. Haggerty's commendation on my course.'[111]

This produced an angry response from Local Unions, who wrote to the national organisation requesting the recall of Haggerty and organiser Joe Vasey. One Local at Crown Hill accused Haggerty of 'using the capitalistic press to forward the policy of Gov. H. D. Hatfield whose interest is entirely with the coal operators of this State and against the miners.' They went on to claim they opposed the presence of Haggerty and Vasey 'as we do a Baldwin thug' – strong criticism indeed.[112] Another Local Union described Haggerty, Cairns, and Vasey as 'incompetent, incapable and unfit' for their task.[113]

The socialist press likewise lambasted the UMWA officials and the strike settlement, on one occasion accusing the UMWA officials of having 'deliberately and even traitorously entered into an agreement with the tyrannical State government.'[114] The criticisms obviously touched a raw nerve, as in June 1913 the editor of the *Socialist and Labor Star*, C. H. Boswell, was arrested after being accused of libelling Haggerty. Boswell had only just been released from detention under martial law.[115] The leadership's dislike of the local socialist press, led to the publication of an 'official organ', *The Miner's Herald*, at Montgomery. The paper preached a conciliatory line on strike action, and bitterly opposed radical political action in all forms, particularly that of Bill Haywood and the IWW, which it described as a 'diabolic cult'.[116] The paper also attacked the local activists who had opposed the Paint Creek settlement, including the socialist editors Thompson and Boswell, who were accused of being 'hangers on', who had no union cards, and were 'complete failures'.[117]

The friction that had built up since the Hatfield settlement continued at the District 17 convention in spring 1914, where allegation and counter allegation flew between the two sides. Indeed, in the aftermath Fred Mooney was stabbed in an attempt to stop him form appearing at a union inquiry.[118] The scale approved by the convention proved unacceptable to the operators, particularly those on Cabin Creek, who were refusing the 'check-off'. In response, 10,000 miners went out on strike, only to be threatened with dismissal by the union leadership. *Coal Age* reported on 9 May that the strikers were told they 'must either return to work pending negotiations . . . or surrender their charters as members of the national organisation', with the result that 'many of the men are returning to work.'[119] As the negotiations continued, both sides agreed to the intervention of

Commissioners of Conciliation from the Department of Labor, who arrived in Charleston on 9 June.[120]

The eventual agreement prevented a strike, but Haggerty and Cairns had to concede a good deal of ground. As they told the Federal President, prior to the arrival of the commissioners: 'The miners made twenty-four separate demands upon the operators, all of which we believe we are entitled to but withdraw all but two of them in the interest of peace.'[121] The final settlement gave no wage increase, a limited check-off, and a board of arbitration for future disputes.[122]

The disillusionment with the official leadership of Districts 17 and 29 culminated in the failure of the national union to accept charges of irregularities in the election of officers. As a result, in August 1915, the dissidents formed a rebel District 30, led by Frank Keeney, with J. L. Workman as Vice President, Lawrence 'Peggy' Dwyer (so-called because of his wooden leg) as Secretary, and Charles Lusk as International Board Representative. Fred Mooney, while in sympathy with the dissidents, declined to join, preferring to continue the battle within the existing union structure.[123] Under the enthusiastic leadership of Keeney and Dwyer, the new District managed to negotiate some closed shop agreements on Cabin Creek, and to attract a large number of members – indeed by the end of the year it was the most powerful organisation on the creek.[124] The District did not consider itself separate from the national union, and continued to send in its dues, although the national union refused to accept these, or recognise the secessionists.[125] By the time of the National Convention in January 1916, however, the dissidents were powerful enough to force the national union to take notice. Although Vice President Frank Hayes launched a strong attack on the seceders, accusing them of having 'scorned that orderly procedure which must ever remain the foundation of any permanent movement'[126], discussions were going on behind the scenes to sort out the difficulties. They resulted in the national organisation temporarily taking over control of Districts 17 and 29.[127]

By the end of 1916 District 30 was dissolved and its members back in the fold, local control was resumed, and elections for officers held in District 17. In a bitter election, which proved that resentments still remained, Keeney was elected President, Mooney Secretary-Treasurer, and William Petry, who Mooney described as 'an habitual drunkard, fat, irresponsible, and prone to make "grandstand plays and then pass the buck"', Vice President.[128]

The election of Keeney and Mooney and the vindication of the critics of the old leadership were completed when the *UMWJ* announced in November 1917 that Haggerty had been forced to resign. The paper reported that the UMWA leadership admitted that it had disagreed with criticisms of Haggerty 'until the fall of 1916, when we became convinced that all was not well for the organisation in West Virginia and that Haggerty was in very close collusion with certain coal interests. Upon investigation we found that Haggerty was engaged in the coal business.'[129] Haggerty had become joint owner of a new operation called the 'New Export Coal Company'. Fellow owners included two judges, a State senator, a sheriff, four UMWA National organisers Joe Vasey, Percy Tetlow, Sam Manet, and Hugh McGinney, District Two President Patrick Gilday, and former President of District 17, Thomas Cairns.[130]

The accession of Keeney to the leadership of District 17 symbolised the growing confidence of the West Virginia miners, especially in the Kanawha region. The Paint Creek strike and its aftermath, while not resulting in a clear victory, had revealed a growing willingness to resist collectively, encouraged by the experience of life in the company towns and the act of struggle itself. While the cultural differences within the communities, particularly between black and white, remained an important point of contrast with more homogeneous coal regions like south Wales, the struggles in these years lessened the divisive impact of social difference upon collective action.

The greater unity across race lines had, as we saw earlier, precedents dating back to the 1880s. The Paint Creek strike saw a resurgence of this tradition with black, white and immigrant miners fighting side by side. R. L. Lewis has shown the prominent role played by black miners in the strike, including Dan Chain, a member of the notorious 'dirty eleven', famous for his ability at turning back strike breakers.[131] The importance of the black strikers was revealed when the UMWA sent in their leading black field representative, George H. Edmunds, to aid in the prosecution of the strike. As Lewis suggests, 'at a time when the southern States were enshrining racial segregation, West Virginia miners were apparently marching to a different drumbeat.'[132]

The Paint Creek strike also reinforced the importance of women in collective action. Throughout this period, and especially in the larger conflicts, women were integral to the prosecution of strikes. In West Virginia, the US coalfields generally and, as we shall see, in south Wales, women marched, harassed those who opposed strikes, and tried to generate wider support for their communities.[133] While the vast majority were denied access to the control and direction of strikes, there were exceptions to this rule, most notably in the shape of Mother Jones, who, as we have seen, re-wrote her gender role to encompass a strong leadership position in West Virginia and other parts of the US. However, alongside their involvement in the more obvious manifestations of struggle, women were vitally important within the tent colonies which sprang up with the mass eviction of strikers. Restricted within the domestic sphere, most of the important tasks of creating a community under canvas fell on the shoulders of the women.[134] This provided the building block upon which the more obvious aspects of struggle could be placed, and underlined the extent to which strikes were genuinely communal actions.

Under the leadership of Keeney and Mooney the UMWA made rapid strides in organisation, which were aided and abetted by the increasing demand for coal, and wartime intervention by the Federal government. One of the most significant gains came when operator Clarence Watson, induced by 'political ambition and war patriotism', allowed the Consolidation Coal Company, and hence most of the Fairmont field, to be organised.[135] This meant that by 1919 as many as half of the State's miners were organised, including most of northern and central West Virginia. The Southern counties, most notably Mingo and Logan, however, remained largely unorganised.[136] It was the attempt to organise these bastions of non-unionism which set in train a mine war which overshadowed even the conflict of 1912–13.

Logan County towered above all others when the District 17 officials looked to organising the south. The County was overseen by the sheriff 'czar' Don Chafin, who ran it like a mini-police State, and in doing so epitomised all of the aspects of the West Virginia situation which the union found so offensive. It was, according to attorney general, Howard B. Lee, 'a leer in the face of liberty, a feudal barony defended by soldiers of fortune'.[137]

The County was dominated by the Island Creek Coal Company, who with the other smaller operators, paid Chafin a fee gathered by a royalty on production, which was used to employ deputy sheriffs dedicated to keeping Logan union-free. A 1919 Inquiry appointed by the State Governor, John J. Cornwell, claimed that the Guyan Coal Operators' Association paid Chafin $ 2,725 per month to appoint twenty-five deputies which were stationed throughout the coalfield.[138] This figure, however, probably underestimated both the amount spent and the number employed. An investigator for the Federal government suggested that Chafin received a cent on every ton of coal shipped out from a non-union Logan which, with the Island Creek company alone producing 95,000 tons a week, would mean substantially more than the Cornwell Commission suggested.[139] Similarly, one miner recalled there being 'three hundred and sixty five gunslingers, paid for out of coal company cash'.[140]

It was not only the use of supposedly public officials for company purposes which outsiders found unacceptable (something which even the spineless Cornwell Commission condemned)[141], but the brutal way in which they operated. Chafin who had been sheriff every other year since the age of eighteen (with intervening years filled by friends to get round local laws), had himself allegedly killed twenty-eight men. Yet, as the Federal Investigator put it, 'there has never been a conviction for murder in Logan County.' He further described how one man was tried for murder four times. During one trial, a gun slipped from the defendant's pocket and went off in court. As in all the other cases, however, the verdict was not guilty.[142]

The victims of the deputies' threats, guns and beatings were mainly those advocating unionism, although political differences at election time could also lead to intimidation.[143] Union sympathisers would be identified by a 'spy' within the workforce and then, at best, sacked and told to leave the County.[144] Outsiders were even easier to identify, and were dealt with more quickly. Thus when an IWW activist arrived in Logan Town in 1921, he was immediately arrested, thrown into jail and then shot. Chafin claimed that the victim had taken a swing at the man who shot him, but another prisoner asserted that he was 'shot down in cold blood'.[145]

It was in this environment, two years earlier, that District 17 determined to sign up union members. In August 1919, under the headline 'United Mine Workers going into Guyan Valley', the *West Virginia Federationist* announced that Fred Mooney had appealed for cooperation from local miners to allow the union to 'throw our entire force into this conflict.'[146] The tensions caused by the announcement of an invigorated organising campaign, and the lack of success thus far, were heightened by various reports of violence emanating from the region, including the beating up of nine men by 'gun thugs' on 27 August.[147]

The result was a gathering of several thousand miners from the central coalfields, at Marmet in Kanawha County on 4 September, intent on marching on Logan and sorting the situation out for themselves. [148] On hearing of the gathering, Keeney, Mooney, and John L. Spivak drove immediately to Marmet where they found the miners well armed, including among their number former soldiers who had 'put on their uniforms for this special occasion'. Keeney was told by a fellow activist from the Paint Creek strike, 'Frank, if you can't protect our organisers, we can.'[149] Keeney attempted to turn the miners back, but was unsuccessful, so Governor Cornwell travelled to the encampment where he told the men they were breaking the law, and that he would call in Federal troops if they did not disperse. He also promised to look into the complaints concerning Logan.[150] He was met with scepticism, with some replying to his call for them to respect the law with 'there is no law in West Virginia except that decreed by the operators, and you know it, Governor.'[151] Although many of the marchers agreed to disperse, a hard-core continued on to Danville, ten miles from the Logan border, where they were turned back by a final appeal from Keeney, and the news that Cornwell had again threatened to call for Federal troops.[152]

The dispersal of the march did nothing to end the miners' grievances, and indeed served to further inflame them, particularly when witnesses called to testify before the Cornwell investigation were intimidated.[153] The union also became frustrated with Cornwell's attitude to the march. He saw it as an act of lawlessness, and became determined to 'fix the responsibility' for what he saw as 'the assembling of a mob of armed men and their march toward the Guyan coalfield.'[154] The union in contrast saw it as an act of self defence against a greater abuse of law and order in Logan County. John L. Lewis, Acting President of the UMWA, informed Cornwell that the national convention had unanimously passed a motion stating that:

> it was their belief that if you would exercise the authority and influence of your office as Governor to . . . guarantee free speech and free assemblage and the right to organize . . . it would not be necessary for free-born American citizens to arm themselves to protect their constitutional rights.[155]

In response to the harassment of witnesses, the miners withdrew their support from the commission and, in the middle of October, sent fifty organisers into Logan. They were met by three hundred armed deputies, and ejected forthwith on a special train, leading District 17 to call for a Federal investigation into Logan County.[156] Cornwell believed that sending in the organisers was a breach of trust and complained to Lewis that Keeney 'suddenly announced he was sending fifty organisers into Logan and at once ceased to participate in the investigation.'[157] Considering the treatment of the witnesses, however, it is not difficult to see why. Cornwell also claimed that the miners were massing arms and ammunition on Cabin Creek and were planning another march on Logan.[158]

The situation was further complicated by the pending national strike of the whole bituminous coal field, which was due to begin on 1 November. President Woodrow Wilson appealed to Lewis to call the strike off, claiming it would be unlawful – an opinion which was sustained by a temporary injunction granted under the Lever Act (which had conveniently remained on the statute book since the War).[159]

Cornwell told Keeney that due to the ruling, any strike would now be 'unlawful', and that the West Virginia miners should 'stand behind the President and the United States Government' and reject the strike call.[160] Keeney countered by explaining that since 1916, the miners' wages had increased at a much lower rate than the operators' profits, and that the District were bound to answer the national union's strike call. 'No one regrets more than I do, this unhappy situation', he wrote, 'but I want to say that our members are loyal American citizens and should have the consideration that is due them.'[161]

The relationship further deteriorated when the UMWA learnt that Cornwell had sent a request for Federal troops directly after meeting with a group of operators.[162] An exasperated Keeney later told the Governor, 'either you are incapable or unwilling to see that the laws of the State and country are upheld in Logan County. My members warned me that I could not get justice from a pawn of the coal operators'. Cornwell claimed this was an 'insolent accusation'.[163]

Cornwell's partiality were ever present during his term in office (between 1917 and 1921). In October 1919, for example, he attempted to secure the Catholic Church's aid in halting the UMWA strike. Cornwell had received a letter from a West Virginia lawyer telling him how he had witnessed the 'breaking up' of the Bethlehem steel strike, after the local priests threatened to excommunicate anybody who went out on strike.[164] Cornwell was impressed by the idea, and wrote to Bishop Donahue asking him whether priests could preach a similar message in West Virginia before the 1 November strike.[165]

The Catholic hierarchy, however, did not approve. Donahue replied that his council had 'resolved unanimously that the Catholic clergy should abstain from any reference to the strike'. Indeed, he suggested that he was 'a little surprised at this unanimity', as 'there were bitter complaints against the treatment of the workers by the officers of the corporations, though these were in connection with the steel strike.'[166] Cornwell, with a remarkable disregard for the truth, replied that there had been a misunderstanding and told Donahue, 'I certainly had no desire to ask any minister to make a pronouncement or take sides in connection with the strike.'[167]

There was no such hedging in Cornwell's reply to the Kanawha Coal Operators' Association. The latter had passed a motion condemning the strike in the most forceful terms :

> the issue is whether the "government of the people by the people and for the people" . . . shall prevail and continue or henceforward the people of the United States shall be subject to the rule of a few men clothed with brief but absolute authority by irresponsible organizations and arbitrarily and tyrannically exercising such authority.[168]

Cornwell obviously agreed as he replied, 'it is gratifying to know that the right-th(ink)ing men, composing, as they do, such organizations as yours, are willing to stand up in this crisis.'[169]

The friendship and support of the operators was underpinned by a paranoia about industrial conflict. Unwilling, or incapable, of seeing the root causes of the trouble, Cornwell consistently stated, as in his comments on the Logan march, that industrial unrest was being caused by a small number of radical, foreign-born agitators. This was, of course, entirely in temper with the national mood during and after the War, when paranoia about radical activities reached fever pitch, and led to widespread suppression of radicals from the SPA, IWW and other groupings.

Cornwell's period in office was plagued by the search for the radicals who, he believed, were inciting the miners. In February 1919, a Reverend Madert from Gary, attempted to correct Cornwell's 'recent prognostications of the impending reign of Anarchism that threatens all our institutions – of your fear of the many thousands of aliens and alien-enemies in this State.' He told the Governor that he knew many foreign-born miners and that he wanted to 'state that none of the above-mentioned anarchist tendencies are in evidence here.'[170] Cornwell was not convinced, however, and claimed that he was constantly receiving 'information of the activity of IWW agents and others . . . for the purpose of propagating their doctrines among our people.'[171]

Possession of what was seen as subversive literature was enough to merit the attention of the State Governor. In May 1919 Cornwell asked the Charleston chief of police to investigate a woman within the city who was accused of 'distributing seditious literature advocating Bolshevistic and Soviet government.'[172] Similarly, after a raid on 'Reds', Cornwell wrote to the Prosecuting Attorney at Chester to ask for copies of the seized literature and received, by return, SPA materials in Finnish, and a Red Flag.[173] To the paranoid Cornwell the latter no doubt had a similar effect as if it had been waved in front of a bull. After all, the Governor had already supported the 'Red Flag Act', House Bill 104, passed early in 1919, which was intended to 'foster the ideals, institutions and government of West Virginia and the United States, and to prohibit the teaching of doctrines and display the flags antagonistic to the form or spirit of their constitution or laws.'[174] Even those who marched against the act were subject to attacks from the State's ruling elite.[175]

If the 'Red Flag Act' was an example of the authoritarian nature of the Cornwell administration, it was in many ways trivial when compared to the treatment of the foreign-born miners identified as troublemakers. Cornwell's reaction was to call for immediate deportation. In November 1919, for example, an operator in Marion County complained that his men were being kept on strike by 'a few anarchists'.[176] With no other evidence, Cornwell replied told a US attorney: 'My information is that trouble at Grant Town is caused by a few aliens who should be deported. I so stated to the Attorney General who wired me last night that Special Agents were enroute there for that purpose.'[177] Three days later the Attorney General was informed that the agents had 'thirty-seven radical aliens' in custody.[178]

Cornwell's information on the activities of the radicals was gained from local law officers, his own spies within the UMWA Locals and, inevitably, the coal operators themselves. The latter were the most common, and excitable, correspondents on the subject. For example on 7 November 1919, the secretary of the KCOA told Cornwell that a Becky Edelson 'of steel strike fame' was coming into the district carrying with her a number of pictures of Fannie Sellers, a UMWA organiser who had been killed in Pennsylvania. Quite how the possession of photographs could be seen as subversive, even under the terms of the 'Red Flag Act' , is a mystery, but Kennedy promised to locate the woman and inform Cornwell when he had done so.[179]

The exaggerated idea of the red threat in the West Virginia coalfields was further encouraged by reports from Military Intelligence, after troops entered the coalfield in Autumn 1919. These reports were compiled with the help of the operators, top law enforcement officers, and Cornwell, and produced predictably colourful comment. The principal information was contained in an actual list of supposed 'radicals', although the grounds for such a description were rather tenuous. Jim Gibson of Mifflin, for example, was described as being 'radical through ignorance'. Others, like UMWA organiser George Barrett, were considered more cunning, 'quietly' spreading their 'radical doctrines among the miners', while black miner A. J. Barker was described as 'not talkative – worst agitator in this section.' James Britt Sr. aroused even greater disapprobation for being 'thrown out of a secret order for refusing to salute the US Flag.' Somewhat mysteriously, it was also noted that his 'past record concerning the Flag (was) bad.'[180]

The compiling of such a report, with no input from anybody in the least sympathetic to the miners, symbolised the extent to which the red threat had obscured the real issues at stake in West Virginia. The most basic of demands were misinterpreted even when they were written down in black and white. On one occasion, for example, one of Cornwell's spies reported that a German was agitating at Raleigh, calling for the removal of guards, and complaining that the company would recoup any pay rise through increased prices at the company store. It was symptomatic of West Virginia in these years, however, that such limited and decidedly unrevolutionary demands could lead to the labelling of the German as a 'very dangerous character'.[181]

One correspondent tried to point out to Cornwell that he should look at the 'cause or number of causes' of labour disorders instead of 'deporting people or keeping them in prison'.[182] Cornwell was unrepentant admonishing his critic by telling him that 'I do not agree that we should not deport foreigners who are lawless and who want to substitute the Russian form of government for our system. If they prefer the Soviet they ought to go back to Russia.'[183]

Despite Cornwell's fears, the November strike did not lead to revolution, either nationally or in West Virginia. On 8 November the temporary injunction was sustained and the UMWA leadership were ordered to end the strike. In West Virginia, as elsewhere, however, many of the miners ignored the call and continued the strike in defiance of the courts. Following further negotiations with the Federal government, a compromise was formulated which provided for a Presidential Commission on the bituminous coal industry, with the power to consider increased wages. This, along with an immediate 14% wage increase, was accepted, and the miners returned to work.[184]

With the ending of the strike in December, attention again shifted to the southern counties of West Virginia, this time to Mingo. The UMWA's organising drive was met with many of the weapons the operators had perfected in the previous forty years: mine guards, violence and, more effectively than ever before, injunctions and legal interference leading to widespread sackings and evictions. All of which were backed up by Cornwell, and his equally malleable successor, Ephraim F. Morgan. The conflict that ensued included some of the bloodiest incidents in US labour history.

One of the principal weapons in the new battle against the union were the so-called 'Yellow Dog' contracts. These were individual contracts which the companies forced the miners to sign, preventing them from joining a union, or encouraging others to do so. They had been in use for a number of years in the State, but only applied on a large scale after the War, due to a decision to uphold their use by the Federal Supreme Court in 1917. Sanctioned by the courts they were subsequently enforced by the Red Jacket Consolidated Coal and Coke Company, the largest operation in Mingo County, soon to be followed by all of the non-union mines in the southern part of the State.[185]

The contracts were complemented by the widespread use of injunctions to prevent the UMWA from getting the miners to 'break' them. One Federal official described how injunctions were 'very sweeping in their prohibition', including one by Judge E. Wardhill Jr. which specified that 'the union's agents were to be restrained, among other things, "from advertising, representing, stating by word, by posted notice, or by placards displayed at any point in the State of West Virginia"', that a strike was in progress.[186]

Sackings and evictions began on a large scale in the spring of 1920, after the UMWA sent a number of organisers into Mingo County. The drive proved particularly successful as the Mingo miners had just been denied the wage increase granted to union miners by the President's coal commission.[187] As a consequence, by May 1920, 50% of the County's 4,000 miners were in the union.[188] The operators responded with further sackings and evictions, forcing the union to establish tent colonies to house the strikers. By the time a strike was called on 1 July 1920 in support of those discharged, 90% had signed union pledge cards, and around 2,800 had been sacked.[189] As a UMWA representative told the 1921 Senate Inquiry, by this point, the conflict was as much a lockout as a strike.[190]

It was in the town of Matewan, six weeks prior to this strike call, that the operators' policy of forcible evictions using Baldwin-Felts agents, led to one of the most violent incidents in the labour war which would, in turn, set in motion a chain of violence culminating in the armed march on Blair Mountain.

On 19 May 1920, twelve armed Baldwin Felts, led by two of the three brothers who ran the agency, arrived in the independent town to evict families from the Stone Mountain Coal Company camp. They were immediately challenged by Matewan's Mayor, Cabel Testerman, and the town's chief of police, 'smiling' Sid Hatfield, both of whom were sympathetic to the miners. Hatfield recalled asking the agents to 'show the authority' for the evictions, which 'they didn't have'. An argument developed during which the agents 'said two hour's notice was all they wanted. We told them they could not throw those people out unless they had papers from the court, to go according to law.'[191] The agents then proceeded by car to carry out the evictions.

Late in the afternoon the agents returned to the railway station to catch the return train to their headquarters at Bluefield. From here the exact sequence of events becomes more controversial. However, it seems that they were again met by Hatfield, who attempted to serve a warrant, charging them with violating a town ordinance by possessing guns. Albert Felts replied by serving a bogus warrant on Hatfield, accusing him of having previously interfered with one of the Felts' agents. Testerman began to protest against the warrant, and was shot in the stomach by Felts. Hatfield then shot Albert Felts through the head, and a fierce gun battle developed between the remaining agents and a number of armed miners who had gathered during the day. When it ended, ten men lay dead or fatally wounded, including the two Felts brothers, five other agents, Testerman, and two miners.[192] On searching the bodies, tempers were further inflamed by the discovery of letters on Albert Felts revealing an attempt to bribe Hatfield, Testerman and Sheriff Blankenship, and a list of spies in the Union Locals.[193]

In the aftermath of the shooting, the union made an immediate appeal for an end to the use of company gunmen, and called for Federal help. Keeney called on the President to intervene, saying that State officials had:

> known perfectly well of the vicious brutality existing, which have resulted in numerous murders and assaults, and have refused to do anything to end the shocking conditions . . . These conditions will not be remedied by the State officials for they ignore all protests made for many years. It is a case now where the Federal government must take a hand . . . Otherwise I fear that the outraged miners and other workers of this State may be driven to other methods.[194]

John L. Lewis also sent a stinging rebuke to Cornwell, telling him that 'for years the terrible evil of this system has been pointed out, but this latest outrage indicates that little or nothing has been done.' He concluded that the blood of the Matewan dead 'must be found on the hands of those who could prevent such murders, but who fail to do so.'[195]

The remaining Felts brother, T. L., accused the UMWA of trying to 'influence public opinion on behalf of those responsible', who he described as having committed 'one of the foulest plots that ever disgraced a State.'[196] The operators also began to circulate stories suggesting that it had been Hatfield, rather than Albert Felts, who had shot Testerman, as part of an elaborate plan to marry the dead man's wife.[197] While Hatfield did marry the former Mrs. Testerman seven days after the funeral, it seems somewhat doubtful that the events in Matewan could have been staged or, if the majority of witnesses are to be believed, that Hatfield shot Testerman.

Taciturn and a crack shot, Hatfield became a hero to the miners. Any person who had stood up to the 'Baldwin thugs' was bound to be popular, but Hatfield had shot at least one of the Felts brothers. He even claimed later that he would 'take credit for all seven' dead agents if need be,[198] and posed with his guns for press photographers.[199] Alongside a rather clinical attitude to the killings, however, Hatfield was not devoid of humour. When he was asked by the operators' lawyer at the 1921 Senate Inquiry how many shots Felts had fired at the beginning of the gun battle, he replied, presumably ironically, 'I didn't have time to count them.'[200]

By the time of the July strike call, it was clear that Mingo was in for a protracted and bloody war. Federal attempts at finding a solution to the strike had foundered upon the operators' intransigence towards the UMWA. As the two Commissioners of Conciliation put in their report to their Director:

> The Williamson Coal Operators' Association refuse to have any dealings whatever with the United Mine Workers' Union; declare their unalterable determination to operate their mines on a non-union basis, and to close down the mines indefinitely rather than to operate them under agreement with the Miners' Union.

The union, while refusing to abandon its plans for organisation had, the commissioners reported, 'made every effort . . . to arrange a conference with the operators before resorting to a strike', but without success. [201]

The strike call was initially successful, with the union effecting what Keeney described as 'a complete tie up'[202] and, by the end of July, nine small operations, employing 400 miners signing the union scale. The larger operations, however, continued to oppose 'any settlement other than surrender of the men,'[203] and 'began to bring in transports'.[204] The strike breakers were of various nationalities and, as in the Paint Creek strike, often brought in under false pretences, being told that there was no strike on and that the mines were working to full capacity. They were met by strikers who attempted to turn them back, with some success. By December, for example, the UMWA had spent over $14,000 paying the return passage of strike breakers.[205]

In the aftermath of Matewan it was also patently clear that the Baldwin-Felts issue was becoming a major factor in the dispute. After talking to 'many and varied' local residents, the two Commissioners of Conciliation discovered that 'all were of the opinion that the source of irritation were the methods of the

Baldwin-Felts Agency guards', who carried out the evictions, 'without due process of law, and by threats and armed force intimidated the workmen and coerced them to accept the conditions of the operators.' Organisers and union sympathisers, they were told, were 'brutally beaten and clubbed', leaving the citizens calling for a Federal investigation.[206]

Nor were the mine guard abuses limited to the strike zone, as unrest spread into non-union Logan and McDowell Counties. Indeed, by the end of July, the two Commissioners noted that the Mingo strike zone was fairly peaceful, with only the odd case of shooting, whereas in McDowell and Logan, 'unbelievable stories are being told from those two counties of the way they are being used by those guards.'[207] One Mingo striker, black union activist Frank Ingham, discovered this first-hand on 10 August, when he was returning from McDowell to Mingo after visiting his sister. He was arrested when changing trains at Welch, threatened, and then thrown in jail. He was later driven from the jail to nearby woods with his hands tied, and questioned about the Matewan incident. When he told them he did not know anything, he was beaten with clubs, kicked in the face, robbed, and left for dead. Fortunately Ingham survived and managed to escape back to Mingo with the help of sympathetic railway workers.[208]

By the end of August the operators were faced with a serious problem, due to the success of the effort to turn back strike breakers. This was exacerbated by their inability to buy off Mingo Sheriff Blankenship, who refused to appoint company mine guards as deputies. Consequently the operators appealed to Cornwell to introduce Federal troops,[209] a policy which was vigorously opposed by union officials.[210] The union was also particularly incensed by charges of lawlessness on the part of union miners and by criticism of Blankenship. Mooney told Cornwell, 'in marked contrast to your own attitude toward the lawless invasion of the County by private gunmen of the operators, Sheriff Blankenship and his deputies have attempted to uphold the law', for which Mooney said, 'he has the earnest and wholehearted support of our officials and membership.'[211]

Characteristically, however, despite the fact that there was greater disturbance in the surrounding counties, Cornwell acquiesced with the operators and, on 28 August, asked the War Department for troops due to, he claimed, 'a noticeable increase in radical activities' in the Mingo field.[212] 500 men were immediately sent from Ohio, of whom 277 were stationed at Williamson, sixty-two at Matewan, and sixty-nine at Thacker.[213]

The arrival of the troops proved to be a turning point in the strike, as they showed clear sympathies for the operators. On 4 September, the District 17 officials complained to the Secretary of War that 'the troops are functioning in the same capacity as the Baldwin-Felts detectives and the State Constabulary. What we desire to know is this, are the Federal troops under orders to act as strike breakers, highway robbers and intimidators?' They cited examples of strikers being ordered from train depots, threats being made with machine guns, and arrests and harassment of union miners attempting to talk to strike breakers.[214]

The military's own reports during their deployment clearly illustrated their partiality. In a report to the Director of Military Intelligence for the period 3–19 September, Lt. Col. William Austin described the strike situation in terms which could easily have been written by the operators. He criticised local Judge Damron and Blankenship for opposing the presence of troops, alleging that the latter's deputies consisted of 'lawless characters', many of whom were UMWA members. The strikers, he alleged, included 'a very considerable number of worthless and criminal natives among the mountaineers, boot-leggers, moon shiners and criminal refugees', while the UMWA was criticised in the most strident terms: 'No condition of slavery ever known is more abject, total and tyrannical than that practised by the Union over its members.'[215]

The Commander of the Federal forces in Mingo, Col. S. Burkhardt Jr., was equally pronounced in his support of the operators. After troops had exchanged fire with strikers on 31 August, he met with the operators and accepted without argument their claim that 'none of the County officers can be depended upon to make arrests or convictions', as well as their call for martial law. He told Cornwell that the latter should be 'declared immediately without any further delay'.[216] The demand for martial law was being made particularly strongly by the operators, who remembered how it had handicapped the union during the Paint Creek strike. Indeed, so keen were they, that the union believed the operators were committing sabotage to force Cornwell's hand. They cited the example of one man caught attempting to blow up a power house, who confessed to having been paid $1,000 by an operator to commit the act.[217]

For the time being Cornwell resisted the calls for martial law and, with a period of relative quiet in the strike zone, was forced to consider the removal of Federal troops. The union were keen on this as the actions of the troops had created an 'unbearable condition' [218] which was seriously undermining their conduct of the strike. The advantage that the troops gave the operators made them equally keen that they should remain. One operator claimed at the end of October that 'the removal of troops, at this time, will result in an attack on our men or the property', adding that 'the general situation has improved very much and, if protection be given those at work, all the mines will soon be at work in a normal manner.'[219] After a further delay due to a killing in the strike zone,[220] however, the troops were finally removed at the beginning of November.

With the departure of the troops, responsibility for law and order returned to the local authorities, and the State police. The latter were under the command of Captain J. R. Brockus who was, predictably, open to the operators' influence.[221] His force, however, was small, and could not seriously influence the strike or the rising tide of violence in the area, which he described in daily reports to Cornwell. These reports clearly reveal the dimensions of the conflict in the strike zone. On 2 November, for example, a union miner was shot through the head by a mine guard at Vulcan,[222] and on 7 November, shots were fired at three strikers who had returned to work, a strike breaker was shot in the neck when visiting the tent colony at Lick Creek, and the tipple of the Thacker Coal Mining Company at Rose Siding was attacked with twelve to fifteen sticks of dynamite.[223] The following day saw shots fired at the motor of the same mine from the Kentucky side of the Tug River.[224]

The operators claimed that the violence was making Matewan a no-go area for their employees. The Red Jacket superintendent told Cornwell that 'our people who have found it necessary to take the trains have in the past few days went (*sic*) across the mountain to Thacker or driven by Motor Car about fifteen miles to Williamson via Pigeon Creek', thus avoiding the town.[225] Under such pressure from the operators, Cornwell again requested Federal troops, claiming 'the situation in Mingo County has again reached the point where the State is powerless to control it,'[226] backing this up with a declaration of martial law on 27 November.[227] The Federal troops began arriving in Mingo the following day.[228]

141

With the arrival of Federal troops for a second time, and the declaration of martial law, the noose began to tighten on the striking miners. The Red Jacket injunction passed by Judge Wadhill had come into force in November, and the first prosecutions took place at the end of that month, with three strikers receiving sixty days each for interfering with strike breakers. As Lunt suggests, Red Jacket were 'undoubtedly' happy with the success of the injunction, as it not only made picketing virtually impossible, but also had 'attrition value' due to the expense and energy wasted on legal challenges to the injunction by the union.[229] This was backed up by the interference of the military and State police which, as in the summer, severely damaged the conduct of the strike. Thus by December the strike was already lost in terms of production, with the operators back to their pre-strike tonnage.[230]

Federal troops were removed for the second time on 16 January 1921,[231] and Mingo remained relatively quiet until the end of March when the *Wheeling Gazette* reported the first trouble for six weeks, with three cases of assault.[232] In contrast, there was more serious violence in early March in other parts of the State. The worst incidents were in Monongalia County, where local union leader, Pat Blevins, was shot dead. Subsequently a number of shots were fired in the district, including several at the home of a relative of the man who killed Blevins. The Prosecuting Attorney for the County, R. P. Posten, requested a division of State police, who were recalled from Mingo.[233]

While the local press claimed the County was becoming a 'Second Mingo',[234] the authorities believed this to be an exaggeration. While this may have been the case in terms of violence, there were definite similarities in terms of the actions and attitudes of public officials. Posten, for example, told the new State Governor, Morgan, that the strike in the County had been in progress since the previous July due to an organising campaign. The organisers, he claimed, 'have been a source of constant annoyance and terror to the people in and about the mining districts.' He clearly cared little about the murder of Blevins who, he claimed, was the strike leader and principal trouble maker. The police had been requested, he told Morgan, after the striking miners had begun firing in revenge.[235]

Morgan, who had entered office on 4 March after being the operators' chosen candidate the previous November, clearly agreed with Posten. He complemented his swift action and told him:

There are several places in the State that the same feeling seems to exist as in Monongalia County. It is a disgrace to the State of West Virginia that there are citizens in so many communities who feel that, if they cannot have their way, they should have the liberty of shooting up houses and destroying property.[236]

For the striking miners in Mingo, March also brought a temporary relief from the battery of legal defeats inflicted by the State and Federal courts. The trial of those involved in the Matewan shootings had begun in a tense atmosphere at Williamson in January. There were rumours that an attempt would be made on the life of Hatfield and the other defendants, which led to counter threats of reprisals by miners.[237] Furthermore, the appearance of company spy C. E. Lively for the prosecution, heightened the mistrust between operator and miner. Lively, a West Virginia native and former UMWA member, had operated a restaurant in Matewan, where striking miners gathered. Lively himself had been an enthusiastic participant at the meetings, and the discovery that he was in the pay of the operators not only meant that he had passed on valuable information, but led to the suspicion that he may have acted as an 'agent provocateur'.[238]

Allegations of intimidation of witnesses and the jury were also rife on both sides. The most prominent example of this involved hotel proprietor, Anse Hatfield. The papers discovered after the Matewan shooting had suggested he was in the pay of the Baldwin-Felts agency, an impression that was reinforced when the agency used his hotel as their headquarters whilst in Matewan. When it was heard that Hatfield was to be the chief witness for the prosecution at the Matewan trial, certain parties decided that his support for the operators had gone to far. According to Mooney, 'one of his chief hobbies was to sit on the hotel porch and snooze during the evening twilight . . . One evening preceding the trials . . . a shot was fired from behind the south end of the freight house which joined the depot', and with remarkable accuracy in the fading twilight, the bullet hit Hatfield in the head and killed him instantly.[239]

Despite the tensions surrounding the trial, there were no attempts on the defendants' lives. The first acquittals were announced at the end of March, and led to celebrations in Matewan. The *Fairmont Times* reported that 'Matewan called it a holiday today', with virtually the whole town turning out to greet the defendants. It went on to describe how 'the throng that gathered about the hillmen when they left the train swayed back and forth from men to children to grasp their hands for an hour after their arrival. Women among the relatives wept alternately from pure joy at their return.'[240]

The pleasure at the not guilty verdicts, however, was short lived. Under the previous Cornwell administration, a State senator who acted as an attorney for the operators, had introduced a bill allowing a judge to summon a jury from a different County to the one in which an offence had been committed. Despite vigorous criticism from the union who saw this as an attempt to secure a prosecution against those accused over the Matewan incident,[241] the bill was passed with the full support of both Cornwell and Morgan, two days after the first acquittals.[242] Consequently, a new trial was arranged for the summer relating to further charges emanating from the shootings.[243] In addition to these changes in the law, the operators had made other moves against Sid Hatfield and Matewan's one policeman, Ed Chambers. Intent on getting the two men out of the relative safety of Mingo County, the operators had them charged over a shooting incident at Mohawk. The two men were to appear at court in Welch at the beginning of August.[244]

Prior to this, in May, trouble had already returned to the Mingo field, and Morgan declared martial law and once again requested Federal troops. However, while the change of personnel in the State house at Charleston may have meant a continuation of the same policies, the new incumbent at the White House, W. G. Harding, was not so willing to use Federal troops at the whim of the Governor. Morgan was told to use his own resources to the full and not treat Federal forces as a national police force.[245]

The absence of the troops proved of little advantage to the strikers, as Morgan constituted a volunteer police force under the command of Brockus. This was openly hostile to the strikers, and worked alongside the State police.[246] The worst example of this hostility occurred at the miners' Lick Creek tent colony on 14 June, after a police car had been fired upon. A force made up of police and volunteers was immediately dispatched to the colony, where they proceeded to wreck the tents and belongings of the strikers, and arrest forty of their number. At some time shots were also exchanged, leading to the death of union activist Alex Breedlove, and the wounding of one police officer. The strikers claimed that Breedlove was murdered in cold blood, after being ordered to hold up his hands.[247]

At the same time as the strikers were suffering at the hands of the forces of law and order, they won a rare legal victory in the State Supreme court, when Morgan's declaration of martial law was successfully challenged because it was being enforced by civil rather than military agencies.[248] Once again, however, the victory proved temporary, as a modified martial law was reintroduced two weeks later, with volunteers enrolled into the State militia under the command of Major T. B. Davis. The militia had the right to arrest and detain those accused of violating martial law.[249]

As in the Paint Creek strike the militia used their powers almost exclusively to thwart and intimidate the miners. A large number of arrests were made including, at the beginning of July, twelve union leaders attending a meeting at Williamson. Morgan told the press that they were arrested after being warned that Davis 'would not permit assemblages in the martial law district'.[250] Alongside allegations of wrongful arrest, Keeney also complained to Morgan that the militia were preventing the distribution of goods in the tent colonies.[251]

To the miners the antics of the State government and the law enforcement agencies were becoming increasingly frustrating, even if somewhat predictable. The murder of Breedlove had been followed by rumours of a gathering of miners on Cabin Creek, who intended to march on Mingo.[252] Although this did not transpire, the feelings of the miners were represented at a number of meetings, and in a vast quantity of letters and proclamations sent to Morgan. 'Do you not realise you were elected Governor of the State of West Virginia, by the People, for the People, and not for the Coal Operators of the southern part of the State alone?' Local 3302 at Bower asked after the Lick Creek raid.[253] Another Local at Mountclare told Morgan that they attacked the 'actions of your special representative and all other officers of constabulary and State troops who did not have brains enough to investigate the shot at Lick Creek tent colony before killing and destroying the miners' property, simply to reek revenge on the miners'.[254]

There were even unsuccessful calls for Morgan's impeachment. Thus a mass meeting at Cannelton on 10 July urged Keeney to 'start some machinery whereby the impeachment of Mr Morgan can be secured',[255] while the Monclo Local, Local 1891 at Gypsy, and Local 4175 at Volga, among numerous others, wrote directly to Morgan threatening the same.[256]

The miners' frustrations came to a head in August. After over a year's struggle against almost insurmountable odds, and despite a remarkable display of solidarity and endurance that saw 2,900 still out on strike,[257] several events occurred which served to underline the powerlessness of the miners and the brutal injustices of the operator/State government conspiracy.

The worst incident occurred on 1 August 1921, when the Baldwin Felts finally exacted their bloody revenge on Sid Hatfield and Ed Chambers. The two men were walking up the court house steps with their wives, to appear in court over the Mohawk charges. As the operators had intended, however, there would be no trial, and Hatfield and Chambers were met on the steps by forty armed gun men, some of whom opened fire before the two men had even reached the third step. [258] The irony that the murders took place on the court house steps was reinforced by the presence of C. E. Lively among those responsible, and the gratuitous violence that accompanied them. Lively reportedly emptied his gun into the fallen Chambers, before being attacked by the latter's wife. The other gun men did likewise, leaving seventeen bullets in Hatfield's body and thirteen in Chambers; so many, in fact, that it was impossible to embalm the bodies.[259] Needless to say, however, nobody was prosecuted for these killings.[260]

The murder of Hatfield was greeted with outrage by many in West Virginia. Local Unions and other organisations bitterly denounced the killings, and accused Morgan of breaking a promise to protect the two men. A letter from the Kanawha Central Labor Union was typical. They told Morgan, 'regardless of this urgent plea for protection and your promise to provide the same, you utterly failed to keep your promise'. They further condemned his 'inactivity since the murders occurred', and demanded an investigation.[261] Morgan replied by accusing the union of being 'biased and prejudiced', and having 'written without that reflection, meditation and cool deliberation that should be used in discussing questions of such importance.' He also claimed, in what turned out to be a hollow assertion, that 'McDowell County has energetic, honest and capable officials, and (I) have no doubt that every proper effort is being made, and will be made, to see that those who violated the law will be properly punished'.[262]

In the aftermath of the Welch murders, the miners became increasingly restless, and on 7 August, around 1,000 attended a mass meeting in Charleston, where they heard speeches by Mooney, Samuel B. Montgomery, and Mother Jones, all of whom attempted to calm tempers.[263] The meeting proposed a solution to the strike based on terms suggested by Keeney the previous month – these included the right to join a union, semi-monthly pay days, the right to elect checkweighmen, and a joint commission to consider wages.[264] The resolution was presented to Morgan, who later rejected it, claiming that the operators had the right to demand that employees should not join a union.[265]

The rejection of the compromise was followed by decisions in the State Supreme Court which upheld the martial law decree in Mingo, as well as the arrest and imprisonment of the UMWA officials in Williamson.[266] There was also a further announcement of mine closures in the union field which, due to the recession, was now operating at only 40% of its normal level of production. This, once again, underlined the importance of organising the non-union counties which were undercutting those which were organised.[267]

These events served to reinforce the restlessness that had come to the fore after the Welch killings. From the middle of August miners across the State began to quit work and head towards Marmet in Kanawha County. By 23 August, officials were reporting armed patrols occupying local roads, raiding stores, and disarming officers.[268] In the next couple of days the miners continued to amass arms and provisions and, on the 25 August, some began marching towards Logan and Mingo. One local paper reported that marching miners had temporarily halted at Indian Creek in Boone County, where they discussed the plan to march on Mingo. The paper noted that there were no obvious leaders and 'every man seemed to be following his own initiative and every marcher was at liberty to deliver a speech.'[269]

The following day Mooney estimated that there were 12,000 armed miners either camped at Lens Creek, below Marmet, or on the march in Boone County, heading south.[270] In fact 2,000 of these had already reached Blair Mountain in Logan, having speeded up their passage by hijacking a train.[271] They were not deterred by the news that Don Chafin was organising a force to meet them. Indeed, the news was greeted with enthusiasm with marchers reportedly singing, to the tune of 'John Brown's Body', 'We'll hang Don Chafin to a sour apple tree'.[272]

While the march had been gathering momentum, frantic efforts were made to call it to a halt. District 17 officials attempted to turn the men back [273] and, on 24 August, after a personal request by Morgan, Mother Jones made a clumsy effort to halt the march on Lens Creek. She claimed to have a Telegram from President Harding promising that, if the miners returned to their homes, he would end the guard system. Many of the marchers, however, suspected that the document was fake, and when Mother Jones refused to show it to either Keeney or Mooney, they demanded that the two leaders telegraph the President's office for verification. The reply came back that it was false, and the march continued. The only effect of the debacle lay in the damage it did to Mother Jones' reputation in the eyes of the miners.[274]

With the failure of Mother Jones to halt the march, Morgan appealed for Federal troops on 25 August, claiming that the situation was 'critical'.[275] The War Department refused this request, but did reply that troops were being prepared in case they were needed later. In the meantime they sent Brigadier General H. H. Bandholtz to Charleston to attempt to solve the problem without the use of Federal forces.[276] On his arrival the following day, Bandholtz wasted little time, contacting Keeney at 5.00 a.m. and telling him to travel to the 'vicinity of Madison, Boone County . . . in your official capacity as President of District 17' where he was to tell the marchers 'the necessity of abandoning their purpose, dispersing and returning to their homes immediately.'[277]

Armed with a letter from Bandholtz warning the marchers of the consequences of refusing to disband, Keeney and Mooney travelled down the length of the march, eventually speaking to a large gathering at a ball park at Danville. The two men were greeted with hostility by some of the miners, but the majority accepted that they should disband.[278] Bandholtz himself visited Racine, Lens Creek, and Paint and Cabin Creeks on 27 August and found that the men were returning to their homes. Content that the march was finished, he left Charleston that evening.[279]

It appears that this would have been the end of the march, had it not been for the actions of a group of State police led by Brockus. Late on the evening of 27 August they arrived at Sharples, on the Logan border, with the intention of serving warrants on one of the town's inhabitants. The result was the 'Sharples Massacre', which left two miners dead and three injured, and the subsequent resumption of the armed march.[280] Quite why the State police, with the

Governor's permission, should have carried out a raid on a town in such a sensitive position, at such a tense time, is somewhat mystifying. Bandholtz, for example, later told the Secretary of War that the withdrawal of the marchers 'would have been satisfactorily achieved' had it not been for 'the ill-advised and ill-timed advance movement of State constabulary on the night of August 27, resulting in bloodshed.' He also criticised the 'tardy sending of trains' which had left many of the marchers stranded in the vicinity.[281]

By 29 August the miners' army was once again streaming towards Logan on foot, horseback, in cars, and on hijacked trains. Medical teams were established by doctors and nurses, and army veterans, numbering around 2,000, many of whom were dressed in their uniforms, helped organise patrols and drill marchers. They headed for Blair Mountain, the gateway to Logan County, where trenches were dug, and they faced Chafin's forces.[282]

With the battle of Blair Mountain about to begin, Morgan was vigorously pressing the Federal authorities for troops. On 29 August he claimed that the march was being led by 'Bolsheviks from Indiana, Ohio and Illinois' and that conditions were 'grave'. He appealed to Bandholtz to 'intercede' on his behalf and persuade the War Department to furnish troops.[283] The authorities again refused to be forced into an unnecessary involvement in the conflict, and told Morgan that troops would only be sent when there was no other alternative.[284] Then, on 30 August, Harding issued a proclamation on the West Virginia violence, warning 'all persons engaged in said unlawful and insurrectionary proceedings to disperse and retire peaceably to their respective abodes on or before 12 o'clock noon of the 1st day of September, 1921'.[285]

It soon became clear, however, that the proclamation would be ignored, as the two sides were already firing at each other, and casualties were being reported. In one instance a party of miners led by the Rev. John Wilburn engaged in a gun battle with a group of Logan deputies, which left three guards dead, and a black miner injured.[286] By 1 September the battle was still in full swing, with firing along a 12 to 15 mile battle front, and no sign of it ending, despite appeals from UMWA Vice President, Philip Murray, who had travelled to meet the marchers.[287] Consequently Bandholtz telegraphed Washington to call for Federal troops.[288]

On 2 September, before the troops arrived, UMWA officials made it clear that the marchers would not fight the Federal forces. Petry told reporters that the marchers had told him 'not a single shot' would be fired at troops, and Murray likewise said that 'the presence of Federal troops will result in immediate quiet being restored. The men engaged in the present conflict against the Governor's misuse of power welcome with open arms the coming of Federal troops.'[289] This proved to be true as the troops reached the area on 2–3 September. Bandholtz reported that 'in establishing themselves in the trouble zone the Federal forces met with no opposition anywhere and do not anticipate any', and that the marchers were surrendering and dispersing.[290] One marcher recalled everyone complying with the military 'like a child taking orders from its mother' because many of the marchers were World War I veterans and 'there was nothing going to make them raise a gun against the US army.' Another marcher, similarly remembered that 'none of the miners wanted to fight the US army so they were disarmed and escorted out of Logan County.'[291]

The fact that the Federal troops did not become involved in the fighting was undoubtedly to the marchers' benefit. The Federal authorities may have been hesitant to send the troops, but when they did, it was a large and threatening force. In addition to over 2,000 troops, a chemical warfare unit and the 88th air squadron were sent to the area.[292] There was in fact some confusion as to whether the latter had been used in the conflict, as there were reports that bombs had been dropped on the marchers.[293] On investigation it turned out that the Federal aircraft were only being used for reconnaissance, and that the Logan forces had used a private plane to drop 'an iron cylinder filled with slugs and bullets', which had failed to explode.[294] As it was, the 88th air squadron, even if it had been used, did not seem very threatening – unless a bystander was unlucky enough to be hit by falling wreckage. Six of the planes crashed before reaching Blair, including two after getting lost in the fog and ending up in Tennessee. Another one crashed in Nicholas County killing four and injuring one.[295]

With the peaceful dispersal of the marchers, the largest armed conflict in the history of US labour came to an end. Over 1,000,000 shots had been fired, although it is unclear how many lives were actually lost. Estimates ranged from four to 110, although it was probably towards the lower end of the spectrum.[296] The relatively low loss of life in relation to the size of the battle, revealed that it was not fought particularly effectively. The miners' army, which was estimated at anything from 6–20,000, was fighting a better equipped force of around 2–3,000.[297] However it seems that it would have found it difficult to cross Logan, let alone Mingo. One of the officers who arrived with the Federal troops noted that the miners had told him 'three more days and we would have been in Logan', but he suggested that 'it would have taken them about three years before they advanced a foot the way they looked.'[298]

If the armed march was not militarily successful, this had a good deal to do with its spontaneous nature. Some have suggested that it was well organised with a clear leadership, under the command of 'Generalissimo' Bill Blizzard, a sub-district President. His brother, for example, later claimed Blizzard had 'engineered the whole thing, organized them under army rules.'[299] However, a more realistic perspective was suggested by another miner who, looking back on these events, told an interviewer, 'now, Bill's one of the finest people that's ever lived . . . But he wasn't the leader anymore than any of the rest of us was, from the way I see it. We were all just leaders, in a manner of speaking.'[300]

It was for exactly this reason that the march was so remarkable. The established leadership, in the shape of Keeney and Mooney, had opposed the march and, after hearing of indictments being prepared on 31 August, wisely fled the State until the situation calmed down.[301] The march was thus a spontaneous, angry uprising, what Savage has described as 'an example of working anarchy'.[302] It was bound together by frustration at the abuses of the operators, brought to a head by the murder of Hatfield and Chambers on the court house steps at Welch. Its scale may have been unique, but it fitted perfectly into a pattern of industrial militancy which had been evolving throughout the previous decades. The more the operator/State government conspiracy attempted to suffocate the peaceful expression of protest, the more the miners were forced to adopt other methods as a way of being heard.

This is illustrated by the fact that once again, only this time on a larger scale, all sections of the workforce marched and fought side by side. Black marchers were prominent, with one operator commenting that 'at any turn you were likely to butt into a colored man with a high-powered rifle.'[303] Likewise, Military Intelligence officers reported that around 10% of the marchers were foreign born, some of whom would be subject to deportation.[304] Nor was the march made up entirely of miners. Philip Murray, for example, attacked

Morgan's claims that only UMWA members were involved, telling reporters:

> Nothing could be further from the truth . . . miners, railroad men, merchants, doctors, ministers of the Gospel, and almost every other element of citizenship of those communities and throughout the State is represented in the force that are fighting for the establishment of true law and order in the State.[305]

Remarkable as the march may have been, in the end it achieved very little. After the miners dispersed, many prominent union activists were arrested, including Keeney, Mooney, and Blizzard. In total over 600 people were indicted, fifty-four on charges of murder and treason.[306] The first to be prosecuted was Blizzard, who was tried at Charles Town in Jefferson County, appropriately, in the same court house which had held the John Brown treason trial. In characteristic fashion, the State was responsible for the prosecution, but it was conducted by the operators' lawyers, who then sent their bill to the State.[307] After a tense five week trial, which attracted national attention, Blizzard was acquitted of the charge of treason in May 1922. Having lost the test case, the litigation dragged on until 1924, but most of the accused were either acquitted or had their charges dropped. Three convictions were obtained, including an eleven year sentence for the Reverend J. W. Wilburn and his son, who were found guilty of murder arising from the shootings on Blair Mountain on 29 August. They were, however, later paroled.[308]

The operators' failure in the courts was not repeated in the strike zone. Despite the vigour of the miners' march, they were unable to win the southern counties for the union. Indeed, quite the opposite happened, as the broader decline in the coal industry's fortunes and the post-war national 'open shop' drive encouraged the West Virginia operators to resist the UMWA. Stories of destitution and misery in the mining communities became commonplace across the coalfield, despite attempts by Morgan to downplay them.[309] Finally, after an unsuccessful national strike, the Mingo dispute was called off in October 1922. This was followed by an assault on the union fields, which led to a cataclysmic fall in union membership. By 1926, the UMWA recorded only 436 members among nearly 120,000 miners.[310]

Probably the worst, and most prolonged, conflict over the assault on the union occurred in the northern coalfield, where in 1924, the operators repudiated the Baltimore Agreement, and began to operate on a non-union basis. There followed the familiar tactics of yellow dog contracts, evictions, mine guards, and interference by the State and legal authorities. Sabotage and violence resulted, and the strike limped on for five years, until 1929, when it collapsed, as demand for the area's coal declined.[311]

By the mid 1920s, therefore, the West Virginia miners were, to a large extent, back where they started. The preceding twenty years had witnessed a growing tide of industrial unrest, definitively shaped by the social and cultural context of West Virginia. Often isolated, culturally mixed, mobile, and governed in an autocratic manner, the miners fought vigorously to gain a voice, and some control over their world. Yet the harshness of this world, and the accompanying denial of the legitimate rights to protest, led to explosions of industrial unrest. As the years progressed the miners' response to their environment, and the experience of struggle itself, helped generate a greater sense of unity – even to the point where the black-white fissure running through the US working-class could be, temporarily at least, overcome. The bloody battles of the mine wars illustrated the results of this learning process.

However, despite their best efforts, the mining communities lacked the power to secure permanently the right to organise, and redress their wrongs. As they had been learning, so had the operators who, by the 1920s, were practised in the art of anti-unionism – whether through brute force, or welfare capitalism. The miners would have to await the changed world of New Deal America, before they could finally turn West Virginia into a union coalfield.

Notes

1 US Senate, *West Virginia Coalfields: Personal Views of Senator Kenyon, and Views of Senators Sterling, Phipps, and Warren*, (Washington D.C., 1922), p. 4.
2 *UMWJ*, 18 Jan 1900, p. 3.
3 W. M. Boal, 'Estimates of Unionism in West Virginia Coal, 1900–1935', *Labor History*, 35, 3 (1994). See table, pp. 438–9. Boal has also tried to calculate union influence in West Virginia by estimating the tonnage produced under union contract. This produces a similar pattern to figures for membership, although sometimes at a higher rate. See pp. 432–7, 440, fig.1.
4 *Ibid.*, pp. 438–9.
5 UMWA, *Proceedings of 25th Annual Convention, 1915*, p. 214

6 R. D. Lunt, *Law and Order vs. The Miners: West Virginia, 1907–33* (Hamden, Archon Books, 1979), p. 70; W. M. Boal, 'Unionism and Productivity in West Virginia Coal Mining', (Unpublished Ph.D dissertation, Stanford University, 1985), p. 16; Boal, 'Estimates of Unionism in West Virginia Coal', pp. 438–9.

7 Lunt, *Law and Order vs. The Miners*, p. 181.

8 S. Brier, 'Interracial Organizing in the West Virginia Coal Industry: The Participation of Black Mine Workers in the Knights of Labor and the United Mine Workers, 1880–1894', in G. M. Fink and M. E. Reed (eds.), *Essays in Southern Labor History: Selected Papers, Southern Labour History Conference, 1976* (Westport, Conn., Greenwood Press, 1976), pp. 18–28, quote, p. 28.

9 *Ibid.*, pp. 29–35; J. Trotter Jr., *Coal, Class and Color: Blacks in Southern West Virginia, 1915–32* (Urbana, University of Illinois Press, 1991), p. 53.

10 A. Roy, *A History of the Coal Miners of the United States: From the Development of the Mines to the Close of the Anthracite Strike of 1902* (Columbus, Trouger Printing Co., 1907), p. 301.

11 R. M. Simon, 'The Development of Underdevelopment: The Coal Industry and its Effect on the West Virginia Economy' (Unpublished Ph.D dissertation, University of Pittsburgh, 1978), pp. 178–185; A. E. Suffern, *Conciliation and Arbitration in the Coal Industry of America*, (Boston, Houghton Mifflin, 1915), pp. 66–7; N. Salvatore, *Eugene V. Debs: Citizen and Socialist* (Urbana, University of Illinois Press, 1982), pp. 172–3; A. Roy, *A History of the Coal Miners of the United States*, pp. 328–9.

12 S. Perlman and P. Taft, *History of Labor in the United States, 1896–1932: Labor Movements* (New York, Macmillan, 1935), p. 326.

13 Suffern, *Conciliation and Arbitration in the Coal Industry of America*, pp. 62–5.

14 US Senate, Committee on Education and Labor, *Conditions in the Paint Creek District, West Virginia*, 63 Congress, 1 Session (Washington D.C., 1913), Pt. 2, p. 1449.

15 N. Robinson, *West Virginia on the Brink of a Labor Struggle* (Charleston, 1912), p. 6.

16 *West Virginia Coalfields, Personal Views of Senator Kenyon, and Views of Senators Sterling, Phipps, and Warren*, p. 5.

17 US Senate, Committee on Education and Labor, *West Virginia Coal Fields Hearings*, 67 Congress, 1 Session, (Washington D.C., 1921–2), 1, p. 9.

18 Vinson also stated that 'At its annual conference in 1912 it changed its policy and its principles from that of a labor union into an organized band of robbers.', *ibid.*, p. 9.

19 *UMWJ*, 5 Apr 1900, p. 8.

20 *UMWJ*, 2 May 1901, p. 4.

21 *UMWJ*, 3 May 1900, p. 8.

22 *UMWJ*, 27 Dec 1900, p. 1.

23 Taylor to Mitchell, 9 Sep 1901, Washington D.C., Catholic University of America, John Mitchell Papers (m/film), Reel 3.

24 Crawford to Mitchell, 30 Aug 1901, *ibid.*

25 Warner to Mitchell, 21 Jul 1901, *ibid.*

26 Letter from Ben Davis, *UMWJ*, 12 Sep 1901, p. 6.

27 Walker to Mitchell, 9 Jul 1901, Mitchell Papers, Reel 3.

28 *UMWJ*, 4 Jul 1901, p. 2; 11 Jul 1901, p. 1.; 1 Aug 1901, p. 1; Crawford to Mitchell, 5 Aug 1901, Mitchell Papers, Reel 3.

29 Hunter to Mitchell, 30 Aug 1901, *ibid.*

30 Crawford to Mitchell, 19 Sep 1901, *ibid.*

31 NEB 11 Apr 1901, *ibid.*, Reel 41.

32 Crawford to Mitchell, 30 Aug 1901, *ibid.*, Reel 3

33 Mitchell to Purcell, 13 Jul 1901; *ibid.*; NEB, 12 Aug 1901, *ibid.*, Reel 41; Manka to Mitchell, 19 Aug 1901; Warner to Mitchell, 29 Aug 1901, *ibid.*, Reel 3.

34 *UMWJ*, 11 Apr 1901, p. 1.

35 Morrison to Mitchell, 5 Jul 1901, 25 Aug 1901, Mitchell papers, Reel 3.

36 Lewis to Mitchell, 2 Oct 1901; Mitchell to Lewis, 2 Oct 1901, *ibid.*

37 Mitchell to Lewis, 17 Oct 1901, *ibid.*.

38 *UMWJ*, 23 Jan 1902, p. 4.

39 J.M. Gowaskie, 'John Mitchell: A Study in Leadership' (Unpublished Ph.D dissertation, Catholic University of America, 1968), pp. 126–8; *UMWJ*, 7 Nov 1901, p. 7.

40 E. M. Steel, 'Mother Jones in the Fairmont Field', *Journal of American History*, 57 (1970), p. 293; Suffern, *Conciliation and Arbitration in the Coal Industry of America* p. 68.

41 Suffern, *Conciliation and Arbitration in the Coal Industry of America*, p. 68.

42 Steel, 'Mother Jones in the Fairmont Field', p. 294.

43 *Ibid.*, pp. 293–298; Gowaskie, 'John Mitchell', pp. 140–43

44 Steel, 'Mother Jones in the Fairmont Field', pp. 300–2; Fox, 'Thomas T. Haggerty and the Formative Years of the UMWA', (Unpublished Ph.D dissertation, West Virginia University, 1975), pp. 217–25.

45 Quoted in J. A. Williams, *West Virginia and the Captains of Industry* (Morgantown, West Virginia University Library Press, 1976), p. 147.

46 Quoted in Steel, 'Mother Jones in the Fairmont Field', pp. 303–4.

47 Perlman and Taft, *History of Labor in the United States*, pp. 328–9.

48 Suffern, *Conciliation and Arbitration in the Coal Industry of America*, p. 69.

49 Gowaskie, 'John Mitchell, pp. 143–4.

50 West Virginia Department of Mines, *Annual Report, 1905* (Charleston, 1905), p. 8; Simon, 'Development of Underdevelopment', pp. 181–2; Suffern, *Conciliation and Arbitration in the Coal Industry of America*, pp. 70–1.

51 Collins to Riley, 18 Jun 1906, Morgantown, West Virginia University (WVU), West Virginia and Regional History Collection, Justus Collins Papers (A+M 1824), Series 1, Box 2, File 7.

52 Herndon to Collins, 13 Jan 1910; 19 Jan 1910, *ibid.*, Box 6, File 36.

53 UMWA, *Proceedings 24th Convention, 1914*, p. 57.

54 *West Virginia Coal Fields Hearings*, 1, p. 19.

55 *UMWJ*, 26 Apr 1912, p. 6.

56 *Charleston Gazette*, 2 May 1912, p. 1; 3 May 1912, p. 1; *UMWJ*, 9 May 1912, p. 6; 16 May 1912, p. 6; 15 Aug 1912, p. 4.

57 R. L. Lewis, *Black Coal Miners in America: Race, Class, and Community Conflict, 1780–1980* (Lexington, University Press of Kentucky, 1987), pp. 139–40.

58 *UMWJ*, 16 May 1912, p. 6.

59 Report by D. J. O'Regan, 5 Aug 1914, p. 2. Washington D.C., National Archive (NA), General Records of the Department of Labor (RG174), Records of Commission on Industrial Relations, Box 17, File 23:13.3.

60 *Charleston Gazette*, 14 Jun 1912, p. 1.

61 F. Mooney, *Struggle in the Coal Fields* [Ed. J. W. Hess] (Morgantown, West Virginia University Library Press, 1967), pp. 16, 25.

62 *Charleston Gazette*, 6 Jun 1912, pp. 1, 6; *UMWJ*, 13 Jun 1912, p. 6.

63 *Wheeling Intelligencer*, 27 Jul 1912, p. 1.; *Wheeling Register*, 27 Jul 1912; *UMWJ* , 1 Aug 1912, p. 1.

64 H. B. Lee, *Bloodletting in Appalachia: The Story of West Virginia's Four Major Mine Wars and Other Thrilling Incidents of its Coal Fields* (Morgantown, West Virginia University Library Press, 1969), pp. 32–3.

65 *Wheeling Register*, 12 Sep 1912, pp. 1, 6.

66 *Wheeling Majority*, 17 Oct 1912, p. 1.

67 *Conditions in the Paint Creek District*, 1, pp. 759–60.

68 Report by D. J O'Regan, p. 2, Records of Commission on Industrial Relations, Box 17, File 23:13.3.

69 *Kanawha Citizen*, 9 Feb 1913, p. 8; *Charleston Gazette*, 8 Feb 1913, p. 1; 9 Feb 1913, p. 1; 10 Feb 1913, pp. 1, 6; *Conditions in the Paint Creek District*, 1, pp. 684–93; pp. 460–65.

70 *Wheeling Register*, 11 Feb 1913, p. 1; *Kanawha Citizen*, 11 Feb 1913, p. 1; Perlman and Taft, *History of Labor in the United States*, p. 333.
71 S. Gompers, 'Russianized West Virginia: Corporate Perversion of American Concepts of Liberty and Human Justice – Organized Labor to the Rescue', *American Federationist*, 20, 10 (Oct 1913), pp. 830, 829.
72 Suffern, *Conciliation and Arbitration in the Coal Industry of America*, p. 100.
73 *Ibid.*, pp. 99–100; Gompers, 'Russianized West Virginia', pp. 829–30.
74 Quoted in *ibid.*, p. 830.
75 Belcher to White, 3 Mar 1913, sent with letter from White to W. B. Wilson, 3 Mar 1913, NA, General Records of the Department of Labor (RG174), File 16/13 E.
76 Lee, *Bloodletting in Appalachia*, pp. 35–41.
77 *Wheeling Register*, 12 Sep 1912, pp. 1, 6.
78 Glasscock to J. McClung, 29 Nov 1912, WVU, W. E. Glasscock Papers (A+M 6 G), Box 28, File 1.
79 Suffern, *Conciliation and Arbitration in the Coal Industry of America*, p. 99.
80 E. L. K. Harris and F. J. Krebs, *From Humble Beginnings: West Virginia State Federation of Labor, 1903–57* (Charleston, West Virginia Labor History Publishing Fund, 1960), p. 74.
81 Report by D. J. O'Regan, pp. 6–7, Records of Commission on Industrial Relations, Box 17, File 23:13.3.
82 *Wheeling Majority*, 17 Oct 1912, p. 1.
83 Report by D. J. O'Regan, p. 5, Records of Commission on Industrial Relations, Box 17, File 23:13.3.
84 *Wheeling Register*, 14 Feb 1913, p. 1; 15 Feb 1913, p. 1; *Wheeling Majority*, 20 Feb 1913, p. 1.
85 Williams, *West Virginia*, pp. 132–3; Lee, *Bloodletting in Appalachia*, p. 44.
86 For example, from Local 1911, Springfield, Illinois, 26 Apr 1913; Local 2741, Hynes, Iowa, 29 Apr 1913; Local 508, Maute, Indiana, n.d.; Alexandria, Va., UMWA Archive, District 17 Correspondence Files.
87 White, Hayes, Perry to Wilson, 9 Apr 1913, General Records of the Department of Labor, File 16/13, Box 23.
88 C. Hayden to Wilson, 25 Apr 1913, *ibid.*
89 D. L. Llewellyn to Wilson, n.d., *ibid.*, File 16/13, Box 24, File 1.
90 M. Jones to Borah, n.d., *ibid.*, File 16/13 E, Box 24.
91 Wilson to D. O'Leary, 23 May 1913, *ibid.*
92 *Socialist and Labor Star*, 13 Jun 1913, p. 1.

93 Williams, *West Virginia*, p. 133, Harris and Krebs, *From Humble Beginnings*, p. 76.
94 Fox, 'Thomas T. Haggerty and the Formative Years of the UMWA', pp. 294–7.
95 Williams, *West Virginia*, p. 134; Suffern, *Conciliation and Arbitration in the Coal Industry of America*, p. 103; Harris and Krebs, *From Humble Beginnings*, p. 75; Perlman and Taft, *History of Labor in the United States*, pp. 334–5.
96 Williams, *West Virginia*, p. 135.
97 Perlman and Taft, *History of Labor in the United States*, p. 335; D. A. Corbin, 'Betrayal in the West Virginia Coal Fields: Eugene V. Debs and the Socialist Party of America, 1912–14', *Journal of American History*, 64, 5 (1978), p. 994.
98 *Ibid.*, p. 994; Fox, 'Thomas T. Haggerty and the Formative Years of the UMWA', pp. 300–1
99 Ibid., pp. 301–2
100 *Socialist and Labor Star*, 30 May 1913, p. 1; *Conditions in the Paint Creek District*, Pt. 2, pp. 2092–4.
101 *Ibid.*, Pt.3, p. 2140.
102 *Wheeling Register*, 22 May 1913, p. 1; 23 May 1913, p. 1.
103 *Wheeling Register*, 20 Jun 1913, p. 1.
104 *Socialist and Labor Star*, 8 Aug 1913, p. 2.
105 *Socialist and Labor Star*, 21 June 1913, p. 1; 4 July 1913, p. 1; *Miners Herald*, 23 Aug 1913, p. 2.
106 UMWA *Proceedings of 23rd Annual Conference, 1912*, p. 303.
107 *Ibid.*, pp. 301–8.
108 *Wheeling Register*, 21 May 1913, p. 1.
109 *Charleston Gazette*, 21 May 1913, p. 1.
110 *Ibid.*, 29 May 1913, p. 1.
111 *Ibid.*, 22 May 1913, p. 6.
112 Letter from Crown Hill Local, 1 Jun 1913, UMWA, District 17 Correspondence Files.
113 Resolution from Local 2537, Kayford, 1 May 1913. See also Letter from Local 1395, Shrewsbury, 17 Jun 1913; Resolution from Local 2537, Eskdale, 1 May 1913. All in ibid.
114 *Socialist and Labor Star*, 6 Jun 1913, p. 1.
115 *Ibid.*, 8 June 1913, p. 1.
116 *Miners Herald*, 26 Dec 1913, p. 4.
117 Quoted in *Socialist and Labor Star*, 1 May 1914, p. 4.
118 Mooney, *Struggle in the Coal Fields*, pp. 42–5; Fox, 'Thomas T. Haggerty and the Formative Years of the UMWA', pp. 328–9.
119 *Coal Age*, 5, 20 (16 May 1914), p. 823.

120 Fox, 'Thomas T. Haggerty and the Formative Years of the UMWA', pp. 333–4; Wilson to Haggerty and Cairns, 5 Jun 1914, General Records of the Department of Labor, File 16/13, Box 23.
121 Haggerty and Cairns to The President, 3 Jun 1914, *ibid*.
122 Fox, 'Thomas T. Haggerty and the Formative Years of the UMWA', p. 334.
123 Mooney, *Struggle in the Coal Fields*, pp. 45–6; D. A. Corbin, '"Frank Keeney is our Leader and we shall not be moved" Rank and File Leadership in the West Virginia Coal Fields', in Fink and Reed, *Essays in Southern Labor History*, p. 145.
124 *Ibid.*, p. 145; Fox, 'Thomas T. Haggerty and the Formative Years of the UMWA', p. 345; Interview with Bert Castle, WVU, Oral History Collection.
125 *Ibid.*
126 UMWA, *Proceeedings of 25th Convention, 1916*, p. 99.
127 *Ibid.*, pp. 516–7; Bert Castle Interview, WVU, Oral History Collection; Corbin, Keeney, '"Frank Keeney is our Leader and we shall not be moved"', p. 145.
128 Mooney, *Struggle in the Coal Fields*, pp. 51–3; Fox, 'Thomas T. Haggerty and the Formative Years of the UMWA', pp. 349–51.
129 *UMWJ*, 15 Nov 1917, p. 15.
130 Fox, 'Thomas T. Haggerty and the Formative Years of the UMWA', pp. 354–5.
131 R. L. Lewis, 'The Black Presence on the Paint-Cabin Creek Strike, 1912–13', *West Virginia History*, 46 (1985–6), pp. 59–71; Lewis, *Black Coal Miners in America*, pp. 139–42.
132 Lewis, 'The Black Presence on the Paint-Cabin Creek Strike', p. 66, p. 71.
133 Corbin, *Life, Work and Rebellion in the Coal Fields: The Southern West Virginia Miners, 1880–1922* (Urbana, University of Illinois Press, 1982), p. 92; C. G. Bindocci, 'A Comparison of the Roles of Women in Anthracite and Bituminous Mining in Pennsylvania, 1900–1920', in K. Tenfelde (ed.), *Towards a Social History of Mining in the 19th and 20th Centuries* (Munich, Verlag C. H. Beck, 1992), pp. 686–7; P. Long, *Where the Sun Never Shines: A History of America's Bloody Coal Industry* (New York, Paragon House, 1991 edn.), pp. 279–80; 284–5; 291–6.
134 Corbin, *Life, Work and Rebellion in the Coalfields*, p. 92. John Sayles' film 'Matewan' (Cinecom Int./MGM, 1987), dealing with the later mine wars, although technically 'fictional', provides a good insight into the role of women in the tent colonies.
135 Lunt, *Law and Order vs. The Miners*, pp. 69–70.
136 *Ibid.*, p. 70; Williams, *West Virginia*, p. 143.

137 Lee, *Bloodletting in Appalachia*, p. 87.
138 *Report and Digest of Evidence Taken by the Commission Appointed by The Governor of West Virginia in Connection with the Logan County Situation, 1919* (Charleston, 1920), pp. 9–10.
139 Walker Report, pp. 6–7, Daily Reports of Field Investigators, Mar-Aug 1923, Suitland, Washington National Records Center (WNRC), Records of US Coal Commission (RG 68), Division of Investigation of Labor Facts, Labour Relations Section, 161, Box 70.
140 National Endowment for the Humanities (NEH), *On Dark and Bloody Ground: An Oral History of the UMWA in Central Appalachia, 1920–35* (Charleston, 1973), p. 19.
141 *Report . . . in Connection with the Logan County Situation, 1919*, p. 65.
142 Walker Report, pp. 6–7, US Coal Commission, 161, Box 70.
143 Lee, *Bloodletting in Appalachia*, p. 90.
144 NEH, *On Dark and Bloody Ground*, p. 73.
145 L. K. Savage, *Thunder in the Mountains: The West Virginia Mine War, 1920–1921* (Charleston, Jalamap Publications, 1984), pp. 123–4.
146 *West Virginia Federationist*, 28 Aug 1919, p. 1.
147 *Ibid.*, p. 4.
148 D. P. Jordan, 'The Mingo War: Labor Violence in the Southern West Virginia Coal Fields, 1919–22', in Fink and Reed, *Essays in Southern Labor History*, p. 106; Mooney, *Struggle in the Coal Fields*, p. 65; J. L. Spivak, *A Man and His Time* (New York, Horizon Press, 1967), p. 67. For Cornwell's recollection of the march see his autobiography *A Mountain Trail* (Philadelphia, Dorrance and Co., 1939), pp. 57–9. It differs very little from the other accounts in terms of facts.
149 Spivak, *A Man and His Time*, pp. 67–8.
150 Jordan, 'The Mingo War', pp. 106–7.
151 Mooney, *Struggle in the Coal Fields*, p. 66.
152 Jordan, 'The Mingo War', p. 107.
153 Keeney to Cornwell, 6 Nov 1919; A. Bays to Cornwell, 1 Feb 1920, WVU, John J. Cornwell Papers (A+M 952), Series 35, Box 138.
154 Cornwell to John L. Lewis, 11 Sep 1919, *ibid.*
155 Lewis to Cornwell, 11 Sep 1919, *ibid.*
156 *West Virginia Federationist*, 16 Oct 1919, p. 1; Keeney to Cornwell, 19 Oct 1919, Cornwell Papers, 35, Box 138.
157 Cornwell to Lewis, 24 Oct 1919, *ibid.*
158 *Ibid.*
159 M. Dubofsky and W. Van Tine, *John L. Lewis: A Biography* (New York, Quadrangle/New York Times Book Co., 1977), pp. 52–6; Lunt, *Law and Order vs. The Miners*, pp. 80–1.
160 Cornwell to Keeney, 26 Oct 1919, Cornwell Papers, 35, Box 138.

161 Keeney to Cornwell, 27 Oct 1919, *ibid.*, Box 136.

162 Keeney to Cornwell, 3 Nov 1919, *ibid.*, Box 138.

163 Keeney to Cornwell, 7 Nov 1919; Cornwell to Keeney, 8 Nov 1919, *ibid.*

164 E. H. Arnold to Cornwell, 25 Oct 1919, *ibid.*, Box 137.

165 Cornwell to Donahue, 29 Oct 1919, *ibid.*

166 Donahue to Cornwell, 30 Oct 1919, *ibid.*

167 Cornwell to Donahue, 1 Nov 1919, *ibid.*

168 Motion sent with letter from D. C. Kennedy, Secretary, K.C.O.A. to Cornwell, 4 Nov 1919, *ibid.*, Box 136.

169 Cornwell to Kennedy, 5 Nov 1919, *ibid.*

170 Madert to Cornwell, 22 Feb 1919, *ibid.*

171 Cornwell to Madert, 24 Feb 1919, *ibid.*

172 Cornwell to Col. J. H. Charnock, 19 May 1919, *ibid.*

173 The Red Flag is actually in the record collection. Cornwell to W. W. Ingram, Ingram to Cornwell, 15 Oct 1919, *ibid.*, Box 138.

174 *Journal of the House of Delegates of the State of West Virginia for the 34th Regular Session, Commencing January 14 1919, and the Extraordinary Session, Commencing March 11 1919* (Charleston, 1919), p. 52.

175 *West Virginia Federationist*, 20 Feb 1919, p. 1.

176 US Attorney Walker to Cornwell, 14 Nov 1919, Cornwell Papers, 35, Box 137.

177 Cornwell to Walker, 14 Nov 1919, *ibid.*

178 Walker to Att. General, 17 Nov 1919, NA, Department of Justice (RG60), File 16–130–83, Part 1.

179 Kennedy to Cornwell, 7 Nov 1919, Cornwell Papers, 35, Box 137.

180 Report on Coal Fields of West Virginia to Director of Military Intelligence, from Col. W. F. Harrell, 16th Infantry, 13 Nov 1919, copy in *ibid.*, Box 138.

181 Report to Cornwell, 17 Nov 1917, *ibid.*, Box 136.

182 P. A. Jacob to Cornwell, 26 Dec 1919, *ibid.*, Box 135.

183 Cornwell to Jacob, 31 Dec 1919, *ibid.*, Box 135.

184 The Commission eventually approved a wage increase of 27% for the majority of union miners. Lunt, *Law and Order vs. The Miners*, pp. 86–90; Dubofsky and Van Tine, *John L. Lewis*, pp. 56–63.

185 Lee, *Bloodletting in Appalachia*, pp. 78–81; Lunt, *Law and Order vs. The Miners*, pp. 15–16, 91–95; W. D. Lane, *Civil War in West Virginia: A Study of Industrial Conflict in the Coal Mines* (New York, B. W. Huebsch 1921), p. 65.

186 'Memorandum on West Virginia Mining Troubles', 6 Sep 1921, by H. Davis, Commissioner of Conciliation, WNRC, Records of Federal Mediation and Conciliation Service (FMCS) (RG280), File 170/1185B.

187 *West Virginia Coal Fields Hearings*, 1, pp. 5–6, 104.

188 Lewis, *Black Coal Miners in America*, p. 157.

189 *Ibid.*, p. 158; *West Virginia Coal Fields Hearings*, 1, pp. 104, 15–16; .

190 *Ibid.*, pp. 5–6.

191 *West Virginia Coal Fields Hearings*, 1, p. 206.

192 With small variations, this is the sequence of events described by Hatfield, *ibid.*, pp. 207–17; Sheriff Blankenship of Mingo County, *Charleston Gazette*, 20 May 1920, p. 1; observing miners, *ibid.*, 21 May 1920; Mooney, *Struggle in the Coal Fields*, pp. 72–7; Lane *Civil War in West Virginia*, p. 48; Lunt, *Law and Order vs. The Miners*, pp. 98–9. A different view was presented by a Felts' informer, Anse Hatfield, *Charleston Gazette*, 20 May 1920; one of the agents, *ibid.*, 21 May 1920, p. 1, and Lee in *Bloodletting in Appalachia*, pp. 52–6, who suggest the miners began the shooting. See also John Sayles' film 'Matewan', for an excellent semi-fictionalised version of these events.

193 Lane, *Civil War in West Virginia*, pp. 74–9; *West Virginia Coal Fields Hearings*, 1, pp. 212–15.

194 *Ibid.*, 22 May 1920, p. 1.

195 *Ibid.*, 21 May 1920, p. 7.

196 *Ibid.*, 29 May 1920, p. 1.

197 *West Virginia Coal Fields Hearings*, 1, pp. 216–17; Lee, *Bloodletting in Appalachia*, p. 57.

198 Quoted in Jordan, 'The Mingo War', p. 108.

199 *West Virginia Coal Fields Hearings*, 1, p. 218.

200 *Ibid.*, p. 216.

201 Report of Commissioners of Conciliation, F. L. Feik and L. R. Thomas, 6 Jul 1920, FMCS, File 170/1185, Part Two.

202 *West Virginia Coal Fields Hearings*, 1, p. 104.

203 J. Purcell and L. R. Thomas, Commissioners of Conciliation, to H.L. Kerwin, Director of Conciliation, 25 Jul 1920, FMCS, File 170/1185, Part Two.

204 *West Virginia Coal Fields Hearings*, 1, p. 104.

205 *Ibid.*, p. 158

206 Report of Commissioners of Conciliation, F. L. Feik and L. R. Thomas, 6 Jul 1920, FMCS, File 170/1185, Part Two.

207 Purcell and Thomas to Kerwin, 25 Jul 1920, *ibid.*

208 Sworn statement to J. Purcell, Commissioner of Conciliation, 24 Aug 1920, *ibid.*, File 170/1185, Part One; *West Virginia Coal Fields Hearings*, 1, pp. 26–38.

209 Lunt, *Law and Order vs. The Miners*, pp. 102–5.

210 Mooney to Cornwell, 19 Jul 1920; Cornwell to Mooney, 19 Jul 1920; Mooney to Cornwell, 20 Jul 1920; Local 1931 to Cornwell, 29 Jul 1920, Cornwell Papers, 35, Box 140.

211 Mooney to Cornwell, 19 Jul 1920, *ibid.*
212 Lt. Col. G. Johnston to War Dept. Chief of Staff, 28 Aug 1920, NA, Records of War Department General Staff (RG165), Military Intelligence Division Correspondence, 1917–41 (MID), Entry 65, File 10634–793, Box 3649, Folder 1.
213 Johnston to Director of MID, 30 Aug 1920, *ibid.*
214 Copy of letter sent to Cornwell by 'No.19' in Washington D.C., 4 Oct 1920, Cornwell Papers, 35, Box 138.
215 Report of Lt. Col. W. A. Austin to Director MID, 22 Sep 1920, MID, File 10634–793, Box 3649, Folder 1.
216 Burkhardt to Cornwell, 13 Aug 1920; 1 Sep 1920, Cornwell Papers, 35, Box 139.
217 Letter from District 17 Officers to Sec. of War, 4 Sep 1920, sent by 'No.19', Washington D.C. to Cornwell, 4 Oct 1920, *ibid.*, Box 138.
218 Keeney to Cornwell, 25 Sep 1920, *ibid.*, Box 141.
219 G. J. Patterson, General Manager, Sycamore Coal Company to Cornwell, 23 Oct 1920, *ibid.*, Box 139.
220 Asst. Chief of Staff, HQ 5th Corp, Indiana to Director MID, 27 Oct 1920, MID, File 10634–793, Folder 2.
221 W. H. Cumming, General Superintendent, Red Jacket Consolidated Coal and Coke Company to Cornwell, 15 Nov 1920, Cornwell Papers, 35, Box 139.
222 Report of Lawlessness, No.2, 1–2 Nov, by Capt. J. R. Brockus, *ibid.*
223 Report of Lawlessness, No.7, 7–8 Nov, *ibid.*
224 Report of Lawlessness, No.8, 8–9 Nov, *ibid.*
225 Cummins to Cornwell, 15 Nov 1920, *ibid.*
226 Cornwell to Maj-Gen. Read, 24 Nov 1920, *ibid.*
227 Proclamation of Martial Law by Cornwell, 27 Nov 1920, *ibid.*
228 Report of Lawlessness, No.27, Nov 27–8, *ibid.*
229 Lunt, *Law and Order vs. The Miners*, p. 116.
230 Jordan, 'The Mingo War', p. 108.
231 *Ibid.*, p. 109.
232 *Wheeling Gazette*, 23 Mar 1921, p. 4.
233 R. P. Posten to Morgan, 11 Mar 1921, WVU, E. F. Morgan Papers (A+M 203), Box 3 File 4.
234 *Fairmont Times*, 11 Mar 1921, pp. 1, 4.
235 Posten to Morgan, 11 Mar 1921, Morgan Papers, Box 3, File 4.
236 Morgan to Posten, 14 Mar 1921, *ibid.*
237 Lee, *Bloodletting in Appalachia*, pp. 59–62.
238 *Ibid.*; Mooney, *Struggle in the Coal Fields*, p. 72.
239 *Ibid.*, pp. 76–7.
240 *Fairmont Times*, 22 Mar 1921, p. 1; *Wheeling Register*, 22 Mar 1921, p. 1.

241 Proclamation by Keeney and Mooney against the bill, 10 Sep 1920, Cornwell Papers, 35, Box 139; Large number of protests from various Local Unions, Morgan Papers, Box 4, Files 3 and 4.
242 See Morgan's justification of the act: Morgan to A. Hayes, Pres. L.U. 1891, 29 Mar 1921, *ibid.*, Box 4, File 3; and the *Wheeling Register*, 24 Mar 1921, p. 1, on succesful passage of the bill through both houses.
243 Corbin, *Life, Work and Rebellion in the Coal Fields*, pp. 216–217.
244 *Ibid.*, 217; Lee, *Bloodletting in Appalachia*, p. 65.
245 Jordan, 'The Mingo War', p. 109; Lunt, *Law and Order vs. The Miners*, p. 118.
246 *Ibid.*, Corbin, *Life, Work and Rebellion in the Coal Fields*, p. 207.
247 Lewis, *Black Coal Miners in America*, pp. 159–60; Mooney, *Struggle in the Coal Fields*, pp. 77–8; *West Virginia Coal Fields Hearings*, 1, pp. 166–7; *Charleston Gazette*, 15 Jun 1921, p. 1; *Wheeling Register*, 14 Jun 1921, p. 1; 15 Jun 1921, p. 1.
248 *Wheeling Register*, 14 Jun 1921, p. 1; Mooney, *Struggle in the Coal Fields*, 1, p. 86; Lunt, *Law and Order vs. The Miners*, p. 119.
249 *Ibid.*, p. 219; Mooney, *Struggle in the Coal Fields*, p. 86.
250 The twelve included David Robb, financial agent of the UMWA, John Brown, who had been imprisoned during the Paint Creek strike, three other national organisers, and local strike leaders. Morgan press release, 9 Jul 1921, Morgan Papers, Box 8, File 1.
251 Morgan to Davis, 11 Jul 1921, *ibid.*, Box 8, File 2.
252 *Charleston Gazette*, 26 Jun 1921, p. 1.
253 Local 3302 to Morgan, 20 Jun 1921, Morgan Papers, Box 1, File 1.
254 Local 4083 to Morgan, 15 Jul 1921, *ibid.*, Box 8, File 2.
255 Various signatories to Keeney, 10 Jul 1921, *ibid.*, Box 8, File 1.
256 Local 4384 to Morgan, 14 Jul 1921; Local 1891 to Morgan, 14 Jul 1921; Local 4175 to Morgan, 16 Jul 1921, *ibid.*, Box 8, File 2.
257 *West Virginia Coal Fields Hearings*, 1, pp. 5–8.
258 Mooney, *Struggle in the Coal Fields*, pp. 87–8; *Bluefield Daily Telegraph*, 2 Aug 1921, p. 1.
259 *Ibid.*, Mooney, *Struggle in the Coal Fields*, p. 88.
260 Lee, *Bloodletting in Appalachia*, pp. 70–2.
261 Kanawha Central Labor Union to Morgan, 8 Aug 1921, Morgan Papers, Box 8, File 4.
262 Morgan to KCLU, 9 August 1921, *ibid.*
263 *Ibid.*, pp. 89–90.
264 Keeney to Morgan, 11 Jul 1921, Morgan Papers, Box 8, File 2.
265 Lunt, *Law and Order vs. The Miners*, pp. 123–4.
266 Jordan, 'The Mingo War', p. 110.

267 *Ibid*; Lunt, *Law and Order vs. The Miners*, p. 124.
268 Sheriff H. A. Walker, Prosecuting Attorney, F. C. Burdette, President of County Court, S. E Childress, and Judge H. K. Black to Morgan 23 Aug 1921, Morgan Papers, Box 9, File 2.
269 C. S. Paisley, Kelly's Creek Colliery Co. to Morgan, 25 Aug 1921; C.C. Dickinson, Dry Branch Coal Co. to Morgan, 26 Aug 1921, *ibid.*; *Bluefield Daily Telegraph*, 26 Aug 1921, p. 1.
270 Mooney, *Struggle in the Coal Fields*, p. 90.
271 *Bluefield Daily Telegraph*, 27 Aug 1921, p. 1.
272 Savage, *Thunder in the Mountains*, pp. 58–9.
273 Mooney, *Struggle in the Coal Fields*, p. 90.
274 *Ibid.*, pp. 90–1; Savage, *Thunder in the Mountains*, pp. 59–60.
275 Morgan to Congressmen W. Goodykoontz and L. S. Echols, 25 Aug 1921, Morgan Papers, Box 9, File 2.
276 Acting Sec. of War to Morgan, 25 Aug 1921, *ibid.*
277 Bandholtz to Keeney, 26 Aug 1921, *ibid.* This reiterated a telephone conversation which had taken place that morning.
278 Mooney, *Struggle in the Coal Fields*, pp. 91–4, *Bluefield Daily Telegraph*, 27 Aug 1921, p. 1.
279 Morgan to Senator Sutherland, 27 Aug 1921, Morgan Papers, Box 9, File 2; Morgan to Pres. Harding and Sec. of War, J. W. Weeks, 29 Aug 1921, *ibid.*, Box 9, File 3.
280 *Ibid.*; Interview with Bert Castle, WVU, Oral History Collection; Lunt, *Law and Order vs. The Miners*, pp. 129–30.
281 Quoted in *Wheeling Register*, 3 Sep 1921, p. 1.
282 Lewis, *Black Coal Miners in America*, p. 162.
283 Morgan to Harding and Weeks, 29 Aug 1921; Morgan to Bandholtz, 29 Aug 1921, Morgan Papers, Box 9, File 3.
284 Senator Sutherland to Morgan, 30 Aug 1921, *ibid.*
285 Copy of proclamation in, Department of Justice, File 16–130–83, Folder 3; Weeks to Morgan, 31 Aug 1921, Morgan Papers, Box 9, File 3.
286 Lunt, *Law and Order vs. The Miners*, pp. 134–5.
287 *Bluefield Daily Telegraph*, 2 Sep 1921, p. 1.
288 *Wheeling Register*, 2 Sep 1921, p. 1; *Charleston Gazette*, 2 Sep 1921, p. 1.
289 *Wheeling Register*, 3 Sep 1921, p. 1.
290 *Ibid.*, 4 Sep 1921, p. 1; 5 Sep 1921, p. 1; 6 Sep 1921, p. 1.
291 NEH, *On Dark and Bloody Ground*, p. 22, p. 35.
292 Maj. B. H. L Williams to Gen. Harbord, 3 Sep 1921; Harris to Commanding Gen. 5th Corp, 6 Sep 1921; Bandholtz to Adj-Gen., 8 Sep 1921, MID, File 10634–793, Box 3649, Folder 4.
293 S. T. Early to War Dept, 3 Sep 1921, *ibid.*

294 Transcription of telephone call between Bandholtz and Maj. Williams, 4 Sep 1921, *ibid.*

295 Johnson to Adj-Gen., 5 Sep 1921, *ibid.*; Williams, *West Virginia*, p. 147; Lunt, *Law and Order vs. The Miners*, pp. 139–40.

296 Lewis, *Black Coal Miners in America*, p. 162; Jordan, 'The Mingo War', p. 112.

297 Corbin, *Life, Work and Rebellion in the Coal Fields*, pp. 218–220; Lee, *Bloodletting in Appalachia*, pp. 94–103.

298 Quoted in Lunt, *Law and Order vs. The Miners*, p. 137.

299 NEH, *On Dark and Bloody Ground*, p. 34; Lee also believed Blizzard was one of the leaders, *Bloodletting in Appalachia*, pp. 98–9.

300 NEH, *On Dark and Bloody Ground*, p. 22.

301 Mooney, *Struggle in the Coal Fields*, pp. 98–9.

302 Savage, *Thunder in the Mountains*, p. 121.

303 Quoted in Lewis, *Black Coal Miners in America*, p. 163. See pp. 157–164 for the role of black workers in the mine wars. See also Trotter, *Coal, Class and Color*, pp. 111–17.

304 Lunt, *Law and Order vs. The Miners*, p. 138.

305 *Wheeling Register*, 3 Sep 1921, p. 1.

306 Williams, *West Virginia*, p. 147.

307 Lunt, *Law and Order vs. The Miners*, p. 159.

308 Lee, *Bloodletting in Appalachia*, pp. 109–15, Jordan, 'The Mingo War', p. 112.

309 See the large amount of correspondence on the issue, FCMS, File 170/1185. For example, see letter from Local 1952 at Blooming Rose, 18 Jan 1922, who had conducted their own investigation and discovered widespread destitution, 'disputing Governor Morgan's said statements to the highest extent.', 170/1185 A; For Morgan's view, see letter to J. J. Davis, Sec. of Labor, 20 Jan 1922, and enclosure, 170/1185 Box.

310 Boal, 'Estimates of Unionism in West Virginia Coal', p. 439.

311 Lee, *Bloodletting in Appalachia*, pp. 143–161; Williams, *West Virginia*, p. 148. For details of strike situation and incidents at Farmington and Grant Town, see H. B. Dynes, Commissioner of Conciliation to H. L. Kerwin, Director of Conciliation, 20 Jan 1925, FMCS, File 170/2535; See Van Bittner on why 1924 agreement was abrogated, (n.d.), WVU, C. E. Smith Papers (A+M 1606), Box 34, File 1.

4

Power in a Union: industrial conflict in the south Wales coalfield, 1900–22

As we have seen, the pattern and form of industrial conflict in West Virginia was decisively influenced by the nature of culture and community in the region. In particular, the formidable displays of mass activity were shaped by the dominance of the operators and the consequent inability to use more traditional methods of labour protest. The different culture, types of community and power relationships in south Wales produced a corresponding variation in the pattern of industrial conflict. As was stated earlier, the communities in south Wales were larger, more homogeneous, less mobile, and less geographically isolated. Furthermore, the different power and social relationships, compared with West Virginia, allowed the miners a greater freedom of voluntary association, and the ability to build their own independent structures within civil society.

The south Wales miners, therefore, were never forced to mount huge armed marches just to establish basic civil rights, particularly that of joining the union. The SWMF was already established by 1900, and conflict took the form of constant strike activity resting on mass solidarity, not periods of quiet punctuated by explosions of unrest. Furthermore, while violence was occasionally present during bitter disputes, it never approached anywhere near the levels experienced in West Virginia.

Although south Wales would later become famous as the most militant coalfield in Britain, the region's miners were in fact slow to organise, only joining the MFGB in 1899, a year after the formation of the SWMF. The explanation for this is not without an echo of the situation in West Virginia, as geography, geology and employer hostility all played a role. The issue of the sliding scale wages system, however, presented as large a barrier as any.[1]

Following the collapse of Thomas Halliday's Amalgamated

Association of Miners in the 1870s, the sliding scale system was adopted, under which wages were related to changes in the selling price of coal. A five person joint committee made up of miners and owners operated the scale, with miners' agents paid by the companies from a levy on wages. Under such circumstances, 'Genuine trade unionism was impossible . . . and . . . the further growth of trade union organisation was delayed for another quarter of a century.'[2] The sliding scale was supported by the most prominent South Wales union leader, William Abraham or 'Mabon', who also became MP for Rhondda in 1885. However the sliding scale was opposed by others, including William Brace, who led the small Monmouthshire and South Wales Miners' District Association. An intense bitterness developed between the two, with Mabon accusing Brace of being an English tool of the MFGB, and suing him for slander. Brace refused to pay the fine, using the case to drum up opposition to Mabon.[3]

The formation of the MFGB in 1889, which vigorously opposed the sliding scale, had done much to increase the divisions within the coalfield. This was further underlined by the 1893 Hauliers' strike which saw police and soldiers drafted into the coalfield. Mabon and nine other miners' agents, including the influential Thomas Richards, also signed a manifesto telling the men to return to work. In contrast, Brace and one other agent were the only officials to support the strike, which was duly defeated.[4] In the aftermath, agitation against the sliding scale continued with the formation of the Amalgamated Society of Colliery Workmen in 1894. However, this was unsuccessful, and it was not until 1898 that the south Wales miners finally served notice on the agreement. Following an unsuccessful five month strike, during which nearly twelve million working days were lost, the SWMF was established, bringing all the region's miners under one union. Mabon became President, with the reconciled Brace as Vice President and Richards as Secretary.[5]

Although the sliding scale system was to remain in place until the establishment of a Conciliation Board in 1903, the SWMF made rapid strides in organisation and entered the new century with over 127,000 members in its twenty districts, out of a total of over 147,000 employed in the region's coal mines.[6] This meant that over 86% of south Wales miners were within the SWMF at the start of the period under consideration – a figure never approached in West Virginia until the mid 1930s. Although with the rapid expansion in employment the proportion of union members fell in the years that followed, membership rarely dropped below 60%, as in 1911–12 and 1921–22, both of which were years which saw major strike defeats. Indeed, the low point of 36% in 1922 was still generally higher than all but the highest levels of organisation in West Virginia; and even then SWMF membership recovered to over 58% the following year.[7]

From the position of a late starter, therefore, the SWMF was cata-pulted to the forefront of the MFGB, making up around 20% of the total membership of the national union.[8] The significance of the coalfield in terms of numbers, however, was surpassed by the remarkably high level of strike activity. Nationally coal miners were more strike-prone than any other section of the working-class throughout the period under discussion, as well as prior to and after it.[9] Between 1901 and 1913, for example, where the best evidence is available, the British mining industry lost four working days per employee per year, compared with 2.1 in textiles, which was the next highest. For the period 1908–13, the rate was even higher at 6.5, although textiles also rose to 3.5.[10]

When the regional make-up of these figures is examined, the true dimension of conflict in south Wales is revealed. Between 1898 and 1913, south Wales saw more working days lost than any other region in every year except 1899 and 1910. Overall, for the slightly longer period of 1894–1913, 33,368 working days were lost through strikes, amounting to 35% of the national total.[11] The sig-nificance of this is revealed by the fact that south Wales employed only 20% of the national labour force. The only other coalfield to have a higher percentage of days lost relative to numbers employed was Scotland with 15% and 13% respectively. The only coalfield of similar size to south Wales was the North-east, where 20% were employed and 19% of working days were lost.[12]

The disparity in strike activity between different mining regions on a national scale was also repeated within the different local regions. Thus Hopkin in his research on south Wales strikes between 1891 and 1913, has suggested that the miners of mid-Glamorgan experienced a far greater increase in the number of strikes and strike participants than those in Monmouthshire.[13]

The pre-eminence of the south Wales miners in terms of strike sta-tistics was obviously of great significance. However, as we saw in the discussion of industrial protest in West Virginia, strike statistics alone convey only part of the total picture. Of equal importance is the intensity of strikes, the motivations of those involved, and the general climate of industrial relations. In the case of south Wales, within the British context, the level of strike activity if anything underplays the degree of industrial militancy and the general climate of conflict between owner and miner.

After the formation of the SWMF, disputes began to congregate around certain specific issues. Between 1899 and 1903, before the introduction of the first Conciliation Board, the MSWCA reported payments from the indemnity fund for twenty-six strikes over non-unionism – more than any other single issue.[14] Nor did this issue, which struck at the heart of the SWMF influence in the coalfield, become any less prominent after 1903.[15] In 1906, for example, the Cambrian lodge resolved to 'tender a month's notice as a protest against non-unionists' after the mine management had failed to deal with the issue.[16] Although a strike was eventually averted, the importance of the issue was shown by the decision of the lodge to 'adhere to our former resolution to indemnify the Company for any loss incurred by them for actions taken by non-unionists against them.'[17]

Alongside the strikes over non-unionism between 1899 and 1903, the MSWCA also reported disputes over various other matters including prices for new seams, cutting prices, allowances and extra payments, as well as sympathy strikes with other strike bound collieries.[18] Underlying all such disputes, particularly as the period progressed, was the worsening economic performance of the ageing and geologically faulted coalfield in the face of stiffening world competition. This saw pressures being placed on wage costs, and the even more vulnerable customary rights.

If the economics of the south Wales coalfield provided the spark for tensions between owner and miner, however, this was more than complemented by what Supple has described as the particular 'obduracy' of the region's coal owners,[19] which went above and beyond the stimulus of economic problems. As one historian has suggested, 'even for those who do not attribute everything to the wickedness of the coal owners . . . the intensity of the pressure exerted by the owners on wage levels is still surprising.'[20] This is particularly true for the period before 1914, as the extent of the economic problems facing the coalfield were still somewhat masked by the increasing general demand for coal on the world market.[21] They may not have mounted machine guns amongst the terraced housing of the south Wales mining towns, or employed armed guards to shoot the union out of the coalfield but, within the very different context, the south Wales owners were every bit as single-minded in pursuit of their desired economic ends as their West Virginia counterparts.

Symbolic of future relations within the coalfield was the owners' abolition of 'Mabon's day' after the 1898 strike. This had been a day's holiday, named after Abraham, which had been taken on the first Monday of each month since 1888. Its ending, K. O. Morgan has suggested, was 'not only an error of monumental if character- istic stupidity by the coalowners', but 'marked the end of an era in the coalfield . . . class harmony . . . would be rapidly eroded by new imperatives of class struggle and industrial conflict', and 'Mabon's world would come crashing down.'[22]

The assault on customary rights and allowances was backed up by the vigorous use of the courts in an attempt to stifle the growth of the SWMF. One of the principal weapons was the Employers and Workmen Act of 1875, which the coal owners used to prosecute strikers for breach of contract.[23] This legislation, which replaced the Master and Servant Act of 1823, was intended to place the employer and employee on an equal footing although, in reality, the employee was still at a disadvantage. Generally, however, the Act did succeed in lessening the number of prosecutions for breach of contract after 1875. The exception to this pattern was the coal industry and, in particular, south Wales.[24]

The frequency of prosecutions under the 1875 Act accelerated in the early 1900s, as the owners attempted to thwart the SWMF and curtail the rising tide of strike activity. Evidence for this can be found in the records of the MSWCA, which show increasing reference to the issue. An example of this occurred at an Association meeting in October 1901. A strike had occurred at one of the member's col- lieries after a collier had been prosecuted for possession of a half match in the pit. The miners complained that the prosecution was unfair because the overman who had discovered the match had struck it, yet had not been prosecuted. Following a strike the company prosecuted the overman, but the miners insisted that he should be sacked. The overman consequently offered his resigna- tion.[25] The MSWCA response says as much about their general atti- tude as the specific point about the 1875 Act. They unanimously

171

agreed that 'the company are not to accept the overman's resignation and that the men be prosecuted for breach of contract.' They
had also asked their solicitor to investigate the possibility of suing
the SWMF, but he reported that there was insufficient evidence.[26]

A later meeting, in July 1902, illustrated the growing emphasis on
the use of the Act. After considering a number of strikes over non-
unionism, the owners' side of the sliding scale committee reported
that they:

> feel very strongly that some steps should be taken in regard to illegal
> stoppages on this question and the Owners' representatives would like
> to impress on the companies affected the importance of prosecuting
> some of the men, as in the particular collieries named the men are still
> out.[27]

If there were any remaining doubts over the wisdom of this policy,
the dissenters were pulled into line by 1903 when such prosecutions
became official MSWCA policy. Payments from the indemnity fund
became conditional upon the company prosecuting strikers who
'broke' their contracts and, following a successful move by the
Lewis Merthyr Company in November 1902, fines were to be
deducted directly from wages. The coming together of these two
aspects, which amounted to a 'decisive tightening of the
Association's procedures', saw the owners making 'the fullest possible use of the legal weapon provided by the 1875 Act'. Despite a
ruling by the House of Lords in 1906, which partially limited its
application, it remained a significant weapon.[28]

If the use of the 1875 Act became a central plank of the owners'
policies after 1900, other legal actions, or threats of, became similarly popular. For example, in October 1901, the MSWCA considered the advantages of recent legal decisions over trade union
liability – presumably the Taff Vale ruling.[29] One member reported
that there were 'stoppages which can be connected with the Miners
Federation and in the view of the decision given in the High Courts
as to the liability of Trades Unions there may be some chance of the
association obtaining a verdict.' They agreed to set up a committee
to discuss the subject.[30] These obviously proved fruitful as the
SWMF was prosecuted under the ruling in 1902, over a one day
strike undertaken in an attempt to regain the monthly 'Mabon's
Day'. The fine of £57,562 was larger than in the original Taff Vale
case.[31]

Impressive as the scale of the legal challenges were, they did not succeed in their aim. As J. Williams has pointed out in his discussion of the law of contract, although prosecutions may have had some deterrent effect, neither strikes nor the growth in SWMF membership were curtailed. Moreover the court decisions served to illustrate the role of the SWMF as 'general protector' of the miners, and the demonstrations which occurred at trials illustrated the division between owner and miners.[32]

The significance of this should not be lost in the comparison with the West Virginia coalfield. On the one hand the aggressiveness of the south Wales owners in pursuing legal action in the early 1900s may have increased the antagonism between owner and miner, just as the outrages of the West Virginia operators fostered a degree of unity among a disparate workforce. In this sense, the level of repression can be seen to have had the opposite effect to that intended. However, on the other hand, the end result illustrates perfectly the different contexts within which protest occurred. Despite being an extremely powerful organisation, with various successes from sympathetic law courts, the MSWCA failed to undermine the SWMF. In contrast, the West Virginia operators, through their control of political, legal and social structures, were able to 'up the tempo' of repression until the UMWA was continually fighting just to maintain its foothold within the State.

The divisions between miner and owner in the south Wales coalfield were becoming more distinct as the new century progressed. The disputes over wages and extra payments were brought into sharper focus by the introduction of the Eight Hours Act on 1 July 1909. The reduction in hours had long been favoured in south Wales, which worked longer hours than any other region, excepting Lancashire.[33] It was equally strongly opposed by the owners, who believed it would further reduce productivity and profits in the coalfield.[34] They made it clear that the reduction of hours would be carried through into the wage rates – when asked during the Parliamentary Inquiry whether wages would be reduced, E. M. Hann, General Manager of Powell Duffryn replied, 'I have no doubt we should try'.[35]

Evidence of this was soon forthcoming. The south Wales owners threatened to end the Conciliation Board Agreement and lock the miners out, to coincide with the implementation of the Act. They demanded a cut in the day men's wages, full utilisation of the sixty-hours clause provided by the Act – to be used in the form of permanent overtime, and a move towards double shifts.[36] The last two were particularly contentious issues, as the south Wales' miners had opposed the double shift system for a number of years.[37] Similarly the MFGB were refusing to recognise the sixty hours clause which, along with the failure to define the eight hours day from bank to bank, had seriously revised their original demands.[38]

An agreement was eventually achieved just before midnight on 30 June, but it did little to address the differences between the two sides, only adding a few clauses to the existing 1905 Agreement. In addition the miners withdrew their opposition to considering double shifts on any ground other than safety.[39] Before long, however, dissension arose over the effects of the Act. In December 1909, the south Wales owners won a significant court case in which they prosecuted a miner for refusing to work a nine hour day, which they claimed was allowed under the sixty hours clause. This decision opened the SWMF up to prosecution for every miner who had not worked one long shift a week since 1 July.[40]

The situation was further aggravated by the long running argument over payments for working in abnormal places for which, ever since 1905, the SWMF had been trying to get a guaranteed minimum wage.[41] A further blow had been struck by a 1908 court decision, Walters v. Ocean Coal Company, which had ruled that any allowances for working in abnormal places were discretionary and not a legal requirement.[42] By 1910, therefore, as the effects of the Eight Hours Act began to feed through, the abnormal places issue became even more controversial, as it placed further downward pressure on wages.

During the latter part of 1909, the miners formulated a programme to offset the fall in wages. Alongside a call for an increase in wages, they requested a minimum wage for abnormal places, payment for small coal, a bonus for night work and, for the first time, a general minimum wage.[43] However, when a new Conciliation Board Agreement was negotiated in April, the owners proved impervious to the miners' demands. The SWMF failed to get an agreement over the minimum wage, small coals or, crucially, abnormal places. Moreover, they agreed to the idea of some afternoon, night and even double shifts.[44] Although the coalfield as a whole voted to support the agreement, it was greeted with little enthusiasm. Several districts voted against, while the SWMF EC came under attack from the growing south Wales rank and file movement, who believed too much had been conceded.[45]

By 1910 the distance between the demands of owner and miner was so great that it became inevitable that the coalfield would experience serious industrial conflict. The Conciliation Agreements were clearly not working any better than the sliding scales – between 1903 and 1910 the boards failed to settle 231 out of the 391 disputes referred to them.[46] The assaults on wages and marginal rights had reached a peak following the introduction of the Eight Hours Act, and were backed up by certain key consolidations in the coalfield, most notably D. A. Thomas' Cambrian Combine, which greatly enhanced the owners' ability to enforce their demands. Moreover, a new generation of young union activists was emerging, reflecting political changes within the communities.

When the tensions finally exploded within the coalfield, they did so in the Rhondda which, more than any other area, experienced the convergence of all of the above factors. The resulting conflict was, in many ways, analogous with the Paint Creek strike in West Virginia, marking a similar watershed in the development of protest. Both were centred upon the most militant areas within the two regions, and both introduced a new period of industrial conflict. There were other similarities, and also key differences, which reveal a great deal about the patterns of protest in these two regions.

The Cambrian dispute began on 1 September 1910 at the Ely Pit, Pen-y-Graig, after a disagreement over the setting of a price list for the new Bute seam. The miners claimed an extra payment due to the large number of abnormal places caused by the amount of stone within the seam.[47] The management refused and proceeded to lock out not only the eighty men who worked on the seam, but all 800 at the pit. After an appeal for solidarity, miners employed at other Naval Colliery pits came out on strike, and the whole Cambrian Combine was only prevented from grinding to a halt by the intervention of Mabon.[48]

A coalfield conference was convened on 17 September which agreed that the Cambrian Combine men should give a month's notice from 1 October, and that a ballot of the whole SWMF should decide whether there would be a general coalfield strike, or just a financial levy to support the strikers. Significantly the latter course was chosen by 76,978 votes to 44,868 – a majority of 32,110.[49] Meanwhile negotiations began at the Conciliation Board which continued into October. On 22 October, following a meeting between various representatives of the miners and owners, including Mabon and D. A. Thomas, a new offer was put to the Combine men.[50] However, this was rejected by the Cambrian Combine Committee (made up of four members from each lodge within the Combine), following a mass meeting.[51] Despite subsequent pressures to reverse the decision, it remained unchanged,[52] revealing both the degree of anger among the men and the extent to which the SWMF leadership were losing control of the situation to more militant, local leaders.

A similar pattern was also emerging in the neighbouring Aberdare valley where a dispute had broken out at pits belonging to Powell Duffryn. This began in the middle of October when, in an already disputatious environment, the management at the Lower Duffryn pit, Mountain Ash, decided to end a forty year custom which allowed the men to take home waste wood. The manner of introduction was as provocative as the act itself. The company called in the police to enforce the new rule before they had even told all the employees. Thus the night shift came up to find the notices and police at the pithead.[53]

A strike ensued, which soon spread to other Powell Duffryn pits.[54] On 21 October a mass meeting drew up a list of grievances with eighteen points, the contents of which revealed a great deal about industrial relations in both Aberdare and the south Wales coalfield generally. At the top were complaints over timber and abnormal places, followed by numerous others relating to the harsh management of the collieries. These included the dismissal of old workmen, victimisation of lodge officials and other miners, violations of the Eight Hours Act, various complaints over price lists, and allegations about the use of 'filthy and abusive language by officials to workmen while following their employment'.[55]

These demands were rejected out of hand by General Manager, Hann,[56] and the situation took a further turn for the worse the following day when Aberdare miners' agent, Charles 'Butt' Stanton, reportedly told Hann over the phone that 'I would like to say that if there is going to be any blacklegging over this there is going to be murder.' Hann, and the press, leapt on this as a threat of murder and broke off negotiations pending its withdrawal.[57] However a mass meeting of strikers had refused to allow Stanton to apologise, or to enter negotiations without him as their representative.[58]

Stanton himself seemed to be enjoying the limelight that the strike had thrust upon him, and was far from cowed. He had become miners' agent at Aberdare in 1900, and had in recent years been a prominent exponent of reorganisation of the SWMF.[59] In 1910, following the discord created by the new Conciliation Agreement, he added to his significant following by consistently criticising the union's leadership; including the famous call to the 'old' leaders to either 'move on or move out'.[60]

Behind Stanton's populism, however, there was a degree of demagoguery. As one miner recalled, 'He was a boisterous man . . . he would threaten employers by beating them up you know, have a fight with them, physical fight and all this sort of thing and therefore he had his following.'[61] There was even a suggestion that he carried a gun.[62] Thus as he led the Aberdare miners in the Autumn of 1910 his talk of 'warfare', 'revolution' and 'rebellion'[63] were underpinned by traits which would, as we shall see later, see him approximating to a Welsh Mussolini.[64]

By the beginning of November the battle lines had been as clearly drawn in Aberdare as the Rhondda. Despite forceful appeals from the SWMF leadership, virtually all the valley's miners were out on strike; the only exception being 400 men employed at the Blaenant colliery.[65] Thus when added to the 12,000 men on strike from 1 November at the Cambrian Combine, and others at Maesteg, nearly 30,000 miners were out in the whole coalfield.[66]

The first serious violence in the Cambrian dispute broke out on 7 November. The miners had decided to prevent not only strike breakers, but colliery officials, and any others concerned with pit maintenance or safety, from entering the mines.[67] On the 7th they attempted to put this into action, organising a demonstration of 2,500, as well as ten squads of fifty pickets.[68] Officials at the Cambrian Colliery, Clydach Vale were brought out after the powerhouse was stoned, and mounted police had missiles thrown at them and were charged by marchers.[69] Women were prominent in the demonstration, with Tom Mann telling of how 'many women were in the procession – a number with infants', some of whom approached the safety men and 'talked to them in pretty emphatic Welsh.'[70] This was to be true of subsequent events with the *South Wales Daily News* going as far as to state that, 'a surprising feature of the whole disturbance was the part played in it by women, who . . . were the ringleaders in many of the assaults and exhorted the men to further violence.'[71]

This was apparent when the procession gathered later in the day outside the Glamorgan colliery at Llwynypia, the last remaining 'open' colliery. This had become the owners' headquarters and inside was the Combine manager, Leonard Llewellyn, a large number of officials, and ninety-nine policemen. When the strikers were prevented from talking to those at work in the pit, they responded by throwing stones at the powerhouse and tearing down fencing surrounding the colliery.[72] Women helped supply many of the missiles by collecting and storing stones in buckets and their aprons.[73] Later in the evening the situation became more serious when police reinforcements arrived from Clydach Vale. They launched a series of baton charges against the demonstrators, who repulsed the attacks and then dispersed. The latter regrouped in Pandy Square in Tonypandy where, at 1.00 a.m., they were again attacked by police. The fighting lasted for over an hour before the square was finally cleared.[74]

Following these incidents, the Chief Constable of Glamorgan, Captain Lionel Lindsay, telegraphed for military reinforcements.[75] When these failed to arrive the following morning, he appealed to the Home Office for troops, speaking of 'many casualties' after the 'Llwynypia Colliery was savagely attacked by a large crowd of strikers'.[76] Much to the later disapprobation of Lindsay and the coal owners,[77] however, the infantry were halted at Swindon. Seventy mounted and 200 Metropolitan police were sent immediately, along with a unit of 200 cavalry, although the latter were stopped at Cardiff, after Lindsay told the Home Office that they could not be accommodated. Home Secretary, Winston Churchill, disabused any notions that Lindsay may have had about the role of the troops, telling him the military would 'not be used until all other means have failed'.[78]

The Government's hesitation was, like their counterparts in the Federal Government when faced with conflict in West Virginia, mainly motivated by a concern not to get unnecessarily involved in local industrial disorders. Churchill was particularly concerned about the possible political repercussions from such an action, especially when past precedents were borne in mind. As Macready recalled, 'The use of troops under such conditions had not been fortunate in the past', as in the case of the Featherstone Riots, 'and the Government, especially in view of the approaching General Election, were anxious that untoward incidents should not occur.'[79]

Underpinning this unwillingness to become involved was, in both regions, the belief that the information being passed on by local agencies was not always to be relied upon. In the case of south Wales, the main source of such information was Lindsay who, before assuming the role of chief constable in 1891, had served with the occupying forces in Egypt. His imperial training was transferred wholesale to the south Wales valleys where, as one historian has suggested, 'at a time when County chief constables were notoriously militaristic and autocratic, Lindsay was in a class of his own.'[80]

Despite appeals by Churchill for calm,[81] the evening of 8 November saw further, and more violent incidents. Once again, several thousand strikers and their families marched to the Glamorgan colliery, where they again demonstrated outside. As with the day before, stones were thrown at the powerhouse, and the mounted and foot police repeatedly charged the demonstration. This led to further 'hand-to-hand conflict' lasting for about two hours. Then, at around 7.00 p.m., a large section of the demonstration flowed back into Tonypandy towards the railway station, having heard that the cavalry were due to arrive there. On the way several shops had their windows smashed and the contents looted, a practice which continued when the crowd discovered the rumour concerning the troops was false. With the police virtually absent, defending the Glamorgan colliery, the 'Tonypandy riot' went on until after 10.00 p.m.[82]

These scenes, however, were not evidence of senseless violence. The demonstration on 8 November, as on the previous night, was intended to stop safety work and it stuck to this aim. Despite claims to the contrary by the owners, at no time did the strikers attempt to occupy the colliery or institute large-scale destruction.[83] Evidence for this comes in a report by Macready to the Home Office, in which he wrote, 'in regard to the recent attacks on mines, I have formed the opinion that they were not as serious as reports would lead one to believe'. He told of how the fencing surrounding the Glamorgan colliery was pulled down, but the powerhouse was not attacked. 'That they did not do this', he wrote, 'is not due to the action of the police but to either the want of leading or disinclination to proceed to extremities on behalf of the mob.'[84]

Similarly the riot in Tonypandy itself was not a display of indiscriminate violence. At no time was there personal violence, arson or serious destruction of property. The violence that did occur was limited to the smashing of windows and looting.[85] This has been underlined by Dai Smith, who has suggested that the crowd acted 'with a measure of control', only attacking certain shops and avoiding others. Thus the first window to be broken was a drapers owned by a senior magistrate. However, a chemist's shop belonging to a locally born former international rugby player was left completely untouched – although every other chemist's was attacked.[86] Furthermore, an element of theatricality entered into the proceedings, with rioters parading in looted clothes, and controlling the riot with whistles. 'These were', Smith suggests, 'revolutionary acts', which were 'evidence of social fracture as much as of industrial dispute.'[87]

At the time, however, it was the idea of senseless violence rather than the revolutionary theatrics which came to characterise these events. This was enhanced by the fact that 8 November also saw serious disturbances in the Aberdare valley. Following a meeting at the Miners' Institute, around 2,000 strikers and their families marched on collieries at Aberaman and Cwmbach. Stoning of the powerhouses and washery occurred, and the police responded by using fire hoses, baton charges, and, at Cwmbach, the electrification of the colliery perimeter fence.[88]

The Home Office had by now effectively assumed control of the strike zone, with Macready in command on the ground. A further 500 Metropolitan police were immediately sent to the area, bringing the total police presence up to 1,100, of whom 120 were mounted. In addition, over 500 military were sent. Two companies of cavalry were stationed at Pontypridd, while infantry companies were quartered at Llwynypia, Aberaman, and Pontypridd, with a further two companies stationed in reserve at Newport.[89]

The sending of troops was initially resented by the local communities and union leaders. Macready reported that when the 18th Hussars held back a crowd at Porth on 9 November, the latter 'showed a rather hostile attitude'.[90] The following day Churchill likewise told Lindsay that 'the cavalry report that they have been badly received by the population in moving about the valley.'[91] The MFGB immediately attacked the deployment, telling Churchill that 'whilst regretting the disturbances which have occurred' they considered the 'civil forces sufficient to deal with such disturbances'.[92] 'Vehement protests' were also forthcoming in Parliament from a number of MPs, including Mabon and Keir Hardie.[93] As in the first troop deployments in the Mingo strike, the communities in the

Rhondda and Aberdare clearly felt themselves under unwarranted occupation.

On establishing themselves, however, the troops were far more impartial than their counterparts in the US. Macready may have shared the military obsession with the idea of left-wing manipulation of the population,[94] but he did attempt to act in, what he saw as, a neutral manner. Negotiations took place with representatives of the strike leaders, [95] and there was even a football match between strikers and soldiers.[96] Moreover, unlike his West Virginia counterpart, Macready was unwilling to accept the owners' propaganda. For example he later recalled how, on arriving in the Rhondda, he was 'inundated with information and advice as to what I should do, all tending towards one conclusion, viz., that the employers were entirely blameless for what was occurring, and that the men should be coerced into submission by force.'[97]

This first impression was reinforced in the following weeks during which 'the information from the managers was in practically every case so exaggerated as to be worthless.'[98] So much so in fact, that Macready stationed officers in various places within the strike zone to investigate the owners' allegations.[99] Using this information he was able to refute inflammatory press reports, such as one in *The Times* concerning a supposed attempt to blow up a manager's house. Similarly, after talking to strikers, he told the Home Office that other reports in the local papers concerning the purchase of revolvers and bomb-making material were false.[100]

The basis for this overbearing attitude was, in Macready's eyes, the extent to which the owners believed they could dominate both the military and police who were in the coalfield. In his final memorandum on the strike, Macready wrote:

> There seemed to be a general idea that the managers were at liberty to carry out any schemes they pleased, such as the importation of 'blacklegs', or fresh work on pits, in short any measure without consideration as to how it might influence the strikers, and that the military would then support such action. Also there was a distinct inclination to direct and opportion the movement of both police and military.[101]

It appears that the owners based this 'inclination' on their existing relationship with Lindsay, who never failed to provide local police when the owners' required them. This was again something which was criticised by Macready, who wrote:

> Another factor which has struck me is that the mine managing class is looked upon by the local police as having a kind of authority over them, and several instances have occurred where a manager has been consulted, and his opinion taken, where clearly the police officer should have acted on his own responsibility.

Significantly, Macready cited as a possible reason for this the fact that the owners themselves paid for extra police when they were required.[102]

While this does not approximate to the company's provision of deputies in West Virginia, the common strand should not be missed. With their different demands, within a more open society, the south Wales owners were nonetheless able to rely on local law enforcement agencies to help combat strikes.

The relative even-handedness of the military in the strike should also be placed in perspective. When the military were deployed it was clearly established that they should only be used as a last resort, if all other methods of crowd control failed. This allowed them to maintain an air of neutrality, which was not available to the police, who were more heavily involved. However, although Macready and the military may have been attempting to act in an even-handed manner, their actions did in fact seriously undermine the ability to conduct the strike. Under Macready's orders picketing was severely limited and strikers were prevented from intercepting strike breakers. Moreover, although the military refused to protect collieries that imported strike breakers on any terms, or start mines up again, they did allow pumping to continue where damage might result if it ceased. They also allowed safety men and engineers to enter the pits once they were deemed necessary by a Government engineer.[103] Thus one of the principal forms of placing pressure on the owners was removed, helping to tip the balance against the strikers.

Even the pretence of impartiality could not be applied to the practical application of the close relationship between Lindsay and the coal owners, nor to the behaviour of the hundreds of police who were sent to restore 'order' in the coalfield during the strike. In the consideration of the 'disorders' of 8 November, it was established that the crowd exhibited a degree of 'control' with only limited, discriminate violence occurring even at the height of the so-called 'riot'. The idea of control, and the discriminate use of force, is not something that was apparent in the activities of the police either then or thereafter.[104]

On both 7 and 8 November serious conflict was precipitated by the frequent baton charges made against the demonstrators. These actions caused numerous injuries and resulted in the death from a fractured skull of miner Samuel Rays.[105] Indeed the batons were used with such vigour that on 9 November 300 more were sent up to Llwynypia to replace those broken the previous day.[106] Similarly, on 8 November in Aberdare, as well as electrifying the perimeter fence, police charged demonstrators, and pushed a large number into a nearby canal, injuring sixty.[107]

The question of police tactics on these and later occasions were raised most forcibly in Parliament by Keir Hardie. Supported by Mabon, fellow Merthyr MP, Edgar Jones, and various others, he asked why 'the whole of the police' at the time of the riot 'were at the colliery guarding the owners' property' and not policing the streets of Tonypandy.[108] The central core of his criticism of police actions, however, concerned the indiscriminate use of violence. In a long-running battle with Churchill lasting into 1911, Hardie and others tried to obtain a Public Inquiry into police activities,[109] presenting a large amount of evidence to support their claims in the process. These included a statement by a Baptist minister which described how police 'under the influence of drink' attacked bystanders, smashed windows and stormed into houses, and even fired a shot into a grocer's shop. One woman was 'knocked down and kicked' by police after returning from a shopping trip, 'after which treatment she suffered from convulsive fits.'[110]

Corroborating evidence came from other sources. A shopkeeper told of police attacking bystanders, while a woman in Pen-y-Graig complained to Hardie that police burst into her house and viciously attacked two men. The force of the attack was such that one of the policemen's truncheons snapped in two, one half of which was still in the woman's possession.[111] The potential embarrassment about the police actions, however, prevented the Government from establishing an Inquiry. In contrast, the strikers were unable to ignore the police intimidation and they continued to voice their concerns over the latter's activities. Thus on 5 December, for example, the Cambrian Lodge set up a committee to 'enquire into the cases of outrages by police.'[112]

The actions of the police help to put the whole Tonypandy incident, and the question of violence in general, into perspective. As we have seen, even at the height of the Tonypandy riots, the behaviour of the strikers was more controlled than that of the police. If we consider further that, other than some less serious clashes on 21/22 November and sporadic other incidents, serious violence did not reoccur, it becomes clear that the association of violence with the twelve-month-long Cambrian dispute gives an entirely unbalanced impression.[113]

This conclusion also has an importance which stretches beyond the specifics of the Cambrian dispute. In a period of pronounced unrest, which would later see troops shoot two railway workers at Llanelli, and the race riots which were described in chapter two, the violence of November 1910 was the worst that the coalfield experienced.[114] Thus, as we shall see, the national minimum wage strike of 1912 passed peacefully in south Wales and thereafter, other than odd clashes with the police, violence was virtually non-existent – in spite of considerable harassment by the authorities. Indeed, the relative peace that followed November 1910 has led Geary to argue that the Cambrian dispute 'marks not the height of anarchy, as is sometimes suggested, but the beginning of a process of moderation'. He suggests this was linked to a national trend whereby the bonding of trade unions to the Labour Party increased the power and voice of the working-class, and helped eliminate the need for violence.[115] While elements of this argument may ring true, as we shall see later, linking the absence of violence with the rise of the Labour Party begs a number of questions – not least why the party did not break through until after the war. Moreover, if we accept that the incidents at Tonypandy have been exaggerated out of all proportion, this in itself removes the high level of violence which the 'moderation' would need to replace.

In fact the absence of violence can be located in the area of empowerment, but not solely through the link to a political party. The comparison with West Virginia illustrates this perfectly. The Paint Creek strike proved a turning point in terms of strike violence because the miners finally managed to organise mass resistance to the operators' abuses. Such was the structure of community and cultural life, and the hugely imbalanced power relations, that armed conflict became the only method for the powerless to defend themselves and challenge the powerful. In contrast the collective culture of south Wales, and the organisations and institutions within it, gave the south Wales miners greater power. Thus violence, which was not an integral part of this culture, was not required on the

184

same scale. This is one of the central differences between the patterns of industrial conflict in these two regions.

Large-scale violence may not have been a significant factor in the rest of the Cambrian dispute, but in common with the Paint Creek strike, tensions within union ranks became apparent during the closing stages of the conflict. The fracture between the established leadership and the more radical elements connected with the strike, came to the fore when an unofficial conference representing 62,000 miners met at the end of November. The talk of widening the strike to cover the whole coalfield, however, came to nothing, and by early January the Aberdare miners were back at work.[116]

Although the unofficial conference was short-lived, the militants' influence was increased by the election of four prominent Rhondda activists on to the SWMF EC. Three of these; Tom Smith, John Hopla and Noah Rees, were active within the Cambrian strike committee, and were elected after the deaths of the existing Rhondda representatives in a train crash in January. The fourth addition to the SWMF EC was Noah Ablett, check-weigher at Mardy, ex-Ruskin student, leading light within the Plebs League and ultimately the outstanding spokesperson for industrial unionism within the coalfield.[117] These four were directly involved in frustrating the ongoing attempts by both the MFGB and SWMF at finding a face-saving compromise to the Cambrian dispute. Indeed, their opposition was such that MFGB representative, Thomas Ashton, claimed that 'two or three representatives from the strike district were grossly insulting. They said the men had been jockeyed and sold', when the SWMF EC discussed a settlement proposed by the MFGB and SWMF leaderships in May 1911.[118]

They were also at the heart of the attempt to link the Cambrian dispute to a broader struggle for a minimum wage for all miners. Although this idea originated with the strikers, it gradually won favour in the wider coalfield, and was official SWMF policy by the time it was taken to an MFGB conference in June 1911. Although the conference rejected the policy, the south Wales miners reaffirmed their support for the minimum wage at their July conference, and selected Noah Ablett and Edward Gill to write a manifesto explaining the south Wales position on the issue. Between thirty and forty strikers from the Rhondda were also elected as 'missionaries' to take the campaign out to the rank and file within other coalfields.[119]

While the efforts on the minimum wage would eventually bear fruit, the Cambrian dispute soon drifted towards what was, from the strikers' point of view, a very unsatisfactory end. The MFGB EC, angered by their reception within parts of the strike zone, had withdrawn its financial support for the dispute following their June conference. This underlined the strikers' isolation, as well as the hardships resulting from nearly twelve months on strike. Consequently, after negotiating with the strike committee, the SWMF EC agreed to order a return to work for 1 September 1911 – As Noah Rees saw it, it was time for the men to 'eat the leek'. The miners thus returned to work with a settlement which gave them 2s 1.3d per ton for the Bute seam, and no guarantees over wages.[120]

The Cambrian dispute, much like 1898 and several subsequent large scale strikes in the coalfield, ended in defeat. Indeed, despite the greater strength of the SWMF relative to the UMWA, the Cambrian strikers managed to secure far less from the owners than the West Virginia miners did in the Paint Creek strike. Although victory in any form would hardly be a common outcome in future West Virginia conflicts, the different results illustrate the fact that the south Wales owners were able to overcome vigorous challenges to their authority.

However, although the Cambrian strikers may have been defeated on their specific demands, as in 1898, the long-term impact of the strike would far outweigh this short-term set back. If 1898 had prepared the way for the SWMF, then 1910–11 clearly established the different approaches to policy. This was most clearly shown by the creation of the URC, which first became public in March 1911, as the dissatisfaction with the SWMF leadership reached its height. Building on the interest shown in the November 1910 unofficial conferences, the URC became the main force agitating for reform of the SWMF structure, linking the abnormal places issue with that of a national minimum wage. The URC initially had a wide political membership, ranging from ILP members of the SWMF EC like Barker, Winstone and Hartshorn, to the proponents of syndicalism like Ablett, Will Mainwaring and Will Hay. The moderate ILP members, however, did not take part in the committee after May 1911, when its emphasis became increasingly one of reorganisation along industrial unionist lines.[121]

Probably the most important contribution of the URC was the publication, in 1912, of *The Miners' Next Step*, which eventually sold over 5,000 copies and played an important part in spreading the south Wales gospel of a national minimum wage, as well as encouraging support for its syndicalist conclusions.[122]

Significant as this minority were within the SWMF, it is important that their influence is not overstated. In elections within the union, it is clear that there was some general dissatisfaction with the existing leadership. Hence, in the autumn 1911, a ballot to elect the coalfield's representatives on the MFGB, rejected the sitting members, Richards, Brace and Onions (SWMF Secretary, Vice President and Treasurer, respectively). However the dissatisfaction clearly had its limits, as the replacements were the moderate ILP supporters Hartshorn and Barker, along with the unpredictable Stanton.[123]

A similar pattern was revealed in 1912 when the industrial unionist wing pushed for reorganisation of the SWMF. After consideration by a committee of twelve, a scheme was presented to the membership for ballot in September. The result was a 10,340 majority for abolition of the existing districts, and the transfer of power to the EC and three-monthly coalfield conferences. However, the significance of this result was undermined by the abstention of 13,000 miners in the anthracite field, and considerable resentment from some of the district agents who would be affected by the changes. When a SWMF conference eventually considered the scheme, the different districts proved reluctant to give up their separate committees, officers, funds and, above all, autonomy. When a second ballot was conducted, therefore, the coalfield rejected re-organisation by 45,508 to 24,106.[124]

The summer of 1912 also saw the resignation of Mabon on grounds of ill health. His replacement, however, was not one of the younger activists but Brace, who defeated Barker in the poll.[125] Brace also regained his place on the executive of the MFGB in the same year, topping the poll, followed by Hartshorn and Barker.[126] The end of Mabonism, therefore, ushered in a new era, but one that showed continuity as well as change.

If the influence of the new activists was more muted outside the Rhondda, the same can not be said for the central demand which arose from the Cambrian dispute; namely the national minimum wage. With the SWMF now united on the policy, attention was again turned on the MFGB who, at the October 1911 conference, agreed to look into the matter. Later that month, at a meeting chaired by Noah Rees, the Cambrian Lodge were clearly pleased by this as they 'resolved that this meeting of the Cambrian Lodge express our satisfaction at the Resolution upon the minimum wage passed at the recent MFGB conference and further hope that all the other districts will spare no efforts to bring this to a successful issue.'[127]

The enthusiasm of the south Wales miners, however, had still to take root within other coalfields. Other regions dragged their feet over the issue and when the demands were finally formulated, south Wales was forced to accept reductions in the wage levels it demanded, and the exclusion of surfacemen from the proposal. These demands were backed by a national ballot in January 1912 which supported strike action by 445,801 to 115,921. The largest vote in favour came from south Wales, where miners voted 103,526 to 8,419 in support of a strike.[128]

Negotiations opened with the owners, under the threat of the first ever national miners' strike. February also saw the intervention of the Government, with a meeting between Prime Minister Asquith and MFGB leaders. Asquith agreed that there 'were cases where a reasonable wage could not be secured', and that some form of district agreement was needed to remedy this. This proved too vague for the miners, while the south Wales owners, along with those of Northumberland, refused to even consider the proposals. The strike thus began at the start of March.[129]

By the end of March, desperate to end the dispute, the Government introduced a Minimum Wage Bill which accepted the idea of a minimum wage, but did not state a wage level, and only provided for negotiation at District Boards. The MFGB balloted its members over continuing the strike, and they voted 244,103 to 201,103 in favour of doing so. The MFGB EC, however, citing the rule that demanded a two-thirds majority for strike action, declared that the strike should be terminated. One of the reasons they were able to do this was that south Wales, which had led the way in the campaign, had voted in large numbers in favour of a return to work – 65,538 to 31,127. Historians have generally agreed that this can be explained by strike weariness, and the depletion of funds, stretching back to the Cambrian dispute.[130]

Although when the act came into operation, the results were disappointing, doing little to increase wages, the strike was nonetheless an important achievement. Church has suggested that the campaign and strike showed that the miners could 'mount and sustain a lengthy national strike', and 'threaten the economy to such a degree that Government felt impelled not only to intervene, as in 1893, but also to legislate on wages.'[131] When it is considered that this whole campaign was the result of the vigorous lobbying and agitating of the SWMF, it is clear that the Fed had become pre-eminent within national mining unionism. The south Wales miners were finally achieving a prominence to match their formidable record of strike activity.

This offers a distinct contrast to West Virginia where, despite long and desperate struggles, Districts 17 and 29 were always seen as a poor cousin within the national organisation. Far from leading the UMWA, the State's miners were a 'problem', who were dictated to, ignored, or else completely misunderstood. Deprived of the same consistently high levels of unionisation by the operators' domination of structures within West Virginia, union activists could only have dreamed of the power of the SWMF and its role within the national union, a national strike, and the national political framework.

And the consequences of this empowerment, based as it was in the different nature of culture and community in south Wales, can be seen in the conduct of the 1912 strike in the region, underlining the earlier discussion of violence. Lindsay requested 3,500 infantry and 500 cavalry to help 'police' the strike – which the cautious Home Secretary, McKenna, refused, preferring instead to station troops nearby, rather than in the coalfield. In the event they were not needed, as the strike passed off without violence.[132]

The themes which came to the fore during, and in the aftermath of the Cambrian and Minimum Wage disputes, remained central for the rest of this period. The pivotal role of the SWMF within the MFGB continued, sustained by an active, if at times inconsistently militant, rank and file. New radical leaders continued to appear, changing policy, yet also co-existing with a more moderate leadership. Underpinning all of this was the continued hostility of the owners, which increased after the war when they finally began to feel the consequences of competition in the bleak post-war economic climate. Some of these factors, as with violence, served to differentiate south Wales from West Virginia, although similarities remained in the intervention of the national State in the industry in both countries, the suppression, even on a different scale, during war time, and the shared hostility of the owners. There was also a final similarity, for despite all of the struggle and sacrifice both regions eventually faced the bitter consequences of economic decline – something which took away even the power of the union.

On the eve of the outbreak of the First World War, the SWMF had a membership of over 153,000, but was still faced with financial problems. The rock of localism, upon which the radicals' reform plans had been smashed, had also prevented the SWMF EC from securing an increase in contributions. At the Annual Conference in April 1914, Union President William Brace spoke of how 'numerically and intellectually we rank high on the Miners' Counsels of this nation, but because of our low financial position we do not command that respect we are entitled to.' Other regions, he claimed, paid more in one week than the south Wales miners did in a month. He accepted, however, that the matter was regrettably now closed until a move came from the mass of miners.[133]

Such criticism was mild compared to that reserved in the same speech for the south Wales owners. He told the delegates:

> Evidently there was only one language that the south Wales coalowners understood; they had no knowledge of the language of humanity, justice or fairplay, but were only amenable to the language of power. When the miners could use their power in these matters, then the Government and the owners, having failed to accept conciliatory methods, must accept demands enforced by industrial and political power.[134]

That this was coming from the supposedly moderate co-founder of the SWMF was an indication of the depth of feeling within the union. It helps to explain why, when the war broke out, the south Wales miners were far from industrially quiescent.

Initially the SWMF responded to the events of August 1914 in a similar way to the rest of the MFGB. At first they were reluctant to grant the Admiralty's request for compromises on work practices.[135] However, when it became clear that efforts by the International Miners' Organisation, and the rest of the European labour movement, would not stop the conflict, the SWMF agreed to compromise. Hence on 6 August, two days after Britain declared war, the SWMF EC agreed to the Admiralty's request to allow an extra hour's work (by utilising the sixty hours clause of the Eight Hours Act).[136] Similarly, a week later, following a 'lengthy explanation of the Admiralty requirements of coal' by a 'Mr Jenkins' from the

Admiralty, the union agreed that the miners at the appropriate pits should work the next Sunday.[137] The SWMF EC thus showed that it would help increase the output of the vital steam coal region but, at the same time, act cautiously over the change of working practices.

The response of the ordinary coal miners during the early months of the war was similar, with widespread recruitment into the forces.[138] This support for the war, however, began to be tested by a number of factors. Between July 1914 and March 1915 the country had experienced rapid inflation with, for example, a 24% increase in food costs. The effects of this were made worse in south Wales by the unsatisfactory Conciliation Board Agreement of 1910 which had prevented an increase in wage rates since 1913.[139]

The combination of these factors convinced the south Wales miners that while they were helping the war effort, the owners were making profits. Looking back on the causes of the 1915 strike, the 1917 Parliamentary Inquiry cited this as one of the main causes. In their report, they suggested that, 'It was this suspected exploitation of their patriotism for the gains of others . . . that caused them to strike.'[140] With the current Conciliation Agreement due to expire at the start of April, therefore, the SWMF set about attempting to redress the balance. A special conference at the start of February posted notices to terminate the Agreement on 1 April, and demanded increases for surfacemen, extra payments for night and afternoon shift work, a new standard rate, a minimum rate of wages 10% above the new standard, and a uniform rate for all hauliers. The demands had been carried with a unanimous vote.[141]

The response of the owners was predictably hard-line. They refused to negotiate with the SWMF, only offering 10% on the 1879 standard for the duration of the war. The stakes were raised in March when the MFGB conference passed a resolution calling for a national 20% wage increase. The south Wales owners then announced that they would not take part in national wage negotiations.[142] At the SWMF annual conference the delegates mandated their representatives to a national conference to 'tender fourteen days notice to terminate contracts to enforce our claim for a War Bonus of 20%'.[143] The subsequent MFGB decision to back down on the insistence on national negotiations had little effect in south Wales, as the owners were refusing to grant an increase.[144]

In the meantime the temperature was rising within the south Wales coalfield. On 17 May the SWMF EC agreed to an Admiralty request that only a one day holiday be taken at whitsun. Five days later, however, they discovered that some miners had refused to work on the Tuesday and Wednesday.[145] The end of May also saw Brace temporarily stand down as SWMF President, to enable him to take up an appointment as Under Secretary at the Home Office. His replacement was ILPer Winstone,[146] who took a harder line on the owners' inflexibility. At a special coalfield conference on 15 June, two weeks before notice ran out, he told delegates that, 'he agreed with those who said it would be a national crime to have a stoppage . . . but if such a calamity takes place, the whole responsibility must be placed upon the shoulders of the South Wales coalowners.'[147]

With a strike imminent, the Government tried desperately to find a solution. Negotiations at the Board of Trade proved unsuccessful, as did those between Minister of Munitions, Lloyd George, and the MFGB, over the Government's plans to place the coalfields under the Munitions of War Act (which, among other things, would outlaw strike activity).[148] When a SWMF special conference met at the end of June to hear about the negotiations, a Government deputation rushed to the coalfield to offer concessions. It was led by Secretary of the Board of Trade, Walter Runciman, and included William Brace and Arthur Henderson. The conference accepted the proposed settlement as the basis for negotiations, agreeing to continue work on a day to day basis.[149]

When the conference met again on the 12 July matters came to a head. The Government had refused to grant a minimum wage, or significant advances. A split SWMF EC recommended acceptance, but a card vote rejected the proposals by 1,894 to 1,037.[150] The following day the Government declared the strike illegal under the Munitions of War Act, and the MFGB appealed for a continuation of day to day working.[151] Neither of these had any effect and on 15 July, 'in the midst of the greatest war in British history – a war in which coal was as essential as munitions or soldiers', 200,000 south Wales miners came out on strike.[152]

The Government were powerless in the face of the strike. Legal action was impossible against such large numbers, so they were forced to seek a quick settlement. Amid conflicting signals, Lloyd George travelled to the coalfield on 19 July and conceded virtually all the miners' claims, including new minimum wages, and an increase.[153] Motivated by the coal owners' abuse of the war-time situation rather than directly political motives, the south Wales miners nevertheless challenged both the owners and the British Government and, in doing so, won a substantial victory.

The repercussions of the 1915 strike were felt the following year when, once again, the south Wales miners complained of large profits being made from increased coal prices. As negotiations reached an impasse in November 1916, there was growing impatience outside the coalfield with the tactics of the south Wales owners. Unwilling to see a repetition of July 1915, the Government assumed control of the south Wales coalfield under the Defence of the Realm Act. This was extended in February 1917 to the rest of the British coalfield.[154] The British miners thus attained access to the government of the coal industry, national wage agreements, and a belief that the longstanding demand for nationalisation would be ceded after the war.[155]

The remaining war years, and those immediately following them, were marked by a growing, if inconsistent, restlessness within the south Wales coalfield. Opposition to conscription became more pronounced in 1917–18, when the Government attempted to 'comb out' further miners. A special conference in October 1917 reflected this unease by rejecting a SWMF EC decision to co-operate with the new conscription. An amendment proposing that the SWMF 'take no part in assisting in the recruiting of colliery workers for the army' was passed by 1,912 votes to 897.[156] However, a coalfield ballot the following month opposed taking strike action against the 'comb out' by 98,946 to 28,903. Similarly in January 1918, when in the light of military set backs, the Government requested the conscription of another 50,000 miners, both the national union and the SWMF reluctantly agreed.[157]

Some of course refused to be conscripted, including Arthur Horner, who instead left for Ireland where he joined the citizen's army. On his return he served a six-month sentence, was released and then court-martialled, serving another two years' hard labour. The communist and SWMF activist was not forgotten, however, as the Mardy Lodge elected him checkweigher in his absence in April 1919.[158]

The opposition to conscription was linked to a general anti-war feeling that resulted from war weariness, and the aspirations encouraged by the Russian revolution. The leftward drift of the union was revealed by the introduction of a new set of rules in early summer 1917, which included the ambitious rule 3a:

> To secure the entire organisation of all workers employed in and about
> collieries situated in the South Wales and Monmouthshire coalfield,
> with a view to the complete abolition of capitalism, and that member-
> ship of the Federation shall be a condition of employment.[159]

The URC was regaining some of its pre-war momentum, as was the
CLC, both of which helped establish radical leaders within the
SWMF.[160] S. O. Davies was elected miners' agent for Dowlais in
October 1918, and worked closely on the SWMF EC with other mil-
itants like Ablett and Frank Hodges.[161] Alongside Horner, A. J.
Cook, who was also destined for national office, increased his
powerbase within the union. A vigorous opponent of the war, Cook
was imprisoned for three months in 1918 for sedition under the
Defence of the Realm Act.[162] This led to an outcry within the
Rhondda and the wider coalfield. The SWMF EC condemned the
sentence and sent a delegation to discuss the matter with the Home
Secretary.[163] Cook was elected as agent for the Rhondda No.1
District in November 1919. In the wider coalfield, however, his
popularity and that of the URC generally, was still limited. At the
SWMF Annual Conference in the spring of 1919, Cook had stood
unsuccessfully, as part of a URC slate, for the Union Vice
Presidency.[164]

The more aggressive stance adopted by the SWMF helped influence a general shift of opinion within the British coalfield. In 1918,
after an MFGB re-organisation, Frank Hodges was elected as full-
time Secretary of the MFGB, where he joined veteran Robert
Smillie, who now became full-time, rather than part-time,
President.[165] Both were socialists and enthusiastic supporters of
nationalisation. Under pressure from south Wales, the MFGB formulated radical demands including a six hour day, a 30% increase
in wages, and nationalisation with joint State and workers' control.
These were tabled in January 1919, and produced a Government
offer of a wage increase and a Royal Commission, chaired by Justice
Sankey, to consider the industry's future. Although nationally the
miners voted 615,184 to 105,082 in favour of strike action, the
MFGB accepted Lloyd George's offer to serve on the proposed
Commission.[166]

The Sankey Commission began its hearings on 3 March, and produced interim reports later in the month. These dealt with the
immediate demands concerning wages and hours. On 20 March, the
day the reports were presented to Parliament, Bonar Law

announced, on behalf of the Government, that the Sankey Report would be adopted 'in spirit and in letter'. After negotiations the MFGB balloted its membership at the beginning of April. They voted by 693,084 to 76,992 to accept the Government offer of an immediate 2s per day raise, and a reduction of one hour per working day, with a further reduction promised in 1921. South Wales voted 142,558 to 19,492 in favour of acceptance.[167]

The Sankey Commission reconvened on the 24 April to consider the question of future organisation of the industry. It produced four reports at the end of June, all of which advocated nationalisation of coal seams. In addition Sankey's individual report recommended full-scale nationalisation of the industry, as did a report signed by the MFGB representatives, and the joint Government/MFGB nominees, R. H. Tawney and Sidney Webb. In his report Sir Arthur Duckham proposed large-scale amalgamations, and limitation of profits, while the Mining Association of Great Britain representatives argued for a return to private ownership, only modified by consultative pit committees.[168]

With seven of the commissioners in favour, and Government commitments to implement the Sankey proposals, the MFGB believed they had a clear case for nationalisation. However, after stalling for nearly two months, Lloyd George announced the rejection of nationalisation, and adopted instead a proposal for amalgamations similar to that proposed by Duckham. The miners genuinely believed they had been betrayed and therefore rejected Lloyd George's proposals. However, with the other members of the Triple Alliance – which allied the miners with the rail and transport workers – unwilling to support strike action, the MFGB EC were reluctant to call a strike. The Government thus succeeded in the real aim behind the Sankey affair which, as Kirby has suggested, was to 'provide the means whereby the miners' exceptional bargaining position could be weakened.'[169]

Intent on returning the industry to private ownership, the Government set about preparing for the change. The Coal Mines (Emergency) Act 1920 arranged the financial basis for the remaining period of control, while the Mining Industry Act of 1920 established, among other things, 31 August 1921 as the date for the return to private ownership. [170] The preparations for decontrol, however, soon brought about conflict with the miners, who began to focus attention on the high domestic and export prices. The issue was first raised in spring 1920, but following negotiations with the Lloyd George and Bonar Law, a wage increase of 20% on gross was accepted by a ballot vote. While nationally the vote for the settlement was narrow, in south Wales there was a huge majority against, and in favour of strike action.[171]

The controversy over coal prices soon reappeared. In an attempt at reducing the gap in profitability between the export and home sales, the Government restored a 10s per ton cut, made the previous November, in the price of household coal, and added another 4s 2d to coal prices generally.[172] With a current Government surplus from the industry of £66 million a year, the MFGB believed that prices would be increased until virtually every colliery was profitable, allowing decontrol to occur with relative ease. In June, therefore, they demanded a substantial wage advance, or a reduction of 14s 2d in the price of coal and the following month they decided to ask for both.[173]

After a large vote in favour of strike action, the miners, along with the Triple Alliance and the Labour Research Department, attempted to build public support for the claim. This was undermined by press hostility, and an announcement that the surplus from the industry would be £33 million, rather than £66 million. Hodges told the MFGB EC that he believed the figures were fixed, but the union was nevertheless forced to drop the demand for a price reduction, calling instead for a tribunal to consider coal prices.[174] In the same month, September, the Government offered a wage increase related to output, along with arbitration. Although the miners refused this offer, the other members of the Triple Alliance decided against supporting strike action. There were also tensions within the MFGB, with Smillie desperately advising against a strike. After a further Government offer, reducing the 'datum line' of output at which a bonus would be paid, was rejected by a large majority, Smillie threatened to resign. This was refused, and a national miners' strike began on the 16 October.[175]

The Government responded by passing an Emergency Powers Act which allowed, with the declaration of a state of emergency, the introduction of 'virtually any "regulations" it liked'. The only limitations were on compulsory industrial or military conscription, making strikes illegal, and changing existing criminal procedures.[176] In spite of this, news that the railwaymen had reversed their decision not to support the miners' strike, forced the Government into making an improved offer. The MFGB EC accepted this and, although a ballot of the membership went narrowly against the offer, the strike was called off on 4 November.[177] This decision, and the general conduct of the strike, created anger within some of the districts. In south Wales over 65% of those who voted had opposed the settlement, as had nearly 83% in Lancashire.[178] In the recriminations that followed, Brace resigned the SWMF Presidency and Hartshorn likewise from the SWMF EC. The latter body accepted the resignations on 13 November, and appointed Winstone as temporary President. The replacement representatives on the MFGB Committee were Morrell and, to the alarm of moderate MFGB officials, Ablett.[179]

The disquiet over the datum line settlement proved well-founded. The linking of wages to production was undermined by the onset of a depression, and the MFGB were still faced with negotiating a permanent settlement with the owners. The situation became more serious when, at the end of February, as a result of the depression, the Government announced that it was bringing forward decontrol to 31 March 1921. Negotiations between the miners and owners made some progress, but became deadlocked over the MFGB demand for pooling profits and thus allowing national agreements, whereas the owners wanted district settlements. With no agreement in sight, the owners posted new wage rates to come into force from 1 April. While some regions did better than others, with Yorkshire even receiving some advances, south Wales, relying as it did on the export trade, was facing wage cuts of up to 45%.[180]

Earlier in March, Smillie had resigned the MFGB Presidency, to be replaced by his deputy, Herbert Smith. In addition, in January, George Barker vacated his seat on the MFGB EC after his election to Parliament, and was replaced by A. J. Cook.[181] It was thus with the pragmatic Smith at the helm, that the miners began another national strike on 1 April. Appeals were made to the other members of the Triple Alliance who, after considering the miners' case, decided to come out in support on 13 April. Furthermore, to place pressure on the owners and Government, the MFGB decided to bring out all safety and maintenance men.[182] The industry was, therefore, brought virtually to a halt. In south Wales, the whole coalfield was paralysed within a week, as strikers organised mass demonstrations and pickets.[183]

Under pressure from the other members of the Triple Alliance, the

MFGB compromised on the issue of safety men. This was followed by negotiations with the Government, which produced an offer involving a subsidy to ease wage cuts in unprofitable districts. The MFGB rejected this and the Triple Alliance announced a new strike date of 15 April. On 14 April, the Rail and Transport leaders met Lloyd George and then, later in the evening, MFGB Secretary Hodges reportedly claimed that the miners would accept a temporary district settlement. With a similar suggestion being made by the Federation of British Industries, Lloyd George wrote to the MFGB on the 15 April requesting talks. The MFGB EC rejected this by nine votes to eight, and the strike continued. Hodges' unauthorised offer, however, provided the pretext for the Rail and Transport leaders to call off the proposed strike. Whether this decision was treachery or, alternatively, pragmatic good sense, is a matter of opinion, however, Friday 15 April 1921 passed into history as 'Black Friday.'[184]

The rest of the 1921 strike fitted a pattern that would be repeated in future years. Deprived of support from other unions, in an unsympathetic economic climate, and facing increasing State interference with the conduct of the strike, the miners were eventually forced back to work. Although the rank and file members rejected proposed settlements, the MFGB EC forced the issue by accepting an agreement which involved a Government subsidy for an initial three months, district wage agreements, alongside some guarantees of minimum wage levels. The miners reluctantly returned to work on 1 July 1921.[185]

The level of State interference in the conduct of the strike is important not only in the history of the British miners, but within this comparison with West Virginia. Overseen by the Government's strike-breaking organisation, the Supply and Transport Committee, the Emergency Powers Act was invoked soon after the strike began. Military and naval leave was cancelled, reserve forces were called up, and a volunteer defence force prepared.[186] Although 'Black Friday' removed the necessity for such elaborate organisation, large numbers of police and military were still deployed. Predictably south Wales received the greatest attention, with extra police, troops and naval ratings drafted in. Labour MPs later complained of naval ratings marching through Abertillery with fixed bayonets and machine guns.[187]

With the Home Office encouraging local police chiefs to deal aggressively with the strikers, Lindsay utilised the Emergency

Powers Act to break up pickets and demonstrations. Collieries were 'protected' by large numbers of police, 'almost always backed up by troops'.[188] The police also made vigorous use of the courts with, by the end of May, over 500 summonses issued under Emergency Regulation 19 (concerning sedition). Hundreds were also charged with intimidation and unlawful assembly. The aim of breaking the strike ran parallel to the attempt to suppress left wing activists, particularly those associated with the CPGB. On 16 May, for example, A. J. Cook's house was raided by the Deputy Chief Constable, and 'a large quantity of correspondence' was taken away.[189]

Cook was later charged with incitement to intimidate a safety worker, incitement to disturb the peace, and unlawful assembly, arising from a speech in which he attacked strike-breaking safety men. Along with a number of other convictions, Cook was sentenced to four months' hard labour, Horner to one month, and George Dolling, Cook's companion in the dock in 1918, two months.[190] The British State had clearly shown that, like its counterpart in the US, it was not afraid to confront and undermine strike activity when it felt threatened. The irony was that, at a time when the British Government was retreating from State control of the industry introduced during the war, it used the structures which originated during the same conflict to control protest. As with the US, therefore, not for the first time (nor the last), the British miners discovered that moves to a 'free' market were accompanied by a strengthening of the apparatus of State repression.

The defeat of the 1921 strike marked a turning point in the fortunes of the coal miners. As Francis and Smith have suggested 'in retrospect' 1918–21 'can be characterised as a final flaring of the power of the mining unions and the attendant boom in coal.'[191] The power of the MFGB, and within it the SWMF, had been based upon the strength of coal, and the decline in the industry's fortunes in the 1920s removed this power. Nowhere was this more apparent than in south Wales, where the disastrous reliance upon the export trade shattered the union's powerbase, and left them fighting unemployment, non-unionism and the vindictiveness of the south Wales coal owners.

The characteristics of the SWMF and industrial disputes after 1921 remained very much those of the previous decade. A vibrant minority, this time around the CPGB and later the MMM, continued to influence union policy.[192] Thus, in July 1921, a coalfield conference voted to urge the MFGB to join the Third International of Labour Unions – a decision which caused Lenin to speculate that 'Perhaps it is the beginning of the real Proletarian mass movement in Great Britain in the Communist sense'.[193] However, neither the affiliation, nor Lenin's hopes came to fruition, even in south Wales. Hence the same summer, on the death of Winstone, Hartshorn was elected SWMF President, a post which he held until 1924.[194] The SWMF continued to be a force within the MFGB with, for example, Cook replacing Hodges as General Secretary in 1921. However, as the defeat of 1926 would show and as the West Virginia miners had discovered in a different way, without the power to challenge the powerful, defeat was the most common outcome of struggle.

Notes

1 C. Williams, 'The South Wales Miners' Federation', *Llafur*, 5, 3, p. 46.
2 Entry on William Abraham, in J. Saville and J. M. Bellamy (eds.), *Dictionary of Labour Biography, Vol. 1* (London, Macmillan, 1972), p. 2; K. O. Morgan, *Rebirth of a Nation: Wales 1880–1980* (Oxford, Oxford University Press, 1981), p. 73.
3 Bellamy and Saville, *Dictionary of Labour Biography, Vol. 1*, p. 2; *ibid.*, Brace entry, p. 52.
4 E. D. Lewis, *The Rhondda Valleys: A Study in Industrial Development, 1800 to the Present Day* (London, Phoenix House, 1959), pp. 169–71; Bellamy and Saville, *Dictionary of Labour Biography, Vol. 1* p. 52; *ibid.*, Richards entry, p. 285.
5 Morgan, *Rebirth of a Nation*, pp. 77–8; Bellamy and Saville, *Dictionary of Labour Biography, Vol. 1*, pp. 52, 2, 285; Strike Statistics from R. Church, *The History of the British Coal Industry, Vol. 3, 1830–1913: Victorian Pre-eminence* (Oxford, Oxford University Press, 1986), pp. 722–3.
6 Union Membership from *ibid.*, pp. 690–1; Numbers employed from B. R. Mitchell and P. Deane, *Abstract of British Historical Statistics* (Cambridge, Cambridge University Press, 1962), pp. 118–19.
7 Percentages calculated by combining figures from *ibid.*, with Church, *The History of the British Coal Industry, Vol. 3*, pp. 690–1. Figures for union membership 1915–23, from SWMF Balance Sheets, Swansea, South Wales Coalfield Archive (SWCA), D.1.
8 Church, *The History of the British Coal Industry, Vol.3*, pp. 690–1.
9 *Ibid.*, pp. 719, 746; Church , 'Edwardian Labour Unrest and Coalfield Militancy, 1890–1913', *Historical Journal*, 30, 4 (1987), pp. 848–9; D. R. Hopkin, 'The Great Unrest in Wales, 1910–1913: Questions of

Evidence', in Hopkin and G. S. Kealey (eds.), *Class, Community and the Labour Movement: Wales and Canada, 1850–1930* (Wales, Llafur/Labour/Le Travail, 1989), p. 255; Table 197, 'Stoppages of Work Due to Industrial Disputes: Summary 1893–1968', Dept. of Employment and Productivity, *British Labour Statistics: Historical Abstracts, 1886–1968* (London, 1971), p. 396.

10 Church, 'Edwardian Labour Unrest and Coalfield Militancy, 1890–1913', p. 848.

11 Church, *The History of the British Coal Industry, Vol. 3*, p. 722.

12 Church, 'Edwardian Labour Unrest and Coalfield Militancy, 1890–1913', p. 85; Hopkin, 'The Great Unrest in Wales, 1910–1913', p. 256.

13 *Ibid.*, pp. 257–9, 270–5.

14 Table listing stoppages and indemnity claims, Jan 1899 - Jan 1903, Aberystwyth, National Library of Wales (NLW), Records of MSWCA, X2.

15 Hopkin, 'The Great Unrest in Wales, 1910–13', p. 261.

16 General Committee, 9 Jun 1906, 15 Jun 1906, Cambrian Lodge Minutes, 31 May 1906 - 12 Oct 1910, A.2.

17 *Ibid.*, 17 Jul 1906.

18 Table listing stoppages and indemnity claims, Jan 1899 - Jan 1903, MSWCA, X2.

19 B. Supple, *The History of the British Coal Industry, Vol. 4, 1913–1946: The Political Economy of Decline* (Oxford, Oxford University Press, 1987), p. 69.

20 L. J. Williams, 'The Coalowners', in D. Smith (ed.), *A People and a Proletariat: Essays in the History of Wales, 1780–1980* (London, Pluto Press, 1980), p. 105

21 *Ibid.*; L. J. Williams, 'The Road to Tonypandy', *Llafur*, 1, 2, p. 47.

22 Morgan, *Rebirth of a Nation*, p. 73.

23 J. Williams, 'Miners and the Law of Contract, 1875–1914', *Llafur*, 4, 2, pp. 36–50.

24 *Ibid.*, pp. 36–40.

25 MSWCA meeting, 18 Oct 1901, MSWCA Minute Book, Aug 1900–Nov 1902, pp. 107–10, MSWCA, MG9.

26 *Ibid.*

27 MSWCA meeting, 5 Jul 1902, *ibid.*, p. 180.

28 Williams, 'Miners and the Law of Contract, 1875–1914', pp. 41–3.

29 For details of the Taff Vale decision, see H. M. Pelling, *A History of British Trade Unionism* (London, Macmillan, 1976 edn.), pp. 123–5. H. A. Clegg, A. Fox and A. F. Thompson, *A History of British Trade Unions Since 1889, Vol. 1* (Oxford, Oxford University Press, 1964), pp. 305–15.

30 MSWCA meeting, 18 Oct 1901, MSWCA Minute Book, Aug 1900–Nov 1902, p. 112, MSWCA, MG9.
31 Pelling, *Popular Politics and Society in Late Victorian Britain* (London, Macmillan, 1968), pp. 111–14.
32 Williams, 'Miners and the Law of Contract, 1875–1914', pp. 46–9.
33 Williams, 'The Road to Tonypandy', p. 49.
34 E. W. Evans, *The Miners of South Wales* (Cardiff, University of Wales Press, 1961), pp. 190–1. See, for example, remarks of MSWCA Committee, MSWCA, Eight Hours Act Correspondence, BA2/5ac.
35 *Report of the Departmental Committee Appointed to Inquire into the Probable Economic Effect of a Limit of Eight Hours to the Working Day of Coal Miners* (Parl. Papers, 1907, Cd.3506, XV, 349), p. 9.
36 Williams, 'The Road to Tonypandy, p. 49; Evans, *The Miners of South Wales*, pp. 193–4.
37 R. P. Arnot, *South Wales Miners; A History of the South Wales Miners' Federation, 1898–1914* (London, Allen and Unwin, 1967), p. 132; Daunton, 'Down the Pit', p. 594; *Report of the Departmental Committee Appointed to Inquire into the Probable Economic Effect of a Limit of Eight Hours to the Working Day of Coal Miners*, XV, pp. 37, 242.
38 Evans, *The Miners of South Wales*, pp. 193–4.
39 *Ibid.*, p. 194; Arnot, *The South Wales Miners, 1898–1914*, pp. 141–2; Williams, 'The Road to Tonypandy', p. 49.
40 Evans, *The Miners of South Wales*, pp. 194–5.
41 M. G. Woodhouse, 'Rank and File Movements among the Miners of South Wales, 1910–1926' (Unpublished D.Phil dissertation, University of Oxford, 1969), pp. 24–5.
42 Pelling, *Popular Politics and Society in Late Victorian Britain*, pp. 111–14.
43 Evans, *The Miners of South Wales*, pp. 196–7.
44 *Ibid.*, pp. 198–200; Woodhouse, 'Rank and File Movements among the Miners of South Wales', pp. 28–34.
45 *Ibid.*, pp. 32–5; M. Barclay, '"Slaves of the Lamp": The Aberdare Miners' Strike, 1910', *Llafur*, 2, 3, p. 25.
46 Woodhouse, 'Rank and File Movements among the Miners of South Wales', p. 9.
47 Lewis, *The Rhondda Valleys*, p. 175.
48 Arnot, *The South Wales Miners, 1898–1914*, pp. 176–8.
49 N. Edwards, *History of the South Wales Miners' Federation, Vol. 1* (London, Lawrence and Wishart, 1938), pp. 35–6.
50 Arnot, *The South Wales Miners, 1898–1914*, pp. 178–9.
51 The Committee had been formed in 1908: See Woodhouse, 'Rank and File Movements among the Miners of South Wales', pp. 47–9, for details.

52 Arnot, *The South Wales Miners, 1898–1914*, p. 179.
53 Barclay,'"Slaves of the Lamp"', pp. 26–8.
54 Arnot, *The South Wales Miners, 1898–1914*, pp. 180–1.
55 For a full list of all 18 demands see Edwards, *History of the South Wales Miners' Federation*, pp. 37–8.
56 Barclay, '"Slaves of the Lamp"', p. 27.
57 *Ibid.*, p. 27; Arnot, *The South Wales Miners, 1898–1914*, p. 181.
58 *Ibid.*; '"Slaves of the Lamp"', p. 28.
59 See Stanton entry, Bellamy and Saville, *Dictionary of Labour Biography, Vol. 1*, pp. 311–12.
60 Woodhouse, 'Rank and File Movements among the Miners of South Wales', pp. 33–6.
61 Interview with Max Goldberg, p. 32, Swansea, South Wales Miners' Library (SWML), Oral History Collection.
62 G. A. Williams, *When Was Wales?: A History of the Welsh* (London, Penguin, 1985), p. 244.
63 Barclay, '"Slaves of the Lamp"', p. 28.
64 Williams, *When was Wales?*, p. 244.
65 Barclay, '"Slaves of the Lamp"', pp. 28–29, 40–1.
66 Woodhouse, 'Rank and File Movements among the Miners of South Wales', p. 53.
67 Smith, 'Tonypandy 1910: Definitions of Community', *Past and Present*, 87 (1980), p. 163.
68 Tom Mann in *Justice*, 12 Nov 1910, p. 7.
69 Smith, 'Tonypandy 1910', p. 164.
70 *Justice*, 12 Nov 1910, p. 7.
71 From 8 Nov 1910, quoted in Woodhouse, 'Rank and File Movements among the Miners of South Wales', p. 55. As in the US coalfields, women in south Wales were prominent in strikes prior to, and throughout, this period, harassing and humiliating strike-breakers via 'rough music' – which involved banging kettles and pans. They also enacted various other forms of public humiliation, including forcing their victims to wear white shirts (known as 'white shirting'), and waving women's clothes on poles. Furthermore, although strikes in south Wales did not involve mass evictions and the move into tent colonies, they still placed an additional domestic burden on women. R. A. N. Jones, 'Women, Community and Collective Action: The "Ceffyl Pren" Tradition', in A. V. John (ed.), *Our Mother's Land: Chapters in Welsh Women's History, 1880–1939* (Cardiff, University of Wales Press, 1991), pp. 17–4. A. V. John, 'A Miner Struggle? Women's Protests in Welsh Mining History', *Llafur*, 4, 1 (1984), pp. 78–82.
72 Arnot, *The South Wales Miners, 1898–1914*, pp. 185–6.
73 Smith, 'Tonypandy 1910', p. 168.

74 *Ibid.*, pp. 164–5; Arnot, *The South Wales Miners, 1898–1914*, p. 186.

75 A. Mor-O'Brien, 'Churchill and the Tonypandy Riots', *Welsh History Review* , 17, 1 (1994), pp. 74–7.

76 *Report and Correspondence on Disturbances in Connection with the South Wales Colliery Strikes* (Parl. Papers, 1911, Cd.5568, LXIV), Lindsay to Home Office, 8 Nov 1910, p. 4.

77 *Ibid.*, MSWCA to Churchill, 10 Nov 1910, p. 15.

78 *Ibid.*, Churchill to Lindsay, 8 Nov 1910; Lindsay to Churchill, 8 Nov 1910, p. 4. Churchill has usually been credited with halting the troops in the first instance. However, Mor O'Brien has suggested that the decision was actually made by Secretary of State for War, Haldane. See 'Churchill and the Tonypandy Riots', pp. 76–8.

79 N. Macready, *Annals of an Active Life, Vol. One* (London, Hutchison, 1924), pp. 136–7. For details of the military deployment at Featherstone during the 1893 Coal strike, in which two miners were killed and fourteen injured, see R. Geary, *Policing Industrial Disputes: 1893 to 1985* (Cambridge, Cambridge University Press, 1985), pp. 6–24.

80 J. Morgan, 'Police and Labour in the Age of Lindsay, 1910–1936', *Llafur*, 5, 1, p. 15.

81 *Report and Correspondence on Disturbances in Connection with the South Wales Colliery Strikes*, Churchill to Lindsay, 8 Nov 1910, p. 5.

82 Smith, 'Tonypandy 1910', pp. 165–6; Arnot, *The South Wales Miners, 1898–1914*, pp. 186–194.

83 *Ibid.*, pp. 192–3; Smith, 'Tonypandy 1910', p. 165.

84 *Report and Correspondence on Disturbances in Connection with the South Wales Colliery Strikes*, Macready to Home Office, 11 Nov 1910, pp. 16–17.

85 Geary, *Policing Industrial Disputes*, p. 31.

86 Smith, 'Tonypandy 1910', pp. 168–9; Holton likewise disagrees with the contemporary view of the riot as senseless violence, B. Holton, *British Syndicalism, 1900–1914: Myths and Realities* (London, Pluto Press, 1976), pp. 81–2.

87 Smith, 'Tonypandy 1910', pp. 179–80, 162.

88 Barclay, '"Slaves of the Lamp"', p. 31.

89 *Report and Correspondence on Disturbances in Connection with the South Wales Colliery Strikes*, Churchill to Lindsay, 9 Nov 1910, p. 7; Churchill to Macready, 9 Nov 1910, p. 8; Macready to Home Office, 9 Nov 1910, p. 9; Churchill to Lindsay, 10 Nov, pp. 12–13; Geary, *Policing Industrial Disputes*, pp. 27–8; Macready, *Annals of an Active Life*, p. 144.

90 *Report and Correspondence on Disturbances in Connection with the South Wales Colliery Strikes*, Macready to Home Office, 9 Nov 1910, p. 9.

91 *Ibid.*, Churchill to Lindsay, 10 Nov 1910, pp. 12–13.
92 *Ibid.*, MFGB to Churchill, pp. 10–11.
93 Lewis, *The Rhondda Valleys*, p. 176.
94 Macready, *Annals of an Active Life*, pp. 141–2.
95 *Ibid.*, pp. 142–3; Woodhouse, 'Rank and File Movements among the Miners of South Wales', p. 57.
96 The strikers would probably have preferred rugby as Macready reported that 'the soldiers were victorious'. *Report and Correspondence on Disturbances in Connection with the South Wales Colliery Strikes*, Macready to Home Office, 15 Nov 1910, pp. 29–30.
97 Macready, *Annals of an Active Life*, p. 142.
98 *Report and Correspondence on Disturbances in Connection with the South Wales Colliery Strikes*, Macready Memorandum, p. 49.
99 Macready, *Annals of an Active Life*, p. 145.
100 *Report and Correspondence on Disturbances in Connection with the South Wales Colliery Strikes*, Macready to Home Office, 15 Nov 1910, pp. 29–30; Macready to Home Office, 19 Nov, pp. 34–5.
101 *Ibid.*, Macready Memorandum, p. 49.
102 *Ibid.*, p. 48.
103 Macready, *Annals of an Active Life*, pp. 147–8.
104 Mor-O'Brien suggests Churchill encouraged the police to deal vigorously (And violently) with the miners – something which the Home Secretary subsequently tried to cover up, even to the point of 'editing' the official published record of these events. 'Churchill and the Tonypandy Riots', pp. 87–9.
105 Arnot, *The South Wales Miners, 1898–1914*, p. 194.
106 Williams, 'The Road to Tonypandy', p. 42.
107 Barclay, '"Slaves of the Lamp"', p. 31.
108 Quoted in Lewis, *The Rhondda Valleys*, p. 176.
109 Arnot, *The South Wales Miners, 1898–1914*, pp. 197–9, 209–10, 213–18, 233–8.
110 Testimony of Revd. D. Jones quoted in full in Geary, *Policing Industrial Disputes*, p. 41.
111 Arnot, *The South Wales Miners, 1898–1914*, p. 214.
112 Cambrian Lodge Minutes, 4 Nov 1910–23 Feb 1912, A.3.
113 Geary, *Policing Industrial Disputes*, p. 29.
114 Morgan, *Rebirth of a Nation*, p. 148.
115 Geary, 'Tonypandy and Llanelli Revisited', *Llafur*, 4, 4, p. 35; For a longer discussion of these ideas, see *Policing Industrial Disputes*, pp. 116–19.
116 Barclay, '"Slaves of the Lamp"', pp. 32–4; Woodhouse, 'Rank and File Movements among the Miners of South Wales', pp. 58–9; Edwards, *History of the South Wales Miners' Federation*, pp. 40–4.

117 Lewis, *The Rhondda Valleys*, pp. 176–7; See entry in J. M. Bellamy and J. Saville (eds.), *Dictionary of Labour Biography, Vol.3* (London, Macmillan, 1976), pp. 2–3; D. Egan, 'Noah Ablett, 1883–1935', *Llafur*, 4, 3, pp. 19–30.

118 Quoted in Arnot, *The South Wales Miners, 1898–1914*, pp. 252–3,. p. 253.

119 Woodhouse, 'Rank and File Movements among the Miners of South Wales', pp. 70–3; Edwards, *History of the South Wales Miners' Federation*, p. 46–7.

120 Rees quote in Lewis, *The Rhondda Valleys*, p. 177; Arnot, *The South Wales Miners, 1898–1914*, pp. 264–8.

121 D. Egan, 'The Unofficial Reform Committee and the Miners' Next Step', *Llafur*, II, 3, pp. 66–7. See also the attached documents, pp. 71–7.

122 Holton, *British Syndicalism, 1900–1914*, p. 88.

123 Arnot, *The South Wales Miners, 1898–1914*, pp. 267–8.

124 H. Francis and D. Smith, *The Fed: a History of the South Wales Miners in the Twentieth Century* (London, Lawrence and Wishart, 1980), pp. 17–21; H. S. Jevons, *The British Coal Trade* (Newton Abbot, David and Charles, 1969 edn.), pp. 130–5; Woodhouse, 'Rank and File Movements among the Miners of South Wales, 1910–1926', pp. 105–8.

125 K. O. Morgan, 'Socialism and Syndicalism: The Welsh Miners' Debate, 1912', *Bulletin of the Society for the Study of Labour History*, 30 (1975), p. 24.

126 Morgan, *Rebirth of a Nation*, p. 153.

127 Lodge Meeting, 18 Oct 1911, Cambrian Lodge Minutes, 4 Nov 1910–23 Feb 1912, A.3.

128 Edwards, *History of the South Wales Miners' Federation*, pp. 54–8; Woodhouse, 'Rank and File Movements among the Miners of South Wales', pp. 80–7.

129 *Ibid.*, pp. 87–8; Church, *The History of the British Coal Industry, Vol. 3*, pp. 743–4; Edwards, *History of the South Wales Miners' Federation*, pp. 62–3.

130 *Ibid.*, pp. 63–5; Woodhouse, 'Rank and File Movements among the Miners of South Wales', pp. 89–91; Holton, *British Syndicalism, 1900–1914*, pp. 117–20; Church, *The History of the British Coal Industry, Vol. 3*, p. 744.

131 *Ibid.*, pp. 744–5.

132 J. Morgan, *Conflict and Order: The Police and Labour Disputes in England and Wales, 1900–1939* (Oxford, Oxford University Press, 1987), pp. 60–3.

133 Presidential Address to Annual Conference, 6 Apr 1914, SWMF Minutes, 1914, SWCA, C.2.

134 *Ibid.*
135 SWMF EC, 1 Aug 1914, 3 Aug 1914, *ibid.*
136 SWMF EC, 6 Aug 1914, *ibid.*
137 SWMF EC, 13 Aug 1914, *ibid.*
138 *Commission of Inquiry into Industrial Unrest: No.7 District – South Wales and Monmouthshire* (Parl. Papers, 1917–18, Cd.8868, XV), pp. 22, 27.
139 Supple, *The History of the British Coal Industry,* Vol. 4, pp. 62–5.
140 *Ibid.,* p. 65; *Commission of Inquiry into Industrial Unrest,* p. 28.
141 Special Conference, 6 Feb 1915, SWMF Minutes 1915, C.2.
142 Edwards, *History of the South Wales Miners' Federation,* pp. 83–4; Supple, *The History of the British Coal Industry,* Vol. 4, p. 65.
143 SWMF Annual Conference, 19/20 Apr 1915, SWMF Minutes, 1915, C.2.
144 Edwards, *History of the South Wales Miners' Federation,* p. 84.
145 SWMF EC, 17 May 1915; 22 May 1915, SWMF Minutes, 1915, C.2.
146 SWMF EC 31 May 1915, 8 Jun 1915, *ibid.*
147 Presidential Address at Special Conference, 15 Jun 1915, *ibid.*
148 Supple, *The History of the British Coal Industry,* Vol. 4, pp. 65–6.
149 Special Conference, 30 Jun 1915, SWMF Minutes, 1915, C.2; Edwards, *History of the South Wales Miners' Federation,* p. 86.
150 Supple, *The History of the British Coal Industry,* Vol. 4, p. 66; Special Conference, 12 Jul 1915, SWMF Minutes, 1915, C.2.
151 SWMF EC, 14 Jul 1915, *ibid.*
152 Supple, *The History of the British Coal Industry,* Vol. 4, p. 66.
153 *Ibid.,* p. 67, Edwards, *History of the South Wales Miners' Federation,* pp. 88–92; Woodhouse, 'Rank and File Movements among the Miners of South Wales', pp. 127–8.
154 Supple, *The History of the British Coal Industry,* Vol. 4, pp. 74–7.
155 M. W. Kirby, *The British Coalmining Industry, 1870–1946: A Political and Economic History* (Hamden Conn., Archon Books,1977), pp. 30–1.
156 Special Conference, 8 Oct 1917, SWMF Minutes, 1917, C.2.
157 Woodhouse, 'Rank and File Movements among the Miners of South Wales', pp. 135–143.
158 See entry in J. M. Bellamy and J. Saville (eds.), *Dictionary of Labour Biography,* Vol. 5 (London, Macmillan, 1979), pp. 112–18; Francis and Smith, *The Fed,* pp. 30–3;
159 SWMF New Rules, 1917, copy in SWCA, M2.
160 Woodhouse, 'Rank and File Movements among the Miners of South Wales', pp. 135–150.

161 See entry in J.M. Bellamy and J. Saville (eds.) *Dictionary of Labour Biography, Vol. 8* (London, Macmillan, 1987), pp. 45–55.

162 Bellamy and Saville, *Dictionary of Labour Biography, Vol. 3*, pp. 38–9.

163 SWMF EC, 23 Mar 1918; 5 Apr 1918; 20 Apr 1918, SWMF Minutes, 1918, C.2.

164 Bellamy and Saville, *Dictionary of Labour Biography, Vol. 3*, p. 39.

165 Woodhouse, 'Rank and File Movements among the Miners of South Wales', pp. 152–4.

166 Kirby, *The British Coalmining Industry, 1870–1946*, pp. 36–7; Edwards, *History of the South Wales Miners' Federation*, pp. 111–15.

167 R. P. Arnot, *The Miners: Years of Struggle – A History of the Miners' Federation of Great Britain from 1910 Onwards* (London, Allen and Unwin, 1953), pp. 189–202.

168 *Ibid.*, pp. 206–9; Supple, *The History of the British Coal Industry, Vol. 4*, p. 136.

169 Kirby, *The British Coalmining Industry, 1870–1946*, pp. 37–8; Arnot, *The Miners: Years of Struggle*, pp. 209–219.

170 Supple, *The History of the British Coal Industry, Vol. 4*, pp. 143–5.

171 Arnot, *The Miners: Years of Struggle*, pp. 232–5.

172 Supple, *The History of the British Coal Industry, Vol. 4*, p. 149.

173 H. A. Clegg, *A History of British Trade Unions since 1889; Vol. 2, 1911–1933* (Oxford, Oxford University Press, 1985), pp. 294–5.

174 Arnot, *The Miners: Years of Struggle*, pp. 246–251.

175 Clegg, *A History of British Trade Unions since 1889; Vol. II*, pp. 295–6.

176 Geary, *Policing Industrial Disputes*, p. 54.

177 Edwards, *History of the South Wales Miners' Federation*, pp. 117–19; Clegg, *A History of British Trade Unions since 1889; Vol. 2*, pp. 296–7; Arnot, *The Miners: Years of Struggle*, pp. 270–5.

178 *Ibid.*, p. 274.

179 R. P. Arnot, *South Wales Miners: A History of the South Wales Miners Federation, 1914–1926* (Cardiff, Cymric Federation Press, 1975), pp. 195–7; Woodhouse, 'Rank and File Movements among the Miners of South Wales', pp. 199–209.

180 Clegg, *A History of British Trade Unions since 1889; Vol. 2*, pp. 297–9; Supple, *The History of the British Coal Industry, Vol. 4*, pp. 151–59.

181 Arnot, *The Miners: Years of Struggle*, pp. 295–6, 281–2.

182 Clegg, *A History of British Trade Unions since 1889; Vol. 2*, pp. 299–300.

183 Woodhouse, 'Rank and File Movements among the Miners of South Wales', pp. 220–1.

184 Clegg, *A History of British Trade Unions since 1889; Vol. 2*, pp. 299–302; Kirby, *The British Coalmining Industry, 1870–1946*, pp. 49–62; Edwards, *History of the South Wales Miners' Federation*, pp. 120–1; Arnot, *The Miners: Years of Struggle*, pp. 310–17.

185 *Ibid.*, p. 318–31; Kirby, *The British Coalmining Industry, 1870–1946*, p. 62; Supple, *The History of the British Coal Industry, Vol. 4*, pp. 161–2.

186 Geary, *Policing Industrial Disputes*, pp. 53–5.

187 Morgan, *Conflict and Order*, pp. 99–107.

188 *Ibid.*, p. 105.

189 *Ibid.*, pp. 192–6; P. Davies, *A. J. Cook* (Manchester, Manchester University Press, 1987), p. 52–3; Woodhouse, 'Rank and File Movements among the Miners of South Wales', pp. 230–1; A. H. Horner, *Incorrigible Rebel* (London, MacGibbon and Kee, 1960), pp. 55–8.

190 *Ibid.*, pp. 55–8; Davies, *A. J. Cook*, pp. 53–7

191 Francis and Smith, *The Fed*, p. 29.

192 For details of the MMM, see Woodhouse, 'Rank and File Movements among the Miners of South Wales', pp. 236–300.

193 Francis and Smith, *The Fed*, pp. 30–1; A copy of the letter is in Arnot, *The South Wales Miners, 1914–1926*, p. 320.

194 Bellamy and Saville, *Dictionary of Labour Biography, Vol. 1*, p. 151.

5

'Citizens of this Great Republic': politics and the West Virginia miners, 1900–22

As we saw earlier, the battle of Blair Mountain marked the culmination of years of struggle on the part of the West Virginia miners, during which they overcame significant barriers to mount a remarkable display of industrial militancy. However, as we also saw, although the form of the march was insurrectionary, the demands and motivations of the miners were far from revolutionary; as UMWA Vice President Philip Murray put it, all sections of the community marched with the miners to 'fight for the establishment of true law and order.'[1]

The relative moderation of these demands, when related to the intensity of the conflict, was characteristic throughout this period, and reflected a general divergence in political identities between the miners of West Virginia and south Wales. In the Mountain State, the campaign for 'law and order' was placed within the context of a vague and loosely defined appeal for American rights and values. These appeals were not located within a wider political or ideological framework, and were frequently presented as self-evident statements of faith, which ignored the fact that the rights and values associated with Americanism could be interpreted in very different ways. No broader political identity was formed, nor did political organisation, or the use of protest at the ballot box, become characteristic in these years. In contrast, as we shall see in the next chapter, the south Wales miners were able to draw on their greater social and cultural collectivity to form a more unified and radical political identity, related to their position as miners in an industrial capitalist society, and resting on political organisation and the flexing of electoral muscles.

All of the barriers against unity at an industrial level, which the West Virginia miners so spectacularly overcame, were even more potent in regard to politics. As we saw earlier, the majority of the State's miners lived in new, unincorporated communities carved into the Appalachian mountains which were isolated both geographically and culturally. Particularly in the early years, they were not part of an existing political framework, nor, as new communities, could they draw on an existing political culture. This was reinforced by the temporary, transitory nature of life in the communities, in particular the remarkable mobility of the inhabitants, many of whom resided only temporarily within the State. When we further recall the fact that the majority of the labour force came from rural origins, and this mobility was often a sign of continued links with an agricultural past, it begins to become clear why, within the semi-agricultural mining towns, the formation of a common political identity would be an extremely difficult process.

This prospect was further impeded by the cultural mix of the communities which, whilst surmountable around a set of demands relating to the specifics of the operators' abuses, was more significant on a political level. For example, as we saw in chapter two, the foreign-born miners included various nationalities and hence, cultures and languages. At a practical level this would inhibit the spread of political ideas within the mining communities, beyond demands which clustered around the UMWA. Moreover, the fact that many of the foreign-born miners intended only a temporary stay in the coalfield had an important impact beyond its immediate effect, limiting the electoral strength of the miners as a whole. If we recall, by the end of the period under discussion, only 10% of this group had become naturalised citizens with the right to vote.[2]

For the black miners, the different pattern of race relations relative to the south, while not granting them social equality, did allow them to vote. As a consequence, like their counterparts with the franchise in other States, the vast majority of black miners voted along race lines for the Republican Party. For historical reasons, the Democratic Party rarely attracted black votes, and the Socialist Party of America (SPA), with its equivocal line towards racism, also secured little black support.[3] Indeed, the link between the black vote and the Republican Party was so strong that there were allegations throughout this period that the operators in southern West Virginia recruited blacks to shift the State's political balance.[4]

The most powerful example of the link with the Republican Party was McDowell County, where in 1910, 34.1% of the voting population were black. There were 5,883 black voters compared with 7,172 native whites and only 250 naturalised foreign-born miners. The majority of blacks resided in the Browns Creek, Northfork, Elkhorn, and Adkin districts, all of which had branches of the 'McDowell County Colored Republican Organisation' (founded in 1904). Commenting on this, the staunchly Republican black newspaper the *McDowell Times* said that 'of the 6,000 Negro voters of McDowell County, 90% will support men and measures endorsed by their leaders and supported by the McDowell Times.'[5]

This was underlined when John J. Cornwell, the sole Democratic Governor in this period, was elected in 1916. Complaining of the increased vote for the Democratic party in the County compared with 1912, an editorial proclaimed 'Black man loyal to the Republican Party', going on to say that 'with less than a dozen traitors, ingrates or jealous cowards among the Negroes, every black man in McDowell County voted the straight Republican ticket.'[6] Nor was black support a one way process. As Trotter has shown, the black community, particularly after the war, won concessions both in terms of representation and legislation. In the class sense, however, this tended to bind black miners into an alliance with the emerging black middle class and, in turn, with the coal operators who dominated the Republican Party.[7]

The native West Virginians within the mining communities discovered that, as with every other aspect of their lives, the coming of the new industrial order destroyed the traditional pattern of politics. Previously their independent, rural way of life had been marked by local political identities, usually based on kinship. Elections were treated as social occasions, often taking place on Sundays or public holidays.[8] The new political framework, created and dominated by the coal interests, ran counter to this in almost every sense. The former mountaineers, therefore, isolated within the coal towns, often clung to their identity as 'descendants of the pioneers' who had first settled the region and who still had a right to own the land.[9] Although this did not necessarily rule out the formation of a common politics with other groups, it did, when combined with the other barriers, make such a process more difficult.

Great though the above were as barriers against the formation of a common political identity, or political organisation, it was inevitably the overarching power of the operators which proved most significant. As we saw earlier, from mining town to State government, a formidable network of repression was in place to deal with recalcitrant UMWA organisers, and any other 'undesirable people', preventing them from organising meetings or distributing propaganda.[10] This obviously applied equally to advocates of political change, particularly if they were outsiders – as the IWW activist murdered in Logan Town in 1921 discovered to his cost.[11]

At the State level, as we saw earlier, particularly under the Cornwell administration, the distinction between industrial and political activity became confused behind a blanket paranoia about 'reds' and 'radicals'. Thus the most limited of demands could lead to the deportation of foreign-born miners, while the response to small quantities of radical literature led to State/Federal activity, and the passing of legislation such as the iniquitous 'Red Flag Act'.[12] Nor were these pressures restricted to the era of the 'red scare'. Although the intensity of repression was greater then, other Governors were equally dismissive of the right to free speech. We only have to remember the actions of Hatfield in suppressing criticism of his imposed 'settlement' of the 1912–13 Paint Creek strike, by smashing the presses and arresting the editor of the Huntington *Socialist and Labor Star*, to realise that the political elite in West Virginia gave dissenters from the gospel of industrial capitalism short shrift.[13]

The operators also interfered with the conduct of elections, particularly those for County posts which provided the basis for the control of the local mining communities. In 1922, for example, a US attorney wrote to the Attorney-General to complain that politics in Logan County was under the control of Sheriff Don Chafin, with 'election results figured up and given out in advance as to what the County will do.'[14] While Logan was probably the worst example of such excesses, electoral abuses were rife, particularly in other southern counties. Thus in 1920, a store owner in McDowell County appealed to W. B. Wilson for Federal aid to ensure fair elections. He reported that mine guards had assaulted local citizens, leaving him concerned that some 'voters in this County will be afraid to go to the polls.'[15] Similarly, in 1916 George Wolfe, manager of the Winding Gulf Colliery Company, wrote to Justus Collins to tell him that there was a 'determined effort to get Robinson votes here, which we had to fight all day', continuing later that 'the net result of the election I cannot give you, except that we took care of our place here very well.'[16]

Nor were the northern counties immune from such shenanigans. In 1908 'labor's champion', Samuel B. Montgomery, State Senator since 1904, was defeated in the Republican primary in Preston County. Having written and sponsored several bills sympathetic to labour's interest, Montgomery had made enemies among the operators. Consequently when the primary took place there were allegations of vote rigging and other malpractices. As the Charleston *Labor Argus* put it, the electoral officers allowed 'beasts of the field, fowls of the air and reptiles of the earth to vote - if they voted for Flynn' (Montgomery's opponent).[17]

A similar fate befell Montgomery's pursuit of the larger prize of the Republican nomination for the State Governorship in the 1920 election. Backed by the State's labour movement, which had been strengthened by the war, a vigorous campaign was launched against the operators' candidate, E. F. Morgan. However Montgomery was defeated by the narrow margin of 43,290 votes to 41,422, thanks to a poor showing in the State's southern counties. John L. Spivak recalled District 17 President Frank Keeney complaining about this to one of the organisers, who replied 'you should look at the river and you'll see what kind of showing we made . . . The ballots are still floating. They didn't even bother to burn them.' They went on to discover that the ballots had been counted by mine guards who, as deputies, were responsible for the conduct of elections. They simply declared every Montgomery vote 'invalid', collected them together and tossed them into the river.[18]

The operators' domination of the political apparatus of the State, which the electoral frauds helped perpetuate, was also a cause of political alienation, and hence a barrier to political action. Both the Democratic and Republican Parties were subservient to the coal interests, as were many of the County and State political offices.[19] This led to the defeat of legislation that the operator's deemed unsympathetic or, when such legislation was passed, as in the case of laws covering scrip and mine guards, ensured non enforcement.[20]

Consequently there was a tendency for the miners to withdraw from the political process and instead turn to the UMWA.[21] This helps explain why the pattern of industrial conflict, most notably in the march on Blair, was so intense and, in many ways, amounted to politics by another means. Indeed the intensity itself helped to focus attention on the specifics of battles in the industrial arena at the expense of a broader, more politicised outlook.

There is also a sense in which the lack of a common politics became a further barrier against its formation – a 'catch 22' – in the sense that political movements or parties not only reflect changes in political identities, but they themselves are agents that stimulate change, helping articulate identity itself.

Considering the remarkably inhospitable circumstances which have been described, it is perhaps surprising that the West Virginia miners engaged in the level of political organisation that they did, rather than vice versa. Although never consistently successful, this activity took place both within the existing party framework and through third party politics.

Prior to this period, in the late 1880s and 1890s, certain areas of the West Virginia coalfield had shown some interest in independent radical politics. Parts of the Kanawha region, in particular, supported the Greenback party, and later the Populists – the latter attracted support for their policy of government ownership of the mines.[22] However with the failure nationally of such attempts, combined with the extension and consolidation of the coal industry, attention was focused on activity within the existing political framework. In addition to the election of Montgomery in 1904, two years later District 17 President, John Nugent, and UMWA attorney, Adam B. Littlepage, were added to the State Senate on the Republican and Democratic tickets respectively. The latter elections led the editor of the *Labor Argus* to announce 'we have elected two of labor's greatest champions to offices where they can compel our enemies to show their hands.'[23]

This was certainly the case, although not quite in the way that the paper's editor had meant. The following year Nugent resigned the District 17 leadership to become State Immigration Commissioner – a post financed and controlled by the operators.[24] The following year also saw, alongside the defeat of Montgomery in the Preston County Republican primary, Littlepage fail to gain the Democratic nomination for the Governorship. Montgomery's Bill to remedy the abuses of the mine guards was also defeated.[25]

These events underlined the operators' stranglehold on the political system and the two established parties, and the difficulties of working within such a framework. Other politicians did run with labour support, such as Democrat Matthew M. Neely, former mayor of Fairmont and future State Governor, who established himself in Northern West Virginia due to splits in the Republican vote during the 'progressive era'. He went on to become a Federal Senator in 1922, with UMWA support, although he reneged on this as the decade progressed.[26] Similarly, Mooney and Blizzard ran unsuccessfully for State office at the end of this period, with the former defeated in 1920 and 1922 as a Republican candidate for the House of Delegates.[27] The black coal miner, John V. Coleman, was slightly more successful, securing election to the House of Delegates in 1918, where he helped influence the passage of a limited anti-lynching law. However, according to Trotter, Coleman was a fairly rare example, with most black mining votes going to buttress the emerging black middle class.[28]

The most vigorous challenge by labour, however, was Montgomery's campaign for the 1920 Republican nomination which, as we saw, ended with great acrimony. Indeed, so strong was the disgust at the manipulations of the ballot that a 'non-partisan' electoral ticket was drawn up for the subsequent elections, with Montgomery at the head, and six Republican and six Democratic candidates for the main State offices. Although defeated by Morgan who secured 150,000 votes, Montgomery came second with a remarkable 81,000 votes, beating the Democrat into third place on 42,500.[29] A similar, independent campaign was run four years later when the veteran radical, Robert M. LaFollette, backed by various labour/left/progressive groups ran against the major parties for the Presidency, and secured nearly five million votes (16.5%).[30] In West Virginia, however, despite efforts by local union leaders, including Mooney who once again ran for the House of Delegates, this time on an independent ticket, the total vote was only 37,724.[31]

Notwithstanding the Montgomery and LaFollette campaigns, the most consistent attempt at creating a genuinely independent labour politics, outside the established parties, was made by the SPA which was at its strongest in the State around the middle of this period. Although partially a response to the disillusion with the political situation within West Virginia, the advance of the SPA was also linked to the national political context, where the party presented an increasingly powerful political alternative. Under the inspirational, if sometimes inconsistent, leadership of Eugene V. Debs, the SPA had not only made electoral advances, but increased its influence within the trade unions, including the powerful UMWA.[32] Thus at the 1912 annual conference the union voted in favour of 'government ownership' of all industries, and added to the constitution the demand that miners be given 'the full social value of our product.' They also, while heavily rejecting the specific support of the SPA, struck out the clause within the UMWA constitution which demanded political neutrality.[33] The more positive stance towards the SPA on behalf of the UMWA, the wider trade union movement, and the electorate generally, proved short-lived, however, as divisions within the SPA, the war, State repression, and social and political changes led to a precipitous collapse in support.[34] This affected West Virginia as much as the rest of the US.

The rise, and indeed fall, of the socialist vote in West Virginia may have mirrored the national pattern, but it did so at a lower level. This point should be stressed as there has been a tendency, in the sparse historiography on the subject, to overemphasise the level and significance of SPA support within the State. Thus Corbin, for example, claims that by the middle of this period the SPA had 'made strong inroads among West Virginia's industrial workers, especially among its coal miners', helping to create 'a growing, viable State Socialist movement.'[35]

This view creates two problems. Firstly, it is permeated by the idea that there should have been an inevitable socialist advance: an idea which is historically inaccurate. Secondly, connected with this, the overestimation of the socialist advance leads to the need to create an artificial explanation for its subsequent decline. In Corbin's case this involves an unconvincing attempt to blame the demise on the 'policies and actions' of Debs during, and in the immediate aftermath of, a short visit to the State during the Paint Creek strike.[36] On the contrary, as was established earlier, given the circumstances within West Virginia, any independent political activity was a remarkable achievement – rather than being somehow inadequate when compared with a mythical ideal type.

The level of the socialist vote in West Virginia is put into stark perspective if we look at the Presidential vote in this period. In 1904, Debs secured only 1,573 (0.7%) votes in West Virginia compared with a national vote of 402,283 (2.98%). This increased to 1.4% (compared with 2.82% nationally) four years later, reaching a high point of 15,248 (5.7%) votes in the election of 1912. This coincided with the national SPA vote of 900,672 (5.99%).[37] Even at the height of the SPA's electoral power, therefore, West Virginia was recording less than the national average, and well below States which had a more vigorous socialist electoral presence. In the same election, for

217

example, Debs received 16.5% of the vote in Nevada, 16.4% in
Oklahoma, 13.5 % in Montana, 13.4% in Arizona, 12.4% in
Washington, 11.7% in California and, 11.3% in Idaho.[38]

In the 1916 election the SPA candidate, Allan L. Benson, polled
less than half the 1912 vote with 6,144 (2.1%), while nationally the
vote dropped to 518,113 (3.18%). In 1920, with the incarcerated
Debs again the candidate, a further drop to a dismal 5,609 (1.1%)
was recorded in West Virginia, compared with a small real increase
nationally to 919,799 (3.42%).[39]

The weakness of the SPA vote revealed in these figures in many
ways speaks for itself. However, State-wide results, particularly
those in Presidential elections, tell only part of the story. If we look
at individual counties in the 1912 election, it becomes clear that the
distribution of the vote was far from even. For example Kanawha
and Fayette Counties, both of which were embroiled in the Paint
Creek dispute, recorded the first and third highest votes for Debs
with 3,071 (20%) and 1,428 (9%) respectively. Similarly Ohio with
1,579 (10.35%) and Harrison with 1,077 (7%) polled over the
average.[40] This was also reflected in the vote for State offices which,
despite Debs' popularity and personal appeal, kept pace with the
Presidential vote.[41] On a State basis the socialist candidate for
Governor, W.B. Hinton, polled 14,900 votes, compared with Debs'
15,248, while all the other major offices attracted over 15,000
votes.[42] On a County level Hinton's vote sometimes exceeded that of
Debs, as in the case of Kanawha where 3,380 votes were cast for the
former, compared with 3,071 for the latter.[43]

If we break down the vote within Kanawha County an even more
interesting pattern emerges. Although the SPA came third overall,
the party's ticket proved more successful within certain electoral districts. In the Cabin Creek district, heart of the strike zone, socialists
were elected to every office, with the ticket polling 2,328 votes compared with 1,142 for the Republicans and 667 for the Democrats.
The Democrats were also pushed into third place in two of the other
eleven districts. All of this was in spite of allegations of electoral
malpractice. Noting the failure to carry Kanawha County as a
whole, the *Wheeling Majority* reported socialist allegations that
their observers had been ejected from some polling stations, 'so they
don't know how many votes were stolen from them.'[44]

Nor was the SPA vote solely explained by the concurrent strike.
The vote may have increased, proportionally, at a higher rate than

218

any other County, but even prior to this certain Kanawha districts had elected socialists. Thus in 1910 two UMWA members were elected as, respectively, Justice of the Peace and Constable in the Washington district.[45] Furthermore, if we recall, it was these districts which at the end of the previous century had voted for radical candidates; something which Williams believes provided the basis for the later socialist successes.[46]

The 1914 elections, deprived of the possible distortion of a Presidential vote, illustrate many of these trends perfectly. While the State-wide vote dropped to 4%,[47] in the vote for Congressman-at-large, Kanawha again recorded the highest vote with 18.42%, followed by Fayette (14.62%) Harrison (11.21%), and Boone (10.91%), which were the only other counties to poll over 10%. In contrast, the socialist candidate E. H. Kintzer only secured 2.28% in Logan and 0.41% in McDowell.[48] Furthermore, scotching Corbin's claim that Debs damaged the SPA during the Paint Creek strike, the Cabin Creek district again returned the complete socialist ticket, increasing their 'straight vote'.[49]

The significance of this pattern should not be missed. The overall socialist vote within the State was based on a disproportionate distribution between and within counties. The fact that these districts have attracted the attention of historians has helped create the distortion in the perceived strength of the socialist vote in the State as a whole.

Of course, this doesn't mean that the Kanawha socialist vote was insignificant. On the contrary, it reveals that a socialist presence could emerge, particularly where a 'radical' tradition already existed. However, Kanawha, and more importantly, specific districts within the County, were an exception rather than the rule in this respect. Indeed, isolated amongst a largely non-socialist voting population, even Kanawha proved unable to sustain a significant socialist presence in subsequent years. Thus in 1916, as the SPA vote in the State dropped from 4% to 2.1% compared with 1914, Kanawaha, for example, fell to only 3.2%. Within this the socialist vote in Cabin Creek was only 11%, compared with 47% two years previously.[50]

These voting figures also underline the lack of correlation between industrial conflict and socialist voting patterns with, once again, the rise in socialist support during the Paint Creek strike being an exception rather than the rule. After all at the height of the Mine Wars the SPA were conspicuous by their absence with the dismal 1.1% vote – Logan, for example, only polled 27 votes for Debs.[51]

Of course it would be wrong, especially if we take into account the difficulties involved in mounting an electoral challenge in West Virginia in these years, to completely write off the socialist influence solely on these electoral figures, revealing though they are. Certainly the socialist press, particularly the *Labor Argus* (which was converted to socialism in 1910) and the *Socialist and Labor Star*, at times, played an active and influential part in not only publicising the abuses within the State, but in encouraging the miners to resist them – hence the unsolicited attention of Hatfield during the Paint Creek strike and, on behalf of the conservative and corrupt local UMWA leadership, the rival *Miners' Herald*.[52]

Furthermore, some of the newer generation of local leaders who came to the fore during the Paint Creek strike, most notably Keeney and Mooney were, for a time at least, associated with the SPA,[53] as were some of the organisers sent in by the national organisation like black SPA activist, George H. Edmunds.[54] Similarly several visits by Debs and other socialist leaders, including in 1912 the MP for the Merthyr Boroughs, Keir Hardie, all raised the profile of the socialists. The latter meeting, for example, took place at Wheeling Fair Grounds after a march by 3,000 workers which proclaimed 'Down with the Mine Guards', and 'The Socialist Party. The only party that never took a cent from big business'.[55]

However, although Italians marched with a red flag at Boomer in 1913,[56] and a District 17 delegate to the UMWA national convention in 1914 declared 'In West Virginia the struggles would not have been won if it had not been for the socialists in that State',[57] the majority of these examples are, as with the electoral pattern, restricted to the middle of this period, and involving events or protagonists from the Kanawha region. The overwhelming impression remains that socialist support was marginal, submerged within a broader non-class based Americanism – the stars and stripes were more in evidence than the red flag.

This is further underlined by the lack of support for the IWW which, as the main left-wing revolutionary alternative, might have been expected to pick up support from socialists disillusioned with, or intimidated from using, the ballot box. However, although Cornwell, Debs, and some historians have seen the IWW hand lurking behind the coal tipples,[58] there is little evidence to support this. Within the local SPA, left-wing elements admitted some sympathy with Haywood but, at the same time, were not opposed to electoral activity.[59] More generally, as IWW activist Ralph Chaplin, in West Virginia at the time of the Paint Creek strike wrote:

> There was little use in proclaiming the virtues of the IWW to the striking coal miners or the hill folks . . . (as) . . . The miners not only had a union already and an industrial union of sorts, but, being in the middle of a two year strike, they were certainly more interested in remaining alive than in listening to arguments in favor of dual organisation.[60]

This was something which even an FBI agent in Charleston at the end of this period agreed with. He reported that he 'never believed that there has been much, if any, outside political agitation at work' in the State.[61]

Not only did the FBI agent refute the suggestion of widespread outside agitation among the West Virginia miners, but he also described what he believed lay behind the miners' actions – in terms not far removed from Chaplin. The local union leadership, he argued, were of 'an extremely radical type'. However, crucially, he continued that:

> All of the radicalism seems to find vent in State issues and the radical elements have been almost completely absorbed in this struggle . . . little or no interest has been manifested in radical issues having a national or international application. Their minds and lives are fully occupied with the struggle immediately at hand . . . teachings and propaganda are directed almost solely against the coal operators of the State, rather than against capitalistic interests everywhere.[62]

The fact that an IWW activist and an FBI agent both stressed the way the miners focused on the specific State issues is as unusual as it is significant, underlining the previous evidence which suggested that due to the significant barriers within the State, the extension of the formidable displays of solidarity and direct action into a wider political movement did not take place, and there was no sustained political activity by the miners either within the existing political framework, or through independent alternatives.

Instead, the focus on the 'struggle immediately at hand', rather than broader class concerns, led to an emphasis on the denial of rights; particularly the right to join the UMWA. The union thus became doubly significant, both as an example of operator

221

interference in the miners' freedom of action, but also, as the only 'alternative source of institutional power', as the potential vehicle, symbolically and practically, for bringing about change.[63] To those engaged in the struggle to establish the union in West Virginia the compromises and contradictions of union policy were often lost beneath a more general faith in the power of the idea of unionism, and its role in remedying the wrongs they experienced. As Winthrop D. Lane put it, 'Keeney has no carefully thought out philosophy of a class struggle . . . His experience is his philosophy. He believes in unionism.'[64]

This struggle for the union and the restoration of rights was placed within a loose frame of reference of what were seen as American values. The system of relations within the State was seen as a throwback to the past, or to the 'old world', what Samuel Gompers stridently called 'Russianized West Virginia'.[65] UMWA Vice President Frank J. Hayes spoke in 1913, of how 'conditions in West Virginia are different from those in other States . . . These conditions have developed a feudal State in the coal mining regions that find no comparison except in the feudalism of the middle ages.'[66] A similar comparison to that was made eight years later by miners at Cannelton who complained of 'inherited laws from the old days in Europe when Saxon or Norman earls administered justice direct with knotted clubs, cleavers and swords.'[67]

Miners at Mountclare compared the situation with British domination in the eighteenth century, complaining that, 'the working people are getting very much agitated over the latest developements (sic) in Mingo; King George the III used the same tactics in '76'.[68] Mother Jones also cited the abuses of monarchy when she was incarcerated during the Paint Creek dispute, claiming that it was 'just what the old monarchy did (to) my grandparents ninety years ago in Ireland.'[69] A Russian born miner argued likewise when, in 1900, he wrote to the *UMWJ* to complain that miners were treated the same as 'in the old country from the Russian government'.[70]

To both native born and foreign born this was seen as un-American, and a betrayal of the meaning of republican America – what Gompers called, in the subtitle to his 1913 piece, 'Corporate perversion of American concepts of Liberty and Human Justice'.[71] Polish born UMWA organiser, Albert Manka, complained that, 'I always thought this was a free country, but I have found there isn't much liberty in the State of West Virginia for a poor working man.'[72] Similarly underneath the headline 'Slave Drivers', the Labor Argus reported that a mass meeting on Cabin Creek had described the guard system as 'unnecessary and un-American'.[73] Most graphically, UMWA Vice President Phillip Murray reported that the marchers on Logan had told him:

> "We fought for America in France. We returned home to find that we, in West Virginia, are not really and truly in America. We have made up our minds to do battle in West Virginia for the purpose of returning the State to the country." Everywhere you go along the fighting line, all that one will hear is "Let us win West Virginia back to America".[74]

On the surface at least, the evocation of America and its symbols seemed straightforward. Independence day was usually marked by marches,[75] and the flag was also prominent with, for example, protesting miners marching behind it during the Fairmont dispute.[76] A striker in the Paint Creek strike eleven years later, emboldened by the flag's symbolic value, hung the stars and stripes outside his tent with the words: 'I don't know any better banner for Americans who are willing to starve for the sake of liberty, to fight under'.[77]

During the same dispute 5,000 miners marching to hear Mother Jones speak did so to the tune of 'America' and 'Star Spangled Banner'.[78] All of the above would have agreed with the sentiments of the miners at Bower who, in a letter to Governor E. F. Morgan, called for a 'course of education in Americanism' in West Virginia, ending with the assertion 'America, the land of the free, is not a place for feudalism of any kind.'[79]

More specifically the miners appealed for their rights as citizens via the application of the Constitution and the Bill of Rights. The Bower miners, for example, included in their letter a call for 'a greater sense of justice and a full measure of the workers' constitutional guarantees to the protection of their rights to organize and combine'.[80] In the same year a local union at Mammoth told the Secretary of Labor that the 'miners ask little' – just fair weighing, the abolition of the mine guards and 'to be treated as Citizens of this Great Republic and knot (sic) Slaves . . . all we wont (sic) is justice and fair play.'[81] As did a local union at Rosebud who demanded of President Harding that he 'restore constitutional rights to the citizens of McDowell and Logan Counties and along the M and K railroad in Monongalia and Preston Counties', as the miners were 'being deprived of the rights to live as citizens'.[82]

In the same vein the Kanawha strikers, after a rally in August 1912, presented Governor W. E. Glasscock with a petition which claimed that the mine guards 'beat, abuse, maim, and hold up citizens without process of law; deny freedom of speech, a provision guaranteed by the Constitution; deny the citizens the right to assemble in a peaceable manner'.[83] An almost identical appeal to that of the Cannelton miners who called for the implementation of 'the Bill of Rights and the Constitution of the United States enjoyed by citizens in all other States of the union', in place of the 'knotted clubs' mentioned earlier, as well as urging Keeney to organise a 'Constitutional League'.[84]

Among the many other complaints, conveyed directly to Governor E. F. Morgan, a local union at Monclo threatened recall proceedings because, they claimed, 'your acts as governor of this State in said strike indicates your intention to defeat the miners in gaining their statutory rights' which 'is in violation of your oath of office'.[85] This was typical, as was the appeal from Mountclare for the 'granting to the miners of this State their lawful and citizens' constitutional rights'.[86]

Heroic figures from the past were also cited in support of the miners' demands. The foreign-born miner who compared the State with his native Russia, for example, concluded, optimistically, that 'as Lincoln said, we will come out on top'.[87] Lincoln was also mentioned in a letter to President Harding in 1922. Margaret Fowles, a miner's wife from Scottdale, concluded her eloquent appeal with, 'no man is fit to preside over the destiny of this Republic who does not recognise with Lincoln that the voice of the people is the voice of God'.[88]

Others, like Keeney, used the example of such historical figures to justify the miners' call to arms. Replying to criticism of a speech he made during which a revolver was inadvertently displayed, Keeney remarked:

> I am still inclined to have my constitutional rights or raise hell. Patrick Henry hinted at the same conviction, and even Thomas Jefferson and a few of his fellow patriots not only believed in raising hell to secure their rights, but actually did so . . . In fact, I'm inclined to the conviction that any one who won't raise hell to protect his rights is a poor citizen.[89]

A conviction shared by Mother Jones who in 1912, for example, told the Kanawha strikers how she led a group of miners up to

Acme. After receiving loud cheers from the audience when she recalled that 'we took a couple of guns because we knew we were going to meet some thugs', she added 'we will prepare for the job, just like Lincoln and Washington did. We took lessons from them'.[90]

The lessons taken from the past and, indeed, the whole appeal to American rights and values were, however, far more ambiguous than they seem at first. Were the miners fighting to receive the same treatment as the rest of America, or were they appealing to a more radical, historical, ideal of America? Moreover, what did this ideal mean? Gompers and Keeney, for example, had very different definitions. In fact these issues were never really worked out and instead the overwhelming impression is of the assertion of these rights and symbols as being somehow absolute and self-evident – as if the myth and reality of America somehow coincided, or were interchangeable.

Yet those responsible for the miners' exploitation in West Virginia themselves espoused Americanism, and laid claim to the same rights and traditions as justification for their actions; as the Revd. G. B. Hammer, who was seemingly reduced to apoplexy after hearing Mother Jones speak, put it, 'Every true and thoughtful American citizen sees that America needs more Americanizing.'[91] This similarity in language is apparent, for example, in the operators' involvement in the American Constitutional Association at the end of this period. They published *The American Citizen* twice monthly, and claimed to support 'American Ideals', 'a greater respect for law and order', 'real patriotism and love of country', as opposed to the (mythical) 'tide of Bolshevism'.[92]

The claim that they were upholding law and order was central to the operator and State government's arguments. Thus Morgan replied to the miners at Bower, 'I assure you that every effort possible is being made to secure the people, and when I say "people" I mean *all the people* of Mingo County, the rights guaranteed to them by our State and federal constitutions.'[93] It is clear that this definition of America, its constitution, and the meaning of citizenship, involved opposing unions, socialists and any others who attempted to protest against the unfettered excesses of business. In their view, it was the UMWA which was un-American.

And it was this definition of the meaning of America, rather than the miners' definition, which was closest to that held by those in power in the US generally. In reality, the US labour movement had consistently appealed to the radical republican tradition and the constitutional order, yet had been restrained by hostile court and government decisions. It was not only in West Virginia in this period, therefore, that workers discovered that they 'did not live in a world shaped according to their preferred version of Americanism'.[94]

If, therefore, it was this America which the West Virginia miners were wanting to return to, they would have encountered a reality which was far removed from the Bower miners' demand for 'full measure of the workers constitutional guarantees to the protection of their rights to organize and combine'. But such issues were never completely worked through. This was not a class conscious version of Americanism, as suggested by Corbin,[95] but rather a vague political language constructed against the odds amidst a severely fragmented social and political culture. With no political movement to help construct a genuinely radical language, or connect it to a wider political discourse, the heterogeneous workforce were only able to unite around a broad belief in law and order, and their rights as citizens of a 'Great Republic' which submerged the ambiguity of such beliefs, and failed to clarify, or place in context, the underlying economic basis for their exploitation.

Notes

1 *Wheeling Register*, 3 Sep 1921, p. 1. (Previously cited, Chapter three, p. 152).

2 See Chapter two, p. 33.

3 F. Barkey, 'The Socialist Party in West Virginia from 1898–1920: A Study in Working-Class Radicalism' (Unpublished Ph.D dissertation, University of Pittsburgh, 1971), p. 168; I. Howe, *Socialism and America* (San Diego, Harcourt Brace Javanovich, 1985), pp. 19–22; S. Miller, 'Socialism and Race'; T. Kornweiber, 'A Reply', in J. H. M. and S. M. Lipset (eds.), *Failure of a Dream?: Essays in the History of American Socialism* (Berkeley, University of California Press,1984 edn.), pp. 223–8, 231–40.

4 W. A. MacCorkle, *The Recollections of Fifty Years of West Virginia* (New York, G. P. Putnam's Sons, 1928), p. 479; R. L. Lewis, *Black Coal Miners in America: Race, Class and Community Conflict, 1790–1980* (Lexington, University Press of Kentucky, 1987), pp. 126–7.

5 *McDowell Times*, 16 May 1913, p. 1.

6 *Ibid.*, 10 Nov 1916, p. 2.

7 J. W. Trotter Jr., *Coal, Class and Color: Blacks in Southern West Virginia, 1915–32* (Urbana, University of Illinois Press, 1991), pp. 216–58.

8 J. C. Campbell, *The Southern Highlander and His Homeland* (Lexington, University Press of Kentucky, 1969 edn.), pp. 100–3; R. D. Eller, *Miners, Millhands, and Mountaineers: Industrialization of the Appalachian South, 1880–1930* (Knoxville, University of Tennessee Press, 1982), p. 235.

9 F. Mooney, *Struggle in the Coal Fields* [ed. J. W. Hess] (Morgantown, West Virginia University Library Press, 1967), p. 16; US Senate, *Conditions in the Paint Creek District, West Virginia*, 63 Congress, 1 Session (Washington D.C., 1913), Pt. 1, p. 790; R. Chaplin, 'Violence in West Virginia', *International Socialist Review*, 13 (Apr 1913), pp. 730–1; J. L. Spivak, *A Man and His Time* (New York, Horizon Press, 1967), p. 57.

10 Collins to Wolfe, 27 Dec 1915, Morgantown, West Virginia University (WVU), West Virginia and Regional History Collection, Justus Collins Papers (A+M 1824), Series 1, Box 13, File 93.

11 See Chapter three, p. 129.

12 *Ibid.*, pp. 216–17.

13 *Ibid.*, pp. 200–1.

14 US Attorney Northcott to Attorney-General, 18 Dec 1922, NA, Department of Justice (RG 60), File 16–130–83, Folder 4; Walker Report, pp. 2–4, Daily Reports of Field Investigators, Mar-Aug 1923, Suitland, Washington National Records Center (WNRC), Records of US Coal Commission (RG 68), Division of Investigation of Labor Facts, Labour Relations Section, 161, Box 70.

15 W. H. Cline to Wilson, Sec. of Labor, 12 Oct 1920, WNRC, Records of Federal Mediation and Conciliation Service (FMCS) (RG 280), File 170/1185, Part One.

16 Wolfe to Collins, 7 Jun 1916, Collins papers, Box 14, File 96.

17 *Labor Argus*, 23 Apr 1908, p. 1; 30 Apr 1908, p. 1.

18 Spivak, *A Man and His Time*, pp. 86–7; E. L. K. Harris and F. J. Krebs, *From Humble Beginnings: West Virginia State Federation of Labor, 1903–1957* (Charleston, West Virginia Labor History Publishing Fund, 1960), pp. 175–7.

19 J. A. Williams, *West Virginia and the Captains of Industry* (Morgantown, West Virginia University Library Press, 1976), pp. 3–16; Eller, *Miners, Millhands and Mountaineers*, pp. 211–17; D. A. Corbin, *Life, Work and Rebellion in the Coal Fields: The Southern West Virginia Miners, 1880–1922* (Urbana, University of Illinois Press, 1981), pp. 12–13.

20 H. B. Lee, *Bloodletting in Appalachia: The Story of West Virginia's Four Major Mine Wars and Other Thrilling Incidents of its Coal Fields* (Morgantown, West Virginia University Library Press, 1969), pp. 10–11; Eller, *Miners, Millhands and Mountaineers*, pp. 217–18; J. B. Thomas, 'Coal Country: the Rise of the Southern Smokeless Coal Industry and its Effect on Area Development' (Unpublished Ph.D dissertation, University of North Carolina, 1971), pp. 224–5.

21 Eller, *Miners, Millhands and Mountaineers*, pp. 234–5; J. A. Williams, *West Virginia: A History* (New York, W. W. Norton and Co.,1976), pp. 142–3.

22 Williams, *West Virginia and the Captains of Industry*, p. 122–4; J. H. M. Laslett, *Labor and the Left: A Study of Socialist and Radical Influences in the American Labor Movement, 1881–1924* (New York, Basic Books, 1970), p. 201.

23 *Labor Argus*, 8 Nov 1906, pp. 1–2.

24 *Ibid.*, 30 May 1907, p. 1.

25 Harris and Krebs, *From Humble Beginnings*, p. 47.

26 *Ibid.*, p. 82; Williams, *West Virginia*, p. 146.

27 Mooney, *Struggle in the Coal Fields*, pp. 129–30.

28 Trotter, *Coal, Class and Color*, pp. 47–49, 226–7, 251–2.

29 Harris and Krebs, *From Humble Beginnings*, p. 177; Lunt, *Law and Order vs. The Miners: West Virginia* (Hamden, Conn., Archon Books, 1979), p. 117.

30 D. P. Thelen, *Robert M. La Follete and the Insurgent Spirit* (Boston, Little Brown, 1976), pp. 181–92; N. Salvatore, *Eugene V. Debs: Citizen and Socialist* (Urbana, University of Illinois Press, 1983), pp. 335–7.

31 Harris and Krebs, *From Humble Beginnings*, pp. 179–80; Mooney put his own defeat down to familiar causes: 'Against me were aligned both the Democrat and Republican political machines, the Ku Klux Klan, The Law and Order League, and the bankers and businessmen of the County'. *Struggle in the Coal Fields*, pp. 129–30.

32 Salvatore, *Eugene V. Debs*, pp. 220–302; R. Ginger, *Eugene V. Debs: A Biography* (New York, Macmillan, 1962 edn.), pp. 220–332; Howe, *Socialism and America*, pp. 3–35.

33 UMWA, *Proceedings of 23rd Annual Convention, 1910*, pp. 191, 215–46, 433–41; Laslett, *Labor and the Left*, pp. 216–19.

34 Laslett, *Labor and the Left*, pp. 218–31; 'End of an Alliance: Selected Correspondence between Socialist Party Secretary Adolph Germer, and UMW of A Leaders in World War One', *Labor History*, 12, 4 (1977), pp. 570–95; Howe, *Socialism and America*, pp. 36–48; Salvatore, *Eugene V. Debs*, pp. 262–345; Ginger, *Eugene V. Debs*, pp. 335–482; J. Weinstein, *The Decline of Socialism in America, 1912–1925* (New York, Monthly Review Press, 1967).

35 The most obvious example of this is D. A. Corbin, 'Betrayal in the West Virginia Coal Fields: Eugene V. Debs and the Socialist Party of America, 1912–1914', *Journal of American History*, 64 (1978), pp. 987–1009. The quote is p. 988. It must be noted, however, that Corbin himself downplays the influence of the SPA in the full length study, *Life, Work and Rebellion in the Coal Fields*, pp. 240–7. Barkey's 'Socialist Party in West Virginia', although less polemical than the Corbin article, also tends to overestimate the SPA strength, see in particular, Chapter IV, 'We had the Revolution'. See also M. Nash, *Conflict and Accommodation: Coal Miners, Steel Workers, and Socialism, 1890–1920* (Westport, Con., Greenwood Press, 1982), pp. 139–48, which falls into a similar trap to the Corbin article. Part of the problem with the Corbin and Nash argument is their over-reliance on the accounts of contemporary socialists who due to the circumstances of struggle, and for reasons of propaganda, exaggerated socialist influence. See, for example, E. H. Kintzer, 'Reconstruction in West Virginia', *International Socialist Review*, 14 (Jul 1913), pp. 23–4.

36 Corbin, 'Betrayal in the West Virginia Coal Fields'. For a detailed critique of this view, see R. J. Fagge, 'Eugene V. Debs in West Virginia, 1913: A Re-appraisal', *West Virginia History*, 52 (1993), pp. 1–18.

37 US Congress, *Presidential Elections since 1789* (Congressional Quarterly, Washington D.C., 1983), pp. 99–107; M. A. Jones, *The Limits of Liberty: American History 1607–1980* (Oxford, Oxford University Press, 1983), p. 650.

38 *Presidential Elections since 1789*, p. 102.

39 *Ibid.*, p. 99–107; Jones, *Limits of Liberty*, p. 650.

40 *Wheeling Majority*, 5 Dec 1912, p. 1.

41 In West Virginia, as elsewhere, Debs' popularity was wider than those who defined themselves as socialists. See, for example, the warm reception he received during his visit to the State in 1913 – even from the local press, *Charleston Gazette*, 20 May 1913, p. 1; *Wheeling Register*, 20 May 1913, p. 1. See also Spivak, *A Man and his Time*, p. 62.

42 *Wheeling Majority*, 5 Dec 1912, p. 1.

43 *Ibid.*

44 *Wheeling Majority*, 14 Nov 1912, p. 1.

45 *Labor Argus*, 17 Nov 1910, p. 1.

46 Williams, *West Virginia and the Captains of Industry*, pp. 123–4.

47 Barkey, 'The Socialist Party in West Virginia', p. 164.

48 *Socialist and Labor Star*, 11 Dec 1914, p. 2.

49 *Ibid.*, 13 Nov 1914, p. 3.

50 Barkey, 'The Socialist Party in West Virginia', pp. 193–5, 251.

51 Nash, *Conflict and Accommodation*, p. 146.

52 See Chapter three, pp. 123–5.

53 Corbin, *Life, Work and Rebellion in the Coal Fields*, p. 240; Interview with Bert Castle, WVU, Oral History Collection.
54 Edmunds, however, also later left the party. R. L. Lewis, 'The Black Presence in the Paint-Cabin Creek Strike 1912–1913', *West Virginia History*, 44 (1985–6), p. 66.
55 *Wheeling Register*, 6 Oct 1912, p. 20.
56 Barkey, 'Socialist Party in West Virginia from 1898–1920', p. 152.
57 UMWA, *Proceedings of 24th Convention, 1914*, p. 408.
58 Debs made his accusations at the height of the controversy over his 1913 visit: see E. V. Debs, 'Debs Denounces Critics', *International Socialist Review*, 14 (Aug 1913), pp. 105–6. Salvatore not only agrees, but believes that the Paint Creek strike 'confirmed all his (Debs') worst fears concerning the nature of IWW organising drives', *Eugene V. Debs*, p. 257. Other historians suggesting a strong IWW presence are Nash, *Conflict and Accomodation*, p. 143; S. Bird, D. Georgakas, and D. Shaffer (eds.), *Solidarity Forever, The IWW: An Oral History of the Wobblies* (London, Lawrence and Wishart, 1987), p. 126.
59 See, for example, H. W. Houston's speech at Holly Grove, 4 Aug 1912, where he proposed both direct action, and use of the ballot box, *Conditions in the Paint Creek District*, Pt. 3, pp. 2258–61; *Socialist and Labor Star*, 4 Mar 1914, p. 4; Barkey, 'The Socialist Party in West Virginia', pp. 146–50; M. Dubofsky's history of the IWW, *We Shall be All: A History of the IWW* (Chicago, 1969), has no mention of IWW activities in West Virginia.
60 R. Chaplin, *Wobbly: The Rough-and-Tumble Story of an American Radical* (Chicago, University of Chicago Press, 1948), p. 121.
61 Report of Agent H. Nathan, NA, Records of War Department General Staff (RG165), Military Intelligence Division Correpondence, 1917–41 (Entry 65), Box 3649, File 10634–793, Folder 5.
62 *Ibid.*
63 Lewis, *Black Coal Miners in America*, pp. 156–7.
64 W. D. Lane, *Civil War in West Virginia: A Story of Industrial Conflict in the Coal Mines* (New York, B. W. Huebsch, 1921), p. 85.
65 S. Gompers, 'Russianized West Virginia', *American Federationist*, 20, 10 (Oct 1913), pp. 825–35. (Previously cited, Chapter three, p. 119.)
66 *Socialist and Labor Star*, 30 Aug 1913, p. 3.
67 Letter from various locals at Mass Meeting to Keeney, 10 Jul 1921, WVU, E.F. Morgan Papers (A+M 203), Box 8, File 1.
68 Mountclare Committee to Morgan, 15 July 1921, Morgan Papers, Box 8, File 2.
69 M. Jones to Borah, n.d., General Records of the Department of Labor, File 16–13 E, Box 24. (Previously cited, Chapter three, p. 122.)
70 *UMWJ*, 15 Nov 1900, p. 4.

71 Gompers, 'Russianized West Virginia', p. 825.
72 *UMWJ*, 11 Oct 1900, p. 4.
73 *Labor Argus*, 8 Jul 1909, p. 1.
74 *Wheeling Register*, 3 Sep 1921, p. 6.
75 For example, at the start of this period miners paraded at Loup Creek on Independence day 'wearing the miners badge', *UMWJ*, 19 Jul 1900, p. 4.
76 E. M. Steel, 'Mother Jones in the Fairmont Field, 1902', *Journal of American History*, 57 (1970), p. 294.
77 *UMWJ*, 12 Sep 1912, p. 2.
78 *Ibid.*, p. 1.
79 Bower Committee to Morgan, 14 Jul 1921, Morgan Papers, Box 8, File 2.
80 Bower Committee to Morgan, 14 Jul 1921, *ibid*.
81 L.U. 404 to Sec. of Labor, 12 Sep 1921, FMCS, File 170/1185 A.
82 Resolutions Committee, Rosebud to Pres. Harding, 2 Sep 1920, *ibid.*, File 170/1185, Part 1.
83 *Conditions in the Paint Creek District*, Pt. 3, p. 2263.
84 Letter from various locals at mass meeting to Keeney, 10 Jul 1921, Morgan Papers, Box 8, File 1.
85 Local 4384, Monclo to Morgan, 14 Jul 1921, *ibid.*, Box 8, File 2.
86 Mountclare Committee to Morgan, 15 Jul 1921, *ibid*.
87 *UMWJ*, 15 Nov 1900, p. 4.
88 Fowles to Harding, 6 Jan 1922, FMCS, File 170/1185 A
89 *West Virginia Federationist*, 26 Feb 1920, p. 1.
90 *Conditions in the Paint Creek District*, Pt. 3, p. 2264.
91 Statement enclosed with letter from A. R. Montgomery to Cornwell, Cornwell Papers, Series 35, Box 136.
92 See leaflet 'The Work of the American Constitutional Association', *ibid.*, Box 135.
93 Morgan to A. M. Wimer, Bower Local, 16 Jul 1921, Morgan Papers, Box 8, File 2.
94 L. Fink, 'Labor, Liberty and the Law: Trade Unionism and the Problem of American Constitutional Order', *Journal of American History*, 74, 1 (1987), pp. 904–25, 906.
95 Corbin, *Life, Work and Rebellion in the Coal Fields*, pp. 244–6.

6

Liberal, Labour, Syndicalist: politics in the south Wales coalfield, 1900–22

In the examination of industrial conflict in south Wales it was clear that, relative to West Virginia, the nature of culture and the type of communities in the region played a decisive role in shaping the pattern of such conflict. Although confronted by what were in British terms particularly fierce owners, the south Wales miners were able to organise within the SWMF, and conduct strikes without the need to resort to the huge armed marches of their West Virginian counterparts. In doing so they became the most militant and influential region within the British coalfields.

As the factors which shaped industrial conflict proved even more effective as a barrier against political organisation in West Virginia, so in south Wales the relative absence of such barriers proved the opposite. The generally larger, older, less isolated, more permanent mining communities in south Wales provided a firmer base for the nurture and spread of political activity. Similarly the overwhelmingly collective culture which developed within these communities was underpinned by the greater cultural homogeneity and the location of this culture within existing traditions of radical political activity which, due to the greater age of the communities were, by the start of this period, part of the miners' common heritage.

The different power relations in south Wales also meant these communities were fully integrated into a political framework and therefore much freer to express the political dimension of this collectivity through party organisation and at the ballot box. Indeed, although the franchise did not admit all miners to the vote throughout this period (and no women were able to vote until 1918), their sheer weight of numbers within certain constituencies gave the mining communities a great deal of electoral influence. Moreover, in contrast to West Virginia, the fact that the union was established proved vital, particularly as the SWMF and MFGB were both actively involved in politics first through the Liberal party and then, after 1909, via the Labour Party. This presented a political structure which, although operating within a far from sympathetic political system, could reflect and help create political identity to a far greater extent than in West Virginia. In addition, other, non-electoral alternatives were available when the shortcomings of the system became apparent.

The south Wales miners had been involved in radical political activity throughout the nineteenth century. Monmouthshire miners formed the underground 'scotch cattle' movement and, in the 1831 Merthyr Rising, miners took part in the initial defeat of the military. Indeed, following the crushing of the rebellion, 23 year old miner, Dic Penderyn, was executed, subsequently becoming the 'first Welsh working-class martyr'. His death was followed by the spread of unions, continuing conflict, and solid support, with other sections of the population, for the Chartist movement.[1]

In electoral terms the Liberals were already winning a majority of the vote in Wales as a whole, and polling even more heavily in the south, by the 1850s. However it was in 1868, backed by the rising tide of radical Nonconformity, and the franchise changes of the 1867 Reform Act, that the Liberals assumed a dominance of political life. Although the Whig element remained in the ascendancy among those elected, there were other more radical successes as in the case of Henry Richard in one of the Merthyr Boroughs seats. This constituency had been particularly affected by the franchise changes, with the electorate leaping from 1,387 to 14,577. As a result the Liberal election committee took the surprising decision to call in the radical Nonconformist Richard from Tregaron.[2]

During the vigorous campaign Richard stood as 'a Welshman, an advanced Liberal and a Nonconformist', welcoming Chartists on to his platform at large, enthusiastic meetings. He also claimed a particular sympathy for the working-class electorate, siding with the miners over contentious issues like double shifts, and declaring himself to be the candidate for 'Wales and the Working Man'. In the event, Richard's appeals proved more than effective, as he topped the poll with 11,683 votes, beating industrialist Richard Fothergill who secured 7,439 votes, and coal owner Henry Bruce, with 5,776. Richard had polled heavily among those miners who were able to vote in Dowlais and Mountain Ash.[3]

Richard, the 'Apostle of Peace', continued to represent the constituency until his death in 1888, his popularity seemingly undiminished. Jack Jones, for example, recalled how around the time of the MPs death, 'granser thought there was no one alive to compare with Henry Richard',[4] while later generations likewise recalled his message – even on the centenary of his death.[5]

The success of Richard within the Merthyr constituency led, in 1874, to an attempt by a more specifically labour candidate to secure the other seat. Thomas Halliday, President of the Amalgamated Association of Miners, polled a creditable 4,912 vote, but still came in behind the second place Forthergill with 6,908.[6]

Further franchise reforms and the redistribution of constituencies in 1884–85, radically altered the nature of electoral politics, giving a larger section of the working-class a vote, and establishing a number of seats where they were in the majority.[7] Almost immediately, in the election of 1885, Mabon was returned as the member for the Rhondda, amid near riotous scenes, defeating Liberal F. L. Davis with over 56% of the vote.[8] Soon after the election, however, it became clear that Mabon and the miners were keen to remain within the Liberal tradition and a joint Liberal and Labour Association was formed.[9]

Mabon's hold on the constituency was such that he was unopposed at the next three elections and won comfortably when challenged by Conservative Robert Hughes in 1900.[10] Described in a miners' manifesto as the 'Labour Member for Wales' and 'the key of the south Wales miners to the British House of Commons',[11] the SWMF President received enthusiastic support from various quarters during the 1900 election, including Sir Henry Campbell-Bannerman and D. A. Thomas.[12] In contrast Hughes was given a rough ride throughout the campaign. At one meeting at Ferndale, for example, 'he was accorded a decidedly hostile reception, and would not be listened to' – despite appeals for calm from a Baptist minister.[13]

The weakness of the Tory challenge was shown at the declaration when cheering crowds sang 'Hem Wlad fy Nhadau' as Mabon swept to victory with nearly 82% of the votes cast.[14] His opponent had, in the meantime, returned to Cardiff, from where he sent a telegram regretting 'his inability to be present owing to Mrs Hughes' indisposition consequent upon the excitement in driving through the constituency'.[15] Mabon was unopposed until 1910.[16]

In general the immediate effect of the 1884–85 reforms revealed the overwhelming commitment of the south Wales miners to the Liberal Party, regardless of whether candidates were miners or not.[17] In Merthyr however, following the unopposed election of D. A. Thomas in March 1888, the death of Richard led to a by-election in October of the same year at which the Liberals offered to allow the local workers to select their own candidate. Amidst a good deal of indecision over who would be chosen, the maverick Pritchard Morgan, recently returned from commercial ventures overseas, stepped forward claiming to be Labour's representative. Taking fright the Liberals promptly withdrew their offer and, in retaliation, the local workers adopted Morgan as their candidate, despite having previously rejected his overtures.[18] Morgan went on to beat the official Liberal candidate, R. F. F. Griffiths, by 59.1% to 40.9%.[19]

Morgan was re-elected as an official Liberal in 1892 and 1895, but the election of 1900 brought a determined challenge from a genuine Labour candidate who was far more in the mould of Richard. The impetus for the challenge came from the ILP who had established themselves, if somewhat shakily, within the constituency during, and in the immediate aftermath of, the momentous 1898 coal strike.[20] With socialists active within newly formed Trades Councils in Aberdare and Merthyr, and the election of ILP member C. B. Stanton as Aberdare miners' agent, the support for running an independent candidate increased.[21] The ILP NAC heard in July 1900 that ILP men within the Trades Council were 'endeavouring to get that body to bring out a Labour candidate'. Moreover they were also told that Keir Hardie, 'had been suggested as a candidate', something which he personally favoured.[22]

Although, under pressure from Bruce Glasier, Hardie decided to accept the nomination to run for Preston, supporters in Merthyr, building on the personal popularity Hardie had gained for his vigorous and practical aid during the 1898 strike, continued with their efforts to get him selected.[23] They were rewarded on 22 September when a joint meeting of the Aberdare and Merthyr Trade Councils selected Hardie by thirty-three votes to seven. However this was only achieved after some wily tactics from chairperson, ILP member Enoch Archer, and the walkout by representatives of 12,000 miners, who had wanted SWMF Vice President William Brace to be their candidate.[24]

Pessimistic about his chances, Hardie concentrated on the Preston seat leaving ILP activists like S. D. Shallard and S. G. Hobson to conduct his campaign. The former recalled that Hardie was 'in the division for exactly one afternoon and two evenings before the polling day',[25] while that latter believed the lack of attention to the constituency gave him 'grave doubts' about Hardie's political wisdom.[26] Hardie nevertheless won a remarkable victory and became the first ILP MP in Wales.

In 1915, looking back on Hardie's first victory at Merthyr, the *Merthyr Pioneer* (paper of the local ILP) suggested that seat had been won because of 'the impression that he (Hardie) had created on people; on the zeal of his workers; and on the fact that Mr Pritchard Morgan was largely out of court with the people.'[27] As a summary of the reasons for Hardie's success this is undoubtedly accurate, particularly concerning the issue of Pritchard Morgan.

In addition to the fact that Morgan was clearly not a Labour representative, he had proved, through his frequent trips abroad and somewhat cavalier attitude, to be a less than satisfactory MP This had led to a bitter rift with the other sitting MP, D. A. Thomas, which undoubtedly helped Hardie. At the end of September Thomas repeated his pledge of 1888 that he would 'not oppose any workman who cared to stand, as that was a distinctly labour constituency'[28] and, more specifically, that he would give Hardie 'his moral support', if he 'received the support of the great bulk of the working men of the constituency.'[29]

During increasingly bitter public exchanges Morgan claimed that he was facing an 'alliance between Mr Thomas and Mr Keir Hardie as a combination of the capital of the Cambrian Collieries and Cadbury's Cocoa'. 'Personally', he went on, 'he doubted which was the better of the two'.[30] Thomas, in a detailed reply to this and other attacks by Morgan, recalled the latter's allegations over Thomas' work load, during the previous election. He added 'of all people Mr Morgan was about the last person who should charge anybody with inadequately performing his duty in Parliament.'[31]

The latter point was also at the forefront of the voters' minds, particularly concerning the latter's absences overseas. Morgan was constantly taunted with cries of 'China' during his campaign – referring to his commercial ventures in that country. At one meeting at the Siloa Chapel, Aberdare, Morgan replied to hecklers 'Well no man in the House of Commons knew more about China than he did, and it was very important to possess the information.'[32] Not the most ingenious reply considering that Morgan was interested in the mining of cheap coal, a fact bound to cause anger among miners reliant on the export trade.[33] This, therefore, contributed to the lively reception he received during the campaign, including one meeting at the Temperance Hall, Merthyr where 'the proceedings were of a somewhat rowdy character, the speaker being subject to considerable interruption.'[34]

While Morgan was an undoubted electoral asset to the ILP campaign, Hardie himself also believed that his own opposition to the Boer War had struck a chord within the constituency.[35] This is something which has been cited by most historians. Bealey and Pelling, for example, suggest that Hardie was returned to Parliament 'not as an exponent of Socialism – though such he remained – but as an opponent of the war.' – something which they link to a general anti-war mood within the whole of Wales.[36] K. O. Morgan, while accepting that Hardie's anti-war stance was not necessarily a handicap within Merthyr, believes that it was only one of several important factors in Hardie's election. Moreover, he also refutes the idea that Wales generally, or the south Wales miners in particular were opposed to the war, suggesting that the latter had 'done very well out of the war'.[37]

In fact the anti-war issue was, at most, only one factor in the Merthyr election. Indeed, as Fox has pointed out, it may have been as important in its effect on the Thomas/Morgan relationship, as an issue in its own right.[38] Thomas had declared the war 'an issue that is dead, a war that is ended',[39] yet Morgan claimed 'Mr Thomas and Mr Keir Hardie were pro-Boers, and he did not want any pro-Boers to vote for him, because he was not a Little Englander'.[40] This did much to break the already strained relations between the two sitting members.

More important than the anti-war issue was Hardie's ability to represent the radical traditions of Merthyr, yet at the same time develop a new angle on them. As he told one audience in 1898, 'my programme is the programme of Labour; my cause is the cause of Labour – the cause of humanity – the cause of God . . . I first learnt my socialism in the New Testament where I still find my chief inspiration', thus combining evangelical fervour and independent working-class politics.[41] Similarly, Jack Jones recalled the appearance of this stranger who 'put us in a different place to where the bosses were living – almost put us apart from our own jollier Welsh miners' leaders', who used the word '"Comrades." From his mouth that word fell charged with pity. At once he made closer contact with his audiences of Welsh-speaking miners than ever their own Welsh-speaking leaders had made.'[42]

This appeal was not primarily over policy, as Hardie and Liberals like D. A. Thomas had, in 1900 at least, much in common. Thomas, in particular, was one of the more radical Liberals in the coalfield,[43] and his election address supported the eight hour day for miners, the extension of the franchise to 'suitably qualified' women, payment of MP's, Old Age Pensions, as well as claiming to 'safeguard and promote the interests of the working-classes.' [44] What Hardie represented was the embodiment of independent working-class politics, Labour with a capital 'L', rather than labour within the paternalistic embrace of the Liberal Party. 'Vote for Labour', he told the Merthyr electorate, then give the second vote to 'the least dangerous man of the other two.'[45]

While this suggestion was not universally accepted, as Hardie's second place in the polls behind Thomas (31.3% to 46.9%) revealed,[46] if we take into account that a large number of miners were disenfranchised due to the 1898 strike,[47] it is clear that his appeal struck some chords within the mining communities. The significance of this was not lost on Mabon who admonished Thomas' support for Hardie, claiming, 'In reality the seat belonged to one of them, but their extreme modesty and consideration for an older member has allowed the seat to be occupied by a stranger.'[48]

The ILP success at Merthyr was very much the exception to the general pattern of south Wales politics at the 1900 election. The only other independent Labour candidacy was John Hodge of the Steel Smelters union in the Gower constituency. He ran only after being rejected as a Liberal candidate, and then proceeded to present a programme which K. O. Morgan suggests was 'nebulous in the extreme.'[49] Despite, or perhaps because of this, Hodge polled a more than respectable 3,853 (47.4%), only 423 behind Liberal J. A. Thomas.[50]

Even Mabon's hold on the Rhondda was an exception in 1900, as he was the only sitting Lib-Lab within south Wales. Moves were made to change this in 1903 however when, under pressure from Liberal chief whip Herbert Gladstone, the South Glamorgan Liberals selected SWMF Vice President William Brace to run at the next election. A year later, with similar pressures applied, SWMF General Secretary Tom Richards was selected to fight a by-election in the West Monmouth seat. He won easily with over 70% of the vote.[51]

In the 1906 general election the Liberal party further tightened its grip on Wales, winning thirty-two out of thirty-four seats.[52] Within this, Mabon, Richards, and Brace – newly elected with over 63% of the vote – ran as Lib-Labs. Another SWMF activist, John Williams, did run in a three way contest in the Gower constituency, building on the precedent of Hodge. Running as an independent Lib-Lab, Williams defeated the second placed Liberal by only 319 votes. On entering Parliament, however, he took the Liberal whip. Thus the only genuine independent Labour candidate, and one of only two non-Liberals in Wales, was once again Keir Hardie in Merthyr.[53]

The fact that both the 1900 and 1906 elections saw only two direct confrontations between Liberal and independent Labour candidates was testimony to the links between the SWMF and the Liberal Party. As early as 1902 the MFGB had devised a scheme to secure greater Parliamentary representation for miners which the SWMF adopted the following year. However, although eleven south Wales seats were targeted, and under a later MFGB scheme, which urged one candidate for every 10,000 members, twelve were 'scheduled' in 1906, in practice the SWMF EC would only allow challenges when seats became vacant. Thus when Liberals in the Brecon seat did not select a miner for the 1906 election, the local miners were prevented from fielding an independent candidate. Similarly, after a conference of trades councils, miners' lodges, and ILP branches selected Vernon Hartshorn to run against Liberal opposition in Mid Glamorgan, the SWMF EC intervened. He was prevented from running in the 1906 and January 1910 general elections, and at by-elections in 1906 and 1908.[54]

The caution over standing miners' candidates as either Liberals, or as independent Labour representatives, is all the more remarkable if we consider that there were, by 1910, eleven constituencies (twelve seats) in south Wales where miners made up over 10% of the electorate. These ranged from the Rhondda seat which had the largest national proportion of miners with 76% (13,590 out of 17,760), to the Brecon seat with 10% (1,400 out of 13,342). In between were West Monmouth (65%), Mid Glamorgan (56%),

East Glamorgan (54%), Merthyr Boroughs (43%), North Monmouth (36%), Gower (26%), South Monmouth (22%), South Glamorgan (19%), and East Carmarthen (17%).[55]

On the surface at least it might have been expected that the 1910 elections would have seen a change in the electoral pattern of the previous decade. After all, following a second national ballot in May 1908, the MFGB officially affiliated to the Labour Representation Committee and the union's MPs took the Labour whip. Within south Wales the enthusiasm for the move was shown by the huge vote of 74,675 to 44,615 in favour of affiliation, an even larger majority than the 1906 margin of 41,843 to 31,527 (when nationally the move was defeated).[56] However in the January election, the SWMF EC withdrew candidates for East and Mid Glamorgan, and East Carmarthen, claiming that they did not want to split the progressive vote while the 'People's budget' was at stake (it also meant that the four Lib-Labs would not be opposed by Liberals).[57]

The National Agent of the Labour Party described the January election results in south Wales in glowing terms: 'In no part of the country has our progress been more marked than in the south Wales District.'[58] In reality however, due to the withdrawal of candidates, the results showed no real change in either substance or the number elected, only in the label applied to the miners' candidates. Thus Mabon, described as the 'Labour and Progressive' candidate by the Liberal *South Wales Daily News*, told an audience that he would represent his constituents 'from a Labour standpoint, and he would be prepared to add to that everything that appertained to Welsh nationalism and every progressive measure, wherever it came from.'[59] When the Rhondda result was announced Mabon claimed his 9,000 majority as 'a tribute to Mr Lloyd George and the cause of progress.'[60]

Likewise Brace seemed more interested in maintaining old alliances than pursuing the independence of the party he now represented. He told an audience at Tonypandy that 'Mr Lloyd George was simply the advance guard of a mighty Welsh nation . . . It required a man to have been born in Wales to have produced such a budget – a budget which breathed of passion for the people.'[61] A similar line to that taken by Williams in Gower who, hearing of his 6,780 majority, spoke of how 'Liberal and Labour combined to achieve a victory of which they may feel proud.'[62]

Only Hardie, in the Merthyr constituency, continued to pursue a genuinely independent course. He told a meeting at Aberdare on New Year's Eve 1909 that, 'so long as the workers were in a minority the Liberals did not think of protecting the rights of the workers. When the workers were being victimised they did not hear much talk about protecting the rights of the individual.'[63] He made a similar point to a meeting in Mountain Ash, at which George Bernard Shaw also spoke, telling them that 'they could not trust the Liberals, for he knew what the Liberal government did when there was no Labour Party in the house, and what it did when there was a Labour Party in the House'.[64]

In another speech at Aberman, Hardie linked the election to the industrial struggles in the coalfield. After saying that he supported the budget, and arguing that the Lords' veto should be abolished, he moved on to industrial matters; 'There was another fight before the Welsh collier', he told the audience, 'when there would be no Liberal or Tories to fight for them, but it would be a fight against the masters on the sixty hours clause, the wages agreement'.[65]

Nor would Hardie have anything to do with the electoral pacts with the Liberals – which had been agreed in the seats held by the Lib-Labs. Although the Liberal candidate Edgar Jones (Thomas had moved to the Cardiff Boroughs seat) believed such an idea was 'desirable', he correctly 'took it that Mr Keir Hardie preferred to run independently'.[66] Indeed in the December election Hardie would later chastise the 'woeful lack of faith in their cause and sad lack of spirit' of the Liberals in running only one candidate. He also threatened that if by the next election candidates had a portion of their expenses paid and 'some form of second ballot . . . he would insist upon having two Labour candidates brought out to fight to the finish the question of which party predominated.'[67]

In the January election the absence of an electoral pact proved no disadvantage to Hardie, despite facing Liberal and Conservative opponents, as well as Pritchard Morgan who, running as an independent Liberal and backed by the Anti-Socialist Union, flooded the constituency with anti-socialist propaganda including leaflets equating socialism with free love.[68] Such claims, however, did little harm as Hardie was elected with 13,841 votes (36.7%), not far behind Jones' 15,448 (41%), with Morgan trailing fourth with only 3,693 (9.7%). This marked a 4.8% increase on Hardie's vote at the 1906 election.[69]

By the time the issue of the Parliament Bill led to a second election in 1910, the south Wales coalfield was affected by the Cambrian Combine dispute. Although the strike saw miners facing up to the Combine owner and former MP for Merthyr, D. A. Thomas, and the Tonypandy riots of November and subsequent dispersal of troops, there was no large scale shift away from the Liberals. The SWMF did back Labour candidates in Mid and East Glamorgan, as well as the sitting MPs. Hartshorn, who finally got to stand in Mid Glamorgan, had already been beaten by 8,920 to 6,210 votes in a by-election in March. He lost once again, by a similar margin, in December. In the East Glamorgan seat C. B. Stanton, busy in the Aberdare strike zone, came bottom of the poll behind both Liberal and Conservative opponents, with only 24.1% of the vote. Dr. J. H. Williams, an independent Labour candidate in the East Carmarthen seat, also came a poor third with only 12.6% of the vote.[70]

Of the sitting MPs, only Williams and Hardie faced Liberal opposition and, once again, only the latter stuck to campaigning on a distinctly Labour platform. On what turned out to be Hardie's last candidacy, he polled his highest percentage with 11,507 (39.6%) votes compared to Jones' 12,258 (42.2%) – only 751 votes between them.[71] In the Gower seat Williams, according to the *Labour Leader*, passed through 'a series of changes of opinion which would do no discredit to a chameleon', which were, it was claimed, 'apt to be embarrassing at times, especially during an election contest'.[72] He managed to hold his seat with a much reduced majority of 953, compared with 6,780 against the Tory challenger in January. The other three former Lib-Labs were all easily re-elected (Richards was in fact returned unopposed).[73]

By 1910, therefore, despite the rising tide of industrial conflict and a vote for affiliation to the Labour Party, the south Wales miners were, in the electoral sense at least, still committed to Lib-Labism rather than Labour. Other than in Merthyr, only Williams could secure election against Liberal opposition, and this was done with a 'chameleon' appeal to the Lib as well as the Lab. For those following a genuinely independent Labour path, the task was all the more difficult. Hartshorn, for example, speaking after the December 1910 election, blamed his defeat on 'the combined opposition of Toryism and the degenerate Liberalism . . . tradition and prejudice, and above all, Chapel influence'.[74]

The weakness of the independent Labour vote at Parliamentary elections was underlined by mixed success in terms of party organisation and local elections. As we saw earlier, a number of ILP branches were formed during the 1898 strike, many of which collapsed soon afterwards.[75] Similarly in 1902, the ILP NAC received a report on an unsuccessful 'south Wales Mission' in which John Penny and Philip Snowden had visited Merthyr, Aberavon, Ferndale, Pontypridd, Swansea and Neath. 'The audiences', they remarked, 'were in most cases small and there seemed considerable apathy.' Their warning of a 'considerable financial deficit on the mission' was later proved well-founded, as the NAC had to pay a bill of £12.[76] By 1904 it was becoming apparent that even the Merthyr branch was in trouble, with a declining membership. [77]

Vigorous campaigning, particularly after the 1906 vote in favour of affiliation to the LRC, did see an increase in ILP influence and the number of branches – by 1906 there were an estimated 49 in south Wales, rising to 84 by April 1908. With five of the ILP's twenty-nine full-time organisers active in the region, a south Wales ILP conference in November 1908 heard that over 2,000 meetings had been organised in the first nine months of the year alone. However amidst internal disharmony, especially between the branches and the umbrella organisation, the organisers were dismissed and the south Wales ILP Federation run down. 'The most interesting aspect of this debate' which followed, Stead suggests, 'was the general admission that four years of organisational activity had not really been successful.'[78]

Labour candidates were making advances in certain parts of the region at a local level. In Merthyr in 1905, for example, twelve Labour candidates were elected in the November elections. This followed the creation, two years earlier, of a local LRC.[79] In the Rhondda there were already six Labour members of the RUDC when, in 1907, the Rhondda No.1 District voted to push for the election of Labour candidates to local offices. Two more candidates were elected later that year.[80] It was following the Cambrian dispute that more significant advances were made, with candidates elected in the wards affected by the riots,[81] and Labour increasing its overall representation to thirty-one seats.[82] Indeed, but for the death of the three Rhondda SWMF EC members (and Labour councillors) at Hopkinstown in 1911, Labour would have assumed control of the RUDC before the outbreak of war.[83]

More widespread Labour advances in local and indeed national elections were hampered by the ineffective organisation of the broader Labour forces, in particular the slow pace of development of LRCs.[84] The lack of cohesion between ILP branches, SWMF lodges and Trades Councils was partly due to the inevitable problems surrounding the creation of a new political organisation. This was, however, exacerbated by the miners' unwillingness to yield influence over the selection of candidates. It was, for example, as late as February 1914 before the SWMF EC agreed to allow other groups as well as the miners to have a say in selecting a candidate for West Monmouth. Even then the vote was only twelve to eight in favour.[85] In fact, where there were successes prior to the war, as in the Rhondda, this was not due to a broad Labour alliance, but to the fact that the SWMF completely dominated the local Labour organisation, paying MPs salaries, and selecting and financing local candidates.[86]

This began to change when the SWMF EC allowed a broader base for the selection of a Labour candidate, which was symptomatic of a more vigorous approach to independent Labour politics immediately prior to the war. Although the Labour Party constitution of 1918 established proper constituency based structures, Stead suggests that 'the meaningful existence of a local Labour Party' in most of Wales 'dates from 1913', when the SWMF EC took advantage of the Trades Union Act of 1913 to declare its commitment to fighting on genuine Labour lines with the backing of genuine Labour organisation in the localities.[87] The SWMF decided to fight eight seats; at Gower, Mid and East Glamorgan, Merthyr Boroughs, Rhondda, and North, South and West Monmouthshire. However, the outbreak of war prevented the final selection of all the candidates, as well as the election of 1915. A genuine battle in the mining constituencies between Labour and Liberal was therefore postponed until after the war.[88]

As a consequence the results of the December 1910 election, which was itself fought amid special circumstances, stand somewhat unrealistically as the pinnacle of Labour pre-war electoral strength. If we recall, this consisted of five Labour MPs, of whom only two were elected against Liberal opposition, and only one of these on a genuinely independent line. In reality this probably underestimated Labour support before 1914, (particularly if we recall the more militant line taken by the SWMF after 1910) and helps explain why there was such a dramatic shift in electoral politics after the war. Certainly the war itself was to be a major influence on change, however we would do well to remember that changes prior to the outbreak of hostilities could only be expressed at the electoral level after 1918.

This point is of great significance in the comparison with West Virginia, where the SPA made its strongest showing in this period. This advance however, as we saw, was regionalised and to prove a temporary, exceptional trend to the general pattern of electoral politics. In contrast the south Wales miners, even at this artificially low point, had established a greater political presence, rooted within the framework of community, providing the building block for further advances. South Wales was headed in an entirely different political direction from West Virginia.

With the outbreak of war, politics in the coalfield was seemingly thrown into turmoil. As with the national Labour movement, the Labour Party, somewhat reluctantly at first, lined up behind the war effort, leading to divisions with elements of the ILP. [89] The latter's *Labour Leader*, for example, decried the decision of the Parliamentary party to co-operate with the Government's recruiting campaign as, 'a grave betrayal of the principles of the party and an outrage upon its traditions and hopes . . . When we read of this decision we bowed our heads with shame.'[90] These splits were more than apparent in the south Wales coalfield where, as we saw earlier, there was, initially at least, general support for the war. Thus most miners' agents including Brace, Richards, Gill, Hodges, Watts Morgan, as well as Stanton and Barker, participated in the recruiting drives.[91]

Even in the Merthyr Boroughs, support for the war ran high. In early August 1914, Edmund Stonelake, one of the first ILP councillors and long-standing Trades Council member, attempted to warn Keir Hardie of the mood within the area. Shortly before a peace meeting in Aberdare, he told Hardie, 'you see . . . this is not like the Boer War; the people are up in arms and want to know why the Germans are allowed to march in and invade defenceless little Belgium.'[92] The meeting did take place with, due to the withdrawal of Stanton, the reluctant Stonelake in the chair. In the event however, Hardie was heckled throughout his speech which was curtailed when scuffles broke out between pro and anti-war elements.[93]

245

The war also helped influence a by-election result in the Merthyr Boroughs the following year which seemed to call into question the strength of the Labour vote in south Wales, within what was one of its strongholds.[94] The by-election was caused by the death of Keir Hardie, after recurring illness, on 26 September 1915.

Due to the electoral truce between the main parties, it seemed, initially at least, as though there would be no contest and it would simply be a case of selecting a new MP. This process began with a ballot of the local miners over five candidates. They were Aberdare miners' agent Stanton, SWMF President James Winstone, Merthyr miners' agent John Williams, Troedyrhiw miners' agent Enoch Morrell, and MFGB President, and Hardie's personal friend, Robert Smillie. After the first ballot the last two were removed, and the miners were polled again. This time Stanton received 4,269 votes, compared with 4,405 for Winstone, and 4,391 for Williams. In a final ballot the SWMF President defeated Stanton 7,832 to 6,232.[95] An LRC meeting subsequently confirmed Winstone's selection.[96]

What had seemed straightforward became more complex when, after the miners' ballot, the increasingly bellicose Stanton resigned as Aberdare miners' agent, complaining of 'a pro-German section in our district that has made my life hell'.[97] He then began to question the validity of the ballot which he claimed was not conducted 'on the square', with ballots handed out in 'a very loose manner'.[98] These charges produced a vigorous response from various quarters. The Aberman Lodge claimed the ballot was 'conducted with all the scrutinising care possible', as did the Cwmneol Lodge where a general meeting 'emphatically' denied that 'the recent ballot was not conducted fairly'.[99] Similarly, MFGB EC member David Gilmour remarked 'I do not think it reflects much credit on Mr. Stanton when he starts off in this fight to cast aspersions on the men with whom he worked for years.'[100] The *Labour Leader* stated simply that Stanton's charges 'will only amuse those who know the facts.'[101]

Stanton, however, with the tacit approval of the other Merthyr MP, Liberal Artemus Jones, announced his intention to run as a pro-war candidate.[102] During the campaign he launched a series of scathing attacks on his former ILP allies. One piece of election propaganda accused Winstone of being the 'nominee of the pro-German, pacifist, friend of-every-other-country-but-their-own Independent Labour Party', whose election 'would become the triumph of German intrigue in Britain.' Stanton, in contrast, was the

'British Candidate', the 'candidate for noble Belgium . . . for pillaged and prostrate Poland . . . for stricken and glorious Serbia.'[103] Stanton called for opposition to this 'small clique of unpatriotic intriguers' and urged voters to instead 'vindicate in an unmistakable manner their British citizenship and their devotion to the Motherland' by voting for him.[104]

In reply to such accusations Winstone (echoing Hardie) described himself as 'a Democrat in Politics, and a Socialist in Economics on the Principles of the New Testament, from which I still draw my chief inspiration.' He denied that he was unpatriotic arguing that 'my patriotism and my love of country may be seen in my life's work without parading it for special occasions.'[105] The principal difference between the two candidates, Winstone suggested, was not over prosecution of the war, but conscription. 'I have done nothing to impede recruiting . . . nothing a Britisher need be ashamed of' he claimed, but he was 'opposed to conscription of any kind.'[106] As evidence for this he revealed that one of his sons was already serving in the army, and another was about to enlist.[107]

Despite these counter claims it is clear that Winstone's ILP membership 'created doubt' about his sincerity in the mind of some of those in favour of the war.[108] This impression was reinforced in some quarters by the presence of Ramsay MacDonald and Fred Jowett at the eve of poll meeting – something which both the *South Wales Daily News* and delegates to the MFGB conference at Southport questioned the wisdom of.[109]

Polling took place on 25 November when, on only a 67.7% turnout due to the large number of servicemen overseas and the use of an old register, Stanton won by 10,286 votes to 6,080 (a majority of 4,206 or 25.6%).[110] The scale of Stanton's victory, however, is not quite as significant as it as first seemed. Several observers pointed out that Stanton secured victory, in large part, due to the absence of Liberal or Conservative opponents, and the fact that only one seat was being contested. In reality, the Labour vote held up fairly well, with Winstone's 37.2% not much below Hardie's highest ever share of 39.6% in December 1910.[111]

In many ways, considering the degree of support for the war at this time, and the way the two campaigns were conducted, this was not a great set back for the Labour cause as it at first seemed. At most it could be seen as a rebuff for the ILP which had taken a more critical approach to the war than the rest of the Labour Party, something which reinforced the impression that it had never been as fully integrated into the political culture as the broader forces of Labour.[112] However, as we have seen, even though the campaign focused on the issue of the ILP, Winstone's vote was far from derisory. Conversely therefore, the 1915 Merthyr by-election result underlined the strength of the Labour Vote.

As we saw in the discussion of industrial conflict, the rest of the war saw an increasing restlessness and growing dissatisfaction within the south Wales coalfield. The first chance to voice such feelings came shortly after the war ended, when Lloyd George called the first general election for eight years. The so-called 'coupon' election of December 1918, however, was hardly a typical election and, to quote Pelling, 'was inevitably a virtual plebiscite for or against Lloyd George, as the architect of victory'.[113] Nevertheless, Labour made significant gains within the newly re-distributed seats in industrial south Wales. Candidates at Rhondda East, Rhondda West, Abertillery, Ebbw Vale and Ogmore (in which Hartshorn finally got into Parliament) were all elected unopposed; while at Caerphilly, Gower, Ogmore, Bedwellty and Pontypool victory was secured against Liberal opposition.[114] All of those elected, however, had been prominent in supporting the war effort.[115] In contrast those Labour candidates who had opposed the war, like Winstone, who had been a prominent critic after the 1915 by-election, went down to defeat. He came second behind Artemus Jones, by the narrow margin of 1,445 votes (5.4%).[116]

By the general election of 1922 the war issue was no longer relevant, and the miners were facing the consequences of economic decline. In an election in which the divided Liberals were generally routed, Labour captured six more mining seats; at Llanelli, Aberavon, Pontypridd, Neath, Aberdare and Merthyr.[117] The new MPs included Ramsay MacDonald at Aberavon, whose 'campaign had aroused almost revivalist fervour amongst the miners of the Afan valley', and Chairman of the ILP and former colleague of Hardie, R. C. Wallhead, at Merthyr.[118] The local Labour activists in Aberdare also revenged themselves on Stanton, when G. H. Hall gained the seat 20,704 votes to 15,487. As Stonelake joyfully recalled, 'The flag-waving miners' Agent – the Britisher – who deserted his party in 1915 was beaten to a frazzle and the young miner won the seat . . . On the declaration of the poll at that election the enthusiasm of the local miners knew no bounds.'[119]

Cemented by the elections of 1923 and 1924, Labour had become overwhelmingly the party of the south Wales miners, and south Wales generally. Backed by a domination of local government,[120] these constituencies became some of Labour's safest in Britain. Indeed, in Rhondda East in the 1930s, for example, the only serious challenge to the Labour Party came not from the Liberals, but the CPGB.[121]

The contrast with West Virginia could not be more stark. Throughout the period 1900–22, the West Virginia miners were unable to sustain independent political activity, even under the umbrella of the two existing parties. The only major independent activity centred on the SPA which momentarily mounted a serious challenge in the Kanawha region, but could never overcome the barriers in its path. In south Wales, in contrast, from Merthyr in 1900 to November 1922, the Labour Party was gradually building a political hegemony based on the votes of the mining valleys.

This difference also extends to other more radical political activities. Whereas the IWW and other syndicalist organisations were virtually non-existent in the West Virginia valleys, in south Wales, as we saw in the discussion of industrial conflict, proponents of revolutionary politics were influential at certain times throughout this period.

The most prominent example of these were the activists in the Rhondda who worked through the Plebs League, Industrial Democracy League (which was active in 1912–13), CLC, Rhondda Socialist Society (which became the South Wales Socialist Society in 1919), and most prominent of all, the URC. The SDF were also a minor influence in the valleys,[122] although it was the CPGB which pulled most of these strands together at the end of this period, and proved the most influential revolutionary party organisation.[123]

Indeed the contrast with West Virginia is made even more pertinent if we consider the fact that some of the inspiration for these organisations came from across the Atlantic. For example Noah Ablett was one of those influenced by Daniel De Leon of the US Socialist Labor Party,[124] while IWW leader 'Big Bill' Haywood was also well received on several visits to the valleys.[125]

The level of support for the revolutionary element was never consistently high, even in the Rhondda, where it was at its strongest. Thus, as we saw earlier, the URC attempts at reorganisation of the SWMF floundered, while the election of officers after the Cambrian dispute, saw the return of reformists rather than revolutionaries.[126]

Similarly the CPGB was influential within the SWMF and had minority support in the coalfield, but was no match for the popularity of the Labour Party. For example, slightly beyond this period, in 1928, veteran SWMF activist, leader of the Welsh Parliamentary Labour Party, and MP for Rhondda East since 1918, D. Watts Morgan, challenged Communist and MFGB EC member, Arthur Horner, to fight a by-election. The two eventually squared up to each other in the 1929 General Election with Watts Morgan winning over 50% of the poll, and Horner coming third with 15.2%, behind the Liberal candidate.[127]

Yet although a minority, the revolutionary groups were at times extremely influential. As G. A. Williams suggested, writing of the election of the imprisoned Horner as the Mardy checkweigher in 1919, the 1917 rule change committing the union to the abolition of capitalism, and the decision to affiliate to RILU, 'This was a spasmodic and minority trend, but at moments of high temper it could carry a majority.'[128]

What this 'trend' built upon was the mixture of anger and frustration at the aggressiveness of the south Wales owners, as well as the potential power of the solid, homogeneous mining communities of, in particular, the Rhondda. As Egan has pointed out, the Rhondda district had a membership of 41,000 members prior to the war which, 'taking their families into account (was) virtually the whole population of the Rhondda Valleys'. This represented a far more direct democracy than the machinations of 'distant Parliaments', as well as a logical fighting unit against the coalowners.[129] Moreover the strength of numbers in the Rhondda, which made up a third of the SWMF, which was in turn the largest region in the MFGB, gave the miners a national influence.[130]

With a sense of such power it is easy to understand why the industrial unionism of the URC could, at times, strike a chord within the steam coal region. As Ablett told one audience, 'the industrial union did not need the backing of the political organisation, therefore it was foolish to swim the river to fill the bucket on the other side.'[131] The emphasis was placed upon strengthening the union and turning it into a revolutionary instrument; a view which received its most famous elucidation in *The Miners' Next Step*. It stated that 'the working-class, if it is to fight effectually, must be an army, not a mob. It must be classified, regimented and brigaded, along the lines indicated by the product.' To do this the pamphlet argued, miners must 'centralise' rather than 'sectionalise our fighting'. Such a move, it was argued, would remove the power from leaders who 'all . . . become corrupt, in spite of their own good intentions'. On nationalisation the pamphlet rejected the policy of the mainstream labour movement, claiming that it would simply create 'a National Trust, with all the force of the government behind it.' Instead, 'Industrial Democracy' was 'the objective' with workers controlling their own industries.[132]

This view was put most forcibly in a highly symbolic debate at the Judge's Hall, Trelaw on 13 November 1912, between George Barker and Edward Gill, both left-wingers formerly associated with the URC, and Ablett and Frank Hodges, two of the most prominent exponents of industrial unionism.[133] The debate concerned the issue of the nationalisation of the mines, and soon came to focus on the differing interpretations of the State and politics. Barker, basing his argument on a draft bill drawn up by a Labour Party barrister, argued that nationalisation would lead to better organisation of the industry, higher wages, improved safety, cheaper coal and 'the elimination of the capitalists altogether from the mining industry of the country.' It would also presuppose, Barker suggested, 'that all other industries also will be nationalised and eventually by getting the State to hold and control the whole of the industries of the country the workers will be emancipated from their servile state.'[134]

In reply Ablett immediately attacked Barker's interpretation of in whose interests the industry should be operated, and the role of the State:

> We on this side are here tonight, not on behalf of the 'community' as at present organised; not on behalf of 'our' country; not even for the sake of the nation; not for any of these, but we are here in the interest of the working-class militant . . . Mr Barker, you would simply place an important section of the working-class in the hands of a State servile to the capitalists' interests, who would use their opportunity to increase the servility we now equally abhor.

Repeating a central claim of *The Miners' Next Step*, Ablett argued that this would mean that in all future industrial conflicts 'you will be faced by the state'. Moreover, 'they will not as the State allow us or want us to organise in a powerful union. The State has never so far allowed its workers to organise so freely as other workers can, and the workers have to recognise this.' He concluded, after quoting Engels on the need for the State to 'irrevocably fall', that:

The roadway to emancipation lies in a different direction than the offices of the Minister of Mines. It lies in the democratic organisation, and eventual control, of the industries by the workers themselves in their organised capacity as trustees for a working-class world that must be the work of the workers themselves from the bottom upward, and not from the top downward, which latter means the servile state.[135]

In reality, particularly if we consider the longer period under examination, the syndicalist position was not as well defined, or as clear cut in relation to Labour supporters, as the above debate makes it seem. For a start, even at its most syndicalist, as in the URC in the middle of this period, it was, as Foote has suggested, 'not necessarily incompatible with labourism, or even the electoral success of the labour movement'.[136] This is graphically underlined by the fact that *The Miners' Next Step* itself noted that the SWMF 'shall engage in political action, both local and national, on the basis of the complete independence of, and hostility to, all capitalist parties', and that:

> Political action must go on side by side with industrial action. Such measures as the Mines Bill, Workmen's Compensation Acts, proposals for nationalising the mines, etc., demand the presence in Parliament of men who directly represent, and are amenable to, the wishes and instructions of the workmen.[137]

Distinctions were also somewhat blurred by the fact that many of the organisations which had syndicalist elements, for a time at least, also contained ILP activists. For example, in 1911, the *Rhondda Socialist* newspaper was started by both ILP and syndicalist sympathisers.[138] Inevitably friction over political tactics were voiced in the paper, as in May 1912, when the secretary of the Rhondda Socialist Newspaper Committee described syndicalism as 'Neo-Anarchism'.[139] However this should not dispel the impression that, except for the most militant exponents, the Labour left and the syndicalists had a good deal in common. This is further illustrated by the way many individuals moved between the two groups. Thus, for example, Ablett was a member of the Labour Party until 1907, as was A. J. Cook until 1913.[140] Similarly Mainwaring, Barker and Hodges moved in the opposite direction to become Labour loyalists.

Moreover such changes did not, necessarily, require an ideological about-turn, just a juggling of the equation balancing industrial and political power. After all, Aneurin Bevan, who was influenced early on by the syndicalist movement, was later able to articulate within the Labour Party a brand of socialism in which the 'belief in the class struggle stayed unshakeable'.[141] Key to this was his understanding that 'politics was about power'.[142] As he put it on the first page of *In Place of Fear*:

> A young miner in a south Wales colliery, my concern was with the one practical question, where does power lie in this particular State of Great Britain, and how can it be attained by the workers? No doubt this is the same question as the one to which the savants of political theory are fond of addressing themselves, but there is a world of difference in the way it shaped itself for young workers like us. The circumstances of our lives made it a burning luminous mark of interrogation. Where was power and which the road to it?[143]

Nor was this pre-occupation with power restricted only to the Labour left and the self-confessed revolutionaries. Virtually all the political activity in this period was concerned with the same question; the differences concerned which roads to take and what power actually meant. This was as true for the Lib-Lab leaders as for those further left; they may have preferred conciliationism, but they were no strangers to strikes or political activity.[144] As William Brace put it in his 1914 Presidential address, the 'Government and the owners, having failed to accept conciliatory methods, must accept demands enforced by industrial and political power'.[145] Nor were the militant elements blind to this. For example, on the death of Tom Richards in 1931, Ablett remarked 'We have lost the greatest man in the Federation: the greatest man in Wales.'[146]

What underpinned this common strand was the sense of power within the mining communities, and the hostility of the coal owners – amid which they formed a strong sense of self-identity. This was why Arthur Horner was described as a miner and trade unionist first, and a communist second.[147] It also explains why the miners' politics concealed a barely disguised arrogance towards other elements of the labour movement for much of this period.

Although the syndicalists, and later the CPGB, were at times able to seize the initiative in this common strand, the eventual road which the mass of miners across the south Wales coalfield chose was that of the Labour Party. What Labour actually came to mean, however, was more complicated. The socialism of the ILP, and later of the Labour Left was one important, but by no means dominant influence. Another input came from the Lib-Labs who had been reluctantly dragged into the party in 1909. As several historians have shown, the continuities in style and content of leadership left an indelible mark on the Labour Party that emerged after the war.[148]

Indeed in the 'translation' of the Liberal past into the Labour future,[149] the most common beneficiary was the middle ground occupied by the likes of Hartshorn and Watts Morgan, where the '"middle position" continually redefined itself and maintains its dominance.'[150] In this sense the shift to Labour was about the independence implied by the capital 'L', which Keir Hardie successfully proffered in Merthyr. It was also the general political expression of the growing self confidence of these valleys, hardened by the conflict which had torn through the coalfield in the previous decades. In an increasingly national political framework, the web of identities – Welsh, English, British, radical, socialist, working-class, miner – which were the substance of these communities became re-defined, and re-shuffled around the appeal of the pragmatic Labour Party. Where the militant minority, particularly the CPGB, were successful, as in the structures of the SWMF, this success owed more to a reputation for strong and able leadership than their revolutionary credentials.[151] In Labour south Wales they were elected as miners first, communists second.

In contrast to their counterparts in West Virginia, therefore, the south Wales miners were able to organise politically, as they had industrially, and establish a political presence firmly rooted within party organisation and electoral representation. This reflected a broader divergence in the political identities of the two regions, for in south Wales, the miners drew on their stronger sense of community and greater civil freedom to form a coherent political identity resting on their occupational and class position. In contrast, the culturally fragmented and politically restricted world of the West Virginia miner, while allowing momentous displays of industrial militancy, could only sustain a fragile and ambiguous alliance around notions of citizenship and exceptionalism, which while relevant to the expression of political protest, were largely unrelated to the position of miners and workers in an aggressive industrial capitalist society.

Notes

1 G. A. Williams, *When was Wales? A History of the Welsh* (London, Penguin, 1985), pp. 191–7; G. A. Williams, *The Welsh in Their History* (London, Croom Helm, 1982), pp. 135–50.
2 Williams, *When was Wales?*, pp. 213–17; K. O. Morgan, *Wales in British Politics, 1868–1922* (Cardiff, University of Wales Press, 1980 edn.), pp. 1–27.
3 *Ibid.*, pp. 23–4; Williams, *When was Wales?*, pp. 216–17; G. A. Williams, *Peace and Power: Henry Richard, A Radical for Our Time* (Cardiff, CND Cymru, 1988), pp. 1–7.
4 J. Jones, *Unfinished Journey* (London, Hamish Hamilton, 1938), p. 27.
5 See Williams, *Peace and Power*, which was published in 1988.
6 K. O. Fox, 'Labour and Merthyr's Khaki Election of 1900', *Welsh History Review*, 2, 4 (1965), p. 352.
7 K. O. Morgan, *Rebirth of a Nation: Wales 1880–1980* (Oxford, Oxford University Press, 1980), pp. 27–8.
8 The *Rhondda Leader*, 13 Oct 1900, p. 4, compared the peaceful election in 1900 with that of 1885, when crowds fought with police and the Riot Act was read.
9 Morgan, *Wales in British Politics*, p. 66.
10 F. W. S. Craig, *British Parliamentary Election Results, 1885–1918* (London, Macmillan, 1974), p. 480.
11 Miners' manifesto in support of Mabon, *South Wales Daily News*, 26 Sep 1900, p. 6.
12 Campbell Bannerman sent his 'heartiest wishes', *Rhondda Leader*, 6 Oct 1900, p. 5; D. A. Thomas was actually one of Mabon's constituents and 'supported Mabon's colours on his way to the booth', *Rhondda Leader*, 13 Oct 1900, p. 3.
13 *Rhondda Leader*, 6 Oct 1900, p. 3.
14 *Ibid.*, 13 Oct 1900, p. 4.
15 *Ibid.*
16 Craig, *British Parliamentary Election Results, 1885–1918*, p. 480.
17 *Ibid.*, pp. 468–84.
18 Fox, 'Labour and Merthyr's Khaki Election of 1900', pp. 353–4; K.O. Morgan, 'The Merthyr of Keir Hardie', in G. Williams, *Merthyr Politics: The Making of a Working-Class Tradition* (Cardiff, University of Wales Press, 1966), pp. 62–3.
19 Craig, *British Parliamentary Election Results, 1885–1918*, p. 458.
20 For a summary of ILP activity in Wales generally from the 1890s to 1906, see D. Hopkin, 'The Rise of Labour in Wales, 1890–1914', *Llafur*, 6, 3 (1994), pp. 125–9.

21 D. Howell, *British Workers and the Independent Labour Party, 1888–1906* (Manchester, Manchester University Press, 1983), pp. 245–6; K. O. Morgan, *Keir Hardie: Radical and Socialist* (London, Weidenfeld and Nicholson, 1984 edn.), pp. 97, 112; Fox, 'Labour and Merthyr's Khaki Election of 1900', pp. 354–7.

22 ILP NAC, 28 Jul 1900, ILP Minute Books, 1893–1909, (M/Film edition), Cambridge, University Library, p. 71.

23 Morgan, *Keir Hardie*, pp. 112–14.

24 ILP NAC, 21–4 Sep 1900, ILP Minute Books, 1893–1900; *Labour Leader*, 29 Sep 1900, p. 309; Fox, 'Labour and Merthyr's Khaki Election of 1900', pp. 354–7.

25 *Labour Leader*, 20 Oct 1900, p. 334.

26 F. W. Bealey and H. M. Pelling, *Labour and Politics 1900–1906: A History of the Labour Representation Committee* (London, Macmillan, 1958), p. 47.

27 *Labour Leader*, 30 Sep 1915, p. 28.

28 *Western Mail*, 26 Sep 1900, p. 5.

29 *Western Mail*, 25 Sep 1900, p. 5.

30 *Ibid.*, 2 Oct 1900, p. 6.

31 *South Wales Daily News*, 1 Oct 1900, p. 6.

32 *Western Mail*, 1 Oct 1900, p. 6.

33 Fox, 'Labour and Merthyr's Khaki Election of 1900', p. 362; Howell, *British Workers and The Independent Labour Party*, p. 250.

34 *Western Mail*, 2 Oct 1900, p. 6.

35 Howell, *British Workers and The Independent Labour Party*, p. 250.

36 Bealey and Pelling, *Labour and Politics 1900–1906*, p. 49; H.M. Pelling, 'Wales and the Boer War', *Welsh History Review*, 4, 4 (1969), pp. 363–5.

37 Morgan, *Rebirth of a Nation*, p. 47; Morgan, *Keir Hardie*, pp. 116–17; Morgan, *Wales in British Politics*, pp. 180–1, 205–6; Morgan, 'Wales and the Boer War: A Reply', *Welsh History Review*, 4, 4 (1969), pp. 367–80.

38 Fox, 'Labour and Merthyr's Khaki Election of 1900', p. 364.

39 *Western Mail*, 27 Sep 1900, p. 3.

40 *Ibid.*, 2 Oct 1900, p. 6.

41 Morgan, 'The Merthyr of Keir Hardie', p. 67.

42 Jones, *Unfinished Journey*, p. 86.

43 D. Tanner, *Political Change and the Labour Party, 1900–1918* (Cambridge, Cambridge University Press, 1990), pp. 208–9.

44 *Western Mail*, 27 Sep 1900, p. 3.

45 *South Wales Daily News*, 29 Sep 1900, p. 6.

46 The result in terms of votes was: Thomas 8,598; Hardie 5,745; Morgan 4,004. Craig, *British Parliamentary Election Results, 1885–1918*, p. 458.

47 Howell, *British Workers and The Independent Labour Party*, pp. 249–50, *Western Mail*, 27 Sep 1900, p. 3.
48 Fox, 'Labour and Merthyr's Khaki Election of 1900', p. 365.
49 Morgan, *Wales in British Politics*, pp. 202, 207.
50 Craig, *British Parliamentary Election Results, 1885–1918*, p. 478.
51 R. Gregory, *The Miners and British Politics, 1906–1914* (Oxford, Oxford university Press, 1968), p. 122; Morgan, *Wales in British Politics*, pp. 209–10; Craig, *British Parliamentary Election Results, 1885–1918*, p. 485.
52 F. W. S. Craig, *British Electoral Facts* (Chichester, Parliamentary Research Services, 1981 edn.), p. 18.
53 *Ibid.*, pp. 480, 485, 481, 478; D. Cleaver, 'Labour and Liberals in the Gower Constituency, 1885–1910', *Welsh History Review*, 12, 3 (1985), pp. 388–410; Morgan, 'The New Liberalism and the Challenge of Labour', *Welsh History Review*, 6, 3 (1973), p. 285.
54 Gregory, *The Miners and British Politics*, pp. 123–7; Morgan, *Wales in British Politics*, pp. 246–7.
55 Gregory, *The Miners and British Politics*, see table, p. 138. The double seat constituency was, of course, Merthyr.
56 R. P. Arnot, *South Wales Miners; A History of the South Wales Miners' Federation, 1898–1914* (London, Allen and Unwin, 1967), p. 149.
57 Gregory, *The Miners and British Politics*, pp. 127–30.
58 *Labour Leader*, 4 Feb 1910, p. 74.
59 *South Wales Daily News*, 1 Jan 1910, p. 8.
60 *Ibid.*, 22 Jan 1910, p. 8.
61 *Ibid.*, 11 Jan 1910, p. 6.
62 *Ibid.*, 22 Jan 1910, p. 8.
63 *Aberdare Leader*, 1 Jan 1910, p. 8.
64 *South Wales Daily News*, 6 Jan 1910, p. 6.
65 *Ibid.*, 6 Jan 1910, p. 6.
66 *Ibid.*, 18 Jan 1910, p. 8.
67 *Aberdare Leader*, 17 Dec 1910, p. 8.
68 *South Wales Daily News*, 20 Jan 1910, p. 7.
69 Craig, *British Parliamentary Election Results, 1885–1918*, p. 458.
70 Gregory, *The Miners and British Politics*, pp. 130–3; Morgan, *Wales in British Politics*, pp. 250–2; Craig, *British Parliamentary Election Results, 1885–1918*, pp. 479, 477, 472.
71 *Ibid.*, p. 458.
72 *Labour Leader*, 9 Dec 1910, p. 774.
73 Craig, *British Parliamentary Election Results, 1885–1918*, pp. 478, 480, 481, 485.
74 *Labour Leader*, 16 Dec 1910, p. 795.

75 Howell suggests a drop from thirty-one to nine branches: *British Workers and The Independent Labour Party*, p. 245.

76 ILP NAC, 1–2 Sep 1902, 28 Feb-1 Mar 1903, ILP Minute Books, 1893–1909.

77 Hopkin, 'The Rise of Labour in Wales', p. 128.

78 Stead, 'Establishing a Heartland – The Labour Party in Wales', in K. D. Brown (ed.), *The First Labour Party, 1906–1914* (London, Croom Helm, 1985), pp. 73–6.

79 Howell, *British Workers and The Independent Labour Party*, p. 252.

80 C. Williams, '"An Able Administrator of Capitalism"? The Labour Party in the Rhondda, 1917–1921', *Llafur*, 4, 4, p. 22.

81 Smith, 'Tonypandy 1910: Definitions of Community', *Past and Present*, 87 (May 1980), p. 181.

82 *Rhondda Socialist*, 10 May 1913, p. 1.

83 Williams, '"An Able Administrator of Capitalism"?', p. 22.

84 Stead, 'Establishing a Heartland', pp. 78–9.

85 SWMF EC Meeting, 23 Feb 1914, SWMF Minutes, 1914, Swansea, South Wales Coalfield Archive (SWCA), C.1; Similar agreed for East Glamorgan, SWMF EC 12 Mar 1914, *ibid.*

86 Williams, '"An Able Administrator of Capitalism"?', p. 20.

87 Stead, 'Establishing a Heartland', pp. 83–4.

88 Gregory, *The Miners and British Politics*, pp. 136–7.

89 For a concise account of Labour and the war, see H. M. Pelling, *A Short History of the Labour Party* (London, Macmillan, 1985 edn.), pp. 35–51.

90 *Labour Leader*, 6 Aug 1914, p. 1.

91 Morgan, *Wales in British Politics*, p. 276.

92 E. Stonelake, *The Autobiography of Edmund Stonelake* [ed. A. Mor-O'Brien] (Bridgend, Mid Glamorgan Education Committee, 1981), p. 157.

93 *Ibid.*, pp. 157–8; A. Mor-O'Brien, 'Keir Hardie, C. B. Stanton and the First World War', *Llafur*, 4, 3, pp. 31–2.

94 This view has been put most recently by A. Mor-O'Brien in 'The Merthyr Boroughs Election, 1915', *Welsh History Review*, 12, 4 (1985), pp. 538–566.

95 *Labour Leader*, 14 Oct 1915, p. 6; 21 Oct 1915, p. 6; 28 Oct 1915, p. 6; 4 Nov 1915, p. 6.

96 *Aberdare Leader*, 13 Nov 1915, p. 6.

97 *Labour Leader*, 4 Nov 1915, p. 6.

98 *Ibid.*, 11 Nov 1915, p. 6; *Aberdare Leader*, 16 Nov 1915, p. 6.

99 *Aberdare Leader*, 13 Nov 1915, p. 7.

100 *Merthyr Pioneer*, 27 Nov 1915, p. 6.

101 *Labour Leader*, 11 Nov 1915, p. 6.

102 *South Wales Daily News*, 5 Nov 1915, p. 7; 23 Nov 1915.

103 *Aberdare Leader*, 20 Nov 1915, p. 6.

104 *Ibid.*, 27 Nov 1915, p. 4.

105 Ibid., 27 Nov 1915, p. 4.

106 *South Wales Daily News*, 19 Nov 1915, p. 6.

107 *Ibid.*, 18 Nov 1915, p. 6.

108 *Ibid.*, 27 Nov 1915, p. 4; 18 Nov 1915, p. 6.

109 *Ibid.*, 24 Nov 1915, p. 6; 27 Nov 1915, p. 6.

110 *Labour Leader*, 2 Dec 1915, p. 1; Craig, *British Parliamentary Election Results, 1885–1918*, p. 485.

111 This point was made by Ramsay MacDonald, and John Williams (one of the defeated candidates in the original miners' ballot) in the *Labour Leader*, 2 Dec 1915, p. 1, p. 5; Myrddin Davies (of the Merthyr ILP), *Ibid.*, 9 Dec 1915, p. 8; and the *South Wales Daily News*, 27 Nov 1915, p. 6; Craig, *British Parliamentary Election Results, 1885–1918*, p. 485

112 See Tanner, *Political Change and the Labour Party*, pp. 214–15, on the limitations of the ILP's appeal.

113 Pelling, *A Short History of the Labour Party*, p. 46.

114 Craig, *British Parliamentary Election Results, 1918–1945* (Chichester, 1983 edn.), pp. 538–568.

115 Morgan, *Wales in British Politics*, p. 283.

116 Winstone died in July 1921, having never gained a seat in Parliament. 25,000 attended his funeral: J. M. Bellamy and J. Saville (eds.), *Dictionary of Labour Biography, Vol.1* (London, Macmillan, 1972), pp. 350–1; Craig, *British Parliamentary Election Results, 1918–1945*, p. 538.

117 The Pontypridd seat had in fact already been won by T. I. Mardy Jones at a by-election the previous July, Craig, *British Parliamentary Election Results, 1918–1945*, p. 562; Morgan, *Rebirth of a Nation*, p. 191.

118 *Ibid.*, p. 191.

119 E. Stonelake, *The Autobiography of Edmund Stonelake*, p. 167.

120 Labour assumed control of the RUDC, for example, in 1919. Williams, '"An Able Admistrator of Capitalism"?', p. 22.

121 Craig, *British Parliamentary Election Results, 1918–1945*, p. 540.

122 B. Holton, *British Syndicalism, 1900–1914: Myths and Realities* (London, Pluto Press, 1976), pp. 79–81; M. G. Woodhouse, 'Rank and File Movements among the Miners of South Wales, 1910–1926' (Unpublished D.Phil. dissertation, University of Oxford, 1969), p. 10; Kenneth Hilton, 'John Spargo, The Social Democratic Federation, and the 1898 South Wales Coal Strike', *Welsh History Review*, 16, 4 (1993), pp. 542–50.

123 For formation of CPGB and role of the different south Wales' groups, see Woodhouse, 'Rank and File Movements among the Miners of South Wales', pp. 187–94.

124 D. Egan, 'Noah Ablett 1883–1935', *Llafur*, 4, 3, p. 22.

125 Holton, *British Syndicalism*, p. 81.

126 See Chapter four, pp. 186–8; Morgan, *Rebirth of a Nation*, pp. 152–3.

127 Horner was beaten by a narrower margin in 1931, but came second with 33.8% of the vote at the by-election in 1933 caused by Morgan's death. The winning candidate, with 61.8% of the vote, was former URC activist, W. H. Mainwaring. Craig, *British Parliamentary Election Results, 1918–1945*, p. 540; Bellamy and Saville, *Dictionary of Labour Biography, Vol. 1*, pp. 246–7.

128 Williams, *When was Wales?*, p. 250.

129 Egan, 'Noah Ablett', pp. 27–8.

130 E. D. Lewis, *The Rhondda Valleys: A Study in Industrial Development, 1800 to the Present Day* (London, Phoenix House, 1959), p. 178.

131 Egan, 'Noah Ablett', p. 28.

132 URC, *The Miners' Next Step: Being a Suggested Scheme for Reorganisation of the Federation* (Tonypandy, 1912), pp. 19, 27, 13, 29.

133 K. O. Morgan, 'Socialism and Syndicalism: The Welsh Miners' Debate, 1912', *Bulletin of the Society for the Study of Labour History*, 30 (1975), pp. 23–4.

134 The whole debate is re-reprinted in *ibid*. These quotes from pp. 26–8.

135 *Ibid.*, pp. 28–31.

136 G. Foote, *The Labour Party's Political Thought: a History* (London, Croom Helm, 1985), p. 92.

137 *The Miners' Next Step*, pp. 19, 20.

138 Woodhouse, 'Rank and File Movements among the Miners of South Wales, 1910–1926', p. 73.

139 *Rhondda Socialist*, 11 May 1912, p. 4.

140 Egan 'Noah Ablett', p. 26; J. M. Bellamy and J. Saville (eds.), *Dictionary of Labour Biography, Vol. 3* (London, Macmillan,1976), p. 38.

141 M. Foot, *Aneurin Bevan, 1945–1960* (London, Paladin, 1975 edn.), p. 17.

142 Foot, *Aneurin Bevan, 1897–1945* (London, 1975 edn.), p. 27.

143 A. Bevan, *In Place of Fear* (London, Heineman, 1952), p. 1.

144 P. Stead, 'Working-Class Leadership in South Wales, 1900–1922', *Welsh History Review*, 6, 3 (1973), p. 342.

145 Presidential Address before Annual Conference, 6–7 Apr 1914, SWMF Minutes, 1914, C.2. (Previously cited, Chapter four, p. 190.)

146 Bellamy and Saville, *Dictionary of Labour Biography, Vol. 1*, p. 285.
147 C. Williams, 'The South Wales Miners Federation', *Llafur*, 5, 3, p. 49.
148 Williams, *The Welsh in Their History*, p. 186; Stead, 'Working-Class Leadership in South Wales', pp. 329–353; P. Stead, 'The Language of Edwardian Politics', in D. Smith (ed.), *A People and a Proletariat: Essays in the History of Wales, 1780–1980* (London, Pluto Press, 1980), pp. 148–65; Williams, '"An Able Adminstrator of Capitalism"?', pp. 20–33; Williams, 'The South Wales Miners Federation', pp. 45–56. D. Smith, *Anuerin Bevan and the World of South Wales* (Cardiff, University of Wales Press, 1993), pp. 67–89.
149 Williams, *The Welsh in their History*, p. 186.
150 Stead, 'Working-Class Leadership in South Wales', p. 344; Williams, 'The South Wales Miners' Federation', pp. 51–2. One of the arguments for nationalization which Hartshorn suggested to the 1919 Sankey Inquiry was that it would halt the growing tide of Bolshevism: *Minutes of Evidence of the Royal Commission on the Coal Industry* (Parl. Papers, 1919 Cd.360, XI, 373), p. 363.
151 Macintyre suggested that the principal appeal of the Communists in the 'Little Moscow' at Mardy was their ability to offer good leadership and to represent 'the sense of cohesion and common purpose that was a feature of such mining communities'. S. Macintyre, *Little Moscows: Communism and Working-Class Militancy in Inter-War Britain* (London, Croom Helm, 1980), pp. 44–5; Stead, 'Working-Class Leadership in South Wales', pp. 351–2.

Conclusion

The preceding pages have revealed that the coal miners of West Virginia and south Wales inhabited very different social and cultural worlds. In this sense, this study contributes to the ongoing battle to rescue miners from the ahistorical stereotypes of the 'Archetypal Proletarian', and place them instead in the real, lived, complex world of industrial capitalism. For all the differences, however, it is important that we do not forget the shared base of the coal industry. Although the act of mining may have differed in these two regions, the instabilities within the industry helped encourage a particularly aggressive attitude towards cost cutting on the part of the coal owners. This laid the basis for the fierce relationship between owner and miner, and the consequent high levels of protest in both these regions.

Less obviously, isolation was a factor in both of these regions, although not in the crude form of the 'Isolated Mass'. In West Virginia the communities were often small, and geographically separate. They were also isolated from neighbouring cultures and traditions, civil and political rights and, in the eyes of the miners, from the broader world of early twentieth-century America. The south Wales communities were less isolated in a geographic sense, and they were also linked to the cultural traditions of the region, and to a national union and national politics. However, there was also a sense of separateness, or isolation, about the way these communities synthesised cultural traditions and created their own definitions of community. Similarly the practice of politics itself, although often using the language of class or labourism, was sometimes more about the world of mining, or south Wales mining. These were not company towns on the frontier of US capitalism, but there was nevertheless something tangibly different about them.

262

Beyond these common strands, however, lay the huge contrasts in the type of community, cultural formations and power relationships found in these two regions. This study has focused on the way these factors help explain variations in the pattern and form of protest in mining communities. In doing so it has offered a more complex picture of what actually constitutes protest, by examining the nature of industrial conflict and the political identities and formations which resulted. As will be clear from reading the text, these patterns could not be accurately represented by counting strike statistics, or studying conflict in isolation from politics.

The resulting picture, shorn of any reliance upon models of political development, is one of different levels of coherence within political identities, and of organisational forms both reflecting and helping to solidify these. This coherence is not based upon notions of ascribed, theoretical class consciousness – something which, ironically, both the West Virginia and south Wales owners were better representatives of than the miners – but an ability to organise self-defence, and to build a strategy to challenge the powerful. For the reasons described in detail in chapter two, the south Wales miners were better able to do this than their counterparts in West Virginia. There was nothing 'correct' or pre-ordained about this path, it was simply the consequence of differences in power, culture and community. However, in future years, as the coal industry collapsed, the south Wales miners found out, much like their counterparts in West Virginia, that it was the first of these, power, or more importantly, powerlessness, which proved most decisive.

Bibliography

1 MANUSCRIPTS

i) United States

Morgantown, West Virginia University Library:
West Virginia and Regional History Collection
Justus Collins Papers (A+M 1824)
John J. Cornwell Papers (A+M 952)
William E. Glasscock Papers (A+M 6G)
Ephraim F. Morgan Papers (A+M 203)
Clarence E. Smith Papers (A+M 1606)
Monongah Mines Relief Fund Records (A+M 1733)
Oral History Collection

Washington D.C., National Archive
Records of Department of Justice (RG 60)
Records of War Department General Staff (RG 165); Military Intelligence
    Division Correspondence, 1917–41 (Entry 65)
General Records of the Department of Labor (RG 174)

Suitland, Ma., Washington National Records Center
Records of US Coal Commission (RG 68)
Records of Bureau of Mines (RG 70)
Records of Federal Mediation and Conciliation Service (RG 280)

Washington D.C., Catholic University of America
John Mitchell Papers (m/film edition)

Alexandria, Va., UMWA Archive
District 17 Correspondence Files

Bibliography

ii) England and Wales

Swansea, University Library: South Wales Coalfield Archive
SWMF Minutes (C1/2)
SWMF Financial Records (D1)
SWMF Rules (M2)
District, Area and Combine Records;
Rhondda No.1 (K10A)
Lodge Records; Cambrian (A2/3)
Workmen's Hall and Institute Minutes; Bargoed, Mardy, Ogmore Vale (A1)

Swansea, South Wales Miners' Library
Oral History Collection

Aberystwyth, National Library of Wales
MSWCA Records

Cambridge, University Library
ILP Minute Books (m/film edition) (P71)

2 PRINTED SOURCES

i) US Government Publications

US Bureau of the Census, *11th Census of the United States: Mineral Industries* (Washington D.C., 1892)

US Bureau of the Census, *13th Census of the United States, Vol. 11: Mines and Quarries, General Reports and Analysis* (Washington D.C., 1913)

US Bureau of the Census, *The Statistical History of the United States from Colonial Times to the Present* (Connecticut, 1965)

US Congress, *Presidential Elections since 1789* (Congressional Quarterly, Washington D.C., 1983)

US Department of Labor, Children's Bureau, *Welfare of Children in the Bituminous Coal Mining Communities in West Virginia* (by N.P. McGill, Bureau Publ. no. 117, Washington D.C., 1923)

US Senate, Committee on Education and Labor, *Conditions in the Paint Creek District, West Virginia*, 63 Congress, 1 Session, 3 pts. (Washington D.C., 1913)

US Senate, Committee on Education and Labor, *West Virginia Coal Fields Hearings*, 67 Congress, 1 Session, 2 pts. (Washington D.C., 1921–22)

US Senate, *West Virginia Coal Fields: Personal Views of Senator Kenyon, and Views of Senators Sterling, Phipps and Warren* 67 Congress, 2 Session, Report 457 (Washington D.C., 1922)

ii) West Virginia State Publications

Bureau/Department of Mines, *Annual Reports*

Bureau of Negro Welfare and Statistics, *Annual Reports*

Department/Board of Health, *Annual and Biennial Reports*

House of Delegates, *Journal of the House of Delegates of the State of West Virginia for the 34th Regular Session, Commencing January 14 ,1919, and the Extraordinary Session, Commencing March 11, 1919* (Charleston, 1919)

Report of Mining Investigation Commission, Appointed by Governor Glasscock on the 28th Day of August, 1912 (Charleston, 1912)

Report and Digest of Evidence Taken by Commission Appointed by the Governor of West Virginia, in Connection with the Logan County Situation, 1919 (Charleston, 1919)

iii) British Government Publications

Commission of Inquiry into Industrial Unrest: No.7 District – Wales and Monmouthshire (Parl. Papers, 1917–18, Cd.8868, XV)

Report and Correspondence on Disturbances in Connection with the South Wales Colliery Strikes (Parl. Papers, 1911, Cd.5568, LXIV)

Report of the Departmental Committee Appointed to Inquire into the Probable Economic Effect of a Limit of Eight Hours to the Working Day of Coal Miners (Parl. Papers, 1907, Cd.3506, XV.349)

Reports of the Royal Commission on the Coal Industry, 1919 (Parl. Papers, 1919, Cd.359, XI.373)

Census of England and Wales, 1911 (Parl. Papers, 1912–13, Cd.7017, I, IX)

Census of England and Wales, 1921; County of Glamorgan (London, 1923)

Department of Employment and Productivity, *British Labour Statistics: Historical Abstract, 1886–1968* (London, 1971)

Home Office, *List of Mines in the United Kingdom of Great Britain and Ireland and the Isle of Man, 1900* (London, 1901)

Home Office, *List of Mines in the United Kingdom of Great Britain and Ireland and the Isle of Man, 1910* (London, 1911)

iii) Other Publications

Craig, F. W. S., *British Parliamentary Election Results, 1885–1918* (London, Macmillan, 1974)

Craig, F. W. S., *British Parliamentary Election Results, 1918–1945* (Chichester, Parliamentary Research Services, 1983 edn.)

Craig, F. W. S., *British Electoral Facts, 1832–1980* (Chichester, Parliamentary Research Services, 1981 edn.)

Gibson, F. A., *Compilation of the Statistics of the Coal Mining Industry of the United Kingdom, the Various Coalfields Thereof, and the Principal Foreign Countries of the World* (Cardiff, 1922)

Hunt, E. E., Tyron, F. G., Willits, J. H. (eds.), *What the Coal Commission Found* (Baltimore, Williams and Williams Co., 1925)

Mitchell, B. R., and Deane, P., *Abstract of Britsh Historical Statistics* (Cambridge, Cambridge University Press, 1962)

RUDC, *Report of the Medical Officer of Health and School Medical Officer for the Year 1914*

UMWA, *Proceedings of Annual and Biennial Conventions*

3 NEWSPAPERS AND JOURNALS

i) West Virginia / US

Black Diamond
Bluefield Daily Telegraph
Coal Age
Charleston Gazette
Fairmont Times
International Socialist Review
Kanawha Citizen
Labor Argus (Charleston)
Miners' Herald
McDowell Times
Socialist and Labor Star (Huntington)
UMWJ
West Virginia Federationist
Wheeling Daily Intelligencer
Wheeling Majority
Wheeling Register

ii) South Wales/ Britain

Aberdare Leader
Justice
Labour Leader
Merthyr Pioneer
Rhondda Leader
Rhondda Socialist
South Wales Daily News
Western Mail

Bibliography

4 AUTOBIOGRAPHIES AND CONTEMPORARY ACCOUNTS

American Constitutional Association, *Life in a West Virginia Coal Field* (Charleston, 1923)

Bevan, A., *In Place of Fear* (London, Heineman, 1952)

Bird, S., Georgakas, D. and Shaffer, D. (eds.), *Solidarity Forever – The IWW: An Oral History of the Wobblies* (London, Lawrence and Wishart, 1987)

Cabell, C. A., 'Building a Model Mining Community', *West Virginia Review* (Apr 1927), 208–10.

Campbell, J. C., *The Southern Highlander and His Homeland* (Lexington, University of Kentucky Press, 1969 edn.)

Chaplin, R., *Wobbly: The Rough-and-Tumble Story of an American Radical* (Chicago, University of Chicago Press, 1948)

Coombes, B. L., *These Poor Hands* (London, Gollancz, 1939)

Conway, A. (ed.), *The Welsh in America: Letters from the Immigrants* (Minneapolis, University of Minnesota Press, 1961)

Cornwell, J. J., *A Mountain Trail* (Philadelphia, Dorrance and Co., 1939)

Gompers, S., 'Russianized West Virginia: Corporate Perversion of American Concepts of Liberty and Justice – Organised Labor to the Rescue', *American Federationist*, 20, 10 (Oct 1913), 825–35.

Griffiths, J., *Pages From Memory* (London, Dent, 1969)

Hindrichs, A. F., *The UMWA and the Non-Union Coal Fields* (New York, Columbia University Press, 1923)

Hodges, F., *My Adventures as a Labour Leader* (London, George Newnes, 1925)

Horner, A. H., *Incorrigible Rebel* (London, MacGibbon and Kee, 1960)

Jevons, H. S., *The British Coal Trade* (Newton Abbot, David and Charles, 1969 edn.)

Jones, J., *Unfinished Journey* (London, Hamish Hamilton, 1938)

Kline, M., 'Growing up on Cabin Creek: An Interview with Arnold Miller', *Goldenseal*, 17, 2 (1981), 35–43.

Laing, J. T., 'The Negro Miner in West Virginia', *Social Forces*, 14 (1936), 417–22.

Lane, W. D., *Civil War in West Virginia: A Story of Industrial Conflict in the Mines* (New York, B. W. Heubsch, 1921)

Lee, H. B., *Bloodletting in Appalachia: The Story of West Virginia's Four Major Mine Wars and Other Thrilling Incidents of its Coal Fields* (Morgantown, West Virginia University Library Press, 1969)

Lewis, H. E., *With Christ Among the Miners: Incidents and Impressions of the Welsh Revival* (London, Allen and Unwin, 1906)

MacCorkle, W. A., *The Recollections of Fifty Years of West Virginia* (New York, G. P. Putnam's Sons, 1928)

Macready, N., *Annals of an Active Life, Vol. 1* (London, Hutchison, 1924)

Bibliography

Mooney, F., *Struggle in the Coal Fields* [ed. J. W. Hess] (Morgantown, West Virginia University Library Press, 1967)

National Endowment for the Humanities, *On Dark and Bloody Ground: An Oral History of the UMWA in Central Appalachia, 1920–1935* (Charleston, 1973)

Robinson, N., *West Virginia on the Brink of a Labor Struggle* (Charleston, West Virginia Mining Association, 1912)

Rogers, J., 'I Remember that Mining Town', *West Virginia Review*, 15 (7 Apr 1938), 203–5.

Ross, M., *Machine Age in the Hills* (New York, Macmillan, 1933)

Roy, A., *A History of the Coal Miners of the United States: From the Development of the Mines to the Close of the Anthracite Strike of 1902* (Columbus, Trouger Printing Co., 1907)

Spivak, J. L., *A Man and His Time* (New York, Horizon Press, 1967)

Stonelake, E., *The Autobiography of Edmund Stonelake* [ed. A. Mor-O'Brien] (Bridgend, Mid Glamorgan Education Committee, 1981)

Suffern, A. E., *Conciliation and Arbitration in the Coal Industry of America* (Boston, Houghton Mifflin, 1915)

Tams, W. P. Jr., *The Smokeless Coal Fields of West Virginia: A Brief History* (Morgantown, West Virginia University Library Press, 1963)

Thomas, D. A., 'The Growth and Direction of Our Foreign Trade in Coal During the Last Half Century', *Journal of the Royal Statistical Society*, 66 (1903), 439–522.

Thurmond, W., *The Logan Coal Field of West Virginia: A Brief History* (Morgantown, West Virginia University Library Press, 1964)

Unofficial Reform Committee, *The Miners' Next Step: Being a Suggested Scheme for the Re-organisation of the Federation* (Tonypandy, 1912)

West Virginia Mining Association, *His Majesty King Coal* (Charleston, 1938)

5 SECONDARY WORKS

Arnot, R. P., *The Miners: Years of Struggle – A History of the Miners' Federation of Great Britain From 1910 Onwards* (London, Allen and Unwin, 1953)

Arnot, R. P., *South Wales Miners: A History of the South Wales Miners' Federation, 1898–1914* (London, Allen and Unwin, 1967)

Arnot R. P., *South Wales Miners: A History of the South Wales Miners' Federation, 1914–1926* (Cardiff, Cymric Federation Press, 1975)

Asteris, M., 'The Rise and Decline of South Wales Coal Exports, 1870–1930', *Welsh History Review*, 13, 1 (1986), 24–43.

Bailey, K. R., 'A Judicious Mixture: Negroes and Immigrants in the West Virginia Mines, 1880–1917', *West Virginia History*, 34 (1973), 141–61.

Bibliography

Baines, D., *Migration in a Mature Economy: Emigration and Internal Migration in England and Wales, 1861–1900* (Cambridge, Cambridge University Press, 1985)

Barclay, M., '"Slaves of the Lamp" – The Aberdare Miners' Strike, 1910', *Llafur*, 2, 3, 24–42.

Baron, A. (ed.), *Work Engendered: Towards a New Labor History* (Ithaca, Cornell University Press, 1991)

Bealey, F. W. and Pelling, H. M., *Labour and Politics, 1900–1906: A History of the Labour Representation Committee* (London, Macmillan, 1958)

Beik, M. E., 'The Competition for Ethnic Community Leadership in a Pennsylvania Bituminous Coal Town, 1890s-1930s', in Tenfelde, *Towards a Social History of Mining*, 223–41.

Bellamy, J. M. and Saville, J. (eds.), *Dictionary of Labour Biography, Volumes 1–8* (London and Basingstoke, Macmillan, 1972–87)

Biagini, E. F. and Reid, A. J., (eds.), *Currents of Radicalism: Popular Radicalism, Organised Labour and Party Politics in Britian, 1850–1914* (Cambridge, Cambridge University Press, 1991)

Billings, D., Blee, K. and Swanson, L., 'Culture, Family, and Community in Preindustrial Appalachia', *Appalachian Journal*, 13, 2 (1986), 154–70.

Bindocci, C. G., 'A Comparison of the Roles of Women in Anthracite and Bituminous Mining in Pennsylvania, 1900–1920', in Tenfelde, *Towards a Social History of Mining*, 682–91.

Brier, S., 'Interracial Organising in the West Virginia Coal Industry: The Participation of Black Mine Workers in the Knights of Labor and the United Mine Workers, 1880–1894', in G. M. Fink and M. E. Reed (eds.), *Essays in Southern Labor History: Selected Papers, Southern Labor History Conference, 1976* (Westport Ct., Greenwood Press, 1977), 18–43.

Breuilly, J., *Labour and Liberalism in Nineteenth-Century Europe: Essays in Comparative History* (Manchester, Manchester University Press, 1992)

Brody, D., *Steelworkers in America: The Non-Union Era* (Cambridge Mass., Harvard University Press, 1960)

Brown, K. D., *The English Labour Movement, 1700–1951* (Dublin, Gill and MacMillan, 1982)

Bulmer, M. I. A., 'Sociological Models of the Mining Community', *Sociological Review*, 23, 1 (1975), 61–92.

Buxton, N. K., *The Economic Development of the British Coal Industry: From the Industrial Revolution to the Present Day* (London, Batsford, 1978)

Campbell, A., *The Lanarkshire Miners: A Social History of their Trade Unions* (Edinburgh, John Donald, 1979).

270

Campbell, J., *Nye Bevan and the Mirage of British Socialism* (London, Weidenfeld and Nicholson, 1987)

Caudill, H. M., *Night Comes to the Cumberlands: A Biography of a Depressed Area* (Boston, Little Brown and Co., 1963 edn.)

Church, R., *The History of the British Coal Industry, Vol. 3, 1830–1913: Victorian Pre-eminence* (Oxford, Oxford University Press, 1986)

Church, R., 'Edwardian Labour Unrest and Coalfield Militancy, 1890–1914', *Historical Journal*, 30, 4 (1987), 841–57.

Clavel, P., *Opposition Planning in Wales and Appalachia* (Cardiff, University of Wales Press, 1983)

Cleaver, D., 'Labour and Liberals in the Gower Constituency, 1885–1910', *Welsh History Review*, 12, 3 (1985), 388–410.

Clegg, H. A., Fox, A. and Thompson, A. F., *A History of British Trade Unions Since 1889: Vol. 1, 1889–1910* (Oxford, Oxford University Press, 1964)

Clegg, H. A., *A History of British Trade Unions Since 1889, Vol. II* (Oxford, Oxford University Press, 1985)

Conley, P., *History of the West Virginia Coal Industry* (Charleston W. Va., Education Foundation, 1960)

Corbin, D. A., '"Frank Keeney is our Leader and we shall not be moved" Rank and File Leadership in the West Virginia Coal Fields', in Fink and Reed, *Essays in Southern Labor History*, 144–58.

Corbin, D. A., *Life, Work and Rebellion in the Coal Fields: The Southern West Virginia Miners, 1880–1920* (Urbana, University of Illinois Press, 1981)

Corbin, D. A., 'Betrayal in the West Virginia Coal Fields: Eugene V. Debs and the Socialist Party of America, 1912–1914', *Journal of American History*, 64 (1978), 987–1009.

Craigo, R. W., 'West Virginia Coal Company Scrip', *Goldenseal*, 5, 4 (1979), 68–71.

Cronin, J. E. and Sirianni, C., (eds.), *Work, Community, and Power: The Experience of Labor in Europe and America, 1900–1925* (Philadelphia, Temple University Press, 1983)

Crook, R., '"Tidy Women": Women in the Rhondda Between the Wars', *Oral History Journal*, 10, 2 (1982), 40–6.

Daunton, M. J., 'Miner's Houses: South Wales and the Great Northern Coalfield, 1880–1914', *International Review of Social History*, 25 (1980), 144–75.

Daunton, M. J., 'Down the Pit: Work in the Great Northern and South Wales Coalfields, 1870–1914', *Economic History Review*, 34 (1981), 578–597.

Davies, E. T., *Religion and the Industrial Revolution in South Wales* (Cardiff, University of Wales Press, 1965)

271

Davies, P., *A. J. Cook* (Manchester, Manchester University Press, 1987)

Davis, M., *Prisoners of the American Dream: Politics and Economy in the History of the US Working-Class* (London, Verso, 1986)

Day, G., 'The Reconstruction of Wales and Appalachia: Development and Regional Identity', *Contemporary Wales* (1987), 73–89.

Dennis, N., Henriquez, F. and Slaughter, C., *Coal is Our Life: An Analysis of a Yorkshire Mining Community* (London, Eyre and Spottiswoode, 1956)

Dubofsky, M., *We Shall Be All: A History of the IWW* (New York, Quadrangle/New York Times Book Co., 1969)

Dubofsky, M. and Van Tine, W., *John L. Lewis: A Biography* (New York, Quadrangle/New York Times Book Co., 1977)

Edwards, N., *History of the South Wales Miners' Federation, Vol. 1* (London, Lawrence and Wishart, 1938)

Egan, D., 'Noah Ablett, 1883–1935', *Llafur*, 4, 3, 19–30.

Egan, D., 'The Unofficial Reform Committee and The Miners' Next Step', *Llafur*, 2, 3, 64–81.

Eller, R. L., *Miners, Millhands and Mountaineers: Industrialization of the Appalachian South, 1880–1930* (Knoxville, University of Tennessee Press, 1981)

Emsley, C. (ed.), *Essays in Comparative History: Economy, Politics and Society in Britain and America, 1850–1920* (Milton Keynes, Open University Press, 1984)

Evans, E. W., *The Miners of South Wales* (Cardiff, University of Wales Press, 1961)

Evans, N., 'Immigrants and Minorities in Wales, 1840–1990: A Comparative Perspective', *Llafur*, 5, 4 (1991), 5–26.

Evans, N., and Jones, D., '"A Blessing for the Miner's Wife": The Campaign for Pithead Baths in the South Wales Coalfield, 1908–50', *Llafur*, 6, 3 (1994), 5–28.

Fagge, R. J., 'A Comparison of the Miners of South Wales and West Virignia, 1900–1922: Patterns of Militancy', in Tenfelde, *Towards a Social History of Mining*, 105–22.

Fagge, R. J., 'Eugene V. Debs in West Virginia, 1913: A Reappraisal', *West Virginia History*, 52 (1993), 1–18.

Feldman, G. D., and Tenfelde, K., (ed.), *Miners, Owners and Politics in Coal Mining: An International Comparison of Industrial Relations* (London, Berg, 1990)

Fink, L., 'Labor, Liberty and the Law: Trade Unionism and the Problem of the American Constitutional Order', *Journal of American History*, 74, 1 (1987), 904–25.

Fishback, P. V., *Soft Coal, Hard Choices: The Economic Welfare of Bituminous Coal Miners* (New York, Oxford University Press, 1992)

Bibliography

Foner, E., 'Why is there no Socialism in the United States?', *History Workshop Journal*, 17 (1984), 57–80.

Foot, M., *Aneurin Bevan, 1897–1945* (London, Paladin, 1975 edn.)

Foot, M., *Aneurin Bevan, 1945–60* (London, Paladin, 1975 edn.)

Foote, G., *The Labour Party's Political Thought: A History* (London, Croom Helm, 1985)

Fox, K. O., 'Labour and Merthyr's Khaki Election of 1900', *Welsh History Review*, 2, 4 (1965), 351–66.

Francis, H., and Smith, D., *The Fed: A History of the South Wales Miners in the Twentieth Century* (London, Lawrence and Wishart, 1980)

Francis, H. *Miners Against Fascism: Wales and the Spanish Civil War* (London, Lawrence and Wishart, 1984)

Gaventa, J., *Power and Powerlessness: Quiescence and Rebellion in an Appalachian Valley* (Urbana, University of Illinois Press, 1980)

Geary, D., *European Labour Protest, 1848–1939* (London, Croom Helm, 1981)

Geary, R., *Policing Industrial Disputes: 1893–1985* (Cambridge, Cambridge University Press, 1985)

Geary, R., 'Tonypandy and Llanelli Revisited', *Llafur*, 4, 4, 34–45.

Ginger, R., *Eugene V. Debs: A Biography* (New York, Collier Books, 1962 edn.)

Gregory, R., *The Miners and British Politics, 1906–1914* (Oxford, Oxford University Press, 1968)

Griffin, A. R., *The British Coalmining Industry: Retrospect and Prospect* (Buxton, Moorland Publishing Co., 1977)

Gutman, H. G., *Work, Culture and Society in Industrializing America: Essays in American Working-Class and Social History* (New York, Vintage Books 1977 edn.)

Hall, B., 'The Welsh Revival of 1904–5: A Critique', in G. J. Cuming and D. Baker (eds.), *Popular Belief and Practice: Papers Read at the Ninth Summer Meeting and Tenth Winter Meeting of the Ecclesiastical History Society* (Cambridge, Cambridge University Press, 1972), 291–301.

Hanagan, M., 'Response to Sean Wilentz', *International Labour and Working-Class History*, 26 (1984), 31–6.

Harris, E. L. K. and Krebs, F. J., *From Humble Beginnings: West Virginia State Federation of Labor, 1903–1957* (Charleston, West Virginia Labor History Publishing Fund, 1960)

Harrison, R. (ed.), *Independent Collier: The Coal Miner as Archetypal Proletarian Reconsidered* (Hassocks, Harvester, 1978)

Harvey, K. A., *The Best-Dressed Miners; Life and Labor in the Maryland Coal region, 1835–1910* (Ithaca, Cornell University Press, 1969)

Hickey, S. H. F., *Workers in Imperial Germany: The Miners of the Ruhr* (Oxford, Oxford University Press, 1985)

Bibliography

Hill, H., 'Myth-Making as Labor History: Herbert Gutman and the United Mine Workers of America', *Politics, Culture and Society*, 2, 2 (1988), 132–195.

Hobsbawm, E. J., *Industry and Empire: From 1750 to the Present Day* (London, Penguin, 1969 edn.)

Hogenkamp, B., 'Miners' Cinemas in South Wales in the 1920's and 1930's', *Llafur*, 4, 2 (1985), 64–76.

Holmes, C., 'The Tredegar Riots of 1911: Anti-Jewish Disturbances in South Wales, *Welsh History Review*, 11, 2 (1982), 214–25.

Holmes, G. M., 'The South Wales Coal Industry, 1850–1914', *Transactions Honourable Society Cymmrodorion* (1976), 162–207.

Holt, J., 'Trade Unionism in the British and US Steel Industries, 1880–1914: A Comparative Study', *Labor History*, 18, 1 (1977), 5–25.

Holton, B., *British Syndicalism 1900–1914: Myths and Realities* (London, Pluto Press, 1976)

Hopkin, D. R., 'The Great Unrest in Wales, 1910–1913: Questions of Evidence', in D. R. Hopkin and G. S. Kealey (eds.), *Class, Community and the Labour Movement: Wales and Canada, 1850–1930* (Wales, Llafur/Labour/Le Travail, 1989), 249–75.

Hopkin, D. R., 'The Rise of Labour in Wales, 1890–1914', *Llafur*, 6, 3 (1994), 120–41.

Howe, I., *Socialism and America* (San Diego, Harcourt Brace Javanovich, 1985)

Howell, D., *British Workers and the Independent Labour Party, 1888–1906* (Manchester, Manchester University Press, 1983)

John, A. V., 'A Miner Struggle? Women's Protests in Welsh Mining History', *Llafur*, 4, 1 (1984), 72–90.

Jones, D., 'Serfdom and Slavery: Women's Work in Wales, 1890–1930', in Hopkin and Kealey, *Class, Community and the Labour Movement*, 86–97.

Jones, D., 'Counting the Cost of Coal: Women's Lives in the Rhondda, 1881–1911', in A. V. John (ed.), *Our Mother's Land: Chapters in Welsh Women's History, 1880–1939* (Cardiff, University of Wales Press, 1991), 109–33.

Jones, M. A., *The Limits of Liberty: American History 1607–1980* (Oxford, Oxford University Press, 1983)

Jones, P. N., *Colliery Settlement in the South Wales Coalfield, 1850–1926* (University of Hull, Occasional Papers in Geography, No.14. Hull, 1969)

Jones, R. A. N., 'Women, Community and Collective Action: The "Ceffyl Pren" Tradition', in John, *Our Mother's Land*, 17–42.

Jordan, D. P., 'The Mingo War: Labor Violence in the Southern West Virginia Coal Fields, 1919–1922', in Fink and Reed, *Essays in Southern Labour History*, 101–43.

Bibliography

Joyce, P., *Work, Society and Politics: The Culture of the Factory in Later Victorian England* (London, Menthuen, 1982 edn.)

Katznelson, I. and Zolberg, A. R., (eds.), *Working-Class Formation: Nineteenth-Century Patterns in Western Europe and the United States* (Princeton, Princeton University Press, 1986)

Kerr, C. and Siegel, A., 'The Inter-Industry Propensity to Strike: An International Comparison', in A. Kornhauser, R. Dubin, and A. M. Ross (eds.), *Industrial Conflict* (New York, McGraw-Hill, 1954)

Kessler-Harris, A., *Out to Work: A History of Wage-Earning Women in the United States* (New York, Oxford University Press, 1982)

Kirby, M. W., *The British Coalmining Industry, 1870–1946: A Political and Economic History* (Hamden, Conn., Archon Books, 1977)

Kirk, N., *Labour and Society in Britain and the USA* (2 Vols.), (Aldershot, Scolar Press, 1994)

Knipe, E. E. and Lewis, H. M., 'The Impact of Coal Mining on the Traditional Mountain Subculture', in J. K. Moreland (ed.), *The Not So Solid South: Anthropological Studies in a Regional Subculture* (Athens, Ga., University of Georgia Press, 1971), 25–37.

Korson, G., *Coal Dust on the Fiddle: Songs and Stories of the Bituminous Industry* (Hatborough, Penn., Folklore Associates, 1965 edn.)

Laslett, J. H. M., *Labor and the Left: A Study of Socialist and Radical Influences in the American Labor Movement, 1881–1924* (New York, Basic Books, 1970)

Laslett, J. H. M., 'End of an Alliance: Selected Correspondence Between SPA and UMW of A Leaders in World War One', *Labor History*, 12, 4 (1971), 570–95.

Laslett, J. H. M., *Nature's Noblemen: The Fortunes of the Independent Collier in Scotland and the American MidWest, 1855–1889* (Los Angeles, Institute of Industrial Relations, University of California, 1983)

Lewis, E. D., *The Rhondda Valleys: A Study in Industrial Development, 1800 to the Present Day* (London, Phoenix House, 1959)

Lewis, H., 'Fatalism or the Coal Industry? Contrasting Views of Appalachian Problems', *Mountain Life and Work*, 45 (1970), 4–15.

Lewis, R. L., 'The Black Presence in the Paint-Cabin Creek Strike, 1912–1913', *West Virginia History*, 46 (1985–6), 59–71.

Lewis, R. L., *Black Coal Miners in America: Race, Class, and Community Conflict, 1780–1980* (Lexington, University of Kentucky Press, 1987)

Lewis, R. L., 'From Peasant to Proletarian: The Migration of Southern Blacks to the Central Appalachian Coalfields', *Journal of Southern History*, 55, 1 (1989), 77–102.

Long, P., *Where the Sun Never Shines: A History of America's Bloody Coal Industry*, (New York, Paragon House, 1991 edn.)

Lunt, R. D., *Law and Order vs. The Miners: West Virginia, 1907–1933* (Hamden, Conn.,Archon Books, 1979)

Macintyre, S., *Little Moscows: Communism and Working-Class Militancy in Inter-War Britain* (London, Croom Helm, 1980)

McKinney, G. B., 'Industrialization and Violence in Appalachia in the 1890's', in J.W. Williamson (ed.), *An Appalachian Symposium* (Boone, N.C., Appalachian Consortium Press, 1977), 131–44.

Matthews, I., 'The World of the Anthracite Miner', *Llafur*, 6, 1 (1992), 96–104.

Milkman, R. (ed.), *Women, Work and Protest: A Century of US Women's Labor History* (London, Routledge and Kegan Paul, 1985)

Miller, D. L. and Sharpless, R. E., *The Kingdom of Coal: Work, Enterprise, and Ethnic Communities in the Mine Fields* (Philadelphia, University of Pennsylvania Press, 1985)

Miller, S., 'Socialism and Race', in J. H. M Laslett, and S. M. Lipset (eds.), *Failure of a Dream? Essays in the History of American Socialism* (Berkeley, University of California Press, 1984 edn.), 231–40.

Mommsen, W. J. and Husung, H. G., (eds.), *The Development of Trade Unionism in Great Britain and Germany, 1880–1914* (London, Allen and Unwin, 1985)

Morgan, J., 'Police and Labour in the Age of Lindsay, 1910–1936', *Llafur*, 5, 1, 15–20.

Morgan, J., *Conflict and Order: The Police and Labour Disputes in England and Wales, 1900–1939* (Oxford, Oxford University Press, 1987)

Morgan, K. O., 'The Merthyr of Keir Hardie', in G. Williams (ed.), *Merthyr Politics: The Making of a Working-Class Tradition* (Cardiff, University of Wales Press, 1962), 58–81.

Morgan, K. O., 'Wales and the Boer War: A Reply', *Welsh History Review*, 4, 4 (1969), 367–80.

Morgan, K. O., 'The New Liberalism and the Challenge of Labour: The Welsh Experience', *Welsh History Review*, 6, 3 (1973), 288–312.

Morgan, K. O., 'Socialism and Syndicalism: The Welsh Miners' Debate, 1912', *Bulletin Society for the Study of Labour History*, 30 (1975), 22–37.

Morgan, K. O., *Keir Hardie: Radical and Socialist* (London, Weidenfeld and Nicholson, 1984 edn.)

Morgan, K. O., *Wales in British Politics, 1868–1922* (Cardiff, University of Wales Press, 1980 edn.)

Morgan, K. O., *Rebirth of a Nation: Wales 1880–1980* (Oxford, Oxford University Press, 1981)

Morgan K. O., *Labour People, Leaders and Lieutenants: Hardie to Kinnock* (Oxford, Oxford University Press, 1987)

Mor-O'Brien, A., 'Keir Hardie, C. B. Stanton and the First World War', *Llafur*, 4, 3, 31–42.

Bibliography

Mor-O'Brien, A., 'The Merthyr Boroughs Election, 1915', *Welsh History Review*, 12, 4 (1985), 538–66.

Mor-O'Brien, A., 'Churchill and the Tonypandy Riots', *Welsh History Review*, 17, 1 (1994), 67–99.

Nash, M., *Conflict and Accomodation: Coal Miners, Steel Workers, and Socialism* (Westport Ct., Greenwood Press, 1982)

Pelling, H. M., *Popular Politics and Society in Late Victorian Britain* (London, Macmillan, 1968)

Pelling, H. M., 'Wales and the Boer War', *Welsh History Review*, 4, 4 (1969), 363–5.

Pelling, H. M., *A History of British Trade Unionism* (London, Macmillan, 1976 edn.)

Pelling, H. M., *A Short History of the Labour Party* (London, Macmillan, 1985 edn.)

Perlman, S. and Taft, P., *History of Labor in the United States, 1896–1932: Labor Movements* (New York, Macmillan, 1935)

Powell, A. K., *The Next Time We Strike: Labor in Utah's Coal Fields, 1900–1933* (Logan, Ut., Utah State University Press,1985)

Price, R., *Labour in British Society: An Interpretative History* (London, Croom Helm, 1986)

Reid, A. J., 'The Division of Labour and Politics in Britain, 1880–1920', in Husung and Mommsen, *The Development of Trade Unionism in Great Britain and Germany*, 150–65.

Reid, A. J., *Social Classes and Social Relations in Britain, 1850–1914* (Basingstoke, Macmillan, 1992)

Reiser, B. and Seeger, P., *Carry it On ! A History in Song and Picture of the Working Men and Women of America* (Poole, Blandford, 1985)

Rimlinger, G. V., 'International Differences in the Strike Propensity of Coal Miners: Experience in Four Countries', *International and Labour Relations Review*, 12, 3 (1959), 389–405.

Roediger, D., *The Wages of Whiteness: Race and the Making of the American Working-Class* (London, Verso, 1991)

Salvatore, N., *Eugene V. Debs: Citizen and Socialist* (Urbana, University of Illinois Press, 1982)

Salvatore, N., 'Response to Sean Wilentz', *International Labour and Working-Class History*, 26 (1984), 25–30.

Samuel, R. (ed.), *Miners, Quarrymen and Saltworkers* (London, Routledge and Kegan Paul, 1977)

Savage, L., *Thunder in the Mountains: The West Virginia Mine Wars, 1920–1921* (Charleston, Jalamap Publications, 1984)

Saxton, A., *The Rise of the White Republic: Class Politics and Mass Culture in Ninetenth Century America* (London, Verso, 1990)

Bibliography

Shifflett, C. A., *Coal Towns: Life, Work and Culture in Company Towns of Southern Appalachia* (Knoxville, University of Tennessee Press, 1991)

Shubert, A., *The Road to Revolution: The Coal Miners of Asturias, 1860–1934* (Urbana, University of Illinois Press, 1987)

Smith, D., 'Tonypandy 1910: Definitions of Community', *Past and Present*, 87 (1980), 158–84.

Smith, D., 'Wales Through the Looking Glass', in *ibid.* (ed.), *A People and a Proletariat: Essays in the History of Wales, 1780–1980* (London, Pluto Press, 1980), 215–39.

Smith, D., *Anuerin Bevan and the World of South Wales* (Cardiff, University of Wales Press, 1993)

Stead, P., 'Working-Class Leadership in South Wales, 1900–1922', *Welsh History Review*, 6, 3 (1973), 329–53.

Stead, P., 'The Language of Edwardian Politics', in Smith, *A People and a Proletariat*, 148–165.

Stead, P., 'Establishing a Heartland – The Labour Party in Wales', in K. D. Brown (ed.), *The First Labour Party, 1906–1914* (London, Croom Helm, 1985), 64–89.

Stedman Jones, G., *Languages of Class: Studies in English Working-Class History, 1832–1982* (Cambridge, Cambridge University Press, 1983)

Steel, E. M., 'Mother Jones in the Fairmont Field, 1902', *Journal of American History*, 57 (1970), 290–307.

Supple, B., *The History of the British Coal Industry, Vol. 4, 1913–1946: The Political Economy of Decline* (Oxford, Oxford University Press, 1987)

Supple, B., 'The Political Economy of Demoralization: The State and the Coalmining Industry in America and Britain Between the Wars', *Economic History Review*, 41, 4 (1988), 566–91.

Taylor, A. J., 'The Coal Industry', in D. H. Aldcroft (ed.), *The Development of British Industry and Foreign Competition* (London, Allen and Unwin, 1968), 37–70.

Taft, P., *The AFL in the Time of Gompers* (New York, Harper and Row, 1957)

Tanner, D., *Political Change and the Labour Party, 1900–1918* (Cambridge, Cambridge University Press, 1990)

Tenfelde, K., (ed.), *Towards a Social History of Mining in the 19th and 20th Centuries* (Munich, Verlag C. H. Beck, 1992)

Thelen, D. P., *Robert M. LaFollette and the Insurgent Spirit* (Boston, Little Brown Co., 1976)

Thomas, B., 'The Migration of Labour into the Glamorganshire Coalfield, 1861–1911', *Economica*, 10 (1930), 275–94.

Bibliography

Thomas, B., 'Wales and the Atlantic Economy', in ibid. (ed.), *The Welsh Economy: Studies in Expansion* (Cardiff, University of Wales Press, 1962)

Thompson, E. P., *The Making of the English Working-Class* (London, Penguin, 1980 edn.)

Thompson, E. P., 'Time, Work-Discipline and Industrial Capitalism', in A. Giddens and D. Held (eds.), *Classes, Power and Conflict: Classical and Contemporary Debates* (Macmillan, Basingstoke, 1982)

Trotter, J. W. Jr., *Coal, Class and Color: Blacks in Southern West Virginia, 1915–32* (Urbana, University of Illinois Press, 1991)

Turner, C., 'Conflicts of Faith? Religion and Labour in Wales, 1890–1914', in Hopkin and Kealey, *Class, Community and the Labour Movement*, 67–85.

Waller, A. L., *Feud: Hatfields, McCoys and Social Change in Appalachia, 1860–1900* (Chapel Hill, University of North Carolina Press, 1988)

Waller, R. J., *The Dukeries Transformed: the Social and Political Development of a Twentieth Century Coalfield* (Oxford, Oxford University Press, 1983)

Walters, R., 'Labour Productivity in the South Wales Steam Coal Industry, 1870–1914', *Economic History Review*, 28, 2 (1975), 280–303.

Weinstein, J., *The Decline of Socialism in America, 1912–1925* (New York, 1967)

Weitz, E. D., 'Class Formation and Labour Protest in the Mining Communities of Southern Illinois and the Ruhr, 1890–1925', *Labor History*, 27, 1 (1985–6), 85–105.

Wilentz, S., *Chants Democratic: New York City and the Rise of the American Working-Class, 1788–1850* (New York, Oxford University Press, 1984)

Wilentz, S., 'Against Exceptionalism: Class Consciousness and the American Labour Movement', *International Labour and Working-Class History*, 26 (1984), 1–24.

Williams, C., ' "An Able Administrator of Capitalism?" The Labour Party in the Rhondda, 1917–1921', *Llafur*, 4, 4, 20–33.

Williams, C., 'The South Wales Miners' Federation', *Llafur*, 5, 3, 45–56.

Williams, G. A., *The Welsh in Their History* (London, Croom Helm, 1982)

Williams, G. A., *When Was Wales? A History of the Welsh* (London, Penguin, 1985)

Williams, G. A., *Peace and Power: Henry Richard, A Radical For Our Time* (Cardiff, CND Cymru, 1988)

Williams, J., 'Miners and the Law of Contract, 1875–1914', *Llafur*, 4, 2, 36–50.

Williams, J. A., *West Virginia and the Captains of Industry* (Morgantown, West Virginia University Library Press, 1976)

Bibliography

Williams, J. A., *West Virginia: A History* (New York, W. W. Norton and Co., 1984 edn.)

Williams, L. J., 'The Coalowners', in Smith, *A People and a Proletariat*, 94–113.

Williams, L. J., 'The Road to Tonypandy', *Llafur*, 1, 2, 3–14.

Williamson, B., *Class, Culture and Community: A Biographical Study of Social Change in Mining* (London, Routledge and Kegan Paul, 1982)

6 UNPUBLISHED THESES

Barkey, F., 'The Socialist Party in West Virginia from 1898–1920', Ph.D., University of Pittsburgh (1971)

Boal, W. M., 'Unionism and Productivity in West Virginia Coal Mining', Ph.D., Stanford University (1985)

Cubby, E. A., 'The Transformation of the Tug and Guyandot Valleys: Economic Development and Social Change in West Virginia, 1888–1921', Ph.D., Syracuse University (1962)

Fishback, P. V. M., 'Employment Conditions of Blacks in the Coal Industry, 1900–1930', Ph.D., University of Washington (1983)

Fox, H. D., 'Thomas T. Haggerty and the Formative Years of the United Mine Workers of America', Ph.D., West Virginia University (1975)

Gowaskie, J. M., 'John Mitchell: A Study in Leadership', Ph.D., Catholic University of America (1968)

Laing, J. T., 'The Negro Miner in West Virginia', Ph.D., Ohio State University (1933)

Lawrence, R. G., 'Appalachian Metamorphosis: Industrializing Society on the Central Appalachian Plateau, 1860–1913', Ph.D., Duke University (1983)

Livingston, W. J. B., 'Coal Miners and Religion: A Study in Logan County', D.Th., Union Theological Seminary, Richmond Va. (1951)

Massay, G. F., 'Coal Consolidation: Profile of the Fairmont Field of West Virginia, 1852–1903', Ph.D., West Virginia University (1970)

Simon, R. M., 'The Development of Underdevelopment: The Coal Industry and its Effect on the West Virginia Economy, 1880–1930', Ph.D., University of Pittsburgh (1978)

Thomas, J. B., 'Coal Country: The Rise of the Southern Smokeless Coal Industry and its Effect on Area Development', Ph.D., University of North Carolina (1971)

Woodhouse, M. G., 'Rank and File Movements among the Miners of South Wales, 1910–1926', D.Phil., University of Oxford (1969)

Bibliography

7.) MISCELLANEOUS

i) Fiction

Jones, L., *Cwmardy* (London, Lawrence and Wishart, 1978 edn.)
Jones, L., *We Live* (London, Lawrence and Wishart, 1978 edn.)

ii) Film

'Matewan' (Dir. John Sayles, US, 1987) Cinecom Int./MGM Video

iii) Music

Gaughan, D., *True and Bold: Songs of the Scottish Miners* (Scottish TUC, 1985)

Index

282

Index

Index

Mardy Institute 87
Marion County 15, 28
Master and Servant Act (1823) 171
Matewan 114–15, 136, 143
McDowell County 14, 139
McDowell Times 72
McGinney, Hugh 127
McKenna 189
measles 63
mechanisation 14
medical facilities 43, 53, 63
Mercer County 15
Merionethshire 35
Merthyr Pioneer 236
Merthyr Rising (1831) 233
Merthyr Tydfil 19, 29, 39
Miller, Arnold 58, 59, 71
Minden 71
mine guards 46, 122
Miners' Federation of Great Britain (MFGB) 167–9, 185–9, 192–8, 239–40
Miners' Herald, The 125, 220
'Miner's Lifeguard' 44–5
Miners' Minority Movement (MMM) 199
Miners' Next Step, The 186, 250, 251, 252
Mingo County 15, 138, 139, 180
Minimum Wage Bill 188
mining accidents 20–1
Mining Association of Great Britain 195
Mining Industry Act (1920) 195
Minter, M.L. 46
Mitchell, John 113, 114, 115
mobility 65–6, 77
Monarch mine 65, 69
Monmouthshire and South Wales Coal Owners' Association (MSWCA) 48, 170, 171, 173
Monongah disaster (1907) 20, 33, 34

Monongalia county 15
Montclare 145
Montgomery, Samuel B. 147, 214, 215, 216
Mooney, Fred 4, 30, 68, 71, 74, 77, 117, 118, 125–30, 139, 143, 147, 148, 151, 152, 216, 220
Moran, Michael 110
Morgan, Governor Ephraim F. 69, 135, 142, 144–9, 152, 214, 216, 223, 224, 225
Morgan, J.P. 17
Morgan, John 85
Morgan, Pritchard 235, 236, 237, 241
Morrell, Enoch 197, 246
mountain people 29–30, 31
Mountain State 39
Mountclare 224
Munitions of War Act 192
Murray, Philip 149–51, 210, 223
music 75
Mynydd Newydd 80

Nantz, S.F. 69
National Federation of Miners and Mine Laborers 110
National Industrial Recovery Act (1933) (USA) 110
National Progressive Union of Miners and Mine Laborers 110
Neely, Matthew M. 215
New Deal 110
New Export Coal Company 127
New River 13, 16, 67, 110
Newlyn Coal Company 56
Newport 15
Nicholas, T.E. 82
nonconformity 80
Norfolk and Western (N and W) Railroad 14, 17
Nugent, John H. 34, 215

United National and Burnyeat,
Brown and Company 18
Unofficial Reform Committee 186,
194, 249
US Children's Bureau 37
US Coal and Coke Company 17, 57
US Coal and Oil Company 17–18,
56
US Coal Commission 36, 41, 58
US Immigration Commission 32
US Steel Corporation 17

Vasey, Joe 123, 125, 127
Vinson, Z.T. 112
violence 30, 69, 70
see also riots

Wadhill, Judge 142
wages
national minimum 174, 187
sliding scale 167–8
West Virginia 20
Walker, John H. 113
Wallhead, R.C. 248
Walters v. Ocean Coal Company
(1908) 174
Wardhill, Judge E., Jr 135
Warner, William 113, 114
Washington, George 225
Watson, Clarence 128
Watts Morgan, D. 245, 250, 254
Webb, Sidney 195
Welsh language 29, 77–8

West Virginia Federationist 129
Wheeling Gazette 142
Wheeling Majority 218
White, John P. 117, 120, 122
White Oak Coal Company 40
whooping cough 63
Widen 57
Wilburn, Reverend J.W. 149, 152
Williams, Dr J.H. 242
Williams, John 239, 240, 246
Williams, John R. 67, 69, 89
Williams, Mr (schoolmaster) 87
Williamson Operators' Association
112, 138
Wilson, William B. 121, 122, 213
Wilson, President Woodrow 131
Winding Gulf 13, 46, 55, 59, 73,
117
Winstone, James 186, 192, 197,
200, 246, 247, 248
Wolfe, George 40, 41, 42, 65, 213
women
employment 62–3
mortality rate 63
role in strikes 128
unpaid work 55, 59
Workers Education Association 86
Workman, J.L. 126
workmen's institutes 64, 83, 87
World War I 190–1
Wren, J.J. 110

Yellow Dog contracts 135